THE EUCHARISTIC FORM OF GOD

The Eucharistic Form *of* God

Hans Urs von Balthasar's Sacramental Theology

JONATHAN MARTIN CIRAULO

University of Notre Dame Press

Notre Dame, Indiana

Library of Congress Control Number: 2021948754

ISBN: 978-0-268-20223-1 (Hardback)
ISBN: 978-0-268-20222-4 (WebPDF)
ISBN: 978-0-268-20225-5 (Epub)

For Allison

La messe. *Comment parler avec dignité de ce mystère adorable? Je l'ai es-*
sayé plusieurs fois, mais cela dépasse mes forces.
—Paul Claudel, *Cahiers*, Vol. 12, *Correspondance*
Paul Claudel–Jacques Rivière, 72

Wanderer tritt still herein;
Schmerz versteinerte die Schwelle.
Da erglänzt in reiner Helle
Auf dem Tische Brot und Wein.
—Georg Trakl, "Ein Winterabend"

CONTENTS

ACKNOWLEDGMENTS

It is only right that this book on the Eucharist begin with thanksgiving. First of all, much gratitude is owed to Cyril O'Regan. Cyril directed my dissertation at the University of Notre Dame, which was the first version of this book, and has served as a model for how to think and to write with greater subtlety and creativity—and how to live with assiduity and humility. Many other mentors and friends from Notre Dame supported me and this project in countless ways, but explicit mention needs to be made of John Betz, Peter Casarella, David Fagerberg, Francesca Murphy, and Mary Catherine Hilkert.

I received several grants that have helped fund travel related to research for this project, particularly from Notre Dame's Rome Global Gateway (on two occasions) and the Nanovic Institute for European Studies. I am especially grateful to Fr. Jacques Servais, SJ, the director of the Casa Balthasar, who was always a gracious host in Rome, and Claudia Müller and other members of the Johannesgemeinschaft, who received me hospitably at the Balthasar Archiv in Basel. Further support for this research was provided by the Adrian Fuerst Faculty Research and Development Fund at Saint Meinrad Seminary and School of Theology. My colleagues and students at Saint Meinrad have provided a welcome home where I could complete this book. In particular, Fr. Alex Crow helped with the final stages of editing and formatting, and Dcn. Dustin Hungerford helped with the index. Mention should also be made of Matthew Levering, the editors at the University of Notre Dame Press, particularly Stephen Little, and the two anonymous reviewers.

Finally, the greatest debt of gratitude is owed to my wife, Allison, who edited this book in its various stages and always fosters an atmosphere in which an intellectual life is able to flourish. My understanding of *Hingabe* comes as much from you, Allison, and our children as it does from Balthasar.

To all of the above, and to many other friends, colleagues, and family members, whom I hope know of my gratitude, I give much thanks for whatever is worthwhile in this book. *Quid autem habes quod non accepisti?* (1 Cor. 4:7).

ABBREVIATIONS

WORKS BY HANS URS VON BALTHASAR

Apok.	*Apokalypse der deutschen Seele*, vols. I–III
CL	*Cosmic Liturgy*
E	*Elucidations*
ET	*Explorations in Theology*, vols. I–V
GL	*The Glory of the Lord*, vols. I–VII
NE	*New Elucidations*
OP	*The Office of Peter and the Structure of the Church*
TD	*Theo-Drama*, vols. I–V
TL	*Theo-Logic*, vols. I–III

WORKS BY OTHERS

Denz.	*Compendium of Creeds, Definitions, and Declarations of the Catholic Church* (Denzinger, 43rd ed.)
SCG	Thomas Aquinas, *Summa contra Gentiles*
ST	Thomas Aquinas, *Summa theologiae*

Introduction

A Theology of Intinction

Among the more puzzling and interminable questions regarding the sacrament of the Eucharist is the enigma of Christ's choice of bread and wine as the "sacramental matter" that perpetuates his corporeal presence on earth. Undoubtedly part of the answer lies in the Last Supper being near or precisely within the Jewish Passover meal, but this or any other historical evidence that could be garnered must remain suggestive, partial, and largely circumstantial. Like any historical event, it remains utterly a part of the realm of the contingent, of the achingly determinate and settled past that now gives only fragmentary clues as to the conscious mental acts that performed them. Why, then, Christ would have chosen these elements has been subject not so much to debate but rather to various heuristic suggestions that range from exploiting the typological significance of these elements to noting the anthropological fittingness of having solid food to nourish the body and drink to enliven the soul, and everything in between.[1] To appropriate this theologoumenon for our purposes here—that is, of finding the place of Hans Urs von Balthasar within the history of Eucharistic theology—we can note that this history can be schematically divided according to how various theologians have reflected one or another of the various properties of these two objects of dominical decision. Without creating procrustean epochs of eucharistic reflection, we can say that there certainly have been times when sacramental theology has tended to reflect the solidity or even desiccation of bread: a theology aimed at precision, comprehensiveness (within a limited frame of reference), and perspicacity. At other times it has been protean, reproducing the unruliness of the liquid state, the inebriation and excesses induced by wine: a theology of praise, heedless of fine distinctions, equally aimed at

1

comprehensiveness, but with a breadth lacking any limitations or strictures. The former is clearly found in the great scholastics, in which the particularity of the sacramental economy is analyzed in rigorous detail and distinguished from all else. The latter is found, differently, in both the patristic era and in the dominant sacramental theologians of the twentieth century, in which the realm of the "sacramental" has been so greatly expanded as to include all else within it.

The overall tenor of Balthasar's own eucharistic theology, to which this book is dedicated, must be understood by his attempts to navigate the great benefits and the dangers of the regnant eucharistic theologies represented by the two sacramental elements. In Balthasar's mind, neither tendency is given exclusive rights to sacramental discourse, as each, without the balance of the other, tends toward pernicious excesses. Balthasar's eucharistic theology is uniquely marked by its simultaneous commitment to both the bread of scholastic precision and order and the wine of mystical flights and the overflowing of sacramentality. He is, at least regarding the scope and intention of his eucharistic theology based on our concocted division (and certainly not denying concomitance or being liturgically insistent), a supremely Utraquist theologian. One could say, at the risk of reducing our chosen metaphor into something overly precious, that Balthasar's eucharistic theology is a theology of *intinction*, of the traditional soaked in the poetic, of the scholastic saturated by the monastic.[2]

Balthasar's entrance into the Society of Jesus in 1929 to begin his formal philosophical education in Pullach (and subsequent theological studies at Fourvière, Lyon) followed immediately upon the submission of his dissertation on German literature, "Geschichte des eschatologischen Problems in der modernen deutschen Literatur."[3] Without rehearsing the well-known malaise that Balthasar himself and many of his generation felt at the perceived vacuity of the regnant theological formation in seminaries, with regard to questions specifically sacramental, we can note that the situation was particularly uninspiring. The manuals on sacramental theology that Balthasar almost certainly used were at least the following two: *De causalitate sacramentorum seu de modo explicandi efficientiam sacramentorum novae legis, textus scholasticorum principaliorum*, edited by M. Gierens;[4] and P. Pourrat, *La Théologie Sacramentaire: Étude de Théologie Positive*.[5] The former is less of a monograph and more of an anthology of scholastic texts regarding sacramental causality; the latter is actually quite historically sensitive and nuanced, as far as the manual genre is concerned. Nevertheless, its scope is firmly restricted to the classical sacramental questions with a posture of Counter-Reformation retrenchment: sacramental efficacy, the sacramental character, the institution of the sacraments, their ministers, intention, and so on. There is no attempt to see the broader context of the sacramental economy within the scope of creation, or as an effect of the Incarnation, or as a reflection of the Triune life. It reflects a eucharistic vision that is confined exclusively to the paten, that risks nothing of the excesses of the chalice, which is jealously guarded from spilling over.

Compare this with Balthasar's previous encounter with sacramental discourse outside the usual theological sources. First, in his studies of German literature, Balthasar was quite aware that the Eucharist was now the common property of European literati, no longer a uniquely ecclesial affair. That is to say, as has been shown quite convincingly, the decline in actual sacramental faith in Europe led not so much to an entirely antisacramental world, but rather to the relocation, and perhaps we should add the confinement, of the sacrament within poetry and literature.[6] For Balthasar, all post-Christian drama can be interpreted as so many Christian "fragments," recalling an integrated past and straining forward toward reintegration.[7] Modern literature, according to Balthasar, is variously a nostalgic look back at a world not yet disenchanted, an epochal reconfiguration and distortion of sacramentality, or even a half-remembered echo of a world in which wine becomes blood. Whatever its modality, Balthasar found an expansive, at times bacchanal, eucharistic "theology" in modern German literature that is as heterodox as it is intoxicating. Again, representative of an exclusively vinous, liquid sacramentality, German literature has allowed the chalice to spill out, to disperse, and thus to resist any containment by rigid oppositions between what counts as, at least potentially, hierophanic. Balthasar's intellectual formation in Vienna before his entrance into the Society of Jesus instilled in him a marked preference for thinking first of the whole rather than the part, or, stated more precisely, of the part only insofar as it is brought into an intelligible unity by the whole. He is primarily indebted to Goethe for this insight, but his early fascination with Plotinus gave him assurances that this style of thought is no Germanic novelty.[8]

To provide a few examples from *Apokalypse*, Balthasar highlights Hölderlin's poetry of sacrifice, of bread and wine; Hegel's fascination with the mystery of eating, whether concerning the Eleusian mysteries or Communion; and also Nietzsche's Zarathustra, who proclaims "the new Lord's Supper" (*das neue Abendmahl*).[9] Balthasar knows that Georg Trakl speaks of "bread and wine for an upright life / God in your soft hands / man places the dark end / all of its guilt and red pain."[10] Finally, Rilke (in whom Balthasar had an enduring interest, following Romano Guardini)[11] spends no little time extolling the sacrality of blood, even if blood is only sacred in an entirely immanent sense, a "Blutmythus" that he shares with Hugo von Hofmannsthal and Stefan George, the latter of whom Balthasar cites as extolling the "magical communion" with the blood of the mediator: "to bodily savor the flesh and blood of a mediator."[12] Although the Eucharist, and its various pagan counterparts and counterfeits, is endlessly variegated in modern literature, perhaps one central motif is that of Communion, of the union and usually dissolution of the finite into the infinite, or vice versa. Hölderlin encapsulates well the unmistakably sacramental tendency of much of modern poetry, but one that is heavily weighted toward the nostalgic, the autochthonous, and ultimately the irruptive:

> Bread is fruit of the earth, yet it is blessed by the sunlight,
> And from the thundering god issues the joy of the wine.
> Therefore with these our thoughts turn to the heavenly, those who
> Once were here and in their own due time will return.
> Therefore do poets, too, solemnly sing of the wine-god,
> And no idly composed praise sounds to the ancient one.[13]

It is a longing for, and perhaps the initial reconstruction of, a world that is permeable to the gods. There is no place here for Real Presence, and ultimately it is based on a Zwinglian metaphysics, but instead of symbol as a placeholder for a fullness that is elsewhere, the symbol alone provides all that could possibly be expected. As Balthasar notes in *Apokalypse*, for Goethe everything that is truly meaningful is a symbol, a symbolic form that is the proper object of creaturely *eros*. But for Goethe as for Rilke, the symbol gives access only to *Deus sive natura* (*Gott-Natur*), and thus whatever sacred may interrupt our sterile modernity, it will always be a sacred immanent to nature rather than received as a gift from without.[14]

Given the stipulated refusal of genuine transcendence in these authors, there was no possibility that Balthasar could have attempted to merge the sacramental thought of modern literature and philosophy with traditional Catholic eucharistic theology (let alone scholasticism). Nevertheless, although it is so many distorted versions of true sacramental piety, the "eucharistic" mysticism of German literature showed itself more dynamic, expansive, and ultimately seductive than anything that could be found in a textbook discussing whether sacramental grace is to be distinguished from sanctifying grace and whether it is something like an infused *habitus*. Not that these questions are unimportant, but they are certainly secondary. They are subservient to and dependent upon the overall logic of sacramental mediation, based as it is on the revelation of Christ as the *Logos* of God in the flesh. Balthasar is worried that much of modern theology had essentially forgotten that the Eucharist is *fons et culmen* not only of popular religiosity but also of the Christian faith's intellectual expression. Thus, because of its restricted scope, standard theological treatments of the Eucharist appeared to be far more attenuated than the counterfeit literary versions that made sacramentality a basic feature of human life.

Balthasar did not need Goethe and Rilke to convince him of the dynamism of sacramental discourse, for he had more proximate literary sources, ones that were already baptized. Although they were still distinguished from traditional theological discourse, a host of Catholic poets and novelists provided Balthasar with a parallel theological education to the one he was receiving in seminary. These sources, although much nearer to orthodox Christianity than were Rilke and Hölderlin, equally tend toward the chalice rather than the paten. Because these sources will recur throughout this book, we only need briefly mention that for Balthasar the likes of Charles Péguy, Paul Claudel, Reinhold Schneider, Georges Bernanos, and Léon Bloy were something of a Christian antidote to the theoretical and metaphysical ailments of modern literature. As Balthasar notes throughout his later *Theo-Drama* I, liturgical cult, pagan or Christian, has always had an intimate relationship with the theater, even if at times a contentious one.[15] This is why, perhaps, we should not be surprised to find cultic themes continuously recurring in even the most avowedly anti-Christian literature. But these Catholic authors repeat, without any sense of anachronism, the fruitful union between theater and the Eucharist that is found in the plays of the Middle Ages and later the *autos sacramentales* of the

Spanish baroque. Commenting on the baroque in particular, but precisely as an analogue for the writings of Schneider, Balthasar writes of the characteristics of all Christian drama: "The resolution of all the tragic tensions under the sign of the forgiving grace, the proximity of the theater and the Eucharist (the primal drama in the world): only in its shadow is it possible to play, to bind and loose aright."[16] Treating the Eucharist as *the* primal cosmic drama, a theme found equally in Claudel as in Bernanos, gives this sacrament a weight that seemed to be utterly lacking in some of the manuals, which treated the Eucharist as a remedial aid to repair an accidental breakdown of human nature—a transitory salve, a means of providing grace.

In 1939, Balthasar wrote a brief review of a German translation of Claudel's *La Messe là-bas* (a translation he must have found unsatisfactory, because he later translated the same work himself): "In true Claudelian style, the liturgical event of the Holy Mass, without the slightest spiritualization or allegorization, is placed here in an immense cosmic frame. *The Mass becomes the center point of the homecoming of the world* [*Mittelpunkt der Heimholung der Welt*]."[17] This radical expansion of the usual role ascribed to the Eucharist, found not only in the poets but also in the great mystics and throughout the patristic period, will be precisely the vision that Balthasar explores in his own sacramental theology while also bringing it into harmony with scholastic theological categories and distinctions. In *Glory of the Lord* IV and especially V, Balthasar traces "the parting of the ways" between theological precision and mystical exceptions that occurred internally to the Church in modernity: "The 'mystic' is now identified increasingly in terms of his subjective experience of glory and is stamped as an exception, while the 'rule' is represented by the strictly logical and intellectualist metaphysics of the Church."[18] Without even a hint of nostalgia for a cohesive patristic past, Balthasar's entire theological project is an attempt to reunite what is only separated at great loss to both religious sentiment and rational reflection. How to bring about this intinction, this reunion, of two styles of thought that have only belatedly diverged will be Balthasar's great effort in his eucharistic theology in particular. As we will analyze in detail in this book, for Balthasar, the Eucharist is truly a midpoint for theological reflection. It is a midpoint in that it measures and preserves the distance between God and the creature, which thus makes it function theologically as a prism that enables the light from other pertinent doctrines, from Trinitarian theology to Christology to eschatology, to refract and thus show their distinctive colors. But the Eucharist is also a midpoint for theological styles, an object that not only allows but positively requires a plurality of theological styles and insights, given that it remains unexhausted by either scholastic precision or monastic devotion.

Hans Urs von Balthasar is not typically regarded as having made a major contribution to sacramental theology, as demonstrated by the relatively small amount of attention the Swiss theologian receives from sacramental and liturgical theologians, especially in English and American scholarship.[19] This fact, however, belies the degree of Balthasar's interest in the subject, because it is present from the earliest of his theological works to his very last. The sacraments in general, or the Eucharist in particular, appear throughout his oeuvre, sometimes only as examples for another point, but also often at key junctures. The sacraments play an essential role in Balthasar's theological speculation, and the Eucharist in particular is a privileged locus where most of his major preoccupations intersect. In virtually everything that he wrote, Balthasar makes such strong claims regarding the importance of the sacraments that any casual reader of him will be alerted to the fact *that* the sacraments are essential to Balthasar. *How* they play such a role, however, is neither explicitly stated nor explored in any great depth, either by Balthasar himself or by the secondary literature. Although this remains true for almost all theological *topoi* treated by Balthasar, regarding the sacraments it is particularly true to say that one cannot isolate a single article or book as the most important or exhaustive. Not only did he never write a book exclusively on the sacraments in general or any one sacrament in particular, but the role they play in his theological project can only be understood when it is seen how the sacraments are interwoven into the wide variety of themes that he treats over his long theological career. The Eucharist is spread throughout his work in bits and pieces. It is both everywhere, in that hardly any work is entirely silent on the Eucharist, and nowhere, in that there exists no Balthasarian *de sacramentis in genere* or *de eucharistia*. This book will provide a synthetic account of Balthasar's eucharistic theology by attending to those particular places where he treats classical questions of sacramental theology and by exploring the implications and interconnection of the Eucharist with his broader theological vision.

WHERE IS BALTHASAR'S SACRAMENTAL THEOLOGY?

Balthasar wrote on the Eucharist in his earliest work, and there is no significant period in which he was not developing some aspect of his eucharistic theology. Furthermore, Balthasar's thoughts on the Eucharist remained quite consistent, and this, combined with the synthetic nature of this project, means that any changes or developments in Balthasar's thought will be noted only parenthetically. My study here operates at the level of both exposition and explicit development. Thus, a major goal of the book will be to articulate what is unique to Balthasar's eucharistic theology, to locate important influences, and to flag significant disagreements with contemporaries and predecessors. Because this book is more thematic and speculative than archival, I do not aim to show in detail historical developments in his thought. Thus, here in the introduction, it is necessary to quickly note the main sites of Balthasar's eucharistic theology.

First, much of Balthasar's early work on the Church Fathers devotes significant attention to the sacraments, and the themes he discovers and develops from the Fathers remain operative for his later systematic work. His book on Origen, *Parole et mystère chez Origène* (1936/1957), is particularly focused on sacramentality, as is his anthology of Origen's work, *Geist und Feuer* (1938).[20] Likewise, his books on Maximus the Confessor, *Kosmische Liturgie* (1941), and Gregory of Nyssa, *Présence et pensée* (1942) both provide strong arguments regarding how the sacraments function centrally in the patristic metaphysical landscape.[21] His articles that treat the Eucharist in the greatest depth include "Seeing, Hearing, and Reading within the Church" (1939);[22] "Liturgy and Awe" (1960);[23] "Eucharistic Congress 1960" (1960);[24] "Seeing, Believing, Eating" (1961);[25] "The Mass: A Sacrifice of the Church?" (1967);[26] "The Mystery of the Eucharist" (1970),[27] which may be his best and most concise summary of his eucharistic theology; "The Veneration of the Holy of Holies" (1971),[28] which looks at the question of the Adoration of the Host; "Spirit and Institution" (1974);[29] "The Worthiness of the Liturgy" (1979);[30] and "Eucharist: Gift of Love" (1986).[31] From the *Glory of the Lord*, there are major sections on the sacraments in *GL* I (1961),[32] many of the portraits in *GL* II and III (both 1962) are focused on issues of sacramentality, especially those on Irenaeus, Denys, Hopkins, and Péguy, and *GL* VII (1969), the final volume, on the New Testament, is as a whole filled with discussion of the Eucharist.[33] In the *Theo-Drama*, the first three volumes contain scattered and important references to the sacraments.[34] *TD* IV (1980) and V (1983) are in a category unto themselves, and even though it has already been stipulated that there is no central place to look for Balthasar's eucharistic theology, were one forced to choose, these two volumes, particularly the latter, would be at the top of the list. *Theo-Logic* I (1947/1985) and II (1985) are sacramental through and through, but *TL* III (1987)[35] treats all of the sacraments explicitly. Finally, the short *Epilogue* (1987) to the *Trilogy* is a highly important work, and contains an important section on flesh and sacramentality.[36]

Even though, again, we are not attempting a comprehensive list of everywhere that Balthasar discusses the Eucharist or the sacraments, it is important to note a few more works that will play an important role in this book. In particular, *A Theology of History* (1950/1959) is key to my chapter 4 on eschatology, and *Mysterium Paschale* (1970) foreshadows and even gives a different light to similar themes found in the *Theo-Drama*. Also, his books *Bernanos* (1954/1988) and *Reinhold Schneider* (1953/1991) are essential locations where Balthasar uses literature to give life to what he calls an "existential sacramental theology," which is explored here in my chapter 2. Mention must also be made of Balthasar's prodigious work in transcribing and editing the massive oeuvre of Adrienne von Speyr, much of which is a direct source for Balthasar's own sacramental theology, and to his numerous translations into German from Spanish, French, English, Italian, Latin, and Greek. With regard to the Eucharist, his most important translations include Pedro Calderón de la Barca's *El Gran Teatro del Mundo*, translated as *Das große Welttheater* (1959);[37] Paul Claudel's *La Messe là-bas*, translated as *Die Messe Des Verbannten* (1981);[38] Jean Corbon's *Liturgie de Source*, translated as *Liturgie aus dem Urquell* (1981);[39] and a translation of the ninth-century work of Paschasius Radbertus on the Eucharist, *De corpore et sanguine domini*, translated as *Vom Leib und Blut des Herrn* (1988).[40]

Scholars of Balthasar's thought have repeatedly noted the importance of the Eucharist for his theology, and the uniqueness of his positions, which has resulted in a substantial number of books,[41] dissertations,[42] and articles[43] on one issue or another of his eucharistic theology. However, these previous studies, albeit providing a foundation for research, even when considered cumulatively do not approximate exhausting Balthasar's eucharistic theology, but rather leave open questions as to how these various elements fit together. The question that remains is whether Balthasar simply had several disparate contributions to make to specific questions regarding the Eucharist, or whether these various strands come together into a coherent eucharistic theology. To decide in favor of the latter, which is the main thesis of this book, is to say that behind Balthasar's particular proposals is a unique vision of the Eucharist that is *essential*, rather than ornamental, to his theological project. To state it succinctly, the "logic" of the Eucharist functions somewhat like a first principle for Balthasar, an inference that then results in particular decisions in his Trinitarian theology, Christology, ecclesiology, anthropology, metaphysics, and eschatology. Balthasar does his theology by thinking *from* the Eucharist, imbuing all of his theology with a eucharistic light. To understand its place in Balthasar's theology, then, it will indeed be necessary to analyze the Eucharist *in se*, but equally important will be to see how it is refracted in these other areas of his thought.

LOOKING FORWARD

In addition to this introduction and a brief conclusion, this book has four central chapters. Chapter 1 begins with what Balthasar calls the "logic of the Eucharist," which is operative at the level of Christ's incarnation and the intra-Trinitarian life of God. This will serve as something of a hermeneutical key for the rest of the book. This "logic" could be summarized as Christ's *Hingabe* ("devotion," "surrender," or, more loosely, "gift of self") toward humanity, and his *Gelöstheit* ("availability"), his readiness to accept a mission of self-distribution. This chapter will then begin with a short section on Christology and its connection to the Eucharist, which provides the entryway into Balthasar's thesis regarding an eternal Eucharist within the life of the Trinity. According to Balthasar, *the* goal of the Incarnation, culminating in the Eucharist (with the cross as the means), is Christ being able to transcend the boundaries between persons, which he accomplishes by becoming literally comestible. This also helps us to understand why Balthasar considers the Eucharist to be a form of *kenosis* for Christ. In addition to a discussion of Christ's downward movement in the Incarnation and his becoming eucharistic, the chapter also has an extensive discussion of Christ's resurrected flesh. Here I will explore Balthasar's attempt at a partial recovery, even if this recovery ultimately functions as a correction, of Luther's notion of Christ's post-Resurrection ubiquity. I then consider Balthasar's claim that it is the Eucharist that gives us the greatest insight into the intra-Trinitarian life of God, in which the divine persons are portrayed as relations of worship and praise, as the total gift of self and surrender (*Hingabe*) from one person to another. This is, for Balthasar, a "eucharistic" relationship that also serves as the condition for the possibility of the ecclesial Eucharist (the theme of the following two chapters).

Chapter 2 begins by continuing a theme from chapter 1, the relationship between Christ and the Eucharist. However, whereas in chapter 1 the issue was what it means for Christ to become Eucharist, touching on questions of the mode of his presence and the state of his resurrected flesh, chapter 2 will address the distribution of the eucharistic Christ to the Church. The major contention of the chapter will be that, for Balthasar, the Holy Spirit's role is the universalization of the particularity of Christ. Thus central to this chapter is Balthasar's proposal for an "existential sacramental theology," which has one meaning when the mode of Christ's presence is under consideration and another when discussing the conditions of fruitful reception. A brief section will give attention to sacramental causality in Balthasar, as a means of arriving at his tension between the objective grace of the sacraments (associated primarily with Christ) and its subjective appropriation by the Christian (with reference to the Holy Spirit). How Balthasar holds together these elements (Christ, Church, Holy Spirit) is elucidated in his theology of the Church's sacrifice in the Mass, which will demonstrate how, according to Balthasar, the Church does not "add" anything to Christ's sacrifice, but rather makes this sacrifice its own by willing, consenting to, Christ's sacrifice. This consent thus implies a reciprocal receptivity, by the power of the Holy Spirit, of the Christian to accept his own (eucharistic) mission. I then conclude the chapter by exploring how Balthasar extends the logic of the Eucharist to individual Christian obedience and mission in the world.

Chapter 3 looks at the visible and tactile experience of the eucharistic liturgy. The question to be addressed is how, and how *not*, the liturgical rites themselves inform Balthasar's theology. The chapter begins by analyzing Balthasar's relationship to the liturgy, from his observation and critique of the liturgical movement before Vatican II to his proposals and interpretation of the liturgical reforms undertaken at the council. This will set the stage for an analysis of Balthasar's aesthetics, with an eye to his clear resistance to any overly aesthetic analysis of the sacramental rites. The development of a Balthasarian sacramental phenomenology will thus be one of the major goals of this chapter. After understanding some of the fundamentals of his aesthetics, I then can begin to make sense of Balthasar's assertion that the sacraments can only appear "marginally" in his *Herrlichkeit*. Balthasar is not deaf to the human and cosmic symbolism in bread and wine, or in general, to the importance of ritual and anthropology, but he resolutely does not consider this approach to be sufficient for sacramental theology. I then highlight the negative limits that Balthasar puts in place regarding an aesthetic presentation of the Eucharist, which are due in part to his strong adherence to the *sacramentum/res* distinction, his indebtedness to Pascal, and the importance of an eschatological delay. In order to extend Balthasar's thought into current debates in sacramental theology, I consider the difference between Louis-Marie Chauvet and Jean-Yves Lacoste, the latter of whom can be considered to extend many of the insights already found in Balthasar. Balthasar is cautious about considering the liturgy and the sacraments as forms of manifestation, but he does have a positive contribution regarding liturgical aesthetics that can also be further developed, which this chapter will attempt to do. Balthasar does provide some indications as to what a Balthasarian "liturgical theology" might look like, so in drawing upon a variety of other sources and developing what is already found in Balthasar, I will conclude with suggestions as to how the texts and rites of the liturgy could and do make their way into theological speculation.

Chapter 4 is dedicated to eschatology. Balthasar is widely recognized as a theologian who made a major contribution to eschatological speculation, but it is less often recognized how *sacramental* his eschatology is. I will argue that the Eucharist in particular has a regulative function for Balthasar's eschatology, ensuring a high level of intrahistorical eschatological fulfillment while also delaying the fullness of that reality. It is his sacramental commitments that distinguish Balthasar's eschatology from those of his contemporaries, such as Rudolf Bultmann and Jürgen Moltmann, among others. In addition to situating his position among the other major eschatological theologians of the twentieth century, I give special attention to those aspects of Balthasar's eschatology that are particularly indebted to eucharistic theology, especially his concept of "sacramental time." Essential to the question of time is the issue of the relationship between finite time, which is more often than not the site of tragedy (what Balthasar calls "the slaughter"), and God's "time," which is constituted by praise and adoration (what Balthasar calls "liturgy"). Thus Balthasar's view on the interplay between "liturgy and slaughter" is a major question for the chapter, because it is the means by which he claims that God is neither untouched by nor subject to the vagaries and, frankly, the horrors of creaturely time. Because Balthasar recurs to his own literary preferences for this question, they will be explored in some depth here. Figures such as Calderón de la Barca and Charles Péguy, and above all the book of Revelation, give Balthasar the material for establishing a maximally liturgical vision that is also highly sensitive to creaturely tragedy. I conclude the chapter by returning to the question of pneumatic flesh, but this time with regard to the resurrected flesh of the saints. This analysis of the *communio sanctorum* is ultimately aimed at Balthasar's affirmation that the Eucharist is not limited to the *ecclesia militans*, but is also a reality for the *ecclesia triumphans*. Thus heaven, for Balthasar, is not the cessation of sacramental life, but rather the heightening of this reality. Thus I end by returning to the concept of an eternal liturgy, an eternal worship, within the divine life, in which the saints are invited to participate.

CONCLUSION

"The Holy Spirit can reopen clogged arteries that have imperceptibly narrowed during the course of theological history. He can also—as if out of the blue—exhibit new, hitherto unnoticed aspects of the ancient tradition that was known from the beginning," states Balthasar.[44] I do not make a judgment as to the Holy Spirit's role in Balthasar's theological project, but it is clear that he viewed the state of sacramental theology in the early twentieth century as such an instance of a clogged theological artery. Thus, subsequent to the scholastic style and tradition of sacramental texts, much of Balthasar's sacramental theology moves at a tangent, charting a new direction and barely skimming the bulk of what was contained in the scholastic manuals. If one is familiar with the standard vocabulary, distinctions, and main questions that have occupied sacramental theology for centuries, Balthasar's voice seems out of place. This is, at least in part, because of his attempt to bring more "vinous" concerns to bear on systematic theology, to refuse to allow mystical insight, liturgical piety, and poetic license to remain extraneous to the theological task. He has new questions, perhaps a new vocabulary, and new answers regarding the mystery of the Eucharist. This new vitality that Balthasar brings to eucharistic theology can be interpreted in a variety of ways. One could interpret Balthasar's various writings on the Eucharist with either a hermeneutics of rupture—to borrow the division used by Pope Benedict XVI concerning the interpretation of Vatican II—such that he is intentionally repudiating not only the scholastic tradition but also perhaps the entire tendency of Western sacramental theology since the early Middle Ages, or with a hermeneutics of continuity, such that Balthasar's audacity to say something new is intended as a compliment and a supplement rather than as a replacement.

His occasional rhetorical excess will lend credence to an interpretation that favors a hard rupture, but it is clear that Balthasar's general theological tendency is toward a generosity that attempts to demonstrate consonance before dissonance. With regard to eucharistic theology, he provides no explicit denunciation of the bulk of the positions held by his scholastic predecessors, even if he never tires in noting their stylistic and perhaps theological deficiencies. He does have qualms regarding very particular issues, but these critiques and counterproposals are directed specifically and are a necessary part of the theological discipline. His "reform" of eucharistic theology, if that indeed is the correct word, is more akin to the reforming work of Ignatius of Loyola than of Martin Luther. It is an attempt not so much to reformulate, trim back, and rearrange the old doctrines but more to show the internal vibrancy and intellectual and spiritual sophistication latent therein. Instead of curtailing the gains made in questions specifically eucharistic, Balthasar aims to make the depth of sacramental discourse relevant for the entire breadth of dogmatic theology, to let the former spill over and fructify the latter. Again, Balthasar is calling for a natural unclogging of the arteries, not a new, artificial bypass that leaves the clog untreated. In the spirit of *Ressourcement* (but without an assumption that any one era of theological expression is wholly preferable to any other),[45] Balthasar's eucharistic theology is one that attempts to recall the range and profundity of earlier sacramental thought that does not exhaust itself solely in discussions regarding causality, institution, form, and matter. His sources, as we will see throughout this book, are just as often poets and novelists as they are the Church Fathers and mystics. Much may appear unfamiliar in Balthasar's presentation of the Eucharist, but usually his thought has some precedent within the tradition. It is this continuity that will be stressed throughout, even at those points when Balthasar may seem to stand alone. The stated goal of my book is to highlight a uniquely Balthasarian eucharistic theology, but I will give attention and emphasis to drawing lines of connection between Balthasar and previous eucharistic theologies, whether there exists a direct dependence or merely a thematic compatibility. Thus I will attempt to portray Balthasar's position as firmly situated within the theological tradition but also as radically innovative with regard to his use of those sources.

Beyond simple exposition of his eucharistic theology, my more constructive goal will be the development of Balthasar's thought. Thus, I will freely expand upon Balthasar's initial insights, bringing to greater systematic clarity those left at the level of suggestion by Balthasar himself, and drawing probable or at least possible conclusions from the various strands of his thought. I will remain faithful to the letter of Balthasar's texts but will be free with regard to supplementation and even correction. The eucharistic speculation that Balthasar has left us is a large set of puzzle pieces, scattered throughout his massive oeuvre, with plenty of missing pieces. Here the puzzle pieces that could be found have been collected, with many of the pieces fitting together quite nicely, and with many others floating around without an obvious place in the whole. Balthasar never chose to put the pieces together himself, which apparently he could have done quite quickly,[46] and here I will instead attempt a coherent portrait of the reassembled puzzle, most of which is Balthasar's original, some of which is my own attempt to fill in the gaps or even extend the edges.

But beyond any particular gaps or remaining questions regarding the Eucharist, the ultimate goal of this book is to demonstrate that Balthasar's importance as a sacramental theologian lies in his seamless integration of eucharistic theology with the rest of his theology. Even better, rather than merely interconnected with the other theological topics, the Eucharist for Balthasar is the center of all theology, and all of his writings are imbued with a sacramental hue. He needs to be supplemented on a variety of particular eucharistic issues, in other words, he does not say everything that needs to be said about this sacrament, but this supplementation and development point back to a fundamental comprehensiveness and expansiveness regarding the Eucharist that is unmatched in the twentieth century. The aim of this book is thus to demonstrate that Balthasar's theology as a whole begins and ends with the Eucharist, both the chalice and the paten, and that many of the most characteristically Balthasarian theological claims are explorations of the startling claim that God makes himself edible and potable.

CHAPTER 1

Balthasar's Eucharistic Theology

Sacramental Foreground and Trinitarian Background

The main backdrop to Balthasar's eucharistic theology is a major shift in sacramental discourse that occurred in the twentieth century. Of the many trends and developments in sacramental theology over the past century, perhaps none is as ubiquitous, both in academic and more popular work, as the change of the noun "sacrament" into its adjectival form, "sacramental." This follows upon the solid foundation of both patristic and medieval conceptions of the sacraments as unexhausted by the seven ecclesial sacraments, or even by the Church's life as a whole. Not only does every aspect of religious life seem to evince a sacrament-like character, but even the structure of created nature can be legitimately named as sacramental. The basic impulse here is that if what the Church proclaims about the sacraments is in fact true, then this must have far greater import and far wider implications than is typically found in a scholastic treatise on the seven sacraments.

However, if there were dangers in the previous contraction of the concept of sacrament to only seven distinct rites (as contemporary consensus never ceases to suggest), there are also dangers of ambiguity in our current age of expansion. If everything manifests a sacramental or eucharistic structure, the particular sacraments seem to be merely different instances, even if privileged ones, of the same universal law. In order to avoid this total undervaluing of the uniqueness of the sacraments, certain clarifications should be made as to the flexibility of the word "sacrament" when it is expanded beyond its typical use. It could be made flexible by using it analogically, but in such a case one would need to ask what is the *primary* referent, the ecclesial sacraments or a sacramental structure of creaturely being? Usually, the expansion of the sacramental category means extending the notion to things that are *less* theologically specified than sacraments (e.g., nature, friendship), but it can also be expanded to cover other data pertaining to divine revelation (e.g., Christology, Trinitarian theology).

How Balthasar navigates this terrain of an expanding notion of the sacramental will be the subject of this chapter, particularly as he considers the Eucharist to be constitutive of both Christology and Trinitarian theology. For Balthasar, the acknowledgment that each distinct doctrinal topic is necessarily presupposed in all the others functions as both a necessary methodological postulate and a concrete imperative for his own writing. Even as this integral view of doctrine is true of all of his theology, his eucharistic theology in particular pushes this confidence in the pervasive coherence of Catholic dogmatics to an extreme limit. It seems that, for Balthasar, the Eucharist is the key to understanding *every* aspect of the *ordo salutis*: "The revelation of the Son has from the very outset a eucharistic structure, which implies also that the Faith that answers this revelation as its echo has the same structure."[1] For all his other differences from Louis-Marie Chauvet, Balthasar would agree with this fundamental intuition: "Against the custom that has prevailed since the rise of the Scholastic 'treatises,' sacramental theology cannot be viewed as just another sector in the field of theology; it is rather, as the Fathers recognized, a *dimension* that recurs throughout the whole of Christian theology, a distinctive way of looking at it."[2] How Balthasar performs this audacious expansion will be seen in what follows, and whether and how it is justifiable will be explored in this chapter's conclusion. Though they share the same intuition, Balthasar's deployment of this principle is markedly different from Chauvet's, in that sacrament is made productive not only in the anthropological arena but also in the Trinitarian.

Linking the Eucharist and the Incarnation as a thematic couple is not unique to Balthasar, functioning as it does as a standard trope in patristic, medieval, and contemporary sacramental theologies. For example, for Thomas Aquinas it is structurally essential that his treatise on the sacraments follows directly after that of the Incarnation, considering that the Incarnation retains a causal influence in the world by means of the sacraments.[3] It is indeed axiomatic to consider the various sacraments as prolongations of the logic of the Incarnation, particularly with regard to the bodily nature of Christ's manifestation. The sacraments are best understood, then, in relationship to the fundamental mystery of the Incarnation, on which they depend and of which they are the expression. What we find in Balthasar, however, is the desire to see this connection move in both directions at once: in addition to the Incarnation shedding light upon the sacraments, Balthasar thinks that the sacraments can give us a hermeneutical key into the shape and the purpose of the Incarnation. In this, Matthias Joseph Scheeben is perhaps Balthasar's closest predecessor: "From the mystery of the Incarnation we pass immediately to the mystery of the Eucharist. Our main reason for proceeding thus is that the relationship of the two mysteries is so close that they serve to complement, illuminate, and clarify each other."[4] Like his nineteenth-century theological forbear, but to a more radical and consistent degree, Balthasar wants to consider Christ in the retrospective light of the sacramental economy.

The idea, for Balthasar and for Scheeben, is that Catholic doctrines have everything to do with one another, and no one specific point of doctrine can be understood without at least implicitly invoking the rest of the totality of belief. This was decidedly *not* the practice of the manualist tradition that began Balthasar's theological formation. In fact, what is distinctive about the manuals (and is, in a way, their strength) is that they depend on being able to separate off one distinct area of doctrine and analyze it in depth, without reference to the other articles of faith, treatments of which could be found elsewhere. For example, Pourrat's widely used 1907 manual on the sacraments, mentioned in the introduction, laments the fact that *sacramentum* was used "indiscriminately" until Peter Lombard. This indiscriminate use included extending the category of sacrament to the Incarnation and "all the mysteries of the Catholic faith." For Pourrat, this was "a confusion which impeded the development of the Catholic doctrine concerning the number of the Sacraments," a confusion that would not be remedied until Peter Lombard.[5] Balthasar does not contest, and in fact commends, Lombard's decision for only seven sacraments, *sensu stricto*.[6] But instead of a "confusion," for Balthasar the "indiscriminate" use of the sacramental category in the patristic and early medieval periods points to an insight that has either been lost or at least partially obscured by the tendency of scholasticism to divide and define the various doctrinal *topoi*. Balthasar does not advocate a return to the imprecisions of the patristics, for Lombard's choice and scholasticism in general have brought enormous gains in precision and even insight, but he does think that the sacraments must be seen again precisely as a part of the central paschal mystery and the mystery of the Trinitarian life of God. In other words, to dedicate an entire treatise to the sacraments without connecting them to the other central mysteries of the faith, as seen in Pourrat, is to effectively view them as peripheral and perhaps secondary aspects of Christianity. This approach, which again presumes that the sacraments are best understood when separated out from their previous entanglement with the other doctrines, effectively hands the sacraments and the liturgy over to the social sciences for examination, which take this separation as a fait accompli. This is precisely what much of sacramental and liturgical studies have become in recent decades, and Balthasar resists this with an unmatched vehemence.

For Aquinas, Christ's humanity is an *instrumentum coniunctum* of the divinity, whereas the sacraments are *instrumenta separata*.[7] The rather unfortunate simile that Thomas uses to describe this relationship is that the *instrumentum coniunctum* is like a hand that can move an object directly by being conjoined to the agent, but an *instrumentum separatum* is like a stick that one uses in order to move something else.[8] For Thomas, this is meant to simply demonstrate the order of causality and how God, the principal agent of grace, does not always cause grace directly and immediately, but prefers to use secondary causes, such as sacraments, which are given the dignity of cooperating as the means by which God's grace is made effective. It is an enormously important metaphysical point and one to which Balthasar would proffer no objection. The use of the term *instrumentum separatum* and the chosen metaphor of the stick help to illustrate the point, but even for Thomas they take on no more than a limited explanatory power.[9] Nevertheless, Balthasar worries that some have taken Thomas's parallel between sacraments and sticks rather literally, not as the heuristic metaphor that it is, which would almost sever the Incarnation–sacrament connection entirely: "Sacraments would be radically misunderstood if one attempted in the least way to disjoin them from the Christ-form as *instrumenta separata*."[10] This disjointed approach, or we could derisively call it the "stick approach," would see the sacraments as arbitrarily chosen (but surely still *conveniens*) instruments by which God does certain things in the world, and even though God happened to choose the distribution of his Son's body and blood as the privileged means of giving grace, any number of alternatives would have been acceptable.

Correlative to treating the sacraments in their own separate treatise, without direct attention to the other doctrines, is that treatises on other topics, for instance *De deo uno*, *De deo trino*, and *De incarnatione*, often enough do not seem to be particularly interested in the sacraments. And although an argument can be made that the whole of Aquinas's *Summa theologiae* is sacramentally oriented, it is simply a fact that the sacraments are almost never mentioned in the *Prima Pars*, giving the impression that how Christ abides with his Church in the Eucharist tells us very little about the life of God *in se*.[11] In contrast, one of Balthasar's most important works on Trinitarian theology, *TD* V, is also his most densely eucharistic. Again, whatever gains have been made by the "divide and conquer" approach to dogmatic theology, a theology more closely hewed to the paten rather than the chalice, what theology also needs is an approach that can point to the inner harmony of the entire system of Catholic doctrines, which is not a simple series of isolated propositions, but a network of mutually implicating beliefs that receive their validity insofar as they support and are reflected in the rest.

A EUCHARISTIC LOGIC

To understand how Balthasar attempts to demonstrate the broader theological relevance of the Eucharist, it will be placed here in a triptych with Trinitarian theology and a theology of the Incarnation. The Trinity/Incarnation/Eucharist triptych is assumed to be one of internal coherence (all pointing to the same mystery) and reciprocal illumination. According to Balthasar, this was the assumption and the method of Irenaeus, and of John the Evangelist: "In this circular motion a line of thought is equally true whether it is followed from below to above or from above to below, from front to back or from back to front. We can say that the eucharist would not be true if Christ's Incarnation were not true, and it would not be true unless man were truly composed of spirit and flesh, *and we can consider the same fact in reverse order.*"[12] To follow this line of thought *in reverse order* would mean that the Incarnation is only understood, in its depths, when seen from the light of the Eucharist, with the Eucharist as its presupposition and interpretation. The Eucharist is, for Balthasar, the entelechy, the internal motivating force and terminus of God taking on flesh: "In the Eucharist of his surrendered Son, God concludes his new and eternal covenant with mankind, committing himself to it utterly and with no reservation."[13]

What connects these key doctrines together, in addition to specific content, is one particular word that occurs nearly everywhere in Balthasar's corpus: *Hingabe*.[14] We must set Balthasar's use of *Hingabe* in relief before entering into the heart of this chapter, for the concept is the governing principle of his eucharistic theology. This peculiar German word is hidden in the English translations because of the variety of possible definitions, from "sacrifice" to "devotion" to "gift of self" to "abandonment." For example, in the English translation of Balthasar's most philosophical text, *Wahrheit*, later published as *Theo-Logic* I, *Hingabe* is variously rendered as "self-abandonment," "surrender," "giving away," and "total self-giving," and in other contexts it is best rendered as "sacrifice."[15] For an example of the wider German context, Jean-Pierre de Caussade's *L'Abandon à la Providence Divine* had been translated into the German as *Hingabe an Gottes Vorsehung* in 1945,[16] but it also must be kept in mind that the etymology of the word, *Hin-Gabe*, contains the connotation of gift and offering, all of which contributes to the depth and the difficulty of this word. We can also note that the words of institution in the German Mass speak of the body "der für euch *hingegeben* wird" (which is given up for you). Balthasar exploits the polyvalence of this word, which enables him to use it to connect various doctrines and concepts that require differing sets of vocabulary in other languages. For our purposes, the Eucharist/Incarnation/Trinity triptych in particular depends heavily on Balthasar's use of this word, for *Hingabe*, according to Balthasar, is perhaps the most fitting word to use for each of these subjects, taking into account the different connotations of the word for each subject. For instance, when discussing the Eucharist, the connotation of "sacrifice" will be in play to a greater extent, and the kenotic aspect of the Incarnation is highlighted with the notion of *Hingabe* as "abandonment" and "surrender,"[17] but for intra-Trinitarian relations, the dominant sense will be that of the "self-gift" between the divine persons. For Balthasar, the advantage of having one, fairly plastic word that can cover all three of these central theological *topoi* is that it demonstrates that even though all language about God is ultimately analogical, and thus subject to the tribunal of the *maior dissimilitudo*, there is still very good reason to think about these three subjects in particular as complementary and mutually enlightening.

Balthasar's privileging of this word has a proximate and a more distant origin. The former is Adrienne von Speyr, and the latter is Caussade, but also the whole tradition of mysticism that emphasizes the soul's *abandonment* (*Gelassenheit*) and various degrees of passivity before God. Balthasar traces this school of spirituality, which he calls the "metaphysics of the saints," from Eckhart to Tauler and Suso, up to Julian of Norwich and even Ignatius of Loyola, but it has such a wide effect that we can say that it "has left its mark on the whole of Christian thinking right up into the modern era."[18] Instead of distinguishing the important differences among these authors, we can focus on Caussade, who, as Balthasar acknowledges, is a synecdoche of the entire movement.[19] Balthasar grants that Caussade successfully avoided the dangers of quietism, and what makes his teaching on *L'Abandon* so remedial to some of the excesses and errors of his predecessors is precisely his insistence on loving surrender (*Hingabe*): "Caussade clearly saw that every attempt to give created reason *more* than the surrender [*Hingabe*] of the perfect fiat (*more* in the sense of a speculative or mystical idealism) would in reality deprive it of its noblest act and clearly turn it into something *less*."[20] Thus Caussade's notion of abandonment, particularly as an index of Ignatian detachment, is one major tributary flowing into Balthasar's conception of *Hingabe*. Caussade's insistence on the soul's perfect disponibility to obey God's will provides a gloss on the Marian *fiat* that is essential to Balthasar's thought, both in his spiritual and dogmatic writings.

This largely Franco-Germanic mystical tradition is thus one essential side to Balthasar's notion of *Hingabe*, but it is precisely only one side. It needs to be supplemented by the other side, which turns the tables and focuses not only on the soul's abandonment to God, but also on God's abandonment for the sinner. This finds its clearest expression, according to Balthasar, in Speyr. Of course, the Marian *fiat* is central to all of Speyr's thought and is the *sine qua non* of a genuinely Christian attitude toward God, but for Speyr and Balthasar, when looked at from a wider perspective, this creaturely *Hingabe* toward the divine will is a fundamentally *secondary* act, second both temporally and logically.[21] Balthasar then finds a place for Ignatian obedience, or Caussade's abandonment, within the wider frame of the primary obedience of Christ to the Father, of the Son's abandonment on the cross. *Hingabe*, then, is a property first of God and only secondarily of the creature. The *Hingabe* of the individual and of the Church will become thematic in chapter 2, but in what follows here, we will explore God's *Hingabe*, first as this is manifest in the Incarnation and cross, all the way to the Eucharist, and ultimately within the intra-Trinitarian life of God.

The Eucharist, when the Trinitarian horizon is kept in view, and the Trinity, presupposing the eucharistic *Hingabe*, function then as two poles that give shape to Balthasar's soteriology. With the Trinitarian *Hingabe* as background and the eucharistic *Hingabe* as foreground, Balthasar thinks two errors can be avoided: first and most importantly, this framework avoids the Hegelian collapse of the immanent and economic Trinity, which has the result whereby "God is entangled in the world process and becomes a tragic, mythological God."[22] In this case, Nietzsche's *Gott ist tot* can be accepted without qualification, and the hard-won theopaschite formula of Constantinople II is traded in for a facile theopaschism. Were Balthasar to adopt this approach, Christ's eucharistic self-gift would be without remainder, and he would exist solely as a sacrificial offering by forsaking his Trinitarian, extrahistorical existence. The other error is the total disassociation of God's inner, Triune life with the event of the cross and the subsequent Eucharist. The Eucharist, in this case, would at worst be arbitrary or even misleading. At best, we could say with Aquinas that it is *conveniens* (which, though not a strict necessity, is indeed a form of necessity), but Balthasar wants to go even a step further than this. Or better, Balthasar wants to give the *argumentum ex convenientia* a basis not only in data congruent with the whole landscape of salvation history but also ultimately in the very nature of the God who originated and will culminate that history. We will see by the end of this chapter that Balthasar attempts to find a solution to this aporia by locating the eucharistic *Hingabe* within God's own intra-Trinitarian life. God pouring himself out eucharistically into creation, then, is not a necessity external to God that impinges upon his freedom, but instead is a gratuitous expression of God's internal, eucharistic love.[23]

MOVEMENT TOWARD THE EUCHARIST

We can now turn to Balthasar's explicit eucharistic Christology, which is encapsulated in the following: "Only the Eucharist really completes the Incarnation."[24] For Balthasar, the Eucharist must have been the entelechy of the Incarnation from the beginning and is thus the completion and fulfillment of what is meant by *verbum caro factum est.* For Balthasar, this connection applies first and foremost to soteriology, that is, to dramatics. Thus, if the drama of the Incarnation was a saving event, the Eucharist is its application or reverberation in history. And, for Balthasar, because this reverberation was the goal from the beginning, the Incarnation was always oriented toward Christ becoming bread, and, more specifically, the cross was not so much an end in itself, but rather the means by which Christ became eucharistic. In this section, we will trace Balthasar's understanding of how the cross is oriented toward the sacrament, and how the sacrament retains the marks of its cruciform origin.

The Cruciform Eucharist and the Eucharistic Cross

In almost every discussion of the Eucharist, Balthasar turns to language that serves to highlight the violent origins of the sacrament. This is not an occasional rhetorical excess, but rather Balthasar's ordinary way of speaking about this sacrament. He rarely says simply "Christ's body and blood," but instead draws on a host of adjectives: it is "torn flesh"[25] or "slaughtered flesh" and "poured-out blood,"[26] and "it is the body in its state of being torn, the blood in its state of being shed that are offered to us as food and drink."[27] The means by which Christ comes to be present is never calmly described as a substantial conversion of the bread into Christ's body (though this is assumed), but always with a reminder that this sacrament comes only as a consequence of the cross: the Eucharist is then the "'liquefying' of Jesus' earthly substance."[28] This language, particularly his repeated claim that Christ "becomes liquid," points to Balthasar's understanding of Christ's eucharistic state as an explicitly kenotic one. There are traditional warrants for a kenotic presentation of the Eucharist, and these will be explored in order to note Balthasar's dependence upon these predecessors and to accentuate his own distinctive voice. First, however, it should be noted that Balthasar's primary intention is to closely imitate

the scriptural language concerning the Eucharist, not to promote an ul-
trarealism if not some form of stercoranism or a eucharistic sadism.
Balthasar's use of hyperbole is his particular mode of signaling the epistemic reserve necessary to the theological task.[29] Balthasar's eucharistic
hyperboles are meant to mirror the scriptural data, and the scriptural intent, which is to invite the reader to enter both speculatively and medita-
tively into the mystery of Christ's appearance in the flesh. Whether this
is justified or not should be judged after examining Balthasar's actual
performance.

Of course, Balthasar's description of Christ's body as "broken" and
his blood as "poured out" comes directly from the institution narratives
themselves, which are set in a clearly sacrificial context that points directly to the coming crucifixion.[30] It is also a notably Johannine theme,
not only Christ's command to eat (τρώγω) his flesh and drink his blood
in John 6, but also the blood and water that come gushing from Christ's
side on the cross (John 19:34–35), which have consistently been understood as symbols of baptism and Eucharist. Furthermore, according to
Aquinas the chief figure of the Eucharist is the paschal lamb, because it is
"Christ crucified who is present in this sacrament: *Christum passum, qui
continetur in hoc sacramento.*"[31] Thus, Balthasar's language is entirely
in keeping with scripture and ecclesial tradition, the latter of which, in
theology, devotion, and the liturgy, have maintained the indissoluble link
between the Eucharist and the cross. For Balthasar, "the two—the cross
and the eucharistic meal—viewed from two angles, are the same."[32] He
also worries that this connection is being lost, which is why he complains
that the Eucharist is "so poorly understood and watered-down by many
theologians and preachers."[33]

There is perhaps no Catholic theologian who would not, at least implicitly, see the Eucharist as derivative and in some way dependent on
Christ's crucifixion. To say otherwise would be to ignore the clear scriptural connections and to militate against the Church's entire tradition on
this matter. The many debates surrounding *how* the crucified Jesus continues to be present in the Church notwithstanding, the assumption has
always been that this relationship is constitutive and necessary if the Eucharist is to be not only the presence of Christ but also the agent to communicate the saving event of the cross. Balthasar takes this connection so
seriously that he views the two not as a sequence, the cross with a later

eucharistic result, but rather as a single event. Balthasar finds his basis
for this in the fact that the Last Supper comes before the Crucifixion, so
that if one had to decide, it would be that the cross is a result of the Eucharist.[34] All that flows from the cross, such as the Church and the sacraments "must not be regarded as a mere result of the Cross-event but as
a constituent element of it."[35] Even further, for Balthasar, the Crucifixion
would be entirely meaningless without the sacrament. The cross is not a
tragedy, a "Nietzschean Yes to the world's ultimate contradiction," because it was not Christ's unexpected and fated destiny that is of utterly no
value in the face of the Absolute.[36] Christ is thus both the one disposed of,
in that he accepts the Father's mission of the cross/Eucharist, and the one
who disposes of himself, in that his sovereign freedom is demonstrated in
the *prior* institution of the Eucharist.[37]

Balthasar's eucharistic theology, particularly when the kenotic aspect is under consideration, is perhaps best represented artistically by
the popular medieval painting of the mystic winepress, which he mentions on multiple occasions.[38] It portrays Christ, the man of sorrows, with
the cross bearing down upon him as he stands in a winepress, treading
grapes. Yet it is not the grapes below that are significant, but Christ, who
is being "juiced" by the weight of the cross. His blood flows copiously
out, through the grapes, and out of the press into a chalice. However, unlike the main scriptural sources for this image (Isaiah 63 and Revelation
14), which at first glance seem to suggest that God is treading on sinners,
in this medieval image it is ultimately the case that God is not only the
one treading but the one trod upon: it is God's blood that is poured out.[39]
This dissolution even of Christ's mortal body so that it can be made permeable and thus communicable is what Balthasar has in mind when he
considers Christ's "liquefaction." Christ is "squished" instead of sinners,
but Balthasar does not understand this in the purely substitutionary sense.
It is not only a transfer of wrath (though this should not be entirely dismissed either); the cross is also the occasion for a purely positive generation of the Church and the sacraments. Yet, this generation is ineluctably
tied to the negative, bloody origin.

The image of the mystic winepress is an instance of the wider phenomenon of devotion to Christ's blood,[40] and though many dismiss this
devotion (which is certainly associated with eucharistic miracles) to
a dark era of piety that is better forgotten, Balthasar thinks that these

devotions "belong, without sentimentality, at the heart of dogmatics."[41] Balthasar takes Catherine of Siena as representative of this tradition, and with her we find that Christ's wounds are not simply healed-over scars, but continuously bleeding wounds that reconstitute the Church and its salvation in every age. Balthasar thinks that this datum of mystical experience needs to be elevated to the "heart of dogmatics" because it points to the cross as "not just a memory receding farther and farther into the past as century follows century but should rather remain the origin of what is forever present and living. . . . In the Eucharist the hour of the Church's birth remains a permanently present reality, coinciding with the hour of Christ's death."[42] The Church thus lives and draws its being from the drama of the cross, a drama that is made present again in the Eucharist. For Balthasar, we cannot forget this dramatic context by, in the case of the Eucharist, forgetting what kind of flesh and blood is present. The blood is not unspecified; it is poured-out blood, it is blood that has been spilled through violence, and the flesh is flesh that has been ripped away from him and pierced by a spear. This pure negativity, in the fashion of Christian paradox, is turned into the source of grace and life. Thus Christ's death is not just one that atones for sin, but is a death that can be shared for the benefit of the world.[43] The full implications of Balthasar's insistence on this violent language regarding the Eucharist will only be appreciated in chapter 4, when we see its connection to eschatological resolution.

In order to give a concrete example as to the centrality of the Eucharist for Balthasar's soteriology, we will briefly explore how the Eucharist, albeit subtly, plays the central role in *Theo-Drama* IV. *TD* IV, which is largely concerned with evaluating and incorporating various soteriological models into Balthasar's own "dramatic soteriology," erupts with references to the Eucharist, precisely at the point when Balthasar begins to present his own solutions. Balthasar notes five predominant soteriological motifs from scripture and tradition: (1) the Son's sacrificial self-gift for the world; (2) the exchange of places (*admirabile commercium*); (3) liberation; (4) incorporation into Trinitarian life (divinization); and (5) the love of God as the primary cause.[44] In his schematic presentation of historical attempts to integrate all five motifs, he notes that where theologians have erred in the past is precisely when they have overemphasized one motif to the detriment of the others. As an example, Anselm, who he thinks has been unjustly maligned and wrongly critiqued by so many in the twentieth century, was at least deficient with regard to how Christ became sin for us (motif 2) and the Trinitarian shape of soteriology (motif 4).[45] In light of this historical survey, Balthasar's own proposal is *not, pace* Karen Kilby,[46] an ultimate, panoptic synthesis that would draw theological speculation to a close, but rather an attempt to take seriously and give proper weight to all the major themes found in scripture and later elaborated upon by tradition. And his proposal finds its most distinctive characteristics not in his own ability to generate creative proposals, but in what is the most obvious datum of ecclesial experience: the Eucharist.

Balthasar does not explicitly make a note of the fact that the Eucharist was absent in the primary soteriological models from the tradition, but this becomes obvious when he chooses it as the centerpiece that holds all five motifs in tension. The effect that this has is to make it clear that the Eucharist was the missing key to a theological evaluation of the drama of salvation, a key that was hiding in plain sight. What is unique about Balthasar, and what would justify calling him, as will be seen in chapter 3, a liturgical theologian, is that the same weight given to the Eucharist in the liturgical structure of Christian life is also present at the highest levels of theological speculation. The Eucharist, because it includes and presupposes the events of Christ's life that lead up to this eucharistic conclusion, acts as the meeting place for all five soteriological motifs, bringing them into a symphonic whole without abolishing the distinctiveness of each note. The first motif, Christ's self-sacrifice, is essentially the definition that Balthasar gives for the Eucharist: "Given the plan to bring about creatures endowed with freedom, the ultimate form of this pouring-forth [of the Son] will be that of the Eucharist, which, as we know it, is intimately connected with the Passion, *pro nobis.*"[47] The second motif, *admirabile commercium*, follows closely upon this, for Balthasar considers the act of the Eucharist to be the result of Christ's taking on of the Father's anger at sin: "God's anger strikes him instead of countless sinners, shattering him as by lightning and distributing him among them; thus God the Father, in the Holy Spirit, creates the Son's Eucharist."[48] Not only does Christ exchange places with sinners by his suffering, but, in the Eucharist, gives them his very self. The third motif, liberation, appears in several different guises—liberation from the evil

one, from the "powers and principalities," and even from unjust socio-
economic structures—but for Balthasar the key is to understand freedom
as contingent upon rather than inimical to obedience. Ultimately, this
means a freedom for the Christian to share in Christ's (eucharistic) mission: "This freedom is perfected by the grace of a sublime participation
in the absolute, divine freedom. This comes about through our being incorporated into the Eucharist that, in the Spirit, Christ makes to the Father."[49] As this last quote indicates, "Eucharist" for Balthasar is much
more than an ecclesial rite, and, especially when it carries the notion of
Hingabe, always has a Trinitarian structure (motif 4). The fifth motif,
God's love as the initiative for salvation, points ultimately to the intra-
Trinitarian eucharistic love, but more proximately to the love of God that
leads Christ to totally pour himself out, not merely in the place of sinners, but precisely out of a nuptial love for sinners: "Only thus, in the pure
gratis of grace, in the pure superfluity [*Überflüssigkeit*] of love, can the
Son be eucharistically poured out, beyond measure [*über-verflüssigt*]."[50]
These five motifs are not exhaustive, but they are expressive of scripture's
general presentation of the economy of salvation through its varying motifs and metaphors, all of which coalesce around Christ's own interpretation of his impending crucifixion: *hoc est enim corpus meum.*

Becoming Bread

Paul established that not only is the bloody and pierced body of Christ to
be considered kenotic ("death, even death on a cross") but that the simple
fact of "being born in the likeness of men" is likewise a kenosis. The criterion seems to be the change in form (μορφή), from the μορφή Θεοῦ
to a μορφή δούλου. How much more, according to Balthasar, should we
consider Christ in the Eucharist as kenotic, as he moves far below the
μορφή δούλου, all the way to being in the form of bread, μορφή ἄρτου.
To call Christ in the Eucharist "in the form of bread" is less controversial
in German than it is in English. *Gestalt*, "form," is also the word for "species," as in the eucharistic species. There is thus no issue, at first glance,
with admitting that Christ is *in Gestalt des Brotes*, "in the form (as in species) of bread," thus warranting a description of his eucharistic presence
as kenotic. Nevertheless, Balthasar goes even further than this, using language his detractors would deem far too reminiscent of the condemned

notion of impanation: "Christ's kenotic condition—as bread to be 'eaten' and wine poured out."[51] His critics, such as Anne Barbeau Gardiner, are correct to identify Speyr as the major influence on Balthasar for this "impanationist" language.[52] Gardiner, however, overstates the connection between Speyr's insights and Protestant sources and is simply mistaken in suggesting that Speyr avoids the "hallowed term" of "transubstantiation."[53] Leaving aside the question of Speyr's influence, several others have claimed that Balthasar either explicitly rejects or cautiously avoids the traditional language of the full conversion, the transubstantiation, of the bread and wine into Christ's body and blood. For instance, Mark Miller suggests that Balthasar "has pushed well off to the sidelines the Catholic preoccupation with form and matter and, even transubstantiation, as an insignificant concern."[54] This interpretation of Balthasar stems from a lack of familiarity with his corpus[55] and perhaps an unwarranted extrapolation based on Balthasar's overall tendency to disparage scholastic distinctions, but this misinterpretation needs to be put to rest, especially as it frames the question about kenosis and impanation.

First, it must be established that Balthasar uses "traditional vocabulary" about the Eucharist, such as transubstantiation, *ex opere operato*, and the substance/accidents distinction, with great frequency.[56] Indeed, Balthasar never explicitly rejects these key terms, even if he is in no way anxious to repeat them whenever possible. For Balthasar, repeating words such as "transubstantiation" is no guarantee that one has penetrated into the mystery of Christ's presence, even though it must be formally affirmed *as a bare minimum*.[57] Thus, in those few instances where Balthasar points to the limited value of these terms, it is not because he is calling into question their validity, but because he thinks that what the Church believes about the Eucharist is far more than formal claims about the how and the when of eucharistic conversion. As a rule, Balthasar accepts the Church's magisterial decisions about "eucharistic mechanics," for instance those of the Council of Trent, and uses them as a springboard for further reflection on the implications of Christ's sacramental presence.[58] For Balthasar, aping formulas without attempting to explore their depths is neither an ecclesial nor a responsible way to do theology.[59] Thus, when Balthasar chooses language that seems to go beyond what the Church has formally taught in the past, it must be kept in mind that he also explicitly affirms all of these teachings regarding the Eucharist.

If, then, Balthasar is to be criticized for his understanding of Christ's sacramental presence, one can only do so based on an internal contradiction
in his thought (between his supposed novelties and the "hallowed terms"
that he also uses) rather than on his willful rejection of Church teachings.

Now that the ground is cleared and Balthasar's intentions are shown
to have been in alignment with the traditional distinctions, we can ask
whether as a matter of fact his theology is in accordance with this deposit.
To return then to Gardiner's critique, there are passages in both Speyr
and Balthasar that seem to suggest impanation, despite their own protestations to the contrary. For instance, Speyr says that Christ "gives to the
Church the act of his *becoming* bread [Brot*werdens*] as well as the state
of *being* bread [Brot*seins*]."[60] She also suggests that there are two forms
of *Hingabe*, "that of being human [*Menschseins*] and that of being bread
[*Brotseins*]."[61] To claim that Christ is incarnate in the bread is contrary to
a Catholic sense of the sacrament, if what is meant by this is that the *substance* of bread remains and that either Christ becomes the substance of
bread (impanation) or exists alongside it (consubstantiation). Although he
does not use Speyr's language of "being bread" nearly as often as he refers to Christ's "flesh and blood," even when utilizing the latter, Johannine
terms, he depends on an assumption garnered from the former approach:
that Christ is somehow limited and is perhaps even "passive" in his eucharistic state. Or, in a word, he takes on the properties of bread, namely,
edibility, lack of self-movement, and utter vulnerability: "In the eucharistic surrender [*Hingabe*] of Jesus' humanity the point is reached where,
through his flesh, the Triune God has been put at man's disposal in this
final readiness on God's part to be taken and incorporated into men."[62]
Ostensibly this is in contrast with Aquinas's position, which is that Christ
is not in this sacrament "moveably," nor is he there "as in a place" (*sicut in
loco*), such that one could say that he is limited or confined by the bread,
for the whole Christ is present under every part of the eucharistic species.[63]
It also appears congruent with what Guitmund of Aversa condemned as
the position of the *impanatores*, who said that "the Lord's body and blood
are truly contained there, but in a hidden way, and they are impanated—if
I may say it in that way—so that they may be consumed."[64]

This difficulty of ascribing the qualities of bread to Christ could be
considered an extension of the question of the orthodoxy of the theopaschite formula (*Unus ex Trinitate crucifixus est*).[65] As understood by the

majority of the tradition, the controversial formula does not imply that the nature of God suffers or is limited by the Crucifixion. Similarly, what we could call a "theopanite formula" (*Unus ex Trinitate panis factus est*) does not by any logical necessity imply that the risen Christ is limited by the eucharistic species. For the question of the cross, the suffering is ascribed to his human nature (but yes, also to the *suppositum* of the divine nature because of the logic of the *communicatio idiomatum*),[66] and for the Eucharist the dimensive and passible aspects belong to the (no longer substantially present) bread and wine. The impetus for these distinctions is the incommensurability of suffering and limitation with God's impassible and infinite nature. Balthasar, again, does not contest the need for these important distinctions, but he does want to trouble the apparent incommensurability of the aspects of the Passion and Eucharist that imply suffering and passivity within the nature of God. Bracketing for the moment questions of Trinitarian theology, Balthasar does not think that Christ is in any way involuntarily "trapped" or limited by his presence in the Eucharist. He does, however, think that he is present there with at least an analogous sense of self-limitation, not involuntarily, but as a positively willed and desired limitation. Further, this limitation of Christ's risen nature is not, for Balthasar, in contrast with Christ's attributes, but is, in fact, a positive mirroring of them. As for the Eucharist, so for the cross: "Therefore everything to do with the sacraments is handed over without defences to human misuse, and was indeed in its essence constituted in the Passion where this human misuse was a factor."[67] That is to say, Balthasar thinks that we should not forget the gains made in Christology in the refusal of a Nestorian mitigation of the scandal of the cross when we turn to the scandal of the altar.

Eucharistic abuse is not the result simply of a lax, post-Constantinian Church that fails to properly catechize its members. Rather, it is inscribed as an inevitability from the very first, as is evident with the Communion of Judas (John 13:26–27). John has no explicit institution narrative, but when read with the other Gospels, it seems to be implied that the "morsel" that Jesus dipped and handed to Judas is, in fact, the Eucharist. This, however, has been debated. Denys and Chrysostom affirm it, but Hilary, for instance, denies it. Augustine also denies that the morsel of John 13 refers to the Eucharist, but this is a rather immaterial objection, for he admits that Judas had received the Eucharist earlier with the disciples.[68]

Lombard and Aquinas follow Augustine on this, that Judas received the Eucharist earlier, but that the morsel of John 13 is only bread.[69] Nevertheless, Balthasar, in concord with Speyr,[70] interprets this passage as the Communion of Judas, which, regardless of the exegetical issues involved, is simply an extension of Thomas's principle (as opposed to, say, Bonaventure) that "sinners eat the body of Christ sacramentally, and not the just only."[71] In other words, Christ is present in the Eucharist, and is received as such, by saints and sinners alike, and does not de-transubstantiate in order to avoid contact with the sinner. For Balthasar, Christ has then made himself vulnerable to misuse, to liturgical abuse, we could say, and as seen in the Communion of Judas, he can be received not only by the rather conventional sinner but even by the great betrayer himself. Thinking with Georges Bernanos, the French Catholic novelist, Balthasar says,

> Bernanos returns to the primal Cross, to that initial and elemental surrender of the pure Flesh to the impure sinner, until he is squarely before the communion of Judas, concerning which John speaks so unambiguously. In fact, this act of eucharistic communion is the only one John mentions, as if this most critical of cases included all other less extreme instances of sinful betrayal, and as if this one case were the proof for a "love that goes to the end" (Jn 13:1). Behind every "use" of the holy Flesh lurks the massive *abuse* of the holy—and also of the saints—at the hands of sinners.[72]

Now it can be seen why Balthasar defines the Eucharist as "the profanation of the holy God."[73] To be subject to the hands of sinners is most certainly another instance of the connection between the cross and Eucharist, but it also exhibits the character of the mission of Christ, which in every instance is one of self-gift, even to the point of passivity.[74] Thus, even as he avoids impanation as a theory of eucharistic physics, Balthasar says that Christ has chosen bread and wine as the mode of his eucharistic presence because it illustrates Christ's desire to hand himself over defenselessly to sinful humanity: "His free self-surrender [*Selbsthingabe*] . . . wants to go 'to the end' (Jn 13:1); and the end is that self-disposition passes over into pure *letting* oneself be disposed of and *being disposed of*."[75] This ability to be disposed of does not, for Balthasar, diminish Christ's power or compromise the elevated status of his humanity, but rather demonstrates that Christ's power and activity is one that is in no way diminished by becoming powerless and passive. The *telos* of the Incarnation, then, was precisely this being eucharistically "scattered"[76] in the world, which was the result of his being first "shattered" by the violence of the cross. Or, in the words of Paul Claudel: "Look, see God striding across the earth like a sower; he takes his heart in both hands and scatters it over the face of the earth!"[77] His scattered Eucharist presence, then, can be properly described, with the requisite qualifications, as Christ's humiliation. Perhaps the most important qualification here is to separate Christ's humiliation in the Eucharist from the question about the sacrifice of the Mass. His "humiliation" in the Eucharist is *not*, for Balthasar, what constitutes the sacrificial nature of the Mass, a question we can turn briefly to now, but the sacrifice of the Mass will be treated in greater depth in chapter 2.

Among the conflicting post-Tridentine interpretations about the sacrifice of the Mass, the Jesuit cardinal Juan de Lugo (1583–1660) emphasized that for the Mass to be properly considered a sacrifice, there must be some form of destruction. Others considered the Communion of the priest to be a sufficient "destruction" as to constitute a sacrifice (Bellarmine), or that the separation of Christ's body and blood in the consecration is itself the sacrifice (Lessius),[78] but for de Lugo, the sacrifice is Christ's dwelling under the form of bread and wine, which is a form of destroying the utility of his human nature: "[The body of Christ] is destroyed in human fashion in so far as it receives a lower state of such a kind as to render it useless for the human purposes of a human body and suitable for other different purposes in the way of food . . . to become eatable which was not eatable."[79] This position, though not Scotistic in itself, became, via Jesuits such as de Lugo, a standard Scotistic position, which explains why Gerard Manley Hopkins seems to echo de Lugo's eucharistic theology.[80] Hopkins says, "The sacrifice would be the Eucharist, and that the victim might be truly victim like, like motionless, helpless, or lifeless, it must be in matter."[81] For this tradition, the sacrifice of the Mass is Christ's renewed humiliation in the Eucharist, his kenotic state that finds him under the species of simple food and drink. Clearly, then, Balthasar is an heir to this tradition but with one important difference: Balthasar, even though he follows the kenotic line of thought, does not attribute this eucharistic kenosis to be the element that makes the Mass sacrificial.

Matthias Joseph Scheeben, although he was taught in the tradition of de Lugo by his teacher, Johann Baptist Franzelin (1816–86), also came to reject this interpretation of the eucharistic sacrifice. And, for him, this was sufficient reason to reject the idea of Christ's kenotic state: "But the humiliation which the ascetics ponder and use for practical ends is something purely external as far as the body of Christ is concerned; it is no more than the absence of all outward splendor, and the possibility of a purely exterior dishonoring."[82] Balthasar, again, agrees that this humiliation is not the sacrifice, but, because of his decoupling of these two concepts, he would contest Scheeben's claim that this dishonor is "purely exterior." Scheeben says that Christ's abasement in the Eucharist "touches only the surface of the mystery, and does not reach down to its inner nature."[83] For Balthasar, on the other hand, Christ's kenotic state in the Eucharist, even if certain qualifications regarding the eucharistic conversion must be put in place, leads us directly to the inner nature of Christ, whose mission and continued state is one of being-expropriated. And this insight, which is very often found in the mystics (or, as Scheeben calls them, "ascetics"), and in poets such as Hopkins, is something that is worth taking seriously in theological reflection. Thus, when someone like Thérèse of Lisieux prays to Christ with the words, "now it is in the Host that I see you consummate your self-annihilation,"[84] Balthasar does not think this should be dismissed as simply pious chatter. Rather, this mystic's prayer brings us to a profound theological insight: that the sufferings of the Lord are not just a past event, but one that is continually present and manifest in the Eucharist.[85]

The full extent of this insight will only be understood in the light of Trinitarian theology and from an examination of the resurrected state of Christ, but it receives its proximate justification not in Christ's humiliation as a sacrifice, but rather as a revelation of his eternal, sacrificial disposition. So to turn again to the symbols of bread and wine, for Balthasar, they were chosen because they reveal something essential about the nature and the disposition of the one who is veiled under them. And we will see in chapter 3 how strongly Balthasar inveighs against an overly symbolic approach to the sacraments, but he does think that the bread and wine are theologically informative. For instance, he says that the tiny bit of bread and wine are symbols, above all, of "nothingness."[86] Or, as Speyr says, bread and wine mirror Christ's self-offering:

This is based on the essence of bread and wine, of water and blood, to pour itself out and let itself be shared out endlessly; in the horizontal outpouring of the water and blood and in the crumbling of the bread to fragments for you and for me and for each one, there is contained the participation in which the Lord distributes himself and in which the one who receives is in turn poured out and distributed with the Lord: to his brethren.[87]

So even in finding theories of impanation to be insufficient with regard to the total conversion of the eucharistic species, Balthasar wants to avoid the impression that bread and wine are arbitrarily chosen vessels in which Christ happens to be contained. Instead, they reveal, when looked at from the perspective of Christ's mission, the prodigality of Christ's kenosis and abasement, which are supremely manifest in the cross and the descent into hell, but are also *always*, by way of analogy, a positive attribute of divinity. And just as the Church does not believe that Christ himself endorsed impanation when he claimed that he was "the bread of life" (John 6:35), nor does the Church itself endorse it when it lauds the Eucharist as the "bread from heaven" or "the bread of angels," so Balthasar can say, without calling into question transubstantiation, that "God makes his Son food for the whole world. In suffering, his whole human substance is 'made fluid' so that it can enter into human beings."[88] And although the Church has had to react against eucharistic heresies, this reaction should not lead to the neglect of the fact that Christ has become food and drink, has poured himself out as an offering and can thus be consumed by saints and sinners alike. Christ as food and drink leads us, according to Balthasar, straight to the heart of the God who has always offered himself as gift for the other, as a gift that is never exhausted. In this Balthasar follows Speyr, who thinks that the ordinary understanding of transubstantiation (the conversion of the substance of bread into the substance of Christ's body) needs to be supplemented by the parallel truth: "For the reverse also happens in the Lord's passage to the host: despite being God, he has chosen to annihilate (*anéantissement*) his divine being into the host."[89] There is then nothing "purely exterior" about Christ's obvious lack of glory in the Eucharist, as Scheeben suggested. For, according to Balthasar, who is here following the Gospel of John, Christ's glory is always one of humility, descent, and expropriation, rather than one of elevation, self-aggrandizement, or self-protection.

There are no theological reasons a priori that should exclude the possibility of considering the Eucharist as kenotic. To claim that this would be beneath God's dignity or somehow in plain contradiction to Christ's attributes could only be the result of forgetting the Crucifixion. In the eleventh century, Guitmund addressed this claim:

> If, however, they [the Berengarians] say that it is not right that Christ be chewed [*atteri*] by the teeth, not because it is impossible, but because it seems to be unworthy [of him], again, I ask, why should this seem unworthy? *Is it because Christ seems to be humbled too much by it?* But shall he who did not deem it unworthy to be irreligiously crushed [*atteri*] by the unfaithful for the salvation of the faithful . . . deem it unworthy, for the salvation of the same faithful, to be chewed [*atteri*] by their teeth as religiously as they are able?[90]

This is not to say that Christ suffers by being chewed in the Eucharist, as some baroque spirituality would have it. "Kenosis," for Balthasar, does not immediately and necessarily connote suffering or pain. Although Christ's passion certainly does include suffering and death, "death on a cross," the Incarnation itself was already Christ's kenotic movement, whereby he left the δόξα of the Father in order to accept the αδοξία, ingloriousness, of appearing as one man among many others. It is "an act of self-concealing" (*intra se latens*).[91] Christ's kenotic state in the Eucharist, for Balthasar, has everything to do with his lack of splendor, his humble state as bread and wine, and thus the fact that he is not immediately recognized as glorious. Yes, he is certainly honored in his eucharistic state by the Church, but this is of the same paradoxical nature as honoring Christ by displaying images of his humiliating crucifixion. And, in the last analysis, Balthasar's appeal to kenosis makes sense only with regard to the Church. Christ is not kenotic so that he could be mishandled by Judas and passed over by the world (though this was certainly inevitable) but in order to be available to the world through the Church. Balthasar again notes the significance of the Last Supper occurring chronologically before the Crucifixion: the Church's participation in Christ's sacrifice "is possible because in his Passion he himself has become available: he is now at the Church's disposal. Before Jesus is delivered into the hands of sinners in accord with the Father's will, he gives himself into the hands of the Church."[92] His eucharistic kenosis is his *Hingabe*, his self-gift without remainder to the Church and to the entire world.

RESURRECTED FLESH

The preceding section may give the impression that Balthasar is only concerned with the presence of the humiliated, crucified Christ in the Eucharist, and not the resurrected Christ. If, as Balthasar says, Christ "distributes his death" in the Eucharist,[93] then how could we affirm that it is the risen and glorified Lord who becomes present on the altar, and not his lifeless, crucified body? This question is, according to Balthasar and indeed almost any sensible theologian, one that could only arise in a mind suffering from a debilitating intellectual scrupulosity. Nevertheless, it must be engaged explicitly here because this is the source of one critique of Balthasar's eucharistic theology. For Alyssa Lyra Pitstick, Balthasar's pairing of Christ's descent into hell with the Eucharist leads to an irreparable injury to the Church's faith: "If the Eucharist is the sacrament of Christ's body and blood, soul and divinity, how can this sacrament represent Christ's descent if His body and soul were separated during it?"[94] Needless to say, Thomas has no problem affirming that it is Christ *crucified* who is present in the Eucharist (*Christum passum qui continetur in hoc sacramento*)[95] *and* that the entire Christ, including his soul and divinity, is present by the power of real concomitance.[96] The Eucharist has always been understood as the *memoriale mortis et resurrectionis*[97] in that it both looks backward and receives its efficacy from the cross, and also looks forward to the second coming of the risen Christ. There is no contradiction then in affirming both that the Christ who is present in the Eucharist is the one who sits at the right hand of the Father in heaven and that the Eucharist, in the words of Pope John Paul II, "is indelibly marked by the event of the Lord's passion and death."[98] Whether or not one agrees with Balthasar's overall presentation of the Eucharist, objecting to it on grounds that it links the Eucharist too closely with Christ's death is to place oneself in a curious position vis-à-vis the entirety of the Church's theology and piety.[99]

There is no reason to doubt that Balthasar thinks that the Christ who is present in the Eucharist is the risen and glorified Christ. However, Balthasar suggests that, instead of establishing some sort of binary between the crucified and risen Christ, we should think of the risen Christ as now even more cruciform than he was on the cross. The cross was not sublated by his resurrection. If, as we have seen, the cross-Eucharist was the entelechy of Christ's mission, then his continued mission in the world is still a cruciform one. He continues to pour himself out, now as food and drink, and does so without the limits that are imposed by the current state of fleshly existence. Thus, if we affirm, as is standard practice, that the Eucharist makes the cross and its effects present for the Church, then this implies that the risen Lord, who still bears the marks of the Crucifixion, now exists in a state on the other side of being torn apart and opened up by the soldier's lance: "In its wounds the body of Christ becomes the freely available habitation of the believers incorporated into it. The wounds are not healed and closed up, but are transfigured and remain open."[100] Christ's liquefaction, then, is not undone by the Resurrection, but is rather magnified, for the "eucharistic gesture of Jesus' self-distribution is a definitive, eschatological and thus irreversible gesture."[101] Even Christ's earthly life, before death, was one characterized precisely by his movement toward the Crucifixion ("everything is moving toward his death"),[102] and his death remains the central reference point of his identity, even though it is now past. Having established the cross-Eucharist pair in Balthasar's thought, we can turn in this section to a consideration of the mode of Christ's presence in the sacrament, particularly because this is understood by Balthasar in existential categories and with specific attention to Christ's resurrected flesh.

Existential Sacramental Theology I: What Is a Person?

Even more decisive for our current question than the permanent cruciform nature of the resurrected Christ is what is implied by what we will call Balthasar's "existential sacramental theology." Even though he distinguishes his position quite clearly from the likes of Sartre or Heidegger, or even religious existentialists such as Kierkegaard, he still claims that the primary goal of *The Glory of the Lord* was to establish "that higher middle way [between rationalism and a religion of feeling] which we can

call 'existential Christianity.'"[103] This predilection toward existential issues is evident in a special way in his sacramental theology. There are two
sides to his existential sacramental theology, one that is Christological and
has the priority, which will be analyzed here, and one that is ecclesiological, which will be discussed in chapter 2. He derives these two sides of his
existential sacramental theology directly from the Gospel of John: "John's
primary concern is to shed light *existentially* on the sacraments, viz., to
show the disposition of Jesus, which they portray and which creates them,
and correspondingly to show the dispositions of the community of disciples, which must respond to the disposition of Jesus."[104] The primary
sense of Balthasar's existential sacramental theology is based on his consistent emphasis on the presence of the person of Christ in the Eucharist,
particularly as he is found in the New Testament. This is just another reason why questions about *how* Christ becomes present are secondary for
Balthasar: the accent, and here Balthasar demonstrates his indebtedness
to the *Exercises* of Ignatius, must always fall on a personal encounter with
Christ.[105] And this Christ is not an a-temporal, cosmic Christ who has
now expanded beyond the confines of Jesus of Nazareth's particular history in the first century, but is precisely the Christ who lived a life framed
by the contingencies of time and culture. The scholastic concept of concomitance was designed precisely to resolve the tension between the affirmation that Christ's "body and blood" are what come to be present in the
Eucharist and the clear assumption that it is not *just* his body and blood
but also his human soul and divine person that are present. By natural
concomitance, says Thomas, "the entire Christ is in this sacrament" (*totus
Christus sit in hoc sacramento*).[106] Balthasar simply extends this logic further to include not only Christ's body, blood, soul, and divinity, but what
also constitutes the *totus Christus*, his saving events of cross and resurrection. He finds this to already be the insight of the Fathers: "The Greek Fathers discerned clearly that Christ, in surrendering his sacrificed flesh and
shed blood for his disciples, was communicating, not merely the material
side of his bodily substance, but the saving events wrought by it. . . . The
fundamental presupposition is that the Person of Jesus is really present;
but along with the Person comes his entire temporal history and, in particular, its climax in Cross and Resurrection."[107]

One major influence on Balthasar's sacramental theology is the
Benedictine monk of Maria Laach, Odo Casel (1886–1948),[108] whose

thought can even be detected in the previous quote. Casel's *Mysterien-theologie* was intended to show how Jesus's historic death can be present in the Church's sacraments, which he saw as developing Leo the Great's axiom, "What was visible in the Lord has passed over into the myster-ies."[109] Balthasar differs slightly from Casel on the question of contem-poraneity with Christ, but they are in agreement about the importance of Leo's axiom. For Balthasar, however, it means far more than the commu-nication of Christ's death, but includes *all* that "was visible in the Lord," such as his miracles, his relationships, and, above all, his mission and his disposition toward his disciples: "The life of Jesus (given for 'many') was made available in a perpetual sacramental form."[110] And when Balthasar says that the *life* of Jesus becomes present, he means the life as narrated in the New Testament. So he moves, as he himself frames it,[111] from Casel to John the Evangelist. John is to be preferred, for he chooses to speak of the sacraments indirectly, with their existence assumed, so as to show their inner logic at work. For instance, "The best point of entry into the Johannine-eucharistic thought is the episode of the foot-washing, which gives us (so to speak) *an anatomy of the Eucharist from John's point of view,* and it cannot possibly be accidental that this episode stands in the Fourth Gospel in the place of the institution narrative that the three others have."[112] The pedilavium as a cross section of the Eucharist means that what is present on the Church's altar is not just body and blood, nor even just divinity, but a singular person and even his intention when he insti-tuted the sacrament. It is Christ in the state of humbling himself before his disciples even to the point of scandal, Christ who has become a ser-vant even to those who would betray and deny him.

The example of the pedilavium is one among many that Balthasar uses. Its primary purpose is to illustrate that Christ's life on earth dem-onstrates that he, as a particular person, meets the communicant in a per-sonal way, just as he did in his earthly ministry. What this signals is a reevaluation of anthropology. According to Balthasar, Christ, the Christ who is present in the Eucharist, is one who has been radically determined by his relationship with others, who cannot be abstracted from his social constellation. This insight forms the basis of his largest sustained treat-ment of ecclesiology, *The Office of Peter and the Structure of the Church (Der antirömische Affekt)* (1974).[113] Here he traces the basic structure of the Church from Jesus's relations as they are found in the New Testament.

Thus, there is the ever-present tension between Peter (office) and John (love), James (tradition) and Paul (freedom).[114] This could be seen as giving undue weight to the arbitrary relations of Christ's life (they could have been otherwise), elevating them to the status of stable structures, but for Balthasar, Christ's relations with his contemporaries are as decisive for him as for any person. Balthasar finds theological justification for this position:

> All men are interrelated in a human constellation. One sole human being would be a contradiction in terms, inconceivable even in the abstract, because to be human means to be with others. The God-man Jesus Christ is no exception: as God *as well as man* he exists only in his relation to the Father in the unity of the divine Holy Spirit. Because of this, Jesus' relation to others cannot be limited solely to his human nature: he stands as an indivisible whole within a constellation of his fellow men. This constellation is an inner determinant; it has relevance for his divine humanity. It is essential, not accidental, to his being and acting.[115]

One would need to look at *Theo-Logic* I to understand the philosophical and anthropological grounding for this position, and consider Balthasar's indebtedness to Maurice Blondel.[116] Suffice it to say here that for Balthasar, to be a human person, and to be a divine person, *mutatis mutandis*, is to be determined by one's relationship to others.[117] As in the case of human persons, so also in the case of the incarnate Christ, for Balthasar, to be a person means to be determined by the contingencies and chance encounters that constitute the historical narrative of one's life. Thus, in the case of Christ, the cross, the Resurrection, his relationship with his mother and the beloved disciple, his investing Peter with authority, and his sending of Paul on a mission are all integral to his identity.

Balthasar's intention is not to show *how* the sacramental life of the Church maps onto an individual life (for, based on the principles we have established, this will be different for everyone), but simply to establish that it does, in fact, create the basic contours of the Christian life. All I wish to do here is express Balthasar's basic premise that in the sacraments this theandric person is encountered in all of his particularity, and this particularity takes on universal significance and application in the sacraments. This is perhaps most evident by viewing baptism as a "new birth," the Eucharist as the sacramental "waybread," and both, along with extreme unction, as giving a special share in Christ's death.[118] This existential sacramental theology serves as the theological basis for two related data of spirituality that shape Balthasar's thought: the experience of the mystics and Ignatian contemplation. For Balthasar, what is present in the Eucharist is neither just "body and blood" nor undifferentiated "grace," for this objective presence exists for the sake of a subjective presence that opens up to contemplative insights. Thus, the encounter with Christ by saints and mystics, which speaks more of a personal and particular experience rather than a general application of objective grace, should be viewed as the norm.[119] Likewise, the imaginative impulse of the Ignatian *Exercises*, which draws directly from the Gospel accounts, is a legitimate and fruitful method for encountering the eucharistic Christ.[120] This is because the Eucharist is Christ in his totality, which includes and does not transcend the particular facts of his historical life.

One definition that Balthasar provides for the sacraments is the following: "Das Sakrament ist kirchliche Gebärde Jesu Chrsti zum Menschen hin" (A sacrament is an ecclesial gesture that Jesus Christ directs to man).[121] Thus far we have seen how it is a gesture from Christ to humanity. That is, we have seen how Balthasar's sacramental theology focuses on the direct and personal presence of Christ. Yet we have skipped over the fact that this gesture is an *ecclesial* gesture, and thus one that finds the Church as the mediator. Thus, a brief word about the Church is necessary to conclude this subsection. Balthasar acknowledges this necessary ecclesial mediation,[122] but he does not wish to blur the fact that Christ still acts immediately and primarily in the sacraments. Though there have been great theological gains by focusing on the inextricable link between the Church and the sacraments, which was, of course, one of the basic insights of de Lubac, this can lead, and certainly has led, to a certain sociological reduction of the sacraments. In some versions, Christ is either left out of the equation or simply equated with the Church, and the sacraments are said to be primarily the self-manifestation of the Church as a social body. The social constitution of the Church can be verified by psychological and social sciences (baptism as a rite of initiation demarcating insider from outsider, etc.), but this fails to arrive at the consequential occurrence of the sacrament: the encounter, yes, ecclesially mediated, between the soul and God. Thus, although Christ does give himself without reserve to the Church, the Church is not given independent authority such that its self-manifestation in the sacraments could be understood only on the ecclesial level and without reference to Christ. This is first because there can be neither a clean separation of Christ and the Church nor their fusion. Thomas says, "Head and members are like one mystical person" (*caput et membra sunt quasi una persona mystica*).[123] The union is clear, *una persona*, as is the distance, *quasi*, for Christ is the *caput*, and the Church the *membra*. The two are not melded into a singularity, but rather the Church receives its identity *only* as Christ's body: it has no existence apart from him (John 15:5). And the sacraments, as artistic representations of the Crucifixion often show, flow directly from the side of the Christ and into the chalice. The Church in this instance is precisely that chalice, which does not constitute the sacrament, but simply catches it and distributes it.[124]

Resurrection: Ubiquity of Pneumatic Flesh

Having established that for Balthasar Christ's cruciform flesh is present in the Eucharist, a flesh that includes the entirety of his person, we can turn directly to his analysis of Christ's *resurrected* flesh. We have already seen Balthasar's attempts to salvage some remnants of impanation, and here we can see how he more directly confronts another condemned eucharistic teaching, namely, Martin Luther's notion of ubiquity. The Council of Trent excluded Luther's particular understanding of ubiquity as a possibility for Catholic theology. Equally, however, it condemned the opposing position of Zwingli, thereby situating the Catholic position as a partial validation of the worthy intentions of both positions. Both Luther and Trent were united against Zwingli, who stated unequivocally that "until the last day Christ cannot be anywhere but at the right hand of God the father. . . . But if Christ is seated there, he is not present here [in the Eucharist]. And if he were here, we could not speak of his return, for he would have returned already."[125] For Zwingli, not only is Christ "at the right hand of the Father," apparently conceived of as a definitive place within the cosmos, he is *only* there, and thus decidedly not present in any way besides symbolically in the Church's Eucharist. Against this, Trent affirmed that "there is no contradiction in the fact that our Savior always

sits at the right hand of the Father in heaven according to his natural way
of existing and that, nevertheless, in his substance he is sacramentally
present to us in many other places."[126] But Luther, before Trent, reacted
to Zwingli not by rejecting his premise that Christ could not possibly
be both at the right hand of the Father and in the Eucharist at the same
time, but by accepting it. Thus, Luther denies that Christ being seated at
the right hand of the Father means anything other than that "he is above
all creatures and in all and beyond all creatures."[127] In other words, it is
a metaphor (*Dextera Dei ubique est*), for "Christ is around us and in us
in all places."[128] This begs the question as to why Christ's presence in the
Eucharist would be any more significant than his presence in a rock,[129]
but Luther's appeal to the notion of ubiquity was meant to safeguard the
possibility that Christ could be substantially present in the Eucharist.
For Trent, one need not decide. There is good reason to affirm both that
Christ's resurrected body is not coextensive with his divinity and that he
is able to be present in the Eucharist without having to "ascend and descend from the heavens through the air."[130]

Even more pointedly than Trent's statement, the concept of Christ's
post-Resurrection ubiquity is rejected in Paul VI's *Mysterium fidei*
(1965). Here the pope says that "it would be wrong for anyone to try to
explain this manner of presence [in the Eucharist] by dreaming up a so-
called 'pneumatic' nature of the glorious body of Christ that would be
present everywhere."[131] Thus, again, the path of ubiquity is forbidden by
the Catholic magisterium. Yet, even with these theological guardrails set
in place, how to understand the relationship between Christ's body as it
exists at the right hand of the Father and his presence in the Eucharist is
not thereby solved or even explored in any great depth. Trent's distinction between Christ's natural mode of existing and his sacramental presence by way of substance, which echoes Thomas's distinction between
Christ's presence *per modum quantitatis* and *per modum substantiae*,[132]
seems more postulated than explanatory. Even Trent found its own solution to be, albeit formally true, paltry in comparison with the reality
under consideration.[133] Balthasar, for his part, thinks that through this
ecclesiastical stammering there is the possibility of arriving at a new insight into Christ's resurrected flesh, and an insight that can, at least in
part, redeem Luther. Thus, with full knowledge of the Church's refusals
of the concept, Balthasar decides that "ubiquity" is precisely the word

that is needed to describe Christ's resurrected body. However, when he uses the term, it is qualified: not just ubiquity pure and simple, but what he calls *eucharistic* ubiquity. Christ's resurrected body and his eucharistic body, for Balthasar, cannot be separated: "There is no fundamental difference between his heavenly and his eucharistic condition."[134] In other words, whatever the distinction between Christ's natural and his substantial presence may mean, it cannot mean that the body that is present in the Eucharist is any other body than the one, post-Resurrection body that sits at the right hand of the Father. The theologically fruitful question to ask here, according to Balthasar, is about the constitution of Christ's body such that differing modes of presence can be predicated of it, that it can be present anywhere at the same time. And for Balthasar it means not just that he can be present in the Eucharist in addition to his presence in his natural body, but rather that everything about his body, no matter its mode, is in fact eucharistic.[135]

Unlike some radical reformers in the sixteenth century, or ancient Docetists for that matter, Balthasar has no sympathies for a "celestial flesh Christology," whereby Christ's incarnate flesh is given not through Mary but from heaven and thus transcends the weaknesses of finite flesh. Instead, Christ's incarnate flesh was subject to the same bonds of finitude as all human bodies, and thus, even though neither the product nor the producer of sin, is partly resistant to the Spirit (Matt. 26:41). After the Crucifixion and Resurrection, however, his body is not only subservient to the Spirit, but thoroughly spiritual.[136] For Balthasar, then, Christ's transition from finite flesh to eucharistic flesh has two primary moments: the cross and the Holy Spirit. His description of Christ being "shattered" on the cross and thus "liquefied," as we have already examined, serves not only to highlight the kenotic element but also to note the expansion of Christ's flesh from limitation to ubiquity, from purely material to spiritual. In other words, in the cross/Resurrection, something happens to Christ's flesh, as is evident from the Gospel accounts themselves. And, as Paul says regarding the hope of resurrection, "It is sown a physical body [σῶμα ψυχικόν], it is raised a spiritual body [σῶμα πνευματικόν]" (1 Cor. 15:44). Balthasar ends *Theo-Drama* IV by quoting these words, and he ties it explicitly to Christ's conquering of death on the cross.[137] First, then, Christ's body that was "in the likeness of sinful flesh" (σαρκὸς ἁμαρτίας) (Rom. 8:3) has been put to death on the cross, which means the destruction of its mortality and limitations.[138] For Balthasar, Christ being "in the likeness of sinful flesh" means that he has accepted a body that simply cannot fully express his inner life because of its inflexibility, and we could say brittleness. Like a glass vase, any expansion would necessarily include a fracturing. Those broken shards can, however, be melted down.[139]

In the Resurrection, Christ arises as a "life-giving spirit" (πνεῦμα ζωοποιοῦν) (1 Cor. 15:45), which reshapes those brittle shards of glass into a body that is now boundless, elastic. His body no longer divides himself from others, but is an instrument for unity with them, "a body that is no longer bound to the earthly demarcations between body and body, between 'I' and 'you.'"[140] This has everything to do with the relationship between the Son and the Holy Spirit, which will only be elaborated upon in chapter 2. Here it suffices to note that for Balthasar, Christ's body being "pneumatic" means that it is joined in a particular way to the mission of the Spirit. Thus, Christ is justly called the "Pneumatic One," which was already publicly verifiable from the moment of his baptism.[141] "Pneumatic" or "spiritual" does not imply "ghostly" or "incorporeal," for Christ's pneumatic flesh is still a body, still corporeal. But, to arrive at some form of precision, Balthasar plays on a distinction between the two German words for body (*Leib*, with its relationship to life, *Leben*; and *Körper*, with the not insignificant connotation of a corpse):

> In his experience of death on the Cross, Jesus seals his total spiritual-intellectual surrender [*totale geistige Hingabe*] to the (vanished) Father with the surrender of his utterly expropriated body [*Körper*]; but he takes this experience with him into his Resurrection body [*Leib*]. As his permanent scars show, this body [*Leib*] is henceforth governed completely by his spirit; thus it expresses nothing other than his constant purpose to self-surrender [*Hingabewillen*] . . . by the operation of the Holy Spirit he has become a eucharistically fruitful body for the reconciled world.[142]

Christ's pneumatic flesh, then, is now truly an expression, we could say *Realsymbol*, of his divine humanity. For Balthasar, this means that Christ's body (*Leib*) is a manifestation and concretization of his *Hingabe*, his sacrificial and self-giving disposition to the Father and the Holy

Spirit, and now also to humanity.[143] Now Christ can give himself, and give himself *bodily*, without limitation and without exhaustion. This is most manifest in the Eucharist, where Christ becomes fully present on innumerable altars, with no limit to his eucharistic presence. But it is also the case for his presence in the saints and in the Church in general, which, for Balthasar, *is* his body. "Eucharistic ubiquity" does not then mean, as it did for Luther, an undifferentiated presence such that his "body" is literally spread evenly across the created order. Even Seneca knew that "to be everywhere is to be nowhere."[144] Instead, Christ's is a body that *can* be everywhere with a concrete and personal presence, while still retaining its corporeality and concreteness. Christ, being pneumatic, is not disincarnated, but is in fact even more bodily because his body is more spiritual.[145] Only now his body expresses what human bodies long to express but cannot do so fully: the complete gift of self to the other to the point of a union without dissolution of otherness.[146]

His speculation can be daring, but on the question of the nature of Christ's pneumatic body Balthasar does exercise a great amount of restraint. He admits that any analysis of Christ's pneumatic flesh can only be analogical, and pieced together from what is found in the New Testament and from what we know about his presence in the sacraments and in the entire *communio sanctorum*. There are, however, certain regulative principles that can be established: "We cannot imagine the state of this ensouled corporality: it has both the particular, human shape and form of the Risen One as well as the eucharistic ubiquity that guarantees room for mankind and the cosmos."[147] What is most important to affirm, for Balthasar, is that Christ's body now "guarantees room for mankind," that is to say, is capacious enough to belong to innumerable others without thereby dissolving Christ's unique identity. The body, Christ's body, does not divide itself from others, as is the law for finite bodies, but serves as the locus for unity and communion. In addition to "ubiquity" and "pneumatic flesh," Balthasar also frequently uses another set of vocabulary to describe the same phenomenon, which we have already mentioned in connection with questions of kenosis: Christ's "liquefaction" (*Verflüßigung*). We are now in a better situation to understand what he means by Christ being "made liquid" or "liquefied." On one occasion he defines fluidity as pure relationality,[148] and it also carries with it the idea of a perfect disponibility. Christ exists now as perfectly in relation to others, and constituted and defined by others who now occupy his very body. In the Incarnation and through the cross, he handed his very being over in obedience to the Father to be used up for the salvation of the world, and in the Eucharist he continues to be present precisely as poured-out, as available. We could say, to retool Charles Taylor's terms, that Christ is not a "buffered self" but a "porous self," which is now perfectly reflected in his porous, permeable body.[149] He now exists in order to be shared, and only *is* as shared: "Christ's body has become finally and definitively Eucharistic . . . its being is not for itself but for the other."[150]

We should not miss the radicality of what Balthasar is suggesting. He *does* mean to call into question the utility and veracity of the distinction between Christ's natural, physical body that sits "at the right hand of the Father" and his substantial presence in the Eucharist. It was perhaps conceivable in a premodern cosmology, but Balthasar thinks that the idea of Christ's resurrected body being *somewhere* in a localized place "in the heavens" is no longer a possibility: "One has here to purge oneself of all mythical pictures of the world which would pin him down to a cosmologically precise place from which he might, as it were, travel to those places, or at least relate himself to those places, where in the celebration of the Mass men commemorate his death and Resurrection." This idea "remains mythical and naïve." Instead, Balthasar says, "He lives on simply as the bodily Eucharist."[151] Christ's body exists now in the Eucharist, in the Church, and anywhere that he is present, without needing to specify *one* place that is just his own, that would belong to Christ and to no one else.[152] The worry that Christ would thereby lose either his particularity or the corporeality of his body by existing as an open space for others is the result of a deficient anthropology.[153] Instead, when the body is conceived of as a place of communion, and a person is defined as being-in-communion, then Christ's eucharistic ubiquity and his pneumatic flesh are the perfect realization of the body's propensity toward becoming self-gift.

Now we can understand the full implications of Balthasar's insistence on Christ's handing-over of his very self, his complete and utter relinquishment of any individuality apart from his mission. Thus, Balthasar wants to take the idea of the *corpus triforme* with utmost seriousness. It is *one* body (*corpus*, not *corpora*) in three forms—natural, ecclesial, and eucharistic—and the natural body cannot be isolated and understood without the others, for the others constitute it.[154] Further, drawing upon the spousal analogue of the relationship between Christ and the Church, Balthasar thinks that they should be understood to have but one flesh.[155] And here we can see that the source for Balthasar's conception of Christ's resurrected body is actually not Luther, but Origen. Christ is not indeterminately spread out, but ecclesially/eucharistically incarnate. Balthasar gathers the following quote into his early (1938) anthology of Origen: "For the body of Christ is not something apart or different from the church which, with its individual members, is his body. But both of these, who are now no longer two but have become one flesh, God has joined together, forbidding man to separate the church from the Lord."[156] If the institution of the Eucharist signals Christ's desire to exist for others and to give himself entirely to the Church, then his resurrected body now perfectly conforms to and reflects this *Hingabe*, which was his from all eternity.

THE LOGIC OF *HINGABE*: TRINITY AS SELF-GIFT

It is at this point, in his seeming collapse of Christ and the Church, that Balthasar is closest to Hegel. Is Christ's pneumatic flesh, which is identified now with the body of the Church and its sacraments, a signal that Christ has passed into the Holy Spirit, which can be identified with the *Gemeinde*?[157] Because of a whole host of interlocking reasons, some of which are decidedly anti-Hegelian,[158] the answer is clearly negative. The first thing to be said is that for Balthasar, no matter how much we can affirm the unity of Christ with the Church, we cannot posit a strict identity between them: there is now, and must always remain, a distance (*diastasis*). This distance is the *sine qua non* of worship.[159] Christ, no matter the extent to which he opens his own identity to the Church, always remains an other in the distance of prayer and obedience.[160] Even more than the necessary condition for worship, according to Balthasar, this distance is an imitation of the proportion between the divine persons.[161] The Church draws its identity solely from Christ, but this act does not empty the source. The Church is not a vampire, draining away Christ's blood, leaving nothing but a desiccated corpse. Rather, as in the image of the life-giving spring, Christ's blood flows out from him without depletion or loss. Nor is the Church Christ's dialectical pair by which he realizes his own identity (as Spirit), as in Hegel.[162] This is why the Eucharist functions so centrally in Balthasar's thought: it illustrates, and more than illustrates, it enacts, the self-giving God who gives his very essence with abandon. Yet, this donation is always marked by plentitude, never loss. The language we have used and the topics that have thus far been explored have focused on Christ's blood (fluidity), but Balthasar retains his theology of intinction and does not forget about the body. Beyond the stylistic and thematic differences associated with bread and wine that were used heuristically in my introduction, we could say that, for Balthasar, there is another good reason that the Church uses both bread and wine as the eucharistic species: the liquid demonstrates Christ being dispersed, poured out, and the bread shows his internal coherence and stability. Christ is entirely poured-out and liquefied, yet he is also crystallized, solidified.[163] He is both pneumatic and fleshly, a pneumatic flesh that transcends earthly dichotomies and thus evades adequate comprehension. Christ gives himself eucharistically to the Church to such a radical degree that he is identified with it, yet without losing his own identity vis-à-vis the Church. This is, for Balthasar, but an earthly mirror for the same dynamic that belongs to the Trinity from all eternity. In this section, then, we will look at the Trinitarian origin of the earthly Eucharist, which stands prior to and is the foundation for the earthly, cruciform Eucharist that we have been examining until now.

Eternal Eucharist

A plethora of theological voices, ancient and modern, and also the basic structure of the liturgical *ordo*, demand that the Eucharist be understood in a properly Trinitarian and not only Christological horizon. Even more than the clear Trinitarian structure of the liturgical rites, there are theological reasons for which one could never understand the Eucharist apart from the Trinity. An established theological tradition, beginning most explicitly with Augustine, insists that there can be no clean separation of the Trinitarian persons. Thus, when we speak of the attributes or actions of any one divine person, it is by appropriation, for the others are co-implicated. Where one is, there are also the others: *opera trinitatis ad extra indivisa sunt*. Other theologians have called into question the idea of appropriations, claiming that it implies that the actions of the economic Trinity, in the end, tell us absolutely nothing about the particularities of the divine persons.[164] But Balthasar actually thinks that the concept can be retained, albeit with significant qualifications. This might seem initially surprising, for Balthasar, unlike Rahner, who critiqued the idea of appropriations, gives far more "personality" and distinction to each of the Trinitarian persons. Nevertheless, when the notion of appropriations is used to highlight the unity of divine action, Balthasar thinks it helpful in avoiding tritheism, but he does fear, as Rahner does, that it is used by scholasticism to erase any meaningful distinctions between the persons.[165] When considering the Incarnation/Eucharist, instead of relying purely on the concept of appropriations, Balthasar thinks that this must be supplemented by the concept of mission, in which the entire Trinitarian life is involved. Nevertheless, whether by appeal to appropriations or to missions, and especially when taking into account the liturgical data, there is every reason to interpret the Eucharist in a Trinitarian setting. In this, Balthasar is not unique. When he says the following, then, it should be interpreted as a standard Catholic and Orthodox position: "What happens, for example, during the celebration of the Eucharist? The Father gives us his Son as food, the Son takes us into his self-gift [*Hingabe*] to the Father, while the Spirit effects the presence of the Son. In the one and the same mystery, then, the Divine Persons operate in inseparable togetherness, yet each one does so in his own proper mode."[166]

Where Balthasar does say something radically new is in his proposal not only to find the entire Trinity in the Eucharist, but also to find the Eucharist in the Trinity. Balthasar's understanding of this issue can be read as an expansion and particular conjugation of Rahner's famous axiom concerning the identity of the immanent and economic Trinity.[167] Balthasar, however, formulates his own axiom, slightly modifying that of Rahner: "*processio* within the Godhead and *missio* outside it are one and the same as far as the Divine Persons are concerned."[168] The missions of the Son and the Spirit are then God's self-exposition, and so the movement of theology is not only one of purifying and abstracting from the data of revelation by moving upward (*ana/ano*), but also a movement upward only to then follow God's exposition downward (*kata*). With regard to the Eucharist, the upward, analogical movement alone would tend to purify elements of revelation that are purely "economic," and thus the sacramental economy would be relegated to the external manifestation of a God who is, in himself, only properly distinguished as subsistent relations and an undivided essence. There is simply no room for the Eucharist in God. The Eucharist, along with the other aspects of God's action in history, such as the Incarnation and Pentecost, belong to the world of history and sin, but not to the unchanged nature of the Godhead. What Balthasar is proposing by saying theology must move downward (catalogically) is that the economic missions of the divine persons are an outward movement of the interpersonal relations. The Eucharist, then, is a window into the very heart of the Triune God.[169]

Balthasar then arrives at his position because of this methodological decision regarding the nature of theology, but he is also drawing upon the witness of the mystics. Balthasar finds Elizabeth of the Trinity saying that "nothing speaks more of the love hidden in the heart of God than the Eucharist."[170] We can also add a quotation from Catherine of Siena about the presence of Christ in the host: "Your bodily eyes could not endure the light, and only your spiritual vision remained, but there you saw and tasted *the depths of the Trinity*, wholly God, wholly human, hidden and veiled under that whiteness."[171] He also finds this idea in Speyr and to a certain extent in Mechthild von Hackeborn.[172] Balthasar repeats this same insight on a number of occasions, claiming that the Eucharist, as the culmination of Christ's descent in the Incarnation, is *the* privileged locus for understanding the Trinitarian life of God. Without the Eucharist, we would not have the Trinitarian understanding that we do: "For what God is has been made known to us and given to us in his Eucharist."[173] Consequently, Balthasar can say without qualification that God *is* a "Eucharistic God."[174] If *missio* is an extension of the eternal *processio* within the temporal and finite world, then the Son's eucharistic self-distribution functions as a mirror of his eternal relations with the Father and the Holy Spirit. However, it must be stated here that when Balthasar speaks of the Eucharist, or worship, or honor within the Trinity, this "catalogical" predication must be balanced by the law of "analogical" speech: whatever *similitudo* there is between God and the world (or God's Eucharist and ours), there is an ultimate and unsurpassable *maior dissimilitudo*. This appeal to analogy is not an a priori safeguard enabling one to import purely anthropological categories onto God with impunity, even if Balthasar can rightly be accused of using imprudent or at least exaggerated language when discussing the Trinitarian relations. Nevertheless, even though Balthasar's understanding of a Trinitarian Eucharist must be tempered by his admission of the irreplaceability of analogical speech, this is not to say that it is imprecise or metaphorical. Instead, for Balthasar, it implies that the economic or earthly manifestations of God's life have their supereminent source within the Triune life, which is not an attenuation of the attributes of the economy, but their maximization. Above all else, this theological method is based on a trust that the Christian experience of revelation actually tells us something positive about God. Speyr says this as eloquently as Balthasar ever did: "We must use what experience we as Christians have of God as access to his nature, as a means of interpreting his being. To renounce this would be to shut ourselves in our earthly world and reject the most precious gifts which give access to God. It would be to hold the strange opinion that God had given us something perfectly good which, on entering heaven, we found to be earthly, temporal, ephemeral and useless."[175]

This comment by Speyr is less controversial when considering the *positive* aspects of the economy. Not in any way the result of sin, but corresponding to a "natural" relationship of the creature to God,[176] worship, prayer, and thanksgiving constitute the creature's relationship to the Creator. For Balthasar, largely drawing on Speyr, worship, prayer, and thanksgiving are attributes of the relations between the divine persons as well.[177] The basic premise behind this assertion is that otherness is a positive quality, as seen principally in the "positive otherness of the Son" from the Father, which "makes possible the positive otherness of creatures."[178] This otherness without discord in the Triune life of God is, for Balthasar, the fulfillment of all distance between God and the creature that is characterized by prayer and adoration. There is then "distance" also in God, a distance between Father, Son, and Spirit, who are not three modalities or attributes of the undivided essence, but consubstantial persons who stand face-to-face with one another. We see this most clearly in Christ's life of prayer to his heavenly Father, which is, again, an expression in the *missio* of the eternal *processio*. Weaving together a series of quotations from Speyr, Balthasar writes,

> When God stands before God we can say "that God shows honor to God" "in a reciprocal glorifying," "in an eternal, reciprocal worship."

"Worship as we know it is a grace that comes from the triune worship. Nothing is more rooted in God than worship." "All worship has its primary basis in the other's otherness. Where there is mere oneness, worship is not possible. The Son does not worship the Father because the Father is like him. . . . Worship is a relation to a Thou."[179]

The Trinity is itself a liturgical reality, with God adoring and praising God. The liturgy of the creature, in whatever form this takes, whether prayer, thanksgiving, or adoration, is a participation in the Son's eternal worship of the Father.[180]

Taking this logic another step further, Balthasar says that "everything that, in the created world, appears shot through with *potentiality* is found *positively* in God."[181] Thus, not only purely positive actions of the creature, such as worship, but even those positive attributes that belong solely to the realm of finitude have their foundation in God.[182] He does not stop here, and extends the argument to include that which seems to be positively opposed to God: "All apparently negative things in the *oikonomia* can be traced back to, and explained by, positive things in the *theologia*."[183] This applies to everything pertaining to Christ's humiliation on the cross and his being torn open so as to become food for the world in the Eucharist. These are indeed negative events, being the results of sin, but they have a prototype within the divine life that functions as the condition for the possibility of Christ undergoing suffering and alienation. If *missio* reflects the *processio*, even the darkness and pain of the former must have some analogue in the latter, even if no negative attributes are ultimately appropriate to God. Thus, with regard to the Eucharist, Balthasar says that "[Christ's] 'having' a human nature, which is given away without reserve in the Eucharist, is therefore nothing other than the earthly representation of the trinitarian poverty, in which everything is always already given away."[184] The "trinitarian poverty" that is manifested in the Eucharist is the Father handing everything, including his very essence, over to the Son and with the Son over to the Spirit. It is the total gift of self, *Hingabe*, that characterizes the divine relations. This leads very quickly to the language of paradox, such that his "poverty" in giving everything away is also his "wealth," in that nothing is lost or depleted.

Balthasar's discussion of a Trinitarian *Hingabe* seems essential to him for two main reasons. First, it establishes that the events of Christ's passion and death were not only possible for him to undergo, but were even fitting expressions of his divinity. This leads directly to the second, which is Balthasar's desire to guard the connection between *oikonomia* and *theologia*. Since it is undoubtedly true that our knowledge of the latter comes to us via the former, the two must be linked more firmly than by simply attributing the saving actions to God's inscrutable will without also reflecting something of his nature. The voluntarism of such a position is obvious, as is its dissociation of God from his own revelation. If God's saving actions in history do in fact reflect his nature, Balthasar thinks that the concept of *Hingabe* is the appropriate one to establish the link.

The generation of the Son by the Father and the spiration of the Spirit by the Father and the Son can be called a *Hingabe* according to a variety of its possible translations: "surrender," "devotion," and "gift." For Balthasar, all of the economic manifestations of the missions of the Son and the Spirit have their origin precisely within this *Hingabe*, which is always already open to otherness, including that of the creature. Thus in the immanent life of the Trinity "the total self-surrender [*Ganzhingabe*] of each Hypostasis to each Other—beginning with the Father's self-surrender [*Selbsthingabe*]—grounds eternal life," and in the economy the "Son's self-surrender [*Hingabe*] through the Father in the Spirit remains the abiding icon of the mystery of God's essence."[185] And because the latter, economic, *Hingabe* finds its completion in the Eucharist, which is the total self-gift and self-dispossession of Christ, so (according to Balthasar's catalogical principle) it is entirely justifiable to call the immanent *Hingabe* by this same name: Eucharist. *The* Eucharist, for Balthasar, is precisely the self-gift of each hypostasis to the others, it is the "blood circulation" in God.[186] The Eucharist was always a matter of God's "blood," but it is only shed violently because of sin. Thus in God there is an eternal Eucharist whereby each person becomes "food" and "nourishment" for the others, in that no person claims anything as a unique possession, but rather hands everything over to the others in a total gift of self.[187] It is this liturgical vision of God that is one of the primary motives and benefits to Balthasar's insistence on the "ever-more" (*je-mehr*) quality of God. As he never ceases to repeat, a belief in the Trinity explodes any conception of a static, immobile God, a God who is merely an object of notional assent. Balthasar, unlike Heidegger, does not contend that the God of the philosophers, the *ipsum esse subsistens*, might not also be the Christian God, but he does agree that a god that is *less* dynamic than creatures may in fact be unworthy of adoration.[188] From at least his early study on Gregory of Nyssa (1942), he became convinced that being and becoming were not an oppositional pair, with the former remaining fixed and the latter subject to movement. If anything, the opposite is true, which has enormous consequences for theology: "Through the Incarnation we learn that all the unsatisfied movement of becoming is itself only repose and fixity when compared to that immense movement of love inside of God: Being is a Super-Becoming."[189]

Balthasar's claims that the divine nature is a "Super-Becoming," that there is an element of "surprise" in God[190] and that God is "enriched" by creation (without implying impoverishment or lack on God's part),[191] are all meant to give texture to his locating liturgy primarily in the divine life, and only derivatively here below. What the Church experiences in liturgy and sacrament is not nonliturgical and nonsacramental in God, but superliturgical and supersacramental. Christ, as the incarnate God-man, gives himself fully to the Church in the Eucharist just as he has been giving himself to the Father from all eternity. His identity as Son *is* the Eucharist.[192] By becoming eucharistic in the economy, the Son of God did not take on self-gift as a new attribute but rather opened up his eternal *Hingabe* as a reality in which creation can participate. There is, therefore, nothing titanic in Christ's kenosis, no metamorphosis in God's nature when the Son is poured out. For Balthasar, then, the *res sacramenti*, the reality of the sacrament that is veiled under the symbolic form of bread and wine, is the Triune life in all its fullness. The Eucharist as a veil is partially translucent. Although one cannot see with bodily eyes, with the eyes of faith one can catch a vague outline of the *dynamis* of the divine life by peering through the veil. And the heart of Balthasar's eucharistic theology is precisely his attempt to sketch that image that can be seen on the other side of the veil, not by ripping the veil and seeing what cannot be seen, but by remaining on *this* side of the veil and gathering the myriad and often paltry findings that we have into a coherent whole. A *theologia viatorum*, which is the only kind possible, can never "give a complete account of the *theologia comprehensorum*."[193]

Interrelation of Doctrines or Metaphorical Eucharist?

To return to a point we made earlier, if one wanted to accuse Balthasar of attempting a panoptic synthesis, one would first need to attend to the fact that his "daring speculations" are drawn from the most basic data of Christian revelation and experience. His portrayal of God as liturgical and eucharistic might not seem like an innovation if one remembered that the way in which God is ordinarily encountered by most Christians is, in fact, in the liturgy and the Eucharist. Balthasar seems to think that God might be very much like how he has shown himself to be: self-giving, willing to be poured out, and excessive. What leads Balthasar to these conclusions is his trust that all Christian doctrines are mutually implicating and bound to one another in such a way that each point implies the rest of the dogmatic structure. Even so, it has often been noted that the sacraments are somehow epistemologically privileged sites for dogmatic reflection, but this project has rarely been consistently and universally carried out, especially with a sacramental maximalism.[194] The closest forerunner to this project would certainly be Scheeben, a fact that Balthasar acknowledges,[195] and it is perhaps safe to admit that the Eastern Orthodox have generally been more attentive and insistent upon an explicit portrayal of all doctrines as interconnected. For Balthasar, then, and he finds this instinct in the Fathers,[196] *all* of theology must be sacramental. The eucharistic anaphora includes the entirety of the *Credo*, and the entire *Credo* should be understood as a liturgical act with a sacramental impulse. Thus *de sacramentis* must be reflected in *de deo uno et trino*, as we have seen in this chapter, and even in *de moribus*, as will be seen in chapter 2. As Balthasar never ceased to say, any specific theological problem and its proposed solution can only be properly judged in light of the entirety of the faith.[197] One's sacramental theology is then not to be judged a success or a failure merely for how well it synthesizes and takes account of strictly sacramental writings in scripture and tradition, but how well it reflects and illuminates the entirety of revelation.

Of course, *how* one connects the Eucharist to the Trinity or any other doctrine is not an a priori given, because the theologian must make judgments about what does, and does not, apply from one doctrine to another. One example is the fact that Louis-Marie Chauvet largely shares Balthasar's concerns about the ability of the sacraments to shed light on human existence and the rest of theology, yet with very different results, stemming from different theological priorities. As we have seen, the two major poles that guide Balthasar's theology are the Trinity and the Eucharist, with *Hingabe* as the mediating concept. And although it seems that Balthasar's intention of bringing the Eucharist and the Trinity into a closer alignment would draw little controversy, the manner in which he does this begs a serious and perhaps devastating question: If the "Eucharist" exists in its fullest expression in God's Triune life, is the ecclesial Eucharist not thereby rendered a metaphor for a different and higher reality?[198] This also resurrects a haunting suggestion raised at the beginning of this chapter and is an issue for most contemporary sacramental theologies, including Balthasar's: If everything is sacramental, then perhaps nothing is. Balthasar notes the danger and acknowledges that perhaps, on the surface, his project looks identical to the manner in which the most representative figures of the Enlightenment handled the data of revelation. Whether carried out by the likes of John Locke or Immanuel Kant, the positive, historical facts of revelation (e.g., the Incarnation, the sacraments) are "translated" into universally applicable and rationally verifiable truths. Is this not exactly what we have seen Balthasar doing, by extracting the concept of self-gift from the Eucharist and finding its universal and necessary source in the Godhead? Is Balthasar's eucharistic theology not a mixture of moral exemplarism and rationalism? Depending on how Balthasar is able to answer this question, the entirety of his eucharistic maximalism could disappear in an instant, revealing that it was all just a smoke screen for a suprahistorical law that is always and everywhere true.

Balthasar's answer redoubles the importance of the Eucharist, and demonstrates once again that although his Trinitarian speculation is indispensable, it is only in the background as the historical, eucharistic drama always remains in the foreground. Again, he stays on *this* side of the veil. So although the Enlightenment's usual handling of positive features of revelation renders them "superfluous as soon as one has arrived at the concept which the form expresses in images," for Balthasar "the idea becomes radiant only in this *conversio ad phantasma*, in this turning to the image which is Christ (and, with him, the Church)."[199] In other words, the theologian cannot kick down the ladder once he has climbed up past and extracted the truth from the seemingly contingent, historical data of

Christ's earthly sojourn. For Balthasar, the Incarnation and the sacramental economy are not pedagogical tools, no matter how much they happen to reveal about the structure of the created order and its relation to its infinite source. Instead, as he says with his typically Johannine accent, "The distinctive Christian factor is that here we not only 'start from' the corporeal and the sensory as from some religious material on which we can then perform the necessary abstractions; rather, we abide in the seeing, hearing, touching, the savouring and eating of this flesh and blood, which has borne and taken away the sin of the world."[200] If then Balthasar moves from the *Hingabe* of the Eucharist to the *Hingabe* within the Trinitarian life, he does not do so by leaving the former behind in favor of the latter. Instead, the knowledge of the latter (and more important than knowledge, participation therein) comes only in and through the liturgical life of the Church, through Christ's self-distribution to the Church and the world. This is also why Balthasar thinks that the indispensable moment of analogy, which moves upward by abstraction, must be supplemented by the catalogical moment, which reaffirms the positivity and permanence of the earthly, historical form. Balthasar's own self-defense on this question mirrors his defense of Denys in *GL* II. Even though he previously had reservations about Denys, by the time of his essay in *GL* II (1962) he shows how the three stages of symbolism, affirmation, and negation are not a movement away from the positivity of ecclesial, liturgical reality, but an intensification thereof. Denys does not move from mediated, ecclesial knowledge to unmediated contemplation, for he acknowledges that on earth "there is only mediated knowledge of God."[201] What Balthasar claims for Denys is equally true of himself: "The whole theology of the Areopogite is for him a single, sacred liturgical act,"[202] which means that the liturgical positivity of the ecclesiastical hierarchy is not abrogated by the dizzying heights of the celestial hierarchy.

Finally, the important point to be made briefly here, and expanded upon in chapter 2, is that the movement from economy to theology is not a move from *mythos* to *logos*. The Church's Eucharist, which is often visibly indistinguishable from theurgy and superstition, is not a mythic version of the logical, divine archetype. For Balthasar, if we are going to use the *mythos/logos* distinction in its broadest sense, *mythos* is as much a part of Trinitarian life as *logos* is of the economic revelation. The expanded and liberal use of "eucharistic" or "sacramental" in Balthasar's vocabulary is not then a dilution of its original meaning, but rather the establishment of a continuum of meaning, from its fullest, perfected archetype in the divine life, to its opening and accommodation to sinful humanity, and everything in between and below that evinces the same fruitful self-giving. Instead then of the Eucharist as a metaphor, it is a pledge and a foretaste of the same reality that has always existed without veils and without having to have first passed through the cross: "The preliminary, earthly forms of this heavenly fruitfulness are more than mere metaphorical pointers, they are a first installment of something final, albeit always under the sign of the Cross."[203] Finally, the Eucharist is not a metaphor because the two primary instances that we have been discussing, the Church's sacrament and the Trinitarian life, are not *two* things, but one. The ecclesial manifestation takes on a different mode than does the Trinitarian *Hingabe*, namely, it is under the form of a veil and is a gift of divinity through Christ's humanity, but it is folded and incorporated into the one *dynamis* of the Triune life.

CONCLUSION: *LA DISPUTA*

This chapter has established that whatever else can be said of Balthasar's eucharistic theology, it operates essentially with the presupposition that a eucharistic maximalism, which is the ordinary mode of Christian piety, can only function beneficially when brought explicitly into theological speculation. I have described first how this occurs by Balthasar's close conjunction of the Eucharist with the Incarnation and its climax at Golgotha, and ultimately how this theological claim gains its credibility only by locating the manifestation of the Eucharist in its Trinitarian prototype. The following chapters, which will attend to more specific, and likely more familiar, issues of sacramental theology, are to be understood only with reference to the parameters and the horizon set by this one. The viability of Balthasar's position, however, can be seen from this basic intention and this general penchant for eucharistic expansion, but it will also be borne out in the manner in which he treats the related issues of sacramental theology. What has been covered in this chapter in the mode of dramatics can be briefly seen from the light of aesthetics.

The various strands of Balthasar's dramatic eucharistic theory can be brought together with the aid of a painting that he knew well: Raphael's *La Disputa del sacramento*. This painting, on the opposite wall from the more well-known *School of Athens* in the Stanza della Segnatura in the Vatican Palace, sets in apposition a debate on the nature of the Eucharist by the pilgrim Church below with the Triune God and the saints in glory above. Balthasar uses *La Disputa* as an example for Maximus the Confessor's theology, but it is equally true of his own work: "The liturgy is the midpoint, around which everything revolves, from which—as the single bright point into which one cannot look—everything is explained, whether left or right, up or down (as in Raphael's *Disputa*) . . . the liturgy is everywhere presupposed as the act that makes real the universal presence of the hypostatic Christ—at the midpoint between God and creation, heaven and earth, new age and old, Church and world."[204]

The painting has a clear break between heaven and earth,[205] marked by a definitive horizon and a thick layer of clouds. Yet, the Host set upon the altar is in a direct descending line below the Father, the Son, and the Holy Spirit.[206] The central feature of both halves of the painting is the same: above it is Christ in a state of glory, and below it is the eucharistic Christ. Below, Christ sits silently and vulnerably as the Church ponders, debates, and perhaps equivocates regarding his eucharistic presence. Above, Christ shows the same eucharistic openness as seen not only from the open wounds in his hands and side and his elevated hands demonstrating receptivity, but also from the fact that Mary and John the Baptist, representing all the saints, are brought into his aura and thus show themselves as extensions of his body and his identity.

Most importantly, the clouds separating heaven and earth function as a curtain, a curtain that one would find in a theater. And although we are given a view so as to see both sides of this curtain, or we could say this veil, the Church below is only granted access to Christ on the altar. The painting can then be seen as partly ironic. The Church throughout the centuries debates the presence of Christ (much of which concerns the essentials, such as the real presence, along with more peripheral issues, such as how the accidents remain, or what happens when a mouse consumes the host), but Raphael gives us the answer in all its simplicity by the top half of the image. What is the Eucharist? The Triune life, which includes the incarnate and now liquefied and pneumatic Christ, who opens his flesh so as to bring the Church to share in his divinity. And among the earthly debaters, it seems to be an artist, Leonardo da Vinci, the first figure to the right of the altar, who understands this best of all, as represented by his arm pointing upward into the Trinitarian economy.[207] This upward gesture, which Balthasar shares with da Vinci in the painting, is a signal that the Eucharist can only be properly understood when it is seen as that which represents a partial tear in the heaven/earth tension, as a reality on earth of what is a properly celestial movement.

To play on the coincidence of the German and English words, for Balthasar, the Mass is truly a *Mass* (or *Maß*), a measurement, a proportion that images the proportion between the divine persons, as is seen by the equal distance between Father and Son, Son and Spirit, and Spirit and Eucharist in *La Disputa*. If *La Disputa* were repainted today, and Balthasar were granted a spot among the eucharistic debaters, he would certainly take his place as one among many. Even though he attempts the most expansive treatment of the eucharistic question, tending to avoid questions of eucharistic physics and other subtleties that have been the predominant issues of sacramental theology for centuries, he would not deny that these issues and debates have their place as responses to questions and heresies. But Balthasar does not think that the heart of eucharistic theology is one that typically arises in the course of disputation or correction. For although the debates against Berengar, or the Albigensians, or the Reformers have clarified doctrine regarding the *how* of the Eucharist, they have not always penetrated very deeply into the question of *why* the Eucharist is the chosen site of divine manifestation.[208] Thus, instead of sacramental theology being done as a reaction to misunderstanding, Balthasar thinks that it is also possible, and indeed essential, to look up beyond the veil that separates heaven and earth and ponder the mystery of the divine self-gift that squanders itself in order to be consumed by the mouths of sinners.

CHAPTER 2

Pneumatic Flesh

The Holy Spirit and the Church's Eucharist

Two major lacunae remain to be filled in from chapter 1, which traced Christ's dramatic act of "becoming eucharistic" through his incarnation and self-gift to the Church, but the existence of this Church-as-recipient was simply stipulated without sustained attention. Likewise, even though the Trinitarian life of God was the culmination of chapter 1's various *topoi*, we really only considered God as a dyad, as the Father–Son pair, leaving the role of the Holy Spirit rather unspecified. This chapter will demonstrate how these two omissions, the Church and the Spirit, were really only one omission, because Balthasar considers the relationship between Church and Spirit to be one of coimplication. This is especially true when the Eucharist comes into consideration. I shall then complete what was lacking by analyzing Balthasar's understanding of the eucharistic drama precisely as it involves the Church, as the Church responds to and participates in Christ's gift, which occurs *in the Holy Spirit*. If until now Balthasar's treatment of the Eucharist could be perhaps characterized as ethereal and seemingly foreign to what is rightly considered normative about this sacrament (namely, that it is an ecclesial reality), then I will here explore the Eucharist precisely as it comes to meet the Church. We have considered the Eucharist as a gift given (without sustained consideration of a recipient), but here the Eucharist is seen as a gift received, presupposing everything that has already been said about its givenness. Thus several familiar and classical sacramental categories will come into focus, namely, the tension between the *opus operatum* and the *opus operantis*, the question of the sacrificial nature of the Mass, and the relationship between sacramental reception and ethics. Before arriving at the major themes already announced, however, certain conceptual clarifications regarding the objectivity of the eucharistic gift and the subjectivity of its reception need to be put in place.

THE TWO HANDS OF THE FATHER:
OBJECTIVITY AND SUBJECTIVITY

Even though all liquids may possess the same essential properties (e.g., flow freely at a constant volume), some are elixirs and some are poisons. And Christ can be said to be "liquefied" in a variety of competing, at times difficult to distinguish, ways. Therefore, in discussing Balthasar's theology of Christ's "eucharistic liquefaction" we also need to concomitantly consider the tension with what we will be calling the modern tendency toward liquidation. Philosophical modernity, especially when it is concerned with preserving theological data, has a version of a "liquid Christ" that possesses very different attributes from Balthasar's. In this section, I will explore what precisely constitutes the difference between these two conceptions of liquefaction, with an eye to the implications that each has for ecclesiology. The question to be explored is how one person, Christ, can be the operative principle of identity for a universal and culturally and historically multifarious collection of peoples called the Church. Or, put differently, how can the objectivity and particularity of one be subjectively relevant for the many? The answer, for both Balthasar and philosophical modernity, concerns the movement from Christ to the Holy Spirit, and thus is only understood within the realm of pneumatology.

Liquefaction: Modern or Eucharistic

Balthasar's most polemical book, *Cordula oder der Ernstfall* (1966) (translated into English as *The Moment of Christian Witness*), contains a fictitious dialogue between a well-disposed commissar, "a figure symbolising the culture of modernity both in its easy secularism and its nightmare terrors,"[1] and a modern Christian who is overly anxious to demonstrate the compatibility of Christianity with modernity, thus de-emphasizing anything particular about the Christian faith. The commissar, who perhaps was initially intent on persecuting the Christian, sees through the mask: "Don't be stupid, my friend. Now I've understood enough. You've liquidated yourselves and spared us the trouble of persecuting you. Dismissed!"[2] In Balthasar's understanding, the modern liquidation of Christianity is designed to make Christ more easily consumable, to make him dissolved and diluted. Or, to change the metaphor, the particularities of Christianity are goods at a liquidation sale of a defunct business: everything must go! As opposed to this modern type of liquidation, which for Balthasar makes martyrdom unlikely if not impossible, his own frequent usage of the concept of liquefaction is intended not to thin Christ out but to make him *more available* in all his particularity, his thick singularity. But, this does not yet solve the problem, for even if the particularity of Christ is made more easily available, that does not mean he becomes any more digestible. The issue becomes even more acute when we turn to how this Christ continues to be present on earth: in the cultic rite of a seemingly sectarian religious body. Can a modern believer participate in the liturgy without the haunting feeling that the accidental and historical aspects of the rite are out of sync with the supposedly universal truths being proclaimed? Louis Dupré notes the dilemma: "Today many, also believers, perceive ritual, sacrament, and sacrifice as quaintly or barbarously out of place. Why would people have to dance to express their dependence on the gods? Or why should gestures of everyday life such as washing and eating ever be considered sacred?"[3]

Without tracing all of the nuances of his position, or evaluating its veracity, we need to first outline Balthasar's understanding of the liquefaction of Christianity that often occurs in philosophical modernity. Since we have already established certain Trinitarian principles in Balthasar's thought in chapter 1, there is no need to demonstrate here that Hegel's *Geist*, which begins as subjective but necessarily makes itself objective in order to become the absolute Spirit, is rejected for its failure to distinguish between the immanent and economic Trinity.[4] Balthasar's concern with theological modernity (as opposed to a more self-consciously philosophical one) is that it likewise tends to move from the objectivity of the Church to the subjectivity of the Spirit (sometimes the Holy Spirit, sometimes the spirit of man, sometimes a mélange of the two). And, as an inheritance of Joachim of Fiore, this tends to be read as an intrahistorical sequence, such that there is a movement from the age of the Son, with its cult and institutions, to that of the Spirit, which is characterized by interiority and a total absence of heteronomy. As Balthasar learned from Henri de Lubac, this makes the Church into a "next-to-last reality."[5] Examples of those who read the scriptural movement from Calvary to Pentecost as both descriptive of the order of revelation and prescriptive for the translation of Christian specificity range from Schleiermacher to Tillich to more recent proponents of Spirit-Christology.[6] It has, in fact, become a universal temptation for theologians who wish to find the relevance of Christianity for those outside of the visible bounds of the Church. The Holy Spirit often appears as an easy tool to bring others into the fold, a fold that, when pneumatological, is wider than the narrowness of the Christological Church. The Church again becomes penultimate.

These pneumatological decisions shape a theology of history and eschatology to a significant extent, which we will treat in chapter 4. Without examining the temporal dimension here, it is to be noted that, for Balthasar, at the base of this modern process of liquidation is a conflation of the human and the divine spirit. This needs to be dealt with not because Balthasar is so clearly opposed to this tendency (though he certainly is), but because his own position can appear to be simply another rendition of it. As I emphasized in chapter 1, if Christ has become so liquefied so as to become eucharistically ubiquitous, and now exists bodily in the Church and its sacraments, then has Balthasar not also moved from the concreteness of Christ as a unique individual to Christ as simply the animating impulse of the Church? We have already rejected this notion because Balthasar insists on a *diastasis* between Christ and the Church, but here the same issue can be put in a pneumatological register: no matter the similarity between the human-, community-, or even world-spirit and the Holy Spirit, an even greater dissimilarity must perdure. Balthasar notes the forgetfulness of the dissimilarity in theologians such as Tillich and Pannenberg, the latter of whom he quotes: "There is no need, nor would it be meaningful, to posit a fundamental separation between human and divine Spirit."[7] The supposed benefits of such a theory are that it allows the Holy Spirit to be interpreted as the *Weltgeist*, the animating force that guides the evolution of creation and creates a positive basis for interreligious dialogue, for presumably all partake of this same Spirit. Though he is sympathetic to these intentions, Balthasar finds the conclusion theologically dubious, given that it imagines two different, even competing, orders of salvation: the mission of the creative Spirit who cooperates in the strivings of humanity and the mission of the Son who creates a Church.

For Balthasar, the Holy Spirit is not on a continuum with the *Weltgeist* or the natural, human soul, because the Holy Spirit is as much about condemning and purifying the spirit of the world as he is about validating it: "With the manifestation of the Holy Spirit of God and of Jesus, we discern a tendency that contradicts the upward-striving natural 'spirit.'"[8] The Holy Spirit is, for Balthasar, every bit as "distant" (first by nature and then compounded by sin) from the creature as Christ is from the Church: "The Spirit is the Spirit of the distance, in that the whole relationship of 'remaining' and 'indwelling' remains correlated to the reality of 'faith' and 'obedience.'"[9] Human *eros*, though good (*pace* Nygren), still needs to be purified by *agape*.[10] Put in more abstract terms, the collapse of this distance is perhaps the essence of Balthasar's understanding of the problem of the process of liquidation in modernity. It gives a priori preference to that which is universal, such as spirit, rendering the supposed parochialism of the historical Christ passé. To consider this same issue with regard to the question of truth, this is essentially a question of how to balance the *mythos/logos* tension. Modernity either ignores *mythos* altogether or attempts to translate it into *logos*, but Balthasar thinks that both the mythological and the logical need to be maintained, at the very least for solid epistemological principles.[11] In this, Balthasar considers himself to be a faithful disciple of Aquinas even as he appropriates the insights of modern phenomenology.[12] All truth, and this is most acutely the case for theological truth, occurs not in "turning away from that which is concretely finite . . . but in turning towards the phenomenal existent (*conversio ad phantasma*) as the only place where the mystery of Being will shine forth for him who himself exists bodily and spiritually."[13]

This is why Balthasar takes issue with Rahner's distinction between the categorical and the transcendental, especially if the distinction between the truth that is found in history and that which is found suprahistorically is mapped onto a Christ/Spirit duality.[14] Instead, Balthasar proposes the inseparability of the categorical and the transcendental, or the realms of *mythos* and *logos*: "It becomes clear, in [Christ], that the *transcendental* is directly present and manifested in the *categorial*. It is impossible, therefore, to postulate an abiding mystery of transcendence *behind* the realm of the 'categorial' that is accessible to reason. . . . On the contrary, the absolute Logos is present in and through history."[15] There is then no access to a pure *logos* abstracted from its manifestation in *mythos*. Here Balthasar is clearly echoing his former mentor, Erich Przywara, who taught that truth is never confined to historical vicissitudes, but it is also never present except *in* history, in the "categorical" order of things. Przywara's formula for this was that truth is always in-and-beyond (*in-über*) history, that *logos* is in-and-beyond *mythos*.[16] To disparage the mythic in favor of the logical is especially impossible when dealing with Christian revelation, which is an unveiling, an *apokalypsis*, of what can be known only insofar as it is unveiled. For Balthasar, Christianity can distinguish itself from Hermeticism only with difficulty.[17]

We can now begin to see some of the direct consequences of Balthasar's insistence on Christ's pneumatic body and his eucharistic ubiquity. He understands that Christianity cannot become "fluid" in the modern sense, whereby particularities are dissolved in favor of universality, but also that it cannot present itself as concerned with only regional truths, which would contradict its missionary impulse. Thus, Balthasar conceives of Christ's flesh as an index for this particularity/universality dialectic. Christ's flesh is totally particular in that it remains corporeal (*leiblich*, not *körperlich*) and bears the marks of his concrete and bloody history, but it is totally universal in that it is now truly pneumatic, risen, and unbounded by (finite) space or time. Just as the Eucharist has always functioned as a symbol for the paradox of unity and plurality within the Church,[18] so for Balthasar it is the epitome of Christ's own singularity-in-universality. And more than signifying it, the Eucharist is also the means by which the singular Christ repeats himself in history. This issue is even more acute, according to Balthasar, when we consider the question of bodies. He asks "how the destiny of a single body-person can be relevant for all body-persons," and after surveying patristic attempts to answer the question, finds the answer: "It is only with the Eucharist that the deepest link is forged . . . the Eucharist is the connecting link between Christ and us."[19] However, though Balthasar thus refuses the temptation toward liquidation in the modern sense, his own version of a eucharistic liquefaction can only be understood accurately when we turn to examine the role of the Holy Spirit in rendering Christ "pneumatic."

The Holy Spirit

From what we have just discussed, it is clear that Balthasar is not going to consider Christ and the sacraments as the *objective* and the Holy Spirit as the *subjective* revelation of God, as several others do.[20] Nevertheless, even if he rejects this rather crude division, he recognizes that there is, indeed, a good deal of truth in it. For example, in *GL* I he includes Christ, the Church, and the sacraments under the heading "The Objective Evidence," and the light of faith and aspects of Christian subjectivity are often linked to the Holy Spirit, and are under the heading of "The Subjective Evidence." There is also ample scriptural evidence that could be used to suggest such a division, because the Holy Spirit is often connected to the human heart or spirit, as in some way connected to our subjective assent and witness to God, and also associated with freedom and liberation.[21] Recognizing this, Balthasar thinks that we would have misunderstood the work of the Holy Spirit in the heart were this considered in isolation from the objective, seemingly "impersonal" aspects of Christ's Church and the sacraments. But even before discussing the interconnection between the missions of Son and Spirit, Balthasar notes that there is no theological reason why we would associate the person of the Holy Spirit as particularly subjective rather than objective: "As fruit, the Spirit is thus the coming to light of the innermost 'subjectivity' of the encounter of Father and Son as well as their 'objectivity,' giving their absolute surrender [*restlos Hingegebenen*] to each other a standard [*Maß*] for their love. But he is that because this standard is also an eternal 'excess' [*Übermaß*] that will eternally spur the two Persons on to renewed surrender [*Hingabe*]."[22]

Everything about the Holy Spirit is entirely "subjective," as an overflowing expression of the subjective love between the Father and Son, but also entirely "objective," as a witness and a measure of this love. Thus, whatever may be gained by this division in the economic sphere, it is of limited and perhaps only heuristic value when discussing the Trinity *in se*. And because we cannot develop Balthasar's pneumatology here in full, but only the Holy Spirit's relationship to the Church and the sacraments, it must be stated rather laconically that the Holy Spirit is, for

Balthasar, simultaneously superobjective and supersubjective, as are the Father and Son.

The cooperation of Son and Spirit in the *ordo salutis* is epitomized, for Balthasar, by the Eucharist. Through the lens of this sacrament we can see the harmony, and the distinction, between these two missions: "It is in the mystery of the Eucharist that we can best see that 'the Father's two hands' do not cease working in concert."[23] In the Eucharist, there is a constant crisscrossing of the various pairs of the dialectic: Christ, body, and objectivity, on the one hand, and Spirit, pneumatic, and subjectivity, on the other. The Eucharist is the bodily Christ, but again, a *pneumatic* body, and this pneumatic body is made present by the operation of the Spirit. And even though he strongly rejects the Joachimite movement from Christ to Spirit, Balthasar does recognize that the incarnate Christ is, because of the "Trinitarian inversion,"[24] subject and obedient to the Spirit. Christ is, from the moment of his incarnation, the "anointed one," the one who is led by the Spirit without any sense of heteronomy.[25] And it is the Spirit who is still the "expositor" of the Son, just as Christ "exposited" the Father. This role of interpretation also includes the task of universalizing and rendering subjectively available all that was objective and particular about Christ. Thus, Christ was led by the Spirit and was eventually made totally pneumatic, but the Spirit moves in the opposite direction, from the pneumatic to the fleshly. The Holy Spirit does not then appeal to human hearts by pointing toward universal truths that are to be subjectively appropriated, but rather toward the specificity and concreteness of Christ.[26] If then Christ points toward the Spirit, the Spirit does not then negate all that belongs to Christ, but in fact blocks all attempts to flee from the bodily and the particular in favor of the purely pneumatic. Body moves toward the Spirit, but the Spirit moves back toward the body.[27] According to Balthasar, any attempt to take refuge in the Spirit as a respite from the corporeal is bound to be frustrated, for the Spirit is always the Spirit *of Christ.*

None of this is to suggest that Balthasar conceives of the Spirit's mission as bound to the visible and institutional structure of the Church and its sacraments, nor should Balthasar's view of the objective nature of the Spirit be read as having direct implications for the salvation or damnation of non-Christians.[28] Rather, Balthasar means to make the Christ–Spirit relationship one that is indissoluble. To reach the Spirit, one must pass through the objectivity of Christ and his Church, and if one wants the incarnate Christ, one will find that "the Spirit gives life, the flesh is of no avail" (John 6:63). The objectivity of sacramental grace is oriented toward the Spirit, toward subjective ratification without which one renders that grace ineffective or worse. Likewise, even if the sacraments aim toward the spiritual, Balthasar does not allow that one could skip over the sacraments by arriving straightaway at a spiritual, subjective union with the Spirit or with Christ: "The personal in Christ can only confront the personal in the individual Christian in union with what appears to be impersonal, the Church and the sacraments."[29] The seemingly impersonal nature of the sacraments, the fact that they are particular, bound to some elements of the earth and some cultural products rather than others, is a signal that they are indeed prolongations of the Incarnation, of the fact that God became flesh at a particular time in a particular place as a particular man. And it is the role of the Holy Spirit to render this particularity a universally significant reality. There is, then, no transcendental/categorical divide for Balthasar. Instead of passing from the categorical concreteness of Christ, the Church, and the sacraments to the transcendental sphere of the Holy Spirit's universality, for Balthasar the categorical in Christ is itself made "transcendental": "Christ's Holy Spirit, working in a mysterious way, universalizes Christ's historical, risen reality as the *universale concretum*, thereby enabling its radiance to penetrate 'to the ends of the earth.'"[30] The concrete is now universal, but, on the other hand, the universal is already specified concretely.

Christ and the Spirit, Balthasar is happy to admit, can be experienced by those outside of the visible structure of the Church. His debt to Teilhard de Chardin, no matter the profound differences in both style and substance between them, should not be overlooked, but this is rarely mentioned.[31] The world is charged with both *logoi spermatikoi* and *spermata pneumatika*, and even if the spirit of the world cannot be strictly identified with the Holy Spirit, natural forms of love and even the normal development of the childhood psyche already illustrate and provide the conditions for strictly "supernatural" revelation.[32] Christ and the Spirit come not only at Bethlehem and Pentecost, respectively, but are essentially interwoven into the natural order of creation. Thus one can experience and partake of the grace of these "seeds" even beyond the borders to the Church. Yet, Balthasar insists that seeds must be understood in relation to the fully grown tree, and not vice versa. Therefore, there is most assuredly *baptismus in voto* and spiritual communion, but these are positively oriented to, and receive their grace from, the actual ecclesial sacraments of baptism and Eucharist, which are their fullest expression.[33] *Spiritual* communion is indeed spiritual *communion*, and the baptism of *desire* is a *baptism* of desire, whereby the personal, spiritual pole receives its relevance from its being inchoately sacramental.[34] Likewise, on the more global scale, whatever the role of *spermata* or of the Spirit's engagement with creation, according to Balthasar, one should judge an artist with regard to the final masterpiece, not the early sketches and outlines: "What is most creative about the Holy Spirit (*Creator Spiritus*) must be marked by the stigma of Cross and Resurrection as it spreads all over the world."[35] If then the Son and the Holy Spirit are like two hands, they are not the two hands of which Jesus speaks in his parable about almsgiving. Rather, here, the left hand not only knows what the right hand is doing, but each presupposes and depends upon the other to complete their common task.

Even when considering the relationship between the Holy Spirit and the Church in the economy of salvation, Balthasar does not stray far from a consideration of the role of the Spirit within the Trinitarian *taxis*. For indeed, the latter is the foundation of the former (even if the order of discovery is the reverse). According to Balthasar, just as the Spirit is the *vinculum amoris* between Father and Son, so the Spirit is what establishes the union of the Church, both at the horizontal level among the members of the Church and vertically, in connecting the Church to Christ. To use Sergei Bulgakov's term, the Holy Spirit is a *copula*, the Spirit as a person exists as the "in-between" of the Father and the Son.[36] The Church is then to be understood in pneumatic terms, in addition to the usual Christological ones (e.g., body of Christ, bride of Christ). For the Church comes to occupy that same space in between the Father and the Son that *is* the Holy Spirit: "Born of the Spirit as we are, we exist in the fire of love in which Father and Son encounter each other; thus, together with the Spirit, we simultaneously bear witness and give glory to this love."[37] The Church is thus a created copy of the Spirit's place between Father and Son, but the Church does this by way of addition, not by replacing the Spirit. It is at this Trinitarian level that all of Balthasar's reflections on the Eucharist need to be situated, for the ecclesial Eucharist is itself a reflection of the love between the divine persons. The role of the Church, we could even say the contribution of the Church, to the Eucharist is then to be located in its movement *to* the Father, *through* the Son, and *in* the Holy Spirit, as the traditional prepositions tell us. It is this *"in"* that animates the Church and makes it more of a theandric society than a purely social body, and that makes the Eucharist understandable as a cooperation between humanity and divinity. At this Trinitarian level, Balthasar gives us an insight into the tension between the objective and the subjective poles of sacramental grace that is far more than the simple requirement of *non ponitur obex.*

THE GIFT AND ITS RECEPTION

A mere *opus operatum* without an *opus operantis*, while it remains a minimal concept necessary as a result of sin, is, from the perspective of God's redemptive plan, a nothing, something that ought not to be. It *does* exist, in an anti-Donatist sense, for the benefit of those who receive grace through it; but it remains fruitless for the unprepared sinner who distributes or receives it.[38]

For Balthasar, everything about the Church is meant to be personal, that is, subjectively appropriated. Certainly, as a rule, this is very often not the case. As the Communion of Judas shows, not only does the objective grace of the sacraments remain unappreciated at times, but it can also be positively scorned. This is of course why the *opus operatum/opus operantis* distinction is helpful: the baptism may be "valid," and thus does not need to be repeated, but it remains fruitless without faith. Yet, for Balthasar, the fruitless sacrament is a profound aberration, a *nothing*, as he says in the extract at the start of this section. Like the presence of evil in the world (and indeed, as a direct result of this), the fruitless sacrament is profoundly illogical. Its existence is widely manifest, but its omnipresence does not lessen the scandal of the disharmony between gift and (lack of) reception. It is also, incidentally, not where sacramental theology should begin. Thus Balthasar wants to recast the tension between *opus operatum* and *opus operantis* in a more explicitly biblical and Trinitarian register where the main concern is not so much about how to balance the objectivity of grace with the need for subjective appropriation, but about the Church's cooperation in the mystery of redemption. This turns the Church's Eucharist into a double gift: a gift of Christ to the Church, but likewise a return-gift of the Church to God. As a gift that is simultaneously its own return-gift (as thanksgiving, *eucharistia*), the Eucharist is for Balthasar the privileged site for the meeting of divinity and humanity, the place where Christ gives himself with utter abandon and the Church ratifies this gratuity with its own eucharistic gift of self. We now turn to this issue as it takes on specificity in the eucharistic exchange.

Ex opere: Objective and Subjective Holiness

If sacramental theology is haunted by any specter, it is the specter of magic. Perhaps more owed to the internal fears of the theologian rather than to popular perception and accusation, magic is always that phenomenon the theologian must show to be dissimilar to the sacraments. Almost universally, the distinction is found in the concept of the *opus operantis*. Whereas magic works on the level of automatism, the sacraments require faith and an active reception in order to "work." Rahner here can be seen as representative: "Insofar as the *opus operatum* of the sacraments encounters the *opus operantis* of the believer or the person who accepts God's act, it is clear that sacraments are only efficacious in faith, hope and love. Hence they have nothing to do with magic rites. They are not magic because they do not coerce God."[39] Balthasar likewise notes that the requirement of personal commitment is sufficient to distinguish the sacraments from magic. Nevertheless, this need to avoid magic can often lead to the following question, asked by Rahner: "So where is the real difference between the *opus operatum* of the sacraments and these other instances of grace being conferred, which we do not call sacraments?"[40] In other words, if God grants grace to the person with an open heart without the sacraments, and the sacraments only grant grace to the extent of that person's goodwill, then why traverse through the sacraments at all? There are a variety of answers to this question, some of which simply appeal to a further nuance between the *opus operatum* and the *opus operantis*, or appeal to Christ's will that specifies the sacraments as privileged distributors of grace, or note the special help given by each particular sacrament. Because Balthasar does not spend as much time worrying about how sacramental grace relates to sanctifying or habitual grace, his solution does not come down to this type of defining or dividing.[41] Rather, he begins not from grace and its various modalities abstractly construed, but with the economy as we encounter it in scripture and the Church. Parallel to this, Balthasar thinks that one should look at the sacraments as they were designed to be used, not by worrying first of all about their aberrant forms. These two streams come together in Mary, who represents for Balthasar the perfect synthesis of the two *opera*, and in such a way that does not render actual sacramental reception suspect, but necessary. In Mary, the operation of grace and its reception are seen as fundamentally eucharistic, whether this occurs in a liturgical context or not.

Bracketing for the moment the question of the relationship between Mary and the Church, we need to first establish Balthasar's Marian theology as a type and symbol of the divine–human relationship perfectly construed. According to Balthasar, to be confounded by the question about whether Mary could have said "no" to Gabriel's message is essentially to miss the harmony between finite and divine freedoms: "No finite freedom can be freer from restrictions than when giving its consent to infinite freedom."[42] Mary's freedom is found in obedience to God's will, which comes not as a heteronomous imposition, but as that which grants her freedom in the first place. Choosing otherwise than God's will, even if as a Promethean expression of one's own freedom, could only be considered as a form of servitude, theologically speaking. For Balthasar, Mary's *fiat mihi* is the most perfect act of obedience, and obedience is the key to understanding his conception of Christian mission. A mission, as seen preeminently in Mary, is not coterminous with one's own natural predilections, skills, or desires, but is rather a gift given from the outside. However, this mission not only gets "absorbed," as it were, into the person so as to become one's own identity, but it is also that which makes someone a *person* at all. Though he does not tie personhood as explicitly to baptismal grace as John Zizioulas does, Balthasar does say that, to modify Tertullian's axiom, persons are made, not born.[43] It is only by affirming the mission that God gives that one have "the greatest possible chance of becoming a person, of laying hold of his own substance, of grasping that most intimate idea of his own self—which otherwise would remain undiscoverable."[44] When the Holy Spirit comes down upon Mary, "there is only a state of agreeing and permitting things to happen, without limit and without setting conditions," which again makes Mary the paradigm of receptivity (not passivity) to grace.[45]

As in C. S. Lewis's depiction in *The Great Divorce* of the denizens of hell separating farther and farther from one another as they seek isolation from their fellows, so too for Balthasar sin precludes solidarity and hardens one's separation from others. Holiness, as the acceptance and enactment of one's mission, on the other hand, necessarily conjoins one to the rest of humanity, which is true in a special sense in the case of Mary.[46] Balthasar finds this to be a major biblical motif, as demonstrated by the bestowal of new names (Abram to Abraham, Jacob to Israel, Simon to Peter): "Their change of name means that they are no longer private, empirical subjects but persons of social and theological significance."[47] This is thus the basis for what he calls the "ecclesialization" (*Kirche-werden*) of Mary, which also finds expression in Vatican II's decision to join the documents on Mary and the Church into one: *Lumen gentium*.[48] According to Balthasar, just as Christ distributes himself eucharistically, so Mary "disappears into the heart of the Church," such that he can say, with Charles Journet, "the entire Church is Marian."[49] The harmony between God's objective grace and subjective reception in obedience is, because of the Marian core, the natural state of the Church. What is unnatural is the dissonance between the two. In this, the Donatists were following a natural intuition: an unholy priest is "grotesque, an impossible possibility, theologically speaking." Nevertheless, the grotesque reality of the Church does not constrict Christ's grace, for he even works through that which is most opposed to him.[50]

The objective/subjective tension, or, in a sacramental key, the interplay between *ex opere operato* and *operantis*, is a matter of the Church catching up with *her*self. The feminine pronoun is entirely apt here, for Balthasar the Church *is* Marian, and thus the imparting of sacramental grace is when the Church is not only revealed to be but actually becomes its own Marian center. The call (*das Wort*) and the response (*die Antwort*) should match, as they do in Mary, such that conversion and baptism, for instance, could be considered the same event.[51] Yet, grace outstrips the sinner such that God's objective condescension and forgiveness precede conversion and holiness.[52] All has been perfectly accomplished by Christ; all has been given over to the Church. Yet, it is not as simple as to add that the Church must now, in each of her members, subjectively appropriate it.

This is certainly true, but it needs to be noted that the Church has also already perfectly received the work of grace in obedience and faith, in the person of Mary. Thus she becomes the *Realsymbol* and foundation for the Church, whereby the Church is always striving to return to the moment of its birth from the side of Christ. According to Balthasar, Mary is the "memory of the Church" in that she continues to "ponder these things in her heart" (Luke 2:19), and whereas the rest of the Church is quick to forget God's saving actions, Mary continues to remember on behalf of the entire Church.[53] This has immediate sacramental relevance, for even if it is impossible to know with certainty whether Mary herself ever received sacramental Communion, "she knows better than any saint or sinner what it means to accept the Son completely into oneself; she stands as it were behind every communion as the *ecclesia immaculata* which makes up to completion and perfection what we have done incompletely and imperfectly."[54] The *opus operatum* and *opus operantis*, Christ's eucharistic gift and its loving reception, are then already perfectly resolved in Mary, in the Church's essential core. The sacraments then unveil the Church. What they unveil, for instance when someone is baptized, is what the Church already was: pure, immaculate. Just as in Augustine's justly famous, though frequently misunderstood, axiom, "receive what you are," so Balthasar says with a uniquely Marian emphasis:

> This is the locus of a great mystery: Mary's hidden presence in the Church's sacraments. Who can lift the veil? The Church, purified through the "washing of water" in baptism, becomes the *immaculata* (Eph 5:26); but this means that she becomes what she always already was in Mary. Bread and wine are transformed into the body and blood of Christ by the descent of the Holy Spirit; but this body was always the flesh that was conceived by the Holy Spirit and born of the Virgin Mary.[55]

There remains, nevertheless, the element of the "grotesque" in the earthly Church, the asymmetry between gift and reception. The sacraments then always retain their status as an objective "other," as something impersonal and foreign to what we would "naturally" project of our own subjective desires. This is a signal that if we are to resolve this disjuncture, that which is objective should not be conformed to the individual's dynamism or even the collective impulses of the majority, but rather the reverse. Genuine Christian experience is the "progressive growth of one's own existence into Christ's existence," and thus even if it corresponds in some measure to one's own desires for self-realization, it has an objective status that comes from God, not from the psyche.[56] This is why so much in the Church, including the sacraments, can only be seen as an utter disappointment: one will *never* find a perfect reflection of one's own private subjectivity, but rather a community, a set of doctrines, a collection of rites, that are established long before the individual's arrival on the scene. As Romano Guardini insisted about the liturgy, and this will be further explored in chapter 3, the individual must continually "renounce his own ideas and his own way" in order to "take part in proceedings of which he does not entirely, if at all, understand the significance."[57] This is a small example of the general rule that Balthasar finds to be essential to the spiritual life, as manifested in Mary: her *fiat* accepts that which is originally strange, perhaps terrifying (like her Son's cross), and makes of this the deepest expression of her own experience and mission. Further, the institutional structure of the Church is *not* to be associated with Christ alone, for the Spirit is the one who leads Christians through what Balthasar calls the "institutional bracket," which is a representation of God's will: "The institutional bracket in which the Spirit has inserted sinners to lead them to what faith, hope and love *really* mean is in its very essence a liberation to be a Christian and is only experienced as a chain and a tutelage when one as a sinner chafes against it."[58] The otherness of the liturgy and the institutional nature of the Church is then an analogue to the inherent asymmetry between the gift of grace and its reception, such that no matter how fervent and "worthy" a communion may be, it can never match Christ's *Hingabe*.[59]

Synergy: The Bridging and Tunneling of the Abyss

So far in this book, we have been attempting to demonstrate that even when Balthasar is radically innovative with regard to the traditional concepts of sacramental theology, he retains them as being at least minimally true. The same holds true when considering the central role that causality has played in Western sacramental theology. Even if Balthasar came to think that theology already has at its disposal a more precise concept to describe the action of God in the sacraments than the usual scholastic terminology, this is a deepening of causal language, not a rejection thereof. Reasoning neither in the manner of Luther's antischolastic polemic nor of Chauvet's distrust of metaphysics, Balthasar thinks that sacramental causality could be better expressed by a term that comes directly from the primal mystery of the hypostatic union: *synergy*. In 1980, the Maronite priest Jean Corbon published *Liturgie de Source*, later translated into English as *The Wellspring of Worship*. Balthasar was so impressed by the book that he decided to not only translate it into German himself and publish it through his publishing house, Johannes Verlag, only one year after the original publication, but also to write an introduction.[60] In that introduction, Balthasar notes the importance of Corbon's use of "synergy," which is worth quoting at length:

> Henceforth, the completed work of the bodily Christ in "heaven" beyond time is one with the work of his members on earth, as celebrated liturgically and in their everyday lives. This is always accomplished by the mysterious syn-ergy, which is only understandable in Christological terms, of the reception (from the Fatherly Source) and the response (by humanity, by the world in the Son).
>
> The reader, in order to penetrate the center of these statements, must consider intensively these concepts of energy and synergy, in order to recognize that, through them, we may leave behind the philosophical concepts of causality (widely used in western sacramental theology), since none of them can explain to us the (christological) "undivided and unmixed" interpenetration of the divine and of the human in the Christian liturgy.[61]

Balthasar will later quote Corbon in his own work and mention explicitly his use of synergy, but Balthasar himself never directly developed the concept of synergy by analyzing it with regard to sacramental cooperation between Christ and the Church.[62] Yet, what Balthasar found in Corbon was already present in his own thought long before, namely, the dynamism of the Holy Spirit that works with the Church and brings the Church into the intra-Trinitarian love between Father and Son, *in* the Holy Spirit. Synergy, as seen in this previous quote, is, first of all, a description of the cooperation between Christ's two natures and wills, but this primary synergy "yields a second, which is both its effect and its response, namely, that between the Spirit and the Church."[63] This pairing of the synergy of the Word and his human nature with the Spirit and the life of the saints was a motif that Balthasar had found in Maximus the Confessor long before his translation of Corbon.[64] And even more basically, it is for Balthasar simply another way of framing the standard Catholic position vis-à-vis Protestantism regarding the harmony of the processes of justification and sanctification, or, on another level, the concept of the *analogia entis*. Thus, in presenting the Catholic position about the relationship between nature and grace at the end of his book on Karl Barth, he insists that the Christian's cooperation with grace *is itself* a grace, and is, in fact, the greatest condescension on the part of God. According to Balthasar, Barth's Protestantism makes him hesitate to acknowledge that grace has "disappeared" into nature, such that the hermetic division between nature and grace is overcome in the eucharistic Christ: "the grace of the Cross and even more the grace of the Eucharist pouring itself into all of the nothingness of our lost natures."[65] Further, Balthasar points to a Trinitarian conception of "distance" that renders the ontological chasm between God and the creature a positive feature when incorporated into the Holy Spirit.[66] The creature can thus be elevated to being a cooperator with divinity without the danger of a Promethean apotheosis or a blurring of the ontological chasm between Creator and creature. This is possible only because otherness, rather than antithetical to, is already an attribute of the Triune God.

It is within these interrelated commitments concerning the distant, yet nonrivalrous, relationship between divine and human action that we can situate Balthasar's rendering of synergy. More germane to a discussion of the Eucharist, and perhaps more frequent in Balthasar's lexicon, is the nuptial bond between Christ and the Church, which is how synergy is deployed at the ecclesiological level. The nuptial imagery that Balthasar frequently appeals to has been subject both to the highest praise and development[67] and to the bitterest and most frequent of critiques,[68] as issues relating to sexuality and gender are wont to do. Staying for the moment at the level of exposition, and avoiding either acrimony or acclamation, it is clear that the nuptial metaphor serves Balthasar's overall aim of affirming both a creaturely participation in the work of salvation and an insistence on the importance of Christ's claim that "without me you can do nothing" (John 15:5). Balthasar's understanding of synergy in a nuptial key serves then to point to love as a higher synthesis beyond the objective/subjective tension or the issue of causality as we have been analyzing them thus far. Albeit, of course, with a theological commitment already in mind,[69] Balthasar notes that at the level of phenomenology, the love between lovers makes of each a beloved, a beloved that cannot be considered a product purely of the subjective love or of a previous objective existence that is finally recognized. Rather, the lover brings the beloved into existence in the mystery and creativity of love: "Many wait only for someone to love them in order to become who they always could have been from the beginning. It may also be that the lover, with his mysterious, creative gaze, is the first to discover in the beloved possibilities completely unknown to their possessor, to whom they would have appeared incredible."[70] The lover has an *objective* image of the beloved in mind, an image that is not the less objective for being ideal, which the beloved may eventually come to subjectively embody. Nevertheless, from beginning to end, this identity was all along the product of the lover: "The beloved . . . will know that the realization of his best potentialities is, not his merit, but the creative work of love, which impelled him to realize them, held before him the mirror and the ideal image, and bestowed the strength to attain the goal. *In this creative happening, every distinction between subjective and objective becomes meaningless.*"[71]

Balthasar finds this at the basic level of two human lovers, but this same production of the beloved's true identity occurs between God and Israel, and thus between Christ and the Church. In the prophet Hosea, for instance, Balthasar notes that God's "foolish love" for Israel, symbolized in Hosea's dedication to the faithless harlot, evinces precisely this logic of a love that purifies and restores the beloved. In Hosea, "God has begun to do something here that will not come to a stop until Golgotha."[72] In the new covenant, it is Mary who is the objective, ideal image that Christ has of his beloved, the Church.[73] This ideal image precedes the Church in that Christ's love is that which empowers the Church to become that which Christ sees it to be. Yet, when the Church, either in an individual or collectively, becomes that which the divine lover saw it to be, this is not to be confused with the notion of "imputed righteousness," for the Church becomes, in reality, this ideal image, which was in any case *always* its true identity. The discussion then shifts away from deciding "how much" God does and "how much" the Church does in the work of sanctification, and is instead situated within Balthasar's categories of activity and receptivity, particularly as this is understood in its Marian and nuptial overtones: "For it is not simply a question of the priority of the objective *opus operatum* of a sacrament over the subjective *opus operantis* of the believer. The real issue is the priority of God's activity in man overall."[74] Instead of one act (God's) requiring the follow-up of another act (the recipient's), Balthasar thinks that, properly speaking, there is only one true *actor* in the sacramental exchange, God. And although the manner in which he develops this is often with his dialogue with Barth in mind,[75] Balthasar does not want to diminish the role played by humanity, but he sees it as one of receptivity, rather than an additional action alongside God's.

Cooperation, or synergy, is then not like two people working alongside and with one another but is better understood as a single action on the part of God that is received by the creature in love and obedience. This obedience, as in Mary's *fiat*, points not to a fusion but to a distance, "a distance expressed in the fact that in all things it is the Lord who commands and the Handmaid who obeys."[76] This receptive obedience, however, is the very opposite of a passive quietism, and is rather the very dynamism of the creature vis-à-vis God: obedience reinscribes the creature in her creatureliness and thus dissimilarity from God, yet paradoxically this redoubling of creatureliness is, in fact, the moment of the creatures "deification."[77] The creature becomes God not by ascent, but in descending with Christ on the cross and Mary in her role as handmaid.[78] Sacramental cooperation is then the highest dignity of the creature, but it is a dignity that consists in allowing God's will to be done, even if this leaves one as "passed over, forgotten, neglected in a corner."[79] This "allowing" of God to carry out his will, especially as this reaches the darkness of the cross, will be the essence of Balthasar's conception of the eucharistic sacrifice, to which we will shortly turn.

Essential to Balthasar's understanding of the creature's cooperation with grace, or Mary's role in the Incarnation in particular, is *Hingabe*. In the Incarnation, Christ's eucharistic gift of self is met simultaneously by Mary's receptivity that was itself a total gift of self: "It is part of her mystery and being that the Word become flesh, not only in but also from her, that her self-giving response to God [*ihre sich hingebende Antwort an Gott*] was understood and required as something involving the whole person, something both spiritual and of the body."[80] Mary's *fiat* is itself a form of eucharistic self-gift, of the same order as is found in Christ and in the Trinitarian persons. As the Son was obedient to the Father, and in his obedience he represents a "super-femininity" toward the Father (which might as well be rendered as a "superreceptivity"), so Mary, in her person and as a type of the Church, is receptive and obedient to Christ's mission. The Incarnation is then the meeting of two total gifts of self: Christ gives himself utterly to the world, and the world, in Mary, hands itself over to Christ by welcoming him without any preconditions. This is why the Church must be understood as "Marial" (*marianisch*),[81] for in Mary there is the perfect cooperation (synergy) between the Spirit and the Church, which is itself bound up with and dependent upon the synergy between Christ's two natures and wills. This Marian receptivity is also why the Church cannot be construed, according to Balthasar, as Christ pure and simple. The Church, even though really Christ's body, remains at a distance from Christ, but a positive distance that mirrors the distance of the Trinitarian persons. It is Mary who ensures this distance because the Church is not simply a modality of Christ, but also lovingly receives him, with the aid of the Holy Spirit. There is then an "irreducible abyss" between the Creator and the creature, and without collapsing the abyss, it is "bridged and tunneled by the power of God's love."[82] The Church then is this correspondence between the two *Hingaben*, Christ's and Mary's, the latter of which becomes normative for all who are brought into the Church: her *fiat* becomes an "infinitely plastic medium to bring forth from it new believers" because her "self-surrender [*Hingabe*] is universalized to become the common source, the productive womb, of all Christian grace."[83] Christ became "infinitely plastic" in his pneumatic distribution in the Eucharist, and this gift requires, as a condition of its reception, that the believer, with Mary, do likewise.

EXISTENTIAL SACRAMENTAL THEOLOGY II

The flow of the first two sections of this chapter has been a movement from a more abstract rendering of the interrelation between the Absolute and the finite to a narrower consideration of the interchange between Christ's self-gift and his reception by the Church. In this section, we reach the concrete and existential significance of Balthasar's position, and the concomitant issue of the eucharistic sacrifice. The parameters of Balthasar's position have been outlined, and now we can see what the real, spiritual concern for him has been all along. Chapter 1 discussed Balthasar's existential sacramental theology in its primary sense: the sacraments understood as expressions of the person of Christ. Again, as he says of John the Evangelist: "John's primary concern is to shed light *existentially* on the sacraments . . . and correspondingly to show the dispositions of the community of disciples, which must respond to the disposition of Jesus."[84] Balthasar indeed notes that Jesus's disposition is the core of this existential analysis of the sacraments, but he himself devotes far more time to exploring the "response," the existential conditions required of the recipient. Balthasar views the sacramental movement as directed so purposefully at the transformation of the communicant that he shifts the usual categories on their heads. Adhering closely to the axiom that *sacramenta sunt propter homines*, Balthasar notes that transubstantiation is not for the sake of the bread and wine, but for those who will receive them. "The accent must fall on this encounter of Christ" because transubstantiation is best understood as a "road to the goal," and not the goal itself.[85] Thus, speaking more evocatively rather than making a technical argument about the sacramental species, Balthasar says that the "matter" of the sacraments is, in fact, the recipient, not primarily the material elements: "The 'matter' that is to be formed is man himself in his concrete situation: as a person who is to enter into God's Kingdom, as a person who is to be washed, nourished, anointed, as a human sinner to whom the great absolution of the Cross must ever anew be applied. . . . In this person a process of formation is at work whose form is Christ himself."[86]

Augustine's axiom that *accedit verbum ad elementum et fit sacramentum* led to the later clarifications about what exactly constituted the *forma* and *materia* of each sacrament. In the case of the Eucharist, the matter is bread and wine, and the form is the dominical words of institution.[87] Balthasar is not contesting these decisions but suggests that when the sacraments are viewed in light of the entire *ordo salutis*, and not just specifying appropriate liturgical practice, then the matter and form can be formulated anew: Christ is the "form" who transforms the communicant (the "matter") into himself. It should not be surprising that

Balthasar considered the standard use of "form" in sacramental theology to be rather limited, particularly compared with his own use of *Gestalt* as the key to theological aesthetics.

In light of his shifting of emphasis away from the sacraments themselves and onto the encounter that takes place with Christ, it must be admitted that there is a certain tendency in Balthasar to minimize the traditional questions of sacramental theology. If then one wonders how transubstantiation can stand considering modern science, or other issues related to eucharistic physics, Balthasar is not the theologian to ask, because he gives the impression that he is more or less uninterested in such questions. In the case of the Eucharist, although the transubstantiation of the elements themselves is always presupposed, Balthasar worries that an excessive focus on this stage risks rendering the sacrament into a magical display of Christ's power rather than an invitation to Communion.[88] Analogously, one can marvel at the nutritional constitution of one's dinner, but without actually eating it, one will go hungry.[89] Again, to arrive at the heart of the Eucharist is to recognize the pneumatic element in it: not only is Christ present as pneumatic flesh, thus not as a mere corpse, but he also must be received in spirit. In the nuptial unity between Christ and the Church, "the flesh alone is of no avail; here the bare sacrament is of no avail; it is only the Spirit, placed by the Lord in flesh and sacrament and received by faith, that makes the fleshly sacramental bridge capable of bearing its load."[90] "Spiritual communion" is therefore not a substitution for "sacramental communion" but a precondition for it.[91]

Sacrifice

Having noted in chapter 1 that Balthasar's understanding of the eucharistic sacrifice does *not* consist in a renewed suffering or in a further humiliation on the part of Christ in the eucharistic species, and having established the key concepts for his ultimate solution, we can now turn explicitly to his conception of the eucharistic sacrifice. Both during Balthasar's lifetime and since, this aspect of his eucharistic theology is the most commented on in the secondary literature, the subject of praise and blame.[92] On the one hand, because of a dominant trend in modern Catholic eucharistic theology that distances itself from sacrificial language (despite, we must add, the enormous burden of its historical importance), Balthasar's insistence on the centrality of sacrifice could perhaps be considered rather archaic. On the other hand, among those who recognize the indispensability of guarding the concept of the sacrifice of the Mass, some consider Balthasar's particular rendition to be a departure from the mainstream tradition.[93] Whereas the first group would consider Balthasar to be insufficiently ecumenical, as insistence on the sacrifice of the Mass remains one of the greatest hurdles to dialogue with mainline Protestantism, the second group would claim that Balthasar has conceded too much to the Protestants by his unwillingness to separate the sacrifice of the Mass from the meal aspect of the Eucharist.[94] This is used as a mark of opprobrium by some, but it is certainly true to say that Balthasar's understanding of sacrifice is less "cultic," that is, derived from Jewish Temple worship, than it is "existential," especially as sacrifice is bonded ineluctably to *Hingabe*.[95]

Although he later adds further commentary and specification, Balthasar's most exhaustive treatment of the sacrifice of the Mass is in his lengthy and programmatic 1967 essay "The Mass, A Sacrifice of the Church?" To briefly summarize, Balthasar is concerned not with how Christ's sacrifice is perpetuated throughout history in the Eucharist, but with the "contribution" to the sacrifice that is implied in the liturgical *offerimus*.[96] He comments on two recent attempts to answer the question, first by Odo Casel and then by Louis Bouyer. He takes issue with Casel, to whom he is largely sympathetic, because Casel's mystery theology seems to collapse the distance between Christ and the Church. For Casel, the contemporaneity of the Church with the sacrifice of Christ on the cross in the liturgical mystery means that it is only Christ who sacrifices as *una mystica persona*. Thus, the Church is "feminine" and receptive only "to the extent that she receives the sphere of the cult mystery but then becomes 'active' in this sphere" by being united in the one sacrifice of Christ.[97] That is to say, Balthasar does not want the sacrifice of the Church to be entirely folded into the sacrifice of Christ, such that the Church both does too much (in actively offering along with Christ) and too little (in not being a receptive other to Christ). The other approach, represented by Bouyer, is to connect the eucharistic sacrifice to its roots in the Old Testament's understanding of sacrifice and in Jewish liturgical practice. This renders Jesus as the Messiah who gathers the new *qahal* (the *ekklesia*) together to offer praise to God. Balthasar is impressed by this line of research and agrees that the continuity between the *berakoth* (Jewish blessings) in the synagogues and the early Christian *eulogia-eucharistia* is too obvious to ignore, and considers the ecclesial and existential aspects to be largely correct. Yet, the problem with this approach, according to Balthasar, is that it is overly "democratic," such that Christ simply appears as the representative of the gathered community.[98]

It is noteworthy that in "The Mass, A Sacrifice of the Church?" Balthasar does not engage with the "destruction" theories of sacrifice that we explored in chapter 1, or any theory that posits some positive action that the Church contributes to the eucharistic sacrifice. This is to say, he is thoroughly committed to understanding the sacrifice in "spiritual" or "existential" terms, in line with Augustine's classic formulation in *De civitate Dei.*[99] Also in line with Augustine, and the Epistle to the Hebrews, is his claim that the Christian notion of sacrifice is *sui generis*; it is "specific to the New Testament," which is again why he ultimately rejects Bouyer's proposal. Thus sacrifice is in the first instance Christ's *Hingabe*, his self-offering that is itself a manifestation of his obedience to the will of another, the Father: "Behold, I have come to do your will" (Heb. 10:9).[100] Yet, the Church's sacrifice is not simply a repetition of this Christological obedience, or a representation of it, in Casel's sense. Balthasar, in line with the overwhelming liturgical evidence, maintains a sacrifice that is proper to the Church itself and is not immediately reducible to that of Christ. The positive *diastasis* between Christ and the Church remains in effect, avoiding any Christomonistic ecclesiology. To do this, Balthasar seeks the "contribution" of the Church not in some additional act, but in its own specific form of feminine receptivity, first exemplified in Mary. In the sense that will be explained, Balthasar says not only that the Marian-ecclesial act of reception is a possible, secondary sacrifice, but is in fact the *conditio sine qua non* for Christ's own sacrifice. Christ, in a radical sense, *needs* the sacrifice of the Church. Christ's self-gift presumes not a *possible* recipient, but an actual and necessary one: construed in Trinitarian terms, the Father, and in ecclesial terms, Mary, the *immaculata.*[101]

In the closely knit set of terms that Balthasar employs for his discussion of sacrifice, such as *Hingabe* and receptivity, none is perhaps as germane as obedience (*Gehorsam*). In fact, the renunciation of one's own will in favor of another's is typically how Balthasar conceives of sacrifice, in regard to the cross and to the Eucharist. Good Friday is the direct result of Holy Thursday: "the Garden of Olives, where the cosmic struggle between the nature of God and the nature of the world took place within a single soul."[102] In accordance with orthodox Dyothelitism, Christ in the garden experienced a conflict between his natural and proper fear of death and the mission on which God the Father had sent him. His obedience, his preference for the will of the Father is thus "the action on which the whole of Jesus' existence is founded, who as God and man brought this aspect of unceasing self-surrender [*unendlicher Selbstübergabe*] from the sphere of the divine into the midst of human existence."[103] That is to say, the eternal *Hingabe* that characterizes the Triune life is now a real creaturely possibility, realized in the union of Christ's two wills and in Mary's creaturely *fiat* to her own mysterious mission and the mission of her Son. As Christ's human will was perfectly obedient to God the Father, so Mary becomes obedient to her Son's mission. Mary, as *Realsymbol* of the Church, thus epitomizes the Church's sacrifice by *allowing* Christ to fulfill his own mission. Balthasar traces Mary's permission and assent to Christ's mission "without limit and without setting conditions" in scenes such as his seeming disobedience in the Temple as a boy, his seeming rejection of her on several occasions, and most definitely at the foot of the cross: "Here there is achieved the ultimate form of the relationship between this Mother and this Son, this Bride and this Bridegroom, this Lord and this Handmaid: she must allow him to go away, not only into physical death, but into the state of abandonment by God."[104] She does not understand why her Son would meet such a horrific end, but in faith and obedience she allows him to sacrifice himself, and this allowance is itself the sacrifice that is proper to her, and thus proper to the Church.

To recall the image we used in chapter 1, Balthasar calls the pedilavium an "anatomy of the Eucharist." This can now be given further precision by taking into account the entire biblical scene. Not only does the Eucharist-as-foot-washing illustrate Christ's humiliation and self-abandonment, that is, Christ's proper sacrifice, but it also brings us directly to the sacrifice of the Church, here represented by Peter. Peter, of course, initially refuses Christ's self-humiliation ("you shall never wash my feet"), but Christ compels him to accept that which is contrary to everything he presumed about his Lord. He, in a sense, *must* allow Christ to wash his feet ("if I do not wash you, you have no part in me"; John

13:8). A crisis comes to Peter, who must decide between the right and proper order of things and communion with Christ, the latter of which appears wholly enigmatic:

> But the only thing that matters now is the *conditio sine qua non*: to let this happen in a state of terror and incomprehension. This is why Jesus compels Peter here to say Yes. The freedom to say No is something purely abstract for the believer, i.e., for the one who loves; if what he wills is love, the fellowship with Jesus, then he must *will* what *he* himself does not want at all: the reversal of the world's order, the Lord's service as a slave.[105]

Christ's is the one, true sacrifice, the Church's sacrifice being used in an analogous sense. But this ecclesial sacrifice, which is represented here by Peter, is its own contribution to the mystery of salvation and is not absorbed into nor a repetition of Christ's sacrifice, as in Casel. His primary difference from Casel is then that in Casel's theory the Church is initially "feminine," but only to the extent that it then takes part in the "masculine" action of Christ's sacrifice. For Balthasar, the Church's sacrifice remains feminine and receptive all the way down, which is to say that the Creator/creature or Christ/Church difference is never abrogated, but retained in its inherent tension.

So what, then, is the "sacrifice of the Church" implied by the liturgical *offerimus*? The answer is at the level of the existential, but it is not at first a creaturely *Hingabe* as a response to Christ's *Hingabe*, even if we will shortly see the place for this. This is again why Balthasar prefers to move above the dialectic between objective grace (*opus operatum*) and its subjective reception (*opus operantis*) toward the higher synthesis of love, because in the classical framework, the "reception" can be falsely considered an *opus*, its own act alongside Christ's. Rather, for Balthasar, the sacrifice of the Church is the same now as it was for Peter then: to allow Christ to carry out his mission. Albeit in no sense in the same mode as a Protestant emphasis on *anamnesis* as a mere recalling of the saving events, the sacrifice of the Church does bring it to contemporaneity with the moment of the Church's birth at the foot of the cross. The "elemental experience" of the Church at the foot of the cross must be a possibility for every generation of the Church, and so it is in the Eucharist:

"The cult mediates us (into) contemporaneity" (*Der Kult vermittelt (in) die Gleichzeitigkeit*). In the Eucharist the ecclesial member can and must, with Mary, "make it known by my presence at the sacrifice of Christ that I *will this death*, in the ecclesial-feminine sense, that I am in agreement with this death. . . . We must—not as sinners, but in the Spirit of the Bride-Church—share in experiencing the absolute pain that we must allow the Beloved to keep his own will to die a vicarious death. The word must penetrate us at this thought."[106]

Christ gives himself totally, and he must be received: "This makes the mouth that consumes him an essential part of the sacrifice of the Lord."[107] This does not require perfect faith in any one priest or in any one communicant in order to make the sacrifice of the Mass validly confected, in a quasi-Donatist sense. Rather, because Mary has always already perfectly received Christ and has herself become the form of the Church, this "burden" is removed concerning validity, but it remains existentially.

Mary thus ensures that the Church remains a constitutive part of Christ's eucharistic self-gift, avoiding a Christomonism whereby Christ gives himself to himself. Balthasar notes that this is a difficult temptation to avoid, as evidenced by the fact that almost the entirety of the Church's tradition has held that Christ received the Eucharist at the Last Supper. Apparently, the reason that the Fathers "make this supposition is that only Christ himself was able to be the receiver in the full and worthy manner that corresponded to his own gift of himself."[108] Rather, and he finds exegetical support for this argument, Balthasar says that it is more likely that Christ fasted at the Last Supper.[109] Christ fasts and humbles himself while commanding his disciples to receive his self-gift. The disciples thus function "as the mouth and the organism that receive his total gift of self [*Gesamthingabe*]. They bring him this 'sacrifice' by carrying out his will to the full."[110] The Communion thus *is* the "Sacrifice of the Mass," but not in Bellarmine's sense. For Bellarmine, the Communion of the priest constitutes the Church's sacrifice, but it is Communion *qua* the destruction and consumption of the host, irrespective of the faith or intention of the priestly recipient. Rather, for Balthasar, Communion is the sacrifice *qua* reception of Christ's self-gift. It is thus Communion *qua* Communion.

The sacrifice is the communion with Christ precisely in the mode established by his mission from the Father, communion in Christ's cross. And lest this existential rendering of sacrifice be considered a vapid rendering of its typical usage, Balthasar assures us that in his understanding of sacrifice, destruction is still involved. And although for one dominant post-Tridentine tradition destruction was considered a constitutive element of a sacrifice (whether of the host, as in Bellarmine, or in the destruction of Christ's human mode of existing, as in de Lugo), for Balthasar too, destruction is a requirement, but it is the destruction of the communicant's own self-involved will.[111] To return to the pedilavium, Balthasar says that in this moment Peter "must choose the last thing that he would have chosen if left to himself."[112] He must renounce *his* own will, but even more than an act of self-renunciation, the sacrifice required is "the renunciation of God." Peter must assent in pure obedience to allowing his Lord to go along a path that contradicts everything he knew, or thought he knew, about him. He must renounce the will he had for Christ, his will that his Lord would be honored and worshipped rather than dishonored and shamefully crucified. This is perhaps plausibly rendered as the original sacrifice required of the first disciples, but we could ask whether this does not stretch credibility to suggest that this is somehow still constitutive of the sacrifice of the Mass. We, of course, have the "whole story," we know that Christ's life ends in his humiliation. Yet, because "the cult mediates us (into) contemporaneity," Balthasar resists rendering the Crucifixion as a fait accompli. Instead, he insists that the Eucharist functions as that which makes the decisive moments of Christ's passion a drama that occurs in the present tense.

Even if in this context "contemporaneity" has a distant Kierkegaardian ring to it, and a proximate relationship to Odo Casel, the main source of Balthasar's use is neither the Danish philosopher nor the Benedictine mystery theologian, but Ignatius of Loyola and his *Exercises*.[113] Because Christ's flesh is made liquid on the cross, the Ignatian "application of the senses," in which one makes use of the imagination to contemplate the events of Christ's life, is just as bodily as it is spiritual.[114] It is not, for Balthasar, a flight of the imagination, but a real entering into the historically past but eucharistically present mystery of redemption. Thus each Christian stands anew with Mary at the foot of the cross, such that one can actually "contribute" to Christ's sacrifice by one's receptivity, or, put in Ignatian terms, one's *indiferencia*.

There is a notable ambiguity in "The Mass, A Sacrifice of the Church?" as to whether the ecclesial sacrifice concerns an *indiferencia* and receptivity with regard to Christ's own historical mission, or whether it concerns a renewed *indiferencia* with regard to one's personal mission *hic et nunc*. Balthasar leaves the two options intertwined, undifferentiated, folded into one another. And perhaps this could be judged an elision of two distinct concepts, but for Balthasar this amalgamation seems to be theologically mandated rather than a conceptual blunder. There need be no antagonism between the objectivity of Christ's mission (in the past) and the contemporary need to respond to God's will for one's life in a particular time and place. Instead, Balthasar insists, one can only truly accept God's will by going through the objective events of incarnation, cross, and resurrection: "His mission is multi-dimensional: it has room enough for everyone."[115] Christ's mission embraces and includes every possible mission of the creature, and the latter's *indiferencia* necessarily implies a receptivity with regard to the former. Of course, Mary's mission is again here exemplary, not only because of her status as *immaculata*, but because her particular mission coincides so perfectly with the historical mission of Christ as to make her the *typos* for all subsequent "sacrifices of the Mass": "Thus there lies in her the identity of communion and offering in sacrifice and also the identity of the sacrifice of Christ and the sacrifice of oneself."[116]

Mary's mission is the direct complement and recipient of Christ's mission, but subsequent believers do not share this same primordial situation. Nevertheless, Balthasar's rendering of sacrifice is such that whenever someone fully surrenders to the will of God, they are co-implicated in Mary's permitting her Son to go to the cross. Again, then, his notion of sacrifice is thoroughly existential, yet in such a way that the solidity of the *ordo salutis* is not mitigated, but rather elevated as the site through which every communicant must pass. The sacrifice that the Church contributes to Christ's eucharistic self-gift is then this *indiferencia* that abandons itself entirely into the hands of the divine providence. We can then see again the importance of Caussade. For even though Balthasar translates Caussade's notion of *l'abandon/Hingabe* by placing it primarily in the Trinitarian and Christological spheres, he also retains its location in human obedience that Caussade originally intended. These two abandonments, God's self-abandonment in Christ for the sake of the world and the creature's abandonment of its own will in favor of divine providence, meet in the eucharistic sacrifice. Here, there is a perfect synergy whereby Christ's flesh is liquefied in order for it to be lovingly received by the Church. The reception of Christ's *Hingabe* is then a mirroring of this self-gift on the part of the creature. It is a participation in Christ's *Hingabe*, Christ's self in a state of *Gelassenheit*, but in a manner that is appropriate to the status of the creature.[117] The creature responds, according to Caussade, by a "state of self-emptying" whereby "there remains with them but one desire: to keep their eyes fixed on the Master they have chosen, to listen to the expression of His will in order to carry it out immediately."[118]

With this broader, existential sense of "sacrifice" operating in Balthasar's eucharistic lexicon, we can see that the "sacrifice of the Mass" occurs exemplarily but not exclusively in the actual liturgy of the Church. This is why Balthasar can say that Mary's *fiat* was itself the first act of Communion.[119] And to tarry with Caussade for a moment longer, this is also why some English translations of *L'Abandon* loosely though justifiably title the work *The Sacrament of the Present Moment*. Every moment can be, for both Caussade and Balthasar, a sacramental encounter. Because Christ exists now *as* eucharistic, all spiritual communions are eucharistic communions. Caussade advises thus: "You seek perfection, and it is in everything that comes to you. Your sufferings, your actions, your leadings are the sacramental 'elements' as it were, under which God gives himself to you."[120] Just as the "matter" of the Eucharist for Balthasar is the communicant, so every moment can be a "eucharistic sacrifice" in which Christ's gift of self is received and returned. It bears repeating that this does not necessitate a sidelining of actual sacramental Communion, but rather an expansion of its sphere of influence.

As always with Balthasar, the issue at hand needs to be reframed in light of the Trinity to understand the full import of the claims being made. The sacrificial exchange is certainly between God and the creature, Christ and the Church, but this exchange is already located within the Trinitarian love of God. First, this means that the "contribution" of the Church to the eucharistic sacrifice must be pneumatically qualified such that it is only by the power of the Holy Spirit that the Church can act in tandem with Christ (but, again, without this implying heteronomy). This also means that the *Hingabe* of the Church is elevated to a higher realm, to be included in the Son's eternal *Hingabe* to the Father. The Holy Spirit is essential at this point, for the *Hingabe* from Son to Father *is* the

Holy Spirit: *ein Geist der Hingabe zum Vater.*[121] In the Holy Spirit, the Church participates in the eternal, Triune love to such an extent that Balthasar renders the true *res* of the eucharistic sacrifice as the Son's gift of self to the Father. This is indeed liturgically justified by the audacious claims of the Roman Liturgy, whereby the Church offers the Son to the Father: *Per ipsum, et cum ipso, et in ipso, est tibi Deo Patri omnipotenti, in unitate Spiritus Sancti, omnis honor et gloria per omnia saecula saeculorum.*[122] In particular, it is the incarnate and crucified Christ that the Church offers to the Father, and in so doing offers itself. So, again, is the Mass a sacrifice? "Yes, it is a sacrifice: it is Christ's sacrifice which he places into the hands of his Church so that she in turn has something to offer to the Father: the only thing of value, the sacrifice of Christ."[123] For the Church too, Christ's sacrifice has become the "only thing of value" because the Church, in Mary, has offered and sacrificed her own will and preferences to the Father with Christ on the cross.

The Mission of Self-Gift: Sacraments and Ethics

Because Balthasar's understanding of sacrifice is personal, spiritual at its core, it is also fundamentally related to the moral life. To round out and complete Balthasar's notion of an existential sacramental theology it is necessary to turn to his portrayal of sacramental life as it is found in a dramatic form in the lives and stories of saints, sinners, and literary figures. His more grandiose conceptions of the Eucharist in the Trinity and as the *telos* of the Incarnation are perhaps where his sacramental theology is operating at its speculative heights, but it can be argued that his central intuition and preoccupation with the sacraments lies in their implications for the Christian life. This becomes most obvious when confronting the anomaly that is his large book on the novelist Georges Bernanos (1888–1948). We have noted that Balthasar's sacramental theology is scattered in bits and pieces throughout his oeuvre, with no one sustained work developing his thought, but one slight exception to this rule is *Bernanos: An Ecclesial Existence*, which is, by far, Balthasar's longest treatment of the sacraments, dedicating almost three hundred continuous pages to the subject, approximately half of the book.[124] Balthasar finds the best expression of an "existential sacramental theology" in the characters portrayed in Bernanos's novels, such that he dedicates a section to exploring Bernanos's dramatic portrayal of each sacrament.[125] Because for Balthasar "the life of saints is theology in practice,"[126] there is no better expression of his own conception of the sacraments than as they are played out in dramatic form. Thus, even though Bernanos's use of "sacrament" is "highly peculiar," and he frequently uses this term to "refer to human experiences that have nothing to do externally with the sacraments of the Church," Bernanos demonstrates the existential profile of the *opus operantis*, of the communicant's reception of Christ's gift.[127] Just as Balthasar noted that John the Evangelist provides an "anatomy of the Eucharist" insofar as it shows what it means for Christ to become eucharistic, so Bernanos provides Balthasar with an "anatomy of the Eucharist" from the side of the recipient: "These forms of the sacramental reality, however, remain existential reflections, as it were, of the actual sacraments of the Church: they are their exegesis through concrete living, so to speak."[128]

Before returning to any particular insight into the Eucharist that Bernanos himself provides, it must be noted that although the pairing of sacraments and ethics is by no means exclusive to Balthasar, his own configuration of the relationship is unique. The Catholic theologian is forced, almost by necessity, to demonstrate that the prophetic critique of the Temple cult not only does not apply to Christian liturgy but that in reality the liturgy itself is intrinsically related to the ideal form of religiosity proclaimed by the prophets. One would be hard-pressed to find a Catholic theologian in the twentieth century who does not share this basic presupposition. According to Chauvet, for example, the "ethical dimension is not simply an extrinsic consequence of the eucharistic process; it belongs to it as an *intrinsic* element."[129] His exploration of the ethics–sacrament connection is rich and variegated, but Chauvet's central intuition is that the gift from God (the Eucharist) intrinsically necessitates, by the very logic of sacramental exchange, a return-gift. This return-gift, however, does not go directly back to God, but must pass by way of one's neighbor in service. The fact that sacramental Communion *requires* (not merely suggests or aids) ethical behavior in the world is also affirmed at the magisterial level from the beginning of modern Catholic social teaching in Leo XIII to the most recent pontiffs.[130]

When Balthasar then insists on this connection, he is one voice among innumerable others. Yet, Balthasar strikes a different tone in his rendering of this relationship, a tone that is in harmony with the perspectives briefly mentioned above, but one that also makes the sacraments/ethics pair even more indissolubly bonded to one another. Instead of noting that the Eucharist somehow requires, as a condition of its reception, ethical action, Balthasar overhauls the category of the ethical and reframes it in a eucharistic mold. Now, instead of considering sacraments and ethics as two distinct categories, there is only the one eucharistic life of Christian obedience modeled on Christ's eucharistic *Hingabe*. Turning now to develop Balthasar's "eucharistic ethics," it should be noted that "ethics" is not a category that sits comfortably in a Balthasarian framework.[131] One could certainly develop a Balthasarian account of the natural law, for example, but an a-theological or pretheological conception of ethics was never Balthasar's explicit concern. It may indeed be correct to say that Balthasar is "very vague on the subject of concrete norms,"[132] as he prefers to speak about the overall pattern and form of Christian conduct, rather than to arbitrate particular ethical decisions. Indeed, even if casuistry is characteristic of Jesuit genetics, in Balthasar it remains recessive. Instead, he thinks more like Caussade, who spoke of the soul's perfect disponibility before the divine will:

> In this state of joyful self-surrender, the only rule is the present moment. In this our soul is as light as a feather, liquid as water, simple as a child, as easily moved as a ball in following these nudges of grace. Such persons have no more consistence and rigidity than molten metal. As such metal takes any form according to the mould into which it is poured, so these souls are pliant and easily shaped to any form that God chooses to give them.[133]

Caussade is quoted at length here because his reflections on the pliability and liquefaction of the surrendered person lucidly convey Balthasar's characterization of Christian ethics as inseparable from obedience. Yet, what Balthasar adds to Caussade is noting that pliability is first of all a characteristic of the eucharistic, pneumatic Christ. Thus whenever these attributes are given to the Christian, it is only by virtue of Christian ethics being a reflection of the eucharistic Christ. Even more than a mirroring, there is a causal relationship between the two: just as in the biological arena like produces like, so the eucharistic Christ causes those who receive him to become eucharistic themselves. Christ's body, itself dissolved, is now a dissolving agent.[134]

When Balthasar says that "Christian ethics must be modeled on Jesus Christ," he means something much more than an *imitatio Christi*, understood in the sense of a moral exemplarism.[135] The Christ who is an ethical model is not just an imitable sage, but the one who "did not count equality with God a thing to be grasped, but emptied himself," and so is understood as a model only in light of the Trinitarian background and the eucharistic foreground: "Christ is the concrete categorical imperative. He is the formally universal norm of ethical action, applicable to everyone. But he is also the personal and concrete norm, who, in virtue of his suffering for us and his eucharistic surrender of his life for us (which imparts it to us—*per ipsum et in ipso*), empowers us inwardly to do the Father's will together with him (*cum ipso*)."[136]

This means that Christian ethics are ineluctably kenotic, kenotic in the full eucharistic sense of the term. This again calls into question the utility for Balthasar of the category of the ethical, particularly when this is linked primarily to action or conduct. For, if Christ is again the model, the greatest deed is not a πρᾶξις but a πάθη: "it consists in his *allowing* something to happen, in *letting* himself be plundered and shared out in Passion and Eucharist."[137] What is required of the disciple is thus this same eucharistic disponibility, receptivity first to the Father's will, but equally to the needs of the world. Although the pneumatization of the flesh occurs only in the *eschaton* (see chapter 4), it is proleptically realized in a eucharistic ethics that tears down the boundaries between one's own will and the will of God, and between one's self and the other selves in the *communio sanctorum*: "This would mean that in the depths of our being the frontiers must now collapse for us too, as they collapsed—or, to put it better, proved to have been obsolete from the outset—for Jesus Christ in the course of his life and death."[138] This is to say, the Christian too must become eucharistic. Thus Augustine's axiom, "Be what you see, and receive what you are," amounts to far more than an affirmation of one's identity as the body of Christ; it also functions in the imperative mood. As Balthasar understands it, eucharistic reception requires that the recipient likewise become Christic, and Christic as specified eucharistically. In other words, one must become bread that is broken and wine that is poured out.

To give greater detail to what exactly Balthasar has in mind, we can return to his exploration of Bernanos and his sacramental dramas (noting that it is Balthasar who considers them sacramental, not necessarily Bernanos).[139] To begin with, Balthasar intentionally pairs his treatment of the Eucharist with that of *viaticum*, because his consideration of the Eucharist particularly concerns its relationship to human suffering and death. This follows directly from everything we saw in chapter 1, namely, the close bond between Christ's passion and his Eucharist: "From the wine press of Gethsemani's anguish, the Blood was made that foams up in the chalice of the Church. For Bernanos, all possible aspects of human existence have their point of reference to this mystery."[140] "Ethical" behavior, as rendered dramatically by Bernanos, is then an imitation of this prototype of Christ, an imitation of Christ's willingness to be exsanguinated for the sake of humanity. Handing oneself over to be squandered is not, however, a masochistic or Promethean abnegation of the self, but rather the full blossoming of one's own personhood and thus well-being. The darkness of Bernanos's characters, the insistence on suffering and agony, are then interpreted by Balthasar as the struggle of the ego against the barriers that it erects around itself against all others. Central to Balthasar's treatment of Bernanos is the concept of the *communio sanctorum* (which is also why Charles Péguy appears so often throughout *Bernanos*): "'Communion of saints' happens when every member of the Body surrenders his whole being and opens it to becoming but a part of the whole, when he allows his integrity to suffer wounds that make possible the passage through him of the Blood circulating throughout the whole."[141] This image, whereby one becomes porous by allowing Christ's blood to flow freely through one's body in the service of the whole, is dramatized by the Country Priest. The priest writes in his diary early in the novel, "I feel that my life, all the sap of my life, will flow to waste in sand."[142] The novel itself makes no reference to the Eucharist at this point, but Balthasar finds here, and in numerous other places where Bernanos's characters suffer on behalf of others, a dramatization of the sacrament.

The eucharistic development of the person, whereby agony, and in particular the death agony, is what "breaks through the dream's layer of fog and presents us with full reality" needs to be carefully distinguished from the clear analogue of Heidegger's *Angst*.[143] Balthasar, knowing how close the German philosopher is to the French novelist, notes that the former undergoes a profound transposition into the latter. In fact, Bernanos becomes *the* Christian answer to secular existentialism: "Bernanos is the trenchant Christian (and not merely existentialist) answer to the philosophical method of Heidegger and Sartre, who exalted anguish and alienation as privileged means and medium for ontological experience."[144] In highlighting this movement from philosophical to theological anguish, Balthasar then makes this profound, if cryptic, metaphysical statement about what Heidegger misses: "what precise Christian meaning the whole experience of anguish may contain and how all Being becomes denuded before God and, once utterly exposed, then becomes immersed in the all-encompassing and graciously enveloping Passion of the Son of God."[145] *Angst* in a theological sense can only be cruciform, and because cruciform, eucharistic. The *Angst* expressed in Bernanos's literary characters is not thus negativity pure and simple, but rather a fruitful self-giving that results in a positive self-realization and donation to the other. For instance, Balthasar finds a "bridge between Saint Thérèse and Heidegger" in Bernanos's *La Joie*, whose character, Chantal, has been "thrown away [(*weg-*)*geworfen*], mercilessly used up, but in the sense of a "vicarious, atoning *representation*."[146]

A sacramental existential theology differs from, say, a Heideggerian reflection on *Dasein* to the extent that although both focus on being thrown, *Geworfenheit*, only the former is a being thrown by God into a particular mission. Being "used up" or the "futility" and "wasteful squandering" of all of one's efforts is a cooperation in the redemptive, eucharistic work of Christ. Bernanos himself "had discovered the truth that loving, *communicating oneself like bread*, all make the loving person into a solitary."[147] This solitariness of one's mission, like Christ's solitude on the cross, is, however, at the service of the *communio sanctorum*. Just as Christ's mission is "multidimensional" and embraces all subsequent missions,[148] and Mary's mission also becomes universal as the form of the Church, so every *homo ecclesiasticus* becomes "deprivatized" insofar as he or she is put to the service of the Church.[149] Thus, although Balthasar's existential analysis necessarily reflects the dark, almost morbid character of Bernanos's novels, the spiritual darkness, humiliations, and personal obscurity are not ends in themselves for Balthasar. They only function at the service of the one thing necessary: mission.

To begin with Christ's mission, there is both an ascending and a descending dimension: looking upward, Christ's mission is one of *obedience* to the Father, and looking downward, his mission is one of *service* for the sake of the world.[150] Obedience to the will of God, which always results in being put to the service of the *ecclesia*, is then the heart of Christian mission and is modeled directly on the eucharistic self-gift of Christ: "*Just as* [καθὼς] I have loved you, you also should love one another" (John 13:34). Again, this does not mean an imitation of this or that feature of Christ's life, but a participation in Christ's *Gestalt*, his self-giving, eucharistic love. All Christian missions, then, allowing for an infinite range of possible permutations, will be eucharistic. If Christian love is a sign to the world of God's love (John 17:21), then this sign is intrinsically united to Christ's sacramental manifestation in the Eucharist.[151] There is a structural and not just formal relationship between Christian charity and Christ's Eucharist, as the classical tradition makes clear by defining the *res sacramenti* precisely as the *vinculum caritatis*.[152]

Balthasar provides us with a summary definition of the Eucharist: "God in the form of his given-ness: *Gott in Gestalt seiner Hingegebenheit*."[153] The Eucharist is God-made-gift, or, rather, because God is eternally self-gift (*Hingabe*), the Eucharist is the presence of God-made-gift in the mode in which he can be received by creatures (despite the appearances, there is indeed a place in Balthasar for the Thomistic axiom *quidquid recipitur ad modum recipientis recipitur*). The question we have been addressing here is simply one of who may receive this gift, and *how* one receives this gift: "There is only one man who may receive such a present as it is intended: he who himself is transformed into the form of given-ness [*in die Gestalt der Hingegebenheit übergeht*], conformed to it by virtue of his own whole-hearted assent, thanks, and acceptance."[154] To receive a gift, at least when this gift is the Eucharist, means to become a gift oneself. The parameters of what this may look like are left unspecified by Balthasar, and thus he does not provide a list of virtues to be cultivated or any type of verification by which one could be assured of receiving a sacrament worthily. A fruitful reception is defined in the broadest categories possible: childlike receptivity.[155] Readiness and receptivity toward God, perfect disponibility to being used (and used up) for the sake of the world is what is required, no more, but also no less. In this sense, the repetition of words such as "obedience" and "receptivity" should not lead one to assume that Balthasar renders Christian mission as entirely imposed from without so as to crush one's individuality and freedom. There is nothing uniform or universal in his conception of mission that is not already particularized. Eucharistic reception, no matter how much it binds one to the body of the Church, then has nothing to do with conformity, either at the sociological or the theological level. For no matter how much Balthasar repeats the word "obedience," this is really a cipher for freedom: "All obedience serves as a preparation for freedom."[156]

Without having to decide beforehand all of the attributes of a fruitful reception of the Eucharist, Balthasar does, of course, retain certain features that are of iconic importance. In particular, even if the Eucharist can be lived existentially in an infinite number of ways, Balthasar retains the importance of the martyr as a representative eucharistic symbol. In part Balthasar seeks to relativize the importance of martyrdom, for instance in highlighting the fact that the suffering of Christians cannot genuinely be extolled above those of other religions, but he does think that martyrdom is Christian mission on display without ornamentation or ambiguity.[157] The martyrs are, as it were, the most eloquent pictures of the heart of the ecclesial Eucharist. Speaking of Thérèse of Lisieux's "existential theology," Balthasar comments that "as far as she is concerned, a thing is not true unless it can be perfected in the moment-to-moment fulfillment of God's will."[158] He does not entirely adopt Thérèse's existential urgency with regard to doctrinal affirmation, but Balthasar does consistently attempt to point to some lived exemplar of whatever theological truth he is elucidating. In the case of the Eucharist, the martyr is frequently enough invoked as that dramatic portrayal of both Christ's own process of becoming Eucharist and the existential profile of eucharistic reception.[159] However, for Balthasar, the theological significance of this has less to do with the suffering of a physical death than it has to do with its manifestation of a prior expropriation of one's will and dedication to one's mission.[160] Thus, to stay with Thérèse, martyrdom is a possibility for all: "All right! *Let us die martyrs!* . . . Martyrdom unrealized by men, known to God alone, undiscoverable by the eye of any creature, martyrdom without honor, without triumph."[161] This martyrdom without honor also shares the anonymity and hiddenness of Christ in the Eucharist. To "become bread" with Christ as a condition of eucharistic reception is a metaphor not only for allowing oneself to be used up by others, to be a nourishment for those who are hungry, but also to be *only* bread, to be something easily passed over and forgotten, and also something that is easily given away. It is to repeat the kenotic movement of the Son.[162] All of this is summarized in the liturgical formula *benedixit, fregit, deditque*, which was printed on Balthasar's own ordination card and was the subject of his first homily as a priest.[163] Later, perhaps based on this first homily, he wrote: "*Benedixit, fregit, deditque* [He blessed, broke, and gave]: Because he blessed, he broke, and because he broke you, he was able to bestow you as gift."[164]

Even though his Ignatian emphasis on discernment makes him hesitant to dictate this or that ethical decision, this does not mean, of course, that Balthasar cedes ethics to the dictates of a practical reason construed without reference to revelation. On the contrary, as Balthasar understands the issue, the unique quality of Christian behavior is not solely in the prior intention or in the larger, theocentric frame of reference, but is actually manifest in a particular way of life and in particular decisions that are supererogatory of what is demanded by practical reason. Otherwise put, Balthasar reserves the right to think and act theologically even in the so-called secular realm, which is so often quarantined by the domain of "reason" in modernity. When he then calls Christ the "concrete categorical imperative," this is a signal that the ethics practiced by the Christian come not from an abstract (and heteronomous) law by which we decide the best organization of human interaction, but rather from the example of the self-giving life of Christ.[165] Balthasar's could be characterized as a virtue ethics in which *phronesis* is marked by habituation to the norm that is the eucharistic Christ.[166] Regarding how one treats one's neighbor, then, the criterion is not based first of all on how one would wish all people would behave (Kant or John Rawls), nor even on some call or imperative that comes directly from the face of the Other (Levinas, or even Buber). The Other, for Balthasar, cannot make the demands of self-abnegation if they are either simply a single individual or even the representative of the moral order.[167]

According to Balthasar, Christian love of neighbor has two major premises: (1) the love with which I love my neighbor does not originate in myself but in God, and (2) the neighbor is to be loved as God, or, said more properly, as a sacrament of God. With regard to the second, Christ is hidden in the neighbor just as he is hidden in the tabernacle. To extend this logic even further, because the Eucharist is constituted by a radical hiddenness, "the poorer and the more needy" my neighbor may be, he is "all the more the Sacrament of Jesus Christ."[168] With regard to the first premise, the love of neighbor, because it is Christ's love, must take a eucharistic form: "to give my neighbor the bread and wine of the word and of my own life."[169] The various ways in which Balthasar deploys a eucharistic logic in his ethics has not even been intimated, nor are those that have been chosen necessarily representative. The point is that Balthasar is issuing a challenge to Christianity's moral imagination. He is convinced that Christianity itself has the resources to conceptualize its relationship to the world and its duty toward the poor and despised.[170] The issue is not that conceptual help or even supplement from philosophy should itself be scorned, but rather that because Christian ethics is based on love, the utmost self-gift of Christ in the Eucharist is the natural exemplar and model of creaturely love. It would be difficult to establish a direct borrowing, and an indirect influence is almost certain, but this is precisely what both John Paul II and Benedict XVI have proposed by stressing the connection between a *"eucharistic form of life* and *moral transformation*."[171] In *Deus caritas est*, in particular, Benedict clearly and unmistakably echoes Balthasar: "The Eucharist draws us into Jesus' act of self-oblation. More than just statically receiving the incarnate *Logos*, we enter into the very dynamic of his self-giving." The official German translation makes this even more evident with its use of *Hingabe*: "Die Eucharistie zieht uns in den *Hingabeakt* Jesu hinein. Wir empfangen nicht nur statisch den inkarnierten *Logos*, sondern werden in die Dynamik seiner *Hingabe* hineingenommen."[172] Ethics, in this conception, is the eucharistic dynamic of Christ's self-gift manifested in the world by those who have handed their very selves over to be used in mission.[173]

To conclude this section on Balthasar's eucharistic vision of Christian mission, it needs to be noted that all of this is true for the individual, but it also applies to Balthasar's vision of the Church as a whole. The Church itself, as a collective body, including its institutional structure, is to evince this same bread-like quality such that it exists in order to be consumed by the world. Balthasar advances this type of porous ecclesiology in its most alarming form in his early book *Razing the Bastions* (1952). In reaction to what he considered the insularity and obduracy of the Church before Vatican II, Balthasar issued his proposal for "a Church no longer barricaded against the world."[174] The book is indeed so radical that it is hard to believe that the Balthasar who today is often enough characterized, by both acclamation and defamation, as a hero of Catholic conservatism, is the same Balthasar who wrote this book that might as well be a Reformation-era pamphlet. Nevertheless, even though the later Balthasar noted the deficiencies of his earlier position, he claimed in 1986, two years before his death, that he was still "fully committed" to this book and its project.[175] In *Razing the Bastions*, Balthasar calls everything about the division between the Church and the world into question, and as the title suggests, proposes a definitive tearing town of the wall of separation between them. The Church is to be so utterly kenotic that it exists only as a mediator between God and the world, and not as an end in itself.

None of this is to say that Balthasar, even in *Razing the Bastions*, explicitly called into question any particular doctrines or ecclesial disciplines or structures.[176] Rather, his intention was to point to the *relative* status of the Church *qua* institution. Not only is the institutional structure to be dismantled eschatologically, but it is relative even now to the salvation of the world. Of course, this is meant not in an antinomian sense such that the objectivity of the Church should be relativized or made to fit certain subjective needs, as should be obvious from our earlier treatment of this issue.[177] What it means, without drawing any specific conclusions as far as implementation, is that the Church as a whole, like Mary, must stand in total (eucharistic) openness to the will of God for the world. Balthasar's program for the renewal of the Church is not isolationism *from* the world, nor is it accommodation *to* the world, but is rather involvement and leavening *in* the world, with the same eucharistic receptivity and self-abandonment required of the individual.[178] Just as the individual's ego becomes shattered and made into a corporate, ecclesial reality, and only thus becomes a person, so the Church as a whole only realizes her identity insofar as she is liquefied for the sake of the world.

CONCLUSION

This chapter has been circling around a host of issues that all basically concern the question of the Church's reception of and participation in the eucharistic gift of Christ. Just as chapter 1 explored how Balthasar's eucharistic theology led him far beyond the usual parameters of sacramental discourse, so here too we see that one cannot understand Balthasar's conception of fruitful sacramental reception without the broader, Trinitarian framework. He is concerned not only with what appears on the surface, such as the conditions set in place for the grace that is given and received, but with the subterranean depths that are implied. Beneath the veil of the sacramental manifestation, as it were, is the dramatic interchange, the communion, between the Triune God and the finite creature. This is again why pneumatology came into consideration in the first section of this chapter, for if the Church is not embedded in the Spirit, it is left not only as an unequal partner to the God who gives, but utterly unable to receive the gift of God. The subjectivity of the communicant does not just confront the sacramental economy as a brute fact, as a foreign objectivity, but, in the Holy Spirit, as the perfection and elevation of all that is most interior. The aporia of the subjective/objective tension in sacramental theology is only resolved in God, and in the Church's participation therein.

Yet, for all this, even as the Church's reception of the Eucharist occurs within a Trinitarian dynamic, the Church is not thereby absorbed by and dissolved into the perichoresis of the divine persons. The creature's synergy with the divine action remains on the properly finite and created level, such that it is marked by a creaturely mode of receptivity and self-abandonment, as we saw in the second section. This Marian reception is the creature's most elevated means of returning a gift to God. The creature's return-gift is precisely this *eucharistia*, this reception and thanksgiving for the great self-gift of God for the sake of the world, which constitutes, for Balthasar, the sacrifice of the Mass (third section of this chapter).

The creature's gift to the Creator, the thanksgiving (*todah*) offering, is then nothing less than the creature's entire self. Balthasar is not ignorant of the lack of nuance and the excess of expression in Thérèse of Lisieux, but she does enact the type of existential sacramental theology that Balthasar has in mind, much like Bernanos does.[179] "By a sort of liturgical deed" Thérèse consecrated herself to divine mercy on the feast of the Holy Trinity, June 9, 1895. One of her desires was that "the Lord should dwell in her as he does in the Host," just as we noted how Balthasar specifies that transubstantiation occurs also in the communicant. Thus she prays:

"I OFFER MYSELF AS A BURNT OFFERING TO YOUR MERCI-FUL LOVE, calling upon you to consume me at every instant, while you let the floods of *infinite tenderness* pent up within you flow into my soul, so that I may become a *Martyr* to your *love*, O my God."[180] Thérèse thus offers herself as the "true matter of the Eucharist," as that which is to be transubstantiated, which is what is enacted liturgically in the Church's Eucharist. This is not to call into question the essential place of the Mass, as if the possibility of eucharistic sacrifice occurring at any time renders this concrete expression void or redundant. Instead, it means that every encounter between the Creator and the creature is one of sacramental interchange. The Eucharist is then not one cultic expression of a transcendental communion, but is the *sine qua non* for all spirituality, for all redemption, for all divinization. Christ exists now only in his pneumatic, eucharistic form, and he can thus only be received eucharistically. For Balthasar, this occurs in its fullness during the Mass, where bodily Communion is not only stipulated but actualized, along with the spiritual Communion.

As should be clear, the eucharistic union of the Church with Christ is decidedly not an erasure of the creature nor any type of Christomonism. According to Balthasar, after the renunciation of the "I," the ego that separates itself from all others, there is then a positive transition from individual to person. On the far side of self-erasure, then, there is self-reception. This discovery of the self, however, is a discovery that the self is not separate from others, nor is it in any way separate from Christ (Gal. 2:20). But because this union with Christ occurs in the Holy Spirit, there is no absorption of the self into Christ, for the Spirit is both *vinculum amoris* between Father and Son (and between Christ and Church) and *vinculum distinctionis*, a bond that unites in love but also distinguishes by that same love. The creaturely insertion into the Trinitarian dynamic is then not like a drop of vinegar into the ocean, whereby union occurs by dissolution, but is instead a positive, creaturely *contribution* to the divine life. Without anticipating too much of the topic of eschatology, to be covered in depth in chapter 4, we can note how Balthasar answers his own question at the end of *TD* V: "What does God gain from the world?"

> An additional gift, given to the Son by the Father, but equally a gift made by the Son to the Father, and by the Spirit to both. [The world]

is a gift because, through the distinct operations of each of the three Persons, the world acquires an inward share in the divine exchange of life; as a result the world is able to take the divine things it has received from God, together with the gift of being created, and return them to God as a divine gift.[181]

In the synergy between the Spirit and the world, the world is able to return thanks, εὐχαριστεῖν, to the Father for the eucharistic prodigality of the Son, and this thanksgiving, in which the creature offers its very self to God, completes the eucharistic exchange. The world then becomes, in God, what it receives eucharistically. The Augustinian notion of the identity between Eucharist and Church then gains significance on a cosmic scale: "The world will not disappear in God; rather, the last sacrament will be the entire triune God revealed in the entirety of glorified creation."[182]

CHAPTER 3

"Truly You Are a Hidden God"

Liturgical Manifestation and Its Limits

"You know also that the beginning is the most important part of any work."[1] We don't need Plato to remind us of this fact, as Balthasar himself begins his *Trilogy* with similar words: "Beginning is a problem not only for the thinking person, the philosopher, a problem that remains with him and determines all his subsequent steps; the beginning is also a primal decision which includes all later ones for the person whose life is based on response and decision."[2] Is it not too late to now turn to the liturgy, when, as almost any recent work on sacramental theology will insist, the liturgy *must* come first? To come to the liturgy, the visible and communal cult of the Church, only at this late stage, when the essentials have already been put in place, might seem to be the result of forgetting the major gains of sacramental and liturgical theology in the twentieth century. And because, as will be made obvious in what follows, this decision for a postponement of the liturgical is based on Balthasar's own inclinations, perhaps we can conclude that he will have nothing to teach us in this regard. Yet, it is precisely Balthasar's bracketing of the question of a visible, liturgical manifestation, resulting in this structural postponement, that will be considered a major decision and intervention with regard to the direction of sacramental theology and liturgical studies. The questions that will emerge in this chapter, from the role of symbolism (and thus the relation of sign to referent), to the tension between the religious community's self-determination and its formation from outside of itself, and above all the analogy between earthly liturgical beauty and divine glory, are thus indicative of Balthasar's theological commitments, which are able to provide a place, albeit a "marginal" one, for the liturgy. First we will trace Balthasar's actual comments on the liturgy and liturgical reform before turning to his negative verdict of an overly aesthetic approach to the liturgy. Then, with the ground cleared and with this potentially damnatory position announced from the outset, we can see how Balthasar, without dissimulation, can be understood positively as something of a liturgical theologian. The chapter will conclude by situating Balthasar's liturgical theology as the hinge between two giants of liturgical reflection: Romano Guardini and Joseph Ratzinger.

SACRAMENTAL AND LITURGICAL SOURCES

Balthasar's rich and variegated understanding of the liturgy is best discovered in how he comments upon and situates himself with regard to other major liturgical sources, particularly the Church Fathers and the liturgical movement. We will see how Balthasar interprets, contextualizes, and ultimately criticizes certain aspects of patristic conceptions of the liturgy and also modern attempts to revive and ameliorate the Roman Rite, before, during, and after Vatican II. First, we must note what Balthasar took positively from the Fathers. What Balthasar found in the theology of the Fathers was a way of doing theology, a style of thought, that exhibited a greater internal dynamism than what he observed in his seminary training, particularly concerning sacramentality: "[A] deep ontological piety according to which existence itself is a prayer . . . a deep understanding of the cultic, of the objectivity of the symbolic and sacramental world order: All of these are the eternal values of the patristic era."[3] It is precisely the more global perspective of the sacramental life of the Church, which extends far beyond the ecclesial rites, that shaped Balthasar's own conception of the scope of the liturgy and its cosmic implications. These are potential antidotes to the scholastic malaise that Balthasar never tired of critiquing, but they also carry within themselves a danger that is equally deleterious to a Catholic vision of the God–world relation. Thus, although the influence of the Fathers on Balthasar's thought is foundational for all of his later theology, he was never interested in *les Pères pour les Pères*, and was always willing, even in his early studies of the Fathers, to critique and depart from them when necessary.

As the heir to the early Greek tradition, Maximus the Confessor is a helpful entry point into Balthasar's understanding of the Church Fathers, particularly as it relates to questions of the liturgy. The title of Balthasar's major 1941 study of Maximus speaks volumes: *Kosmische Liturgie*. He assures us years later that this book did not receive its title "without serious premeditation."[4] In Maximus, Balthasar discerns the meeting of a variety of his favorite streams of patristic thought, particularly those of Origen, Evagrius, and Denys, and the decisions of the councils, particularly Chalcedon. Balthasar consistently attempts to interpret Origen and Denys as ecclesial theologians,[5] but they lack the concrete, material side that emerges only in Maximus's "Chalcedonian Origenism":

> That is the reason why the symbolism of the *Mystagogia* begins with a building: with a visible church made of stone—something that would have been unthinkable for Origen; and that is why Maximus insists, in a very simple way, on real participation in the liturgy within this building. The "gnostic soul," too, is urgently encouraged to stick to the liturgical order in order to realize his own perfection, by projecting his own subjectivity onto the "objective" pole of cultic worship.[6]

Because the liturgy, for Maximus and for many of the Fathers, is "the midpoint, around which everything revolves,"[7] misunderstanding the place of the liturgy will cause the whole system to shift out of alignment. Maximus is the Church Father, for Balthasar, who most closely views the liturgy as the union of the terrestrial (thus the emphasis in the *Mystagogia* on the physical aspects of the liturgy) and the celestial (the physical as symbolic of the spiritual), or as later Western theology would define it, *res et sacramentum*.

Nevertheless, even if Maximus is the Greek Father who best valorizes the earthly liturgy, not even he entirely avoids the snares of the Alexandrian tradition and its spiritualizing tendency. Balthasar notes this in 1941, but expresses it even more insistently several decades later: "The unambiguous tendency, from Clement of Alexandria *via* Origen, Evagrius, both Gregories and Maximus, is to transcend the visible liturgy and to find its 'truth' in an individual-Gnostic immediate relationship to God."[8] This has been, as he notes, something that Christianity as a whole has never quite overcome, and much of Balthasar's own theology is his attempt to insist on the need for Christian spirituality to be rooted in the concreteness of the flesh.[9] The problem with the Alexandrian appeal to the symbolic side of liturgy, even if this is considered preferable to a disjunctive scholastic view of the sign, is that it often serves as a means for negating the earthly, historical liturgy in favor of the cosmic liturgy in which it participates.[10] The earthly liturgy tends toward the cosmic liturgy of the divine life, and even reflects that celestial liturgy here below, but with the ultimate goal of abolishing itself and fusing with the Absolute. Even Alexander Schmemann notes that this is the tendency in his own Orthodox Church, a problem that he labels as a liturgical crisis: "Worship is experienced as a departure out of the world for a little while, as a 'vent' or a break in earthly existence, opened up for the inlet of grace."[11] Ironically, even the opulent symbolism of the patristic era, intended to illustrate the transformation of the cosmos by the inhabitation of the divine life, can lead to a denigration of finitude based on an otherworldly liturgical escapism.

The figure that best represents a contemporary attempt to rehabilitate patristic understandings of the sacraments for Balthasar is Odo Casel. Both the promises and the dangers that Balthasar noted in the Fathers reemerge with greater urgency in Casel. One of Casel's main points is to illustrate that Christ's saving deeds are made present to the Church in the form of the mysteries, or sacraments. The sacrifice of the Mass for Casel, as we explored in chapter 2, is not a new sacrifice that the Church offers, but rather the mode by which the Church participates in Christ's one, original sacrifice on the cross. It is, essentially, the relationship between archetype and image, with the latter participating in the former. However, like Plato, who leaves participation (μέθεξις) rather underdefined and ambiguous, Casel does not specify *how* this participation takes place, and again, like Plato, he tends to resort to the mythological or at least the inexplicable for answers.[12] Balthasar did note that Casel was "anxious to avoid" an overt Platonism to solve this difficulty,[13] but according to Balthasar, without substantial correction, Casel's theory can appear as Platonic, magical, or both.[14] Casel, who puts such great weight on the symbolism of the eucharistic cult, says the following, revealing a latent antimaterialistic spiritualism: "There is nothing external or material mixed up in [the liturgy]. For behind the visible, objective action is a wholly spiritual reality: the person of Christ, the Word incarnate, who, under the veil of mystical figures, presents his loving act of devotion to the Father in dying."[15]

Much of what worried Balthasar in some of the Greek Fathers applies equally to his hesitancy about the liturgical movement in the early twentieth century, a movement that sought to renew the Roman Rite based on historical research and concrete liturgical reforms. Balthasar never aligned himself with the liturgical movement, and when he does discuss it, it is almost always with an eye to critique, which tends to center around two issues that are closely united: first, that the liturgical movement seems to drink from the streams of romanticism, and second that it subordinates the person to the community, a motive that derives from idealism.[16] Balthasar agrees with what is a presupposition of most of the liturgical movement: the liturgy is a gift from above. Yet, for Balthasar, its vertical origin does not necessitate that the rites themselves be considered divinely mandated. Were the rites akin to revelation, then the liturgical movement would be correct in trying to find *the* liturgy, whether this is the medieval Roman Rite (e.g., Prosper Guéranger and Solesmes), a patristic rite as it is found in the liturgical manuscripts, such as the *Apostolic Tradition* (e.g., Botte and even to some extent Jungmann),[17] or some basic *ordo* that all liturgical families share (e.g., the more recent ecumenical work of Gordon Lathrop).[18] The liturgy, however, is *both* a gift from God *and* "the work of human hands." It is a moment of synergy or cooperation between Christ and the Church, the Bridegroom and the Bride.[19] For Balthasar there exists no ideal liturgy, whether in the past or in the temporal future, for the Church is always attempting to attune its life (including its cultic expression) to that of Christ. There are obviously internally self-regulative aspects of the liturgy, one could even say a basic *ordo*, but Balthasar thinks that the liturgy, as a whole, must be directed and ordered by an extraliturgical reality, that of the form of Christ.[20]

Though many, including Balthasar, will accuse the postconciliar liturgy of devolving into a "closed circle," Balthasar made essentially the same critique earlier of the liturgical movement.[21] Without the goal of holiness and mission, the liturgical movement could simply result in making the liturgy a controllable site of human activity, a place less for worship and devotion and more for self-reflection, introspection, and perhaps even a need for domination. Balthasar provides an example of the *"Volksschott-Bewegung,"* which provided Latin/German missalettes in Germany, with the goal of increasing understanding and participation in the Mass: "De facto, the 'Schott' missal has become a kind of new iconostasis for us. We follow the real unfolding of the liturgy or the Scripture. . . . We control the situation and thereby stand outside it. We have the word in black on white, but the word does not have us. We grasp; we are not ourselves grasped. We hold the libretto in our hand and could prompt 'priest' and 'people,' but we ourselves are not 'people' or 'priest.'"[22]

Balthasar certainly thought that understanding and participating in the Mass was desirable, and he was not in principle opposed to Mass in the vernacular or missalettes with translations. What he worried about was tipping the balance away from *receptivity* in the Christian life and towards *activity*. Instead, for Balthasar, first (and not just chronologically, but by priority) there is God's initiative and Mary's receptivity, which then, and only then, creates the possibility of the Church's activity and cooperation. To put this theological point in Thomas's words, operative grace (e.g., the grace of conversion) precedes cooperative participation in God's grace (through meritorious good works).[23]

In general, Balthasar has very little to suggest about liturgical renewal, especially before Vatican II. His "contribution" to the liturgical movement, if any, was always one of cautioning against rather quick assumptions about our ability to shape the liturgy in order to achieve predetermined results. In his estimation, much of the push to increase participation only resulted in newer forms of artificiality and nonparticipation. This, however, is a symptom of the real issue: the underlying romanticism of the liturgical movement, which paradoxically makes it akin to the strictest traditionalism. In both cases, the liturgy is considered as *a-cosmic*, as a flight from the entirely secular world into an entirely holy realm. This is made psychologically possible by the antiquarianism of the liturgy: if we cannot have heaven now, the Middle Ages or perhaps the fourth century will do! To this end, on the occasion of a eucharistic congress in 1960, Balthasar wrote: "Dear brothers and sisters, have we not perhaps narrowed down the breadth of the Christian liturgy in the last decades in a way that flees from the world, out of sheer concern for the sacrality of our liturgical services? Have we not coddled and dressed up the liturgy in an aseptic, sterilized, germ-free environment, and did not

Hitler take us at our word in a terrible way? . . . The Church is not a club; either she is the world, or she does not exist."[24]

For this reason, Balthasar consistently emphasizes the difference between a church and the Temple.[25] The Temple is in *a* place; a Christian church can be set up anywhere: it is like a tent that can be erected by the pilgrim Church, which transverses the world with ease, making any and every place holy.[26] As it is with space, so also with time: the Church is rather indifferent to times. No age, patristic or medieval, is a preferable time. Thus, no matter how beautiful the liturgy of a bygone era ("'What is beautiful must also die,' and embalming does not help it"),[27] the liturgy cannot be the repristination of a supposed past, but an encounter with the living Christ in the present tense.

Balthasar's preference for *now* as the only liturgical time is meant to counteract the liturgical movement's preference for *then* (medieval or patristic), and thus he calls for an end to liturgical romanticism and its conceptual dependency on idealism. This idealism becomes even more acute after Vatican II. Balthasar, of course, was not invited to the council, but there is no reason to assume that he would not have applauded the *Constitution on the Sacred Liturgy (Sacrosanctum concilium)*.[28] The document incorporates much of what was good and helpful in the liturgical movement, for instance in its desire for the "full, active participation" of the laity and in the removal of unnecessary accretions in the liturgy, and it also views the liturgy within the larger economy of salvation. It also, importantly for Balthasar, does not overemphasize the corporate aspect of liturgical prayer to the neglect of personal devotion and silence.[29] Nevertheless, Balthasar remained highly critical of the implementation of the new form of the liturgy, citing not only the tendency toward the insipid but the more pernicious theological undercurrent to this expression. Having a refined aesthetic sensibility, Balthasar was particularly sensitive to the "element lacking in good taste [that] has crept into the liturgy since the (falsely interpreted) Council,"[30] to say nothing of the prevalence of flagrant liturgical abuse.[31]

All of these issues, from bad taste to liturgical abuses, are simply symptoms of a deeper, systemic problem. The cause of these liturgical deformations is a *theological* one, and will therefore only be solved by a theological remedy and not by liturgical adjustments, major or minor. This is why Balthasar virtually equates the postconciliar liturgical abuses that are careless with liturgical norms and regulations with traditionalists who are obsessed with them. Both try to impress upon the liturgy their own form, their own imprint.[32] Some, and this is more common after the council, will shape the liturgy according to their own predilections and desires, but others, traditionalists, will seek to form it according to a venerable tradition. But in either case, the community's own desires to form the liturgy take precedence over Christ's initiative, or, at the most dangerous, are equated: "For them [traditionalists] the dignity of the form—a perhaps wonderfully polished, aesthetic dignity—predominates over the perennially new, nonobjectifiable dignity of the divine event."[33]

Ultimately, for Balthasar, what has too frequently occurred since Vatican II is that the liturgy has now validated all of Feuerbach's intuitions: religion is, ultimately, self-worship. The congregation now worships itself, its own ideal spirit. Or, if we take a step behind Feuerbach, we can ask an even more haunting question with Thomas O'Meara: "And thereby we ponder if, as in other cultural areas, we are not liturgically the prodigal children of Hegel."[34] Whether or not one agrees with O'Meara's assessment, Balthasar does note that an element of self-reflection and self-awareness has crept into the Church's liturgies in a manner that is unparalleled by previous ages. If scholasticism failed to see the intrinsic relationship between the Church and the Eucharist, an error addressed by de Lubac's *Corpus Mysticum*, liturgical idealism fails to adequately differentiate the two, thereby collapsing Christ and the Church. The Eucharist is then not an Other who is worshipped (Christ), but a solidification of the community's own spirit, its own self-projection.[35] Karl Barth, long before Vatican II, made the claim that Catholicism and liberal Protestantism are two sides of the same coin, a claim Balthasar strongly contested.[36] But, with the liturgical changes after the council, Balthasar wonders whether the Church is starting to prove Barth correct: "It is 'church,' feeling very satisfied with herself; the spiritual self-indulgence of the community—precisely the kind of thing for which we used to reproach the pietistic and liberal Protestant services. What if the malicious analyses of Karl Barth were, after all, correct in lumping together Schleiermacher and Catholicism—as a self-glorifying *Corpus Mysticum*?"[37] This liturgical idealism, according to Balthasar, denies that the distance between Christ and the Church, the distance between the individual and the community, and the difference between matter and spirit could have a positive basis that is the condition of the possibility of communion, a communion that forbids one pole from absorbing the other.

We have seen how Balthasar reacts to his main liturgical sources, and have thus highlighted Balthasar's concerns and misgivings with regard to these sources, but he also does offer his own thoughts on the liturgy, which reveal his own particular liturgical sensibility. To state it tersely, Balthasar's understanding of the liturgy is notably Western and decidedly Roman. And if there is one word that characterizes the Roman Rite, it is "sober," which is precisely the word that Balthasar insists on when he offers his liturgical suggestions: "And the more soberly the Eucharist is celebrated—without superfluous ornamentation, but also without hyper-liturgical rigidity—as, for instance, the first Christians celebrated it—the more comprehensible the event becomes, the more legible the figure."[38] We might expect Balthasar to provide a, or perhaps even *the*, aesthetic commentary on the liturgy, and to reflect on how the beauty of the liturgy reveals the glory of God, but he consistently refuses to do so. More often than not, as in the quote just above, Balthasar's liturgical suggestions amount to no more than an appeal to dignity, sobriety, and personal holiness. As would be expected, from those who remember attending his masses, he himself would celebrate the liturgy simply and quietly.[39]

The liturgy that Balthasar suggests is one that is simple, reliant on the tradition of the Church instead of attempting to always create something new, and also thoroughly modern, in the sense of its freedom from artificial anachronisms.[40] This does not dispense the Church from attempting to create beautiful liturgical forms in each era, and Balthasar does acknowledge a few noteworthy examples from the twentieth century and was himself a friend to and proponent of contemporary artists,[41] but he thinks that these forms will emerge at first from small centers of holiness in the Church: "In the vast, teeming pluralism of our postmodern times, the task will be achieved, if at all, only in enclaves, though enclaves have the capacity to propagate themselves, like ripples on the surface of the water."[42] As he had already noted in his early essay on art from 1927, "Katholische Religion und Kunst," *Hingabe* is required for a genuinely Catholic form of art.[43] For Balthasar, as we explored in chapter 2, the objective holiness of the Church, its offices and institutions, exist for the sake of the subjective holiness of the saints. The former is entirely ancillary to the latter and thus can never become an end in itself. All of this is to say simply that Balthasar reverses the priority of the relationship between liturgy and holiness. For him, it is not that a certain type of liturgy (whether progressive or traditional) can produce a certain type of effect (if we use contemporary music, people will participate more, or if we use the Tridentine Rite, people will necessarily be more reverent), but rather that the holiness and receptivity of the Church to the Holy Spirit will lead to a worthy and prayerful liturgy.

This trust in holiness, perhaps theologically accurate, has little practical purchase, and perhaps even underestimates the degree to which the *form* of the liturgy has an active and determining role in the shaping of the subjectivities for those who participate in them. Nevertheless, Balthasar believed that a parish that truly seeks the face of the Lord would inevitably drift toward worthy liturgical forms. Holiness, for Balthasar, has a way of naturally purifying elements that are antithetical to itself. The Church "has the incorruptible ear for what is fitting, for what is appropriate for herself."[44] This is so when the Church is true to itself, which means that it operates with a Marian receptivity, and thus avoids any productionist attitudes with regard to the liturgy. In practical terms, "the worthiness of the liturgy increases in proportion to the participants' awareness of their own unworthiness. It is impossible, then, to manipulate or technically produce this worthiness."[45] We will return to this particular form of Balthasar's liturgical theology later in the chapter, but here it is simply important to note how his theological principle of Marian receptivity leads to his preference for a simple, sober Mass in which God's initiative is highlighted.[46] The liturgy is, in a sense, a partial disappearing act for the congregation, according to Balthasar: "Whatever form the response of our liturgy takes, it can only be the expression of the most pure and selfless reception possible of the divine majesty of his grace."[47]

THEOLOGICAL AESTHETICS AND ITS LIMITS

Turning directly to Balthasar's theological analysis of the liturgy, and specifically his evaluation of the *visible* aspect of the liturgy, it is evident that his position is partly an amalgamation of insights that he critically borrowed from the Fathers and from more contemporary sources. Nevertheless, although Balthasar seldom thinks without historical commentary, his indebtedness to others should not obscure the fact that his appropriation of others is never done uncritically, but is rather always filtered through his own distinctive lens. Balthasar's theological aesthetics, found embryonically in *Apokalypse* and fully developed in *Herrlichkeit*, is applied without sentimentality to discriminate and separate the wheat from the chaff, even, for example, in his most beloved Maximus. The criterion, then, by which patristic concepts such as *typos*, *mystagogia*, and *mysterion*, and scholastic ones such as *signum* and *sacramentum* are all critically evaluated is his theological aesthetics, which represents not just a valorization of all that is beautiful but a careful discrimination about how, and how not, to put objects of beauty, including the liturgy, to theological use. In this section, I will explore the limits that Balthasar's aesthetics establish for sacramental theology in order to clear the ground for the more positive, fruitful aspect of his thought in the next section. The proscriptive elements of Balthasar's liturgical methodology come first for two reasons: first, it is what emerges most clearly in Balthasar's thought and was evidently more pressing on his mind than a positive construction, and second, Balthasar's words of caution most directly address contemporary issues in sacramental and liturgical theology, and can potentially have a salubrious effect on some tendencies in recent thought.

When Balthasar began *Herrlichkeit*, he was already highly conversant in the thought of phenomenology, particularly as represented by Edmund Husserl, Max Scheler, and Martin Heidegger.[48] Yet, he chose, it seems intentionally, *not* to use phenomenology as his primary tool for his theological aesthetics, but rather Goethe and his concept of *Gestalt*.[49] And although Goethe and his terminology are employed by Balthasar, even to the extent that Balthasar claims Goethe as the discrimen between himself and Rahner, the contribution of Goethe turns out to be more terminological and perhaps methodological rather than pertaining to any of the specific content of Balthasar's *theological* aesthetics. This is also true regarding his philosophy, particularly as seen in *Wahrheit*, but it is doubly so for his theology: the objective form of what is revealed takes precedence over any anthropological preconditions that might dictate the manner in which the form is revealed. The anthropological element is in no way ignored, but it is subordinated to the primacy of the revealed form: "Our first principle must always be the indissolubility of form, and our second the fact that such form is determined by many antecedent conditions."[50] This is another manner of expressing the more generic polarity in Balthasar's thought between objectivity and subjectivity, which are always in a creative interplay, with the former enjoying some manner of precedence, but never in abstraction from the latter. With regard to data belonging to revelation, then, Balthasar will emphasize first their unexpected and irruptive quality when considering human expectations, but also how this data fulfills and perfects all that is genuinely human (*gratia non tollit*). Therefore, the liturgy and the sacraments cannot be approached as merely common phenomena, but will only be understood when perceived (*wahrnehmen*) by the eyes of faith.[51] Or, to expand the categories of phenomenology itself, it will require a particularly *sacramental* phenomenology that is equipped to handle the interplay between visibility and invisibility in the liturgical rites.

One major qualm that Balthasar has with post-Kantian philosophy, and this would include Husserl and Heidegger despite their protestations to the contrary, is that it brackets out, a priori, that which is "unknowable." It does this with seemingly impeccable motives: Why entertain the possibility of a reality to which we have no access? When this is done, though, "we wholly lose the phenomenon of objective self-manifestation, the self-revelation of the object from the heart of its own depths, and everything runs aground in shallow functionalism."[52] To turn "to the things themselves" is, of course, the rallying cry of phenomenology, which is why Balthasar's thought is rightly brought into parallel with it. The simple fact of the matter, however, is that phenomenology, particularly in its classical formulations by both Husserl and Heidegger, not only seems to have no place for revelation, but is positively hostile to it. As Ferdinand Ulrich aptly noted, for all of Heidegger's talk of fervent expectation for the divine, ultimately he absolutizes expectation in an "ultimate disobedience in the sense of a radical rejection of history," a history in which the Word *has* spoken.[53] If phenomenology was itself to have a fruitful relationship with Christianity, it necessarily had its "theological turn," as represented by figures, such as Jean-Luc Marion, who attempt to retool and expand the possibilities of the phenomenological enterprise.[54] Balthasar thinks that Marion goes too far down the phenomenological path, particularly in his agreement with Heidegger about the bankruptcy of metaphysics, which is not an insignificant point, but there is nevertheless much that links Balthasar and recent phenomenology that is open to revelation.

Like his philosophical guide, Erich Przywara, Balthasar thinks that Christianity and its metaphysics stand in tension between idealism and realism, or we could say between idealism and phenomenology.[55] And even if Christianity needs some aspects of idealism and abstraction, and some of the fruits of this approach were borne out in the patristic era, it remains fundamentally hostile to any negation of finite existence: because Christianity is dedicated to a "theological vision of Being which remains bound to 'myth,'" ultimate knowledge comes not from turning away from finitude, "but in turning toward the phenomenal existent (*conversio ad phantasma*) as the only place where the mystery of Being will shine forth for him who himself exists bodily and spiritually."[56] Our knowledge of revelation then comes from the concrete realism of particular phenomena: the commandments of Moses, Jesus the Nazarene, the Church. The danger, however, with a purely phenomenological approach is that it tends toward viewing the phenomena of revelation as simply one set of phenomena, however special and privileged, among others: "Thus understood, the rationality of faith rests totally on the persuasive character of the revelatory signs, their power to convince man's reason."[57] It is certainly not just that "an evil and adulterous generation seeks a sign" (Matt. 12:39), as if Christianity transcended phenomenal appearance, but rather that the dialectic between affirmation of the sign and its negation needs to be supplemented by a higher perspective. This is precisely what Balthasar attempts to do with his concept of *Gestalt*. The form has an objective coherence in which it attests to its own validity and is not therefore justified outside of itself. Yet, the form is not grasped by all who visually behold it, for certain subjective, eidetic, dispositions are required for a truly perceptive vision. Instead, then, of the tension inherent in the sign, his use of *Gestalt* is meant to show that the properly "phenomenological" aspect of any form also reveals its inner signification: "The content [*Gehalt*] does not lie behind the form [*Gestalt*], but within it."[58] Access "within" the form, however, is not granted without some prior capacitation.

Turning to a more specifically theological interpretation of the issue, Balthasar shows how God's self-manifestation, both in the Old and the New Testaments, is understood by this category of the form, which is neither a pure *Deus absconditus* nor a simple manifestation (*Schein*). Particularly about Christ and his self-abasement, Balthasar notes that inasmuch as this is the form of God's self-revelation, it is also one that is thoroughly hidden: "among you stands one whom you know not" (John 1:26). And even though Balthasar is a thoroughly Johannine theologian, he does recognize that John's interpretation of Christ as an event of δόξα is a "developed theology," whereas the original historical event does not shine immediately with Taboric light. Instead, "we can see that this lack of glory is what the 'form of a slave' wishes to make present, displaying it only through its absolute hiddenness."[59] That is to say, Balthasar's phenomenology, to the extent that he has one, is one that is heavily weighted toward the Pascalian. This Pascalian edge is precisely Balthasar's attention to the nonappearance and darkness of God in the scriptures, including the revelation in Christ: "The closer we come to Christ, the more the visibility fades."[60] Rather than a pure negation and flight toward blindness and absurdity, Pascal's genius is his insistence that the Christian must learn a "seeing in not-seeing," must learn to accept a "veiled vision" rather than an unmediated one.[61] This is, of course, most especially true of Christ in the Eucharist, which is at the heart of Pascal's reflections: "Jesus has decided to dwell here in the most strange and the most obscure secret of all, which is the species of the Eucharist. It is this sacrament that St John, in Revelation, calls a hidden manna, and I believe that Isaiah saw him [Christ] in this state, for he says in the spirit of prophecy: 'Truly you are a hidden God.'"[62]

Pascal's *theological* aesthetic, then, which Balthasar incorporates in good measure, is "an aesthetic that has room in its heart for the most demanding asceticism."[63] This "ascetic aestheticism" is the restraint and the patience to accept the givenness of the object, and in the case of Christian revelation, the givenness of revelation that must be understood according to the mode of its own manner of being given. This is why, to return to the Gospel of John, the δόξα of God in Christ is precisely the darkness and obscurity of the cross (*videbunt in quem transfixerunt*): "Henceforward, nothing more of God will be visible: this will be his total disclosure, but also his total concealment."[64] The cross, as the measure and the summit of all divine revelation, necessitates this asceticism, an asceticism that allows for a revelation that is totally otherwise than expected.

What is needed in approaching theological phenomena, in addition to asceticism concerning the visible, is the *lumen fidei*. It is faith, then, that grants the ability to see the form: "The light of God which faith has *sees* the form as it is, and, indeed, it can demonstrate that the evidence of the thing's rightness emerges from the thing itself and sheds its own light outwards from it."[65] This is indeed why Balthasar was less concerned with the possibilities of phenomenology, at least as articulated by Husserl and Heidegger, because phenomenology, when applied in its pure form to theological data, inevitably reduces the form of God's appearance to the limits of a mental capacity, or even *Dasein*, to grasp such a form. In this, especially in the case of Husserl, it remains ineluctably Kantian. Faith, however, as a supernatural virtue, elevates human capacity to perceive that which is impossible to perceive otherwise: "The grace of the Holy Spirit creates the faculty that can apprehend this form."[66] This is heavily indebted to Rousselot and his teaching on *les yeux de la foi*,[67] but is also cognate with Newman's (who was a major influence on Rousselot) evaluation on the first principles that condition our ability or inability to understand. Just as "a good and a bad man will think very different things probable," so also the phenomena of revelation admit of many competing interpretations.[68] Christ crucified, who is a "stumbling block to Jews and folly to Gentiles" (1 Cor. 1:23), can only be seen as the form that he truly is when he is loved.[69] Marion expresses this well: "Seeing is the result of the decision to see, and this decision, made by me, nevertheless comes to me from elsewhere. I must make the decision to make a decision, will to be willing, in order to arrive at seeing. Revelation comes to me *from elsewhere*."[70] Proper vision is then utterly sustained by revelation, in terms of both the object presented and the capacity of perception.

The Marginalization of the Sacraments

Given his hesitations about and modifications of the phenomenological project in light of Christian revelation, it is no wonder that Balthasar's reservations will continue, and in fact be heightened, when he turns to the question of the sacraments and the liturgy. What, then, gives itself to be perceived in the liturgical rites? For Balthasar, at least initially, it seems that the answer is *nothing*, that the liturgy shows us nothing of its inner significance: "The Eucharist is a pure 'mystery of faith.' The only thing which can be perceived in it is the symbol of eating and drinking; no subjective experience can be produced as a criterion for its objective truth. That is why, in the context of a theological doctrine of perception and vision, *the Eucharist can be dealt with only marginally [nur am Rande zu handeln]*."[71]

Balthasar has overstated his case, and it will be seen how he significantly nuances this position. But the overstatement serves the purpose of drawing attention to naïve assumptions that the visibility of the liturgy provides its own interpretation within itself. Instead, for Balthasar, without *les yeux de la foi*, one would only see bread and wine in the sacramental species, and not Christ's body and blood. Balthasar is here thinking within the traditional division of the sacraments as *sacramentum tantum*, *res et sacramentum*, and *res tantum*.[72] We, by the fact of being *viatores* and not *comprehensores*, currently have no immediate access to the *res tantum*, which will only be realized in the fullness of the eschaton (and thus to be deferred until chapter 4), but only to the Eucharist as it is given to us in its double reality as *res et sacramentum*, which could appropriately be called a "symbolic reality" in its singular manifestation.[73] The Eucharist, and all the sacraments for that matter, still lends itself to possible misinterpretation because of the permanence of its symbolic valence. The consecrated Eucharist still appears as *sacramentum tantum*, as a sacred sign alone. Though its *res* has changed, in that it is no longer bread and wine, it still manifests only the properties of these species to the undiscerning eye and to the undiscerning microscope, blind as it is to the question of substances.[74] It does appear, to any alert observer, as a sacred rite and as consecrated bread that is both offered to a (real or imagined) god and that receives a special blessing from that god. Thus it is clear that the invisible is as much in play in the liturgy as the visible. There are invocations of the long-dead, prayers to a god that is neither seen nor responds in kind. There are offerings made to this god, which are carried to the god by unseen messengers (*angeloi*), who then exchange this offering for the body and the blood of the god's only son. It seems that the Word overrides visibility and gives access to the invisible: the priest speaks of a *corpus meum*, but the *meum* is a *meum* from elsewhere, as the abrupt change from the third to the first person indicates.[75] The Word renders the invisible as palpable as the visible, and in fact crosses out the latter, declaring that the merely visible, at least in this instance, is a veil and not a manifestation, a *Schein*, not an *Erscheinung*.[76]

If the Word crosses out the visible or at least puts it in brackets, then the liturgy again only attains a marginal place in an aesthetic analysis.

Visibility will be given a place, an essential place, but this must come only after this initial ascetic bracketing of the visible. Augustine shares Balthasar's position in this regard. In his oft-quoted *Sermo* 272, Augustine begins with a negation of the visible: "So what you can see, then, is bread and a cup; that's what even your eyes tell you; but as for what your faith asks to be instructed about, the bread is the body of Christ, the cup the blood of Christ."[77] But then later, after establishing Christ's saving presence in the Eucharist, he asks: "So why in bread?" The bread and the wine *then* take on theological significance, contributing an essential component to an understanding of the gift of the Eucharist. This is why, again, the question about the liturgical manifestation has been delayed until our chapter 3, until after we have seen how Balthasar establishes the Eucharist as the meeting point of humanity with the Trinitarian life of God. This is also why we must first establish the negative limits of Balthasar's liturgical aesthetics, before approaching the positive opportunities. What must be said first and last about the sacraments, according to Balthasar, is the reality of Christ's total self-gift, and although the symbolic aspect cannot be neglected, it should not be given inflated importance either: "The happening [of the sacrament] has an external and, hence, sensible and symbolic side: the water of baptism is important because it really washes, and so on. But we ought not to exaggerate the symbolism of the elements as such, statically considered; the *continere gratiam* (Dz 849) should not have to suffer on this account."[78] The phenomenological approach, then, has its limits. It cannot reach, and as seen particularly in the thought of Louis-Marie Chauvet it positively rejects, the question of causality and metaphysics.[79] It then attempts to overburden the symbolic value with remnants of causal language, essentially constructing an ersatz lexicon of sacramental mediation.

We will see Balthasar's valorization of the sign-quality of the sacraments, and the fittingness of the chosen elements themselves, but for Balthasar, the first thing that is immediately obvious about the liturgy and the sacraments is the gap between their signification and their effect. This theme recurs throughout theological history and is in no way a scholastic deformation.[80] Tertullian can here provide one example:

There is indeed nothing which so hardens men's minds as *the simplicity of God's works* [*simplicitas divinorum operum*] *as they are observed in action, compared with the magnificence promised in their effects.* So in this case too, because with such complete simplicity, without display [*sine pompa*], without any unusual equipment, and (not least) without anything to pay, a man is sent down into the water, is washed to the accompaniment of very few words, and comes up little or no cleaner than he was, his attainment to eternity is regarded as beyond belief. On the contrary, if I mistake not, the solemn ceremonies, or even the secret rites, of idolatry work up for themselves credence and prestige by pretentious magnificence and by the fees that are charged.[81]

For Tertullian, it is the *idolaters* who attempt to make their rites credible by "pretentious magnificence," but the Christian sacraments are praised for their simplicity (a reflection of God's own simplicity) and for the asymmetrical relationship between the marvels that are promised by the sacraments and the poverty of their performance. This is due, in part, to the Church's situation as *viator*, but it also confirms for Balthasar a basic law of the experience of God: "In these and all other Biblical experiences of God, the element that impels the subject forward lies, precisely, in the superabundance of their content, as compared with man's limited capacity to grasp it." This awakens in the person a longing "for the Always-More that resides in what has already been bestowed."[82] What is perceptible ("which we have heard, which we have seen with our eyes") is also constantly outstripped by what is actually bestowed in its contents and in its effects ("That which was from the beginning"), even if the former is the only means of access to the latter (1 John 1:1).

Even more than a simple inability to adequately see, Balthasar also elevates the long tradition of noting how the sacraments even give rise to deception on the part of the perceiving intellect. Guitmund of Aversa attests to this against the Berengarians: "Thus by acting in a way contrary to the sight of flesh in this so necessary a sacrament, we might learn to transcend the visible and hurry to the invisible, hold as more certain what is hidden and what the truth, which never lies, teaches, rather than what the false eye presents to us."[83] Or, the same is stated more elegantly by Aquinas, as translated by Gerard Manley Hopkins: "Godhead here in hiding, whom I do adore, / Masked by these bare shadows, shape and nothing more, / See, Lord, at thy service low lies here a heart. / Lost, all lost in wonder at the God thou art. / Seeing, touching, tasting are in thee deceived: / How says trusty hearing? that shall be believed."[84] Only hearing the Word (*auditu solo*) can lead to adoration of the hidden deity (*latens Deitas*), for all other senses (*visus, tactus, gustus*) are defective (*fallitur*). Balthasar reflects upon the *Adoro te devote*:

> the flesh of a Jewish individual, a crucified flesh and blood, shared out and made available as ordinary food, bread and wine. The "enlightening" brought about by the revelation of infinite freedom's plan, which is also the peripeteia of human destiny, does not put an end to divine latency in favor of some universal knowledge attainable without a decision on freedom's part. *God is now more profoundly latent*, and thus he makes both a greater gift of love to finite freedom and a greater challenge to it.[85]

For Balthasar, then, the sacraments do not change what is a fundamental law of the relationship between God and the world, but in fact heighten the paradoxes. Pascal is, again, the guide. Pascal, according to Balthasar, steers a middle course between a Platonic *theoria*, which abstracts from the visible manifestation in order to ascend to contemplative heights (which, again, he sees as a temptation in much of the patristic era), and Luther's *latere sub contrario*, whereby God's manifestation remains incognito in its manifestation. Pascal says, "Just as Jesus Christ remained unknown among men. . . . So, too, the Eucharist in the midst of ordinary bread."[86] Yes, Christ is hidden in the Eucharist (*latens Deitas*), but this hiddenness is not a simple negation or refusal to appear, but rather a manifestation in itself, a manifestation of the humility of God. The "law of Christian contemplation," which Balthasar learns from Pascal, is "to let itself be constantly determined by the form of evidence proper to its object. 'In your light we see light'—even if your light must assume the mode of darkness!"[87] Balthasar's "phenomenological" method, then, like all phenomenology, is one that lets the phenomenon appear without prior determination and restraint, and thus instead of covering over the hidden manifestation in the sacraments, Balthasar highlights it.

Balthasar's position, insofar as he differs from some of his contemporaries, can be seen in his retention of a gap between causality and signification. The debate can be brought into relief by focusing on the interpretation of Thomas's claim, which he says is a common belief (*communiter dicitur*) that the sacraments cause what they signify (*efficiunt quod figurant*).[88] For Thomas, of course, this was a way of uniting the seemingly disparate categories of sign and cause, and even Thomas's objectors recognize that this was a significant achievement in its own right.[89] Yet, theologians in the twentieth century began to conclude that Thomas did not go far enough with this insight because Thomas, even as he attempts to unite the two categories, still retains separation between them. According to Rahner, "The axiom that Thomas formulates in this connection, *efficiunt quod figurant*, is a fine one, but one which surely calls for considerable further thinking out."[90] The move from Thomas's position that sacraments cause *what* they signify to sacraments causing *by* signifying is not in itself problematic for Balthasar.[91] But Balthasar does resist, quite adamantly, the claim that the sacramental sign is itself, without remainder, the cause of grace: "It may be true that the separation of the forms of bread and wine is a symbolic sign, referring to Christ's sacrificial death; but it is scarcely possible to say that this sign has the power to bring about an effective *presence* of this sacrificial death."[92] It does not need to be decided here to what extent Rahner or Schillebeeckx or Chauvet collapse sign and cause, but it is clear that the adoption of many of their ideas has led to clear anthropological or psychological reductions of the mystery of the sacraments.[93] David N. Power explains: "The drawback of this new emphasis on sign was that it associated sign with cause more closely than did Thomas himself. When some writers began to appeal to the human sciences and especially to studies on rite and symbol to explain the role of the sacraments in the church, nothing seemed to be left that could not be given a humanistic or empirical explanation."[94] This led to the controversies surrounding the proposals of transsignification and transfinalization, condemned by Paul VI in *Mysterium fidei*[95] insofar as they are meant to replace, and not simply supplement, transubstantiation.[96] For Balthasar, on the other hand, no matter how closely we should view the relationship between sign and cause, we have already begun with the wrong problematic if we are asking what the visible manifestation of the rites mean on the purely anthropological level and *then* seek to find a theological connection. Balthasar takes his leave from Thomas on a number of points in sacramental theology, and is even a bit uneasy with the traditional language of causality, but, as we saw in chapter 2, he adheres closely to Thomas's position on this issue. According to Thomas, unlike pagan sacraments, the sacraments of the New Law are not outward manifestations of a prethematic faith, but are rather determined precisely *by God*.[97] Likewise, it is a mistake to too closely align *sacramentum* and *signum*, because the former is a heightening and a purifying of the latter.[98] In other words, the efficacy of the sacramental rites is not determined by the ability of the recipient to understand the natural symbolism of the elements, because it is the *Word* that gives form and symbolism to the elements, making it a sacrament (*accedit verbum ad elementum et fit sacramentum*).

All of this is to say that Balthasar, from his earliest works on the Fathers, throughout the heady days of proposals of "transfinalization," and to his most mature position throughout the *Trilogy*, was consistently worried about an emphasis on the sacramental rites that attributed too much to their sign quality or visible manifestation, which has often led to psychological or anthropological "explanations" for the sacraments. He writes in 1961: "It is here [in the divine act of constituting the sacramental sign] that the full weight of the sacrament lies and not, *as many today understand it in aestheticist fashion*, in the encounter between the sacramental symbols and the 'great archetypes of the psyche.'"[99] Balthasar's asceticism in this regard, in his self-limitation about the extent to which aesthetics can be put to theological use, is instructive. In recent decades, when sacramental theology has been turning more and more to ritual studies and linguistics for support,[100] we need to hear again Balthasar's insistence that the sacraments can *only* be properly understood when they are set within the drama of a divine simplicity that effaces itself before the world in order to initiate creation's return to its origin. Within this narrative arc, ritual studies and every social science can indeed be appropriated and made productive, but only after stipulating that Christ's form in the sacramental rites is manifested in a mode that is wholly *sui generis*. This includes, then, an understanding that the word (which is a *theological* word) transgresses to a significant extent the visibility of the rite, but also that there is an essential, *theological* reason for a lack of vision: Christ's humility. This is the role that Balthasar's use of *Gestalt* plays, especially when considering the Eucharist: it is only by being familiar, by the power of the Holy Spirit, with the form of Christ as the manifestation of God the Father that we have the capacity to see him and his saving deeds in the visible liturgy itself. The liturgy cannot be seen by any passerby, one must learn to see correctly, learn to see that a sharing of bread and wine is also a *manducatio spiritualis*. Balthasar provides a helpful metaphor for the relationship between Christ and the sacraments: "All the sacraments have their initial, visible life-form in the earthly form of Christ's mission itself. They are distilled from herbs, as it were, which we first held physically in our hands. If afterwards we are no longer able to perceive sensually in the distilled essence the herbs' original form, nevertheless we do know whence the essence is derived: indeed, from its fragrance and taste we clearly see it betray its origin."[101]

The one who knows the herb (Christ) is able to discern its presence in the distilled form (the sacraments) because of the long familiarity with its original state. Then, and only then, can we say that the rites of the Church are a manifestation of Christ and the future kingdom of God. The distinction being made is simply that between the bodily senses and the spiritual senses, which, though fundamentally related to one another,[102] must not be confused. Balthasar considers the relationship between the two to be analogous to Paul's distinction "between the fleshly and the pneumatic man."[103] For Balthasar, this is particularly true concerning the perception of the liturgy and was true of the great liturgical commentators. For instance, according to Maximus, "if a person has [the spiritual senses], he 'realizes' in an experiential way the mystical content of the liturgy, the true meaning of Jesus' gift of himself in the Eucharist—not by exaggerating the external liturgy, but through a concurrent 'divine perception' (αἴσηθσις θεῖα) that is aware of the intelligible content *in* the symbolic ceremony."[104] There is a need, then, for a "divine perception," the spiritual senses, or as will be developed later in this chapter, a "sacramental phenomenology" that is enabled to perceive the liturgy aright.[105]

Corpus Triforme: Triply Hidden

It is not only the eucharistic body of Christ that needs the "eyes of faith" to be perceived appropriately, but every form, all three forms, of Christ's body: natural, eucharistic, and ecclesial. The separation of these three forms has led to a certain mischief in Catholic theology, a fact that Balthasar learned from his mentor, Henri de Lubac.[106] Thus, although the three need to be conceptually distinguished, for Balthasar, they are all subject to the *one* form of Christ (it is *corpus*, not *corpora, triforme*). Christ's hiddenness has already been mentioned, and his body, the Church, is likewise hidden in the world. The *corpus triforme*, then, is not a simple manner of three forms of Christ's manifestation, but also three forms of his hiddenness.[107] Balthasar's Pascalian conception of hiddenness is not the same as simple invisibility but is rather a visible, manifest hiddenness, a hidden form of visibility: "We must never forget that, even in the forms that mediate him, Christ himself is and remains the appearance of the God who does not appear, and that the mediating forms, too, are likewise vehicles of the non-appearing power and efficacy of the gracious God."[108] The Church is, of course, a visible institution with all the characteristics of any other social body.[109] Still, this sociological exterior will never lead one to, and in fact may lead in the opposite direction from, the Niceno-Constantinopolitan Creed's claim that the Church is *una, sancta, catholica, et apostolica*. The innumerable divisions within Christianity, and even within Catholicism itself, make the claim to *una* almost laughable, and the same could be said for its (far too evident) lack of sanctity and catholicity.[110] That is why, according to Balthasar, the Catholic must start with "the a priori of the Church's understanding," which means that "the Church is first of all a *mysterium* (as Jesus is God's only begotten Son first of all and not as an afterthought), and as this *mysterium* she is Christ's Body and his Bride."[111]

In the previous chapters, we saw how Balthasar provides a more direct link between the sacraments and Christ, such that the sacraments are above all expressions of the life of Christ, and of the Church only secondarily. This important qualification notwithstanding, Balthasar does conceive of the sacraments and the liturgy as the manifestation (or in Rahner's terms, *Leibhaftigwerdung*) of the life of the Church. He understands this precisely in the sense of the interpenetration of the various senses of the *corpus triforme*, and, in particular, de Lubac's formulation that *l'Église fait l'Eucharistie et l'Eucharistie fait l'Église*. Not only does the Church have the commission and power to validly confect (*fait*) the Eucharist, but the Eucharist itself is the center, and, as John Paul II's *Ecclesia de Eucharistia* affirmed, it has a "causal influence" on the Church.[112] Furthermore, along with Semmelroth, Schillebeeckx, de Lubac, and the majority of Catholic ecclesiologists of the twentieth century, Balthasar thinks that it is helpful to conceive of the Church as not only producing and being produced by the sacraments, but as a sacrament in its own right.[113] More than just a sacrament, the Church is the primordial, or originary sacrament (*Ursakrament*). This could be interpreted in a variety of ways, including the idea that the Church, as the community of believers, is most properly considered a sacrament, with the particular sacraments as simple modes of ratifying and dramatizing the spirit of the community. This would be Hegel's choice, but there are religious precedents in the Anabaptists (particularly another Balthasar, Hubmaier)[114] and more contemporary, atheistic advocates, such as Slavoj Žižek. This is not what Balthasar has in mind, for the Church as *Ursakrament* does not mean that it is the unveiling of what is hidden in the particular sacraments, but that it is the most hidden form of sacramentality. The Church operates by the same logic of hiddenness as the other sacraments, and even grounds their hiddenness: "It is as if the individual sacraments were becoming concealed within the total sacrament of the Church, to operate from that concealment."[115] The movement from sacraments to Church does not grant the observer a privileged view, because the Church is itself relativized in light of the form of Christ. There is not a descending emanation from Christ to the Church to the sacraments, so that one could reverse the order and say that the sacraments manifest the life of the Church and the Church that of Christ. Rather, for Balthasar, the sacraments of the Church and the Church itself are at an equal distance from (and thus proximity to) Christ: "So what the individual sacrament mediates is not the Church but Christ's self-dedication to the Church."[116] Balthasar has thus removed another possible justification for the sacraments: they cannot even be justified on the basis of the community of the Church. To call the Church a *sacramentum* is not to put an end to the process of sacramental referral, for the Church is not the terminus of sacramental signification, but rather it serves, in the hands of Balthasar, to intensify the question of the referent even further. If the Church is not the referent, the *res sacramenti*, then the Church is itself an ecstatic reality, existing under the constant mode of self-transcendence.[117]

The question that Balthasar is pressing is this: Who is the privileged hermeneut of the *corpus triforme*? It is immediately evident in the Gospels that there are some who see Christ correctly, and others who misinterpret him and mistake him for only a partial aspect of his identity (carpenter's son) or miss him altogether (a gardener). This continues to be true for the eucharistic body of Christ (just some bread) and his ecclesial body ("they are filled with new wine"). As Balthasar notes, the world may only see the failings and institutional structure of the Church, "but this does not mean that the Church in her true nature, the holy Church, has to interpret herself in this way."[118] That is to say, the Church retains an interpretive autonomy, a right to self-understanding that claims for itself a reality that exceeds sociological or rationalistic verification. This helps us to understand Balthasar's partial approval but also major qualification about the extent to which the historical-critical method can be helpful to biblical studies, and understand his cautioning against the use of secular sciences (sociology, history, or psychology) as the primary tools for understanding the Church and the sacraments. The Church can, of course, be reduced, and there is no rational criterion by which to judge whether this reduction is justified or not. This is why the Church's liturgy calls the Eucharist a *mysterium fidei,* and why the Church is called a "bride" and a "body," both of which are relative terms understood only in relation to "groom" and "head," respectively. Especially in modernity, when the Church has been analyzed from every possible angle, the Christian is forced more than ever to have faith without the aid of the Church's social respectability and privileged status: "One cannot deny that it is more difficult today to be objectively a Christian than it was in earlier times. There is no longer any shelter. . . . The heart of the Church herself is laid bare and even pierced like that of her Lord, so that anyone who wishes to take shelter in her enters into something naked and wounded."[119] Just as the Church has lost a liturgical naïveté, no longer able to hold onto the celestial origins of the rites, so there has been a loss of presumed ecclesiological trust: "Ultimately, the Church has no walls about her but stands defenselessly open to the world."[120] These losses are, and there is no reason to deny it, a form of trauma, and there is every reason to grieve.

There are healthy and unhealthy ways of dealing with trauma, and the trauma caused by the loss of the Church's external credibility would not be dealt with productively by resorting to an invisible Church with no relationship to the visibly deformed historical Church. Those who support such an approach would likely appeal to Augustine, but it would be a gross misreading of *De civitate Dei*. For Balthasar, one must maintain the visibility of the Church, even when this visibility seems to speak of a reality more demonic than angelic. It is true that "the Johannine Church is the secret heart of the Church of Peter. The rite exists for the sake of the inner mystery; the visible sacrifice of the Church exists for the sake of the invisible sacrifice of the Cross."[121] But this does not turn the visible into a dispensable cloak: "This visibility is not merely an external, exoteric one but an essential visibility that can never be abolished," because the Church exists as "a visible, sacramental sign. She is the training of the world in redemption."[122] For Balthasar, this ecclesial visibility, which is the foundation for sacramental visibility, is a continuation of the principle of incarnation, but stands between the incarnate Christ in his state of humility and the future state of glory.[123] The question that is forced upon the Christian by various social and historical sciences (and today we should perhaps add journalistic) is whether one can *still* believe in the Church and its liturgy despite all the evidence that points to an entirely mundane, if not noxious, social organization and cultic expression. Although one could, and perhaps should, furnish evidence in favor of the Church as a remarkable exception to social laws (thus avoiding the need to appeal to *credo quia absurdum*), the radical humiliation of the Church in recent centuries, for Balthasar, points to the need for a purity of vision that is able to see the whole of reality in light of Christ:

> The object of God's dramatic struggle with human freedom over the purity of vision (through the darkness of faith) is not simply the isolated figure of Jesus but also the whole cosmos that crystallizes around him as its center: his Church, with her mysteries discernible only to a deeper gaze and her disconcerting obscurities veiling her true essence from unpracticed eyes. . . . Catholic dramatics includes the struggle to achieve a comprehensive, hence, properly "catholic" vision that leaves nothing out and is capable of reading Church and world in light of their center: Christ.[124]

Ecclesiology, then, is not an escape-hatch for difficulties found in sacramental theology. In retreating from the darkness of the sacraments, one does not find illumination in the Church, but rather the source of the enigma.

Balthasar among the Phenomenologists: *Res et Sacramentum*

In this final subsection discussing the negative limits of Balthasar's method of sacramental theology, before turning to his positive contribution, it will be helpful to see Balthasar's position as it is played out anew in a postmodern setting. This is important for two reasons: first, sacramental theologies that can be broadly labeled as "postmodern" have become enormously influential and widely accepted, especially in Anglo-American scholarship,[125] and second, a successor who carries Balthasar's banner can be readily found in the philosopher/theologian Jean-Yves Lacoste.[126] Also, as others have noted, Balthasar's theological project in general is congenial to postmodernity.[127] The extent of Balthasar's "phenomenology" has been noted, but this could only have been done in scare quotes. However, when analyzing Lacoste's extension of Balthasar's thought, phenomenology can be discussed without qualification. For in fact, in the postmodern setting of sacramental theology, the question has revolved around the extent to which phenomenology, and what type of phenomenology, can contribute to an understanding of the liturgy and the sacraments. Thus, if Lacoste is Balthasar's representative on this question (consciously or not), this must be seen as an alternative answer to the same question posed by Chauvet, whose approach has dominated contemporary (especially American) sacramental theology.[128] It is not a simple binary between Lacoste and Chauvet, but they can stand here for two opposing decisions about sacramental theology: either phenomenology as the hermeneutical key for sacramental theology (Chauvet) or sacramental theology as a limit and an expansion of phenomenology (Lacoste).

There are many serviceable summaries of Chauvet's thought, and no such summary will be attempted here. Yet, concerning our present question about the phenomenality of the sacraments, Chauvet's position can be understood by acknowledging both his polemical intention and his constructive proposal. Following Heidegger primarily, but a Heidegger read forward as interpreted by Derrida and various linguistic and cultural theorists, Chauvet believes that philosophical and theological thought must be freed from its metaphysical past (that can never be fully overcome) that imagined some underlying substance (ὑποκείμενον, *sub-stantia*) "beneath" the appearances. This is, of course, true also for eucharistic theologies, which have continuously returned to "metaphysical" language, such as causality and the substance/accident distinction, in order to discuss the presence of Christ *apart from* the phenomenality of the eucharistic species and the eucharistic liturgy in general. For Chauvet, though, we must move from substance language (*esse*) and, with Heidegger, turn to the language of presence (*ad-esse*), looking at the ways in which Christ is made present in the appearance of the rite itself. Heidegger frees himself from technological thinking, and so Chauvet follows this same path in what he views as the liberation of the sacraments from a technical, productionist view of grace. Thus, instead of quickly passing by the species of bread and wine, Chauvet wants us to see Christ as mediated *in* the bread and wine as their natural symbolic qualities are elevated and heightened. Just as Heidegger's jug, which gathers the fourfold, so "bread is never so much bread as in the gesture of thankful oblation where it gathers within itself heaven and earth, believers . . . and the giver whom they acknowledge to be God."[129] Symbol is now no longer mere ornamentation in the giving of grace, or just simply *conveniens*, but is constitutive of that gift and in fact *is* the gift. Christ is then not present in the Eucharist by being "accidentally" hidden under bread and wine, but is present precisely within the symbolic network of bread that is broken and wine that is poured out. It is bread as food and wine as drink, not inert containers, that carry supernatural grace. The fraction rite, for example, points to Christ's presence and absence, in that he comes as bread that is broken and distributed, in bread that shows Christ coming through the mode of being opened. The sacraments *are* insofar as they function within the symbolic network of the Church, as intralinguistic realities that mediate access to God and block our logocentric dreams of an unmediated, bodiless, communion with the divine. Instead, the sacraments reaffirm the law of symbolic mediation, the law that is not transgressed by Christian revelation but validated thereby.

The concept of *sign* that has been so prevalent in sacramental theology (*sacramentum = sacrum signum*), according to Chauvet, has necessitated the *sacramentum et res* distinction, such that the former points to the latter, which is a separate reality from itself. The concept of *symbol*, particularly as this is played out in Heidegger's later work, however, is able to finally abolish this harmful divide, so that Christ's presence is not a separate reality from that which points to his presence. Instead, Christ is present *symbolically*, which is not to be distinguished from him being present *really*. We can see then quite clearly how Chauvet differs from Balthasar on the question of the symbolic value of the visible rites: for Balthasar they are (at least initially) peripheral; for Chauvet they are central. Chauvet thus pursues this symbolic approach as far as he is able, often with results that illuminate the liturgical rites in unexpected and remarkably fruitful ways. Yet even Chauvet acknowledges that this symbolic, phenomenological approach has a limit: "This symbolic approach is obviously *insufficient* for expressing the significance of the Eucharistic presence."[130] However, it remains unclear what exactly Chauvet finds to be lacking, given his own criteria, in his symbolic approach.[131] Certainly, we cannot expect that an idea of Christ's *objective* and extralinguistic presence would come in to supply the lack, as Chauvet already marked this as a symptom of a noxious metaphysical impulse. Another caveat is that Chauvet's understanding of God and God's symbolic disclosure is not a simple baptism of Heidegger's reflections on being, but rather that the two forms of thought are "homologous."[132] Nevertheless, even with these two caveats, it is clear that Chauvet thinks we can understand the sacraments *within* Heidegger's world and not outside of it. Just as Thomas incorporated much of Aristotelian thought into this sacramental theology, but also changed Aristotle when necessary, so Chauvet thinks that Heidegger can today provide the method for a nonidolatrous sacramental theology that is able to validate all that has been neglected by metaphysics: symbol, language, and the body.

There are immediate difficulties with comparing Chauvet and Lacoste. We are dealing with two theologians whose debts to Heidegger are massive, yet we are not dealing with one Heidegger but two, and two different uses of these different Heideggers. Chauvet's Heidegger makes no "turn," or perhaps the turn has always-already been made, but judging simply from citations and what themes are made productive, Chauvet's Heidegger is not really the Heidegger of *Being and Time*, but the Heidegger of "Building, Dwelling, Thinking." This is a Heidegger who is *almost* indistinguishable from Wittgenstein,[133] one whose meditations on language and symbol give us an indispensable glimpse into what it means to be utterly constituted by language and culture. Being for Chauvet's Heidegger is less a *Dasein* thrown toward death and more of a Being that finds language to be its house. Lacoste, on the other hand, considers the later Heidegger's use of the *Geviert* to be a flight toward mythology and as a potential betrayal of the original insights of *Being and Time*. The Heidegger that Lacoste prefers is precisely the tragic Heidegger, and so instead of language as the house of Being, there is no house at all, for we are all homeless (*Unzuhause*). Or better, we do have a house, but this is only for the purpose of keeping us under house arrest, and although we may wish to escape these confines, may long to leave the house, we know that there is nowhere to go, that there is no other home than that which seems to be a trap for us. The logic of *in-der-Welt-sein* is the logic of existing with the status of the foreigner, but a foreigner who neither comes from elsewhere nor is going anywhere else.[134] Further, for Chauvet, Heidegger is no atheist, and although he does not provide any place for God within philosophy, he maintains a "respectful silence" before God. There are thus no antecedent reasons for disallowing Heidegger's influence on theology, for this Heidegger harbors no antipathy to Christian faith, but is a potential ally. Lacoste, on the other hand, as seen most explicitly in his *Experience and the Absolute*, allows Heidegger's prohibition against using his philosophy for theological purposes to stand. Phenomenology, therefore, deals with an atheistic world. Heidegger here is not pious and silent before God but intentionally excludes God from the world, banishes him and refuses to permit him reentrance. More specifically, as evident from how he erases the obvious eucharistic imagery from his commentary on Georg Trakl's poem "Ein Winterabend" in his essay "Die Sprache," Heidegger is either blind or hostile to the sacraments.[135]

Lacoste nevertheless finds Heidegger to be useful precisely because of his atheism, because of his willingness to describe the world as it is, or at least as it is according to phenomenology. Lacoste says, "The central but not exclusive intention of *Being and Time* is to unveil the fundamental structures of experience such as they are everywhere, always, and for everyone."[136] Whether Lacoste considers the world to be based in atheism because of an understanding of the extent of the fall or because of a Barthian streak in his thought,[137] pointing out that the fundamental structures of experience do not admit of an experience of God allows Lacoste to say that standing before God, *esse coram Deo*, or simply "liturgy," is always supererogatory and excessive of the laws of immanence. Heidegger is thus presupposed in order to be transcended. We could say, with a touch of irony, that *Being and Time* functions as Lacoste's postmodern version of the scholastic pure nature, but instead of obediential potency and a velleity for the supernatural, we have *angst* as the fundamental mood and an immanent frame with its tragic finitude and obliviousness of the infinite.[138] Instead of a homology between Heidegger's Being and the Christian God, we have, it seems, an antagonism, with the former refusing to give a fair hearing to the latter, and the latter as subverting and transforming the former. Thus, if Chauvet tried to bring the sacraments into Heidegger's world, Lacoste says that the liturgical experience in general, and the sacraments in particular, brackets being-in-the-world. That is why the fundamental mood of liturgy, for Lacoste, is boredom: boredom demonstrates that liturgical time is wasted time, that it operates by a different logic than what is existentially ubiquitous: "The liturgy makes words [we could add "symbols"] un-everyday."[139]

Lacoste does admit that the sacraments can, in fact, be analyzed in the same manner in which Heidegger understands the jug, or the bridge, or the peasant's shoes. With Chauvet, he notes the symbolic power of bread, about the "fruit of the earth and work of human hands," and how the offered bread can indeed unite the *Geviert* in Heidegger's sense. But then comes the cut: "Nothing of all this is sacramental. And neither is anything sacramental in the definition and the description of the *Thing* provided by Heidegger."[140] Whereas what Chauvet meant to show by the title of his major book, *Symbol and Sacrament*, was the unity of these two concepts, for Lacoste, the symbol and the sacrament dance to two very different rhythms.[141] A symbol, for Lacoste, is an a-theological concept: anything can be a symbol without thereby becoming a sacrament. Bread and wine may, in and of themselves, as symbols, evoke an immanent sacred, as in Heidegger's gods, but *not* a transcendent sacred of which Christ spoke when he said *hoc est enim corpus meum*. The sacrament, which is not exhausted by the categories of the "thing" or the "symbol," is, for Lacoste, a Christian concept that can be understood not by hermeneutical sophistication, but only by initiation, by baptism. As Balthasar notes, although the sacraments effect an "ontic" change, they also impart a "noetic" shift, which is why the Fathers called baptism "illumination."[142] The uninitiated will only ever see bread and wine, potent symbols, but those with the "eyes of faith" will "see," or rather "perceive," Christ's body and blood.[143] To see sacraments as things (*Dingen*, in Heidegger's sense) is to glimpse "only a fraction of what they are,"[144] and, in fact, is to miss the phenomenon of the sacrament. Unlike Chauvet who moves forward from Heidegger to Derrida, Lacoste often enough moves backward from Heidegger to Husserl. And from Husserl he learns that one needs an intuition when attending to phenomena. To see a work of art *as* a work of art is to really allow the thing to appear, and likewise to know that one stands before a sacrament, to have a sacramental intuition, or a sacramental intentionality, is to see it as it truly is. This means that one must, at least implicitly, operate with the classical distinction between the *res sacramenti* and the *sacramentum tantum*. According to Lacoste, the *sacramentum*, the pure sign quality of the sacrament, is not to be in any way negated or denied, but we must note that it remains within the world, that is, Heidegger's world, while the *res*, which is not a *Ding*, is "totally outside of the world."[145] And though there is then a necessary eschatological deferment regarding a direct experience of the *res*, when Christians adore the Eucharist they "open up a tear in the flesh of the world."[146] For Lacoste, sacraments are precisely those instances where the world that can be subject to phenomenological analysis shows its own limits, where that horizon begins to appear less like an open expanse and more like a wall, a wall that begins to crack.

According to Lacoste, the work of sacramental theology is a dangerous one, with many false paths and temptations, and what is most frightening is that one of these temptations comes from what is really a positive feature of the sacraments: their symbolic value. This is, in fact, what is most obvious about them. It is data available as much to the sociologist or anthropologist as it is to the theologian: "No visible difference seems assuredly to be able to separate the solemnity of a pagan libation and that of a eucharistic memorial."[147] What makes sacramental theology a difficult task is that it is concerned principally with the nonobvious, with taking a step beyond that which gives itself immediately for contemplation. Those who have refused to take this step, those who seem to have been overwhelmed by appearance and sign, such as Berengar of Tours,[148] have thus essentially failed in their tasks.[149] Lacoste's warning, which is a logical extension of Balthasar's own position, is the following:

> To be satisfied by the sacrament [he means *sacramentum*] independently of its "thing" [he means *res*, not *Ding*], consequently, will always be possible: the sacramental symbols are pregnant, all are able

to be integrated into our experience of ourselves and our world, all can receive a religious signification, and we will always be able to reinterpret theology in anthropological terms. *It is dangerous to enter into the sacramental order—we always run the risk, precisely, of not actually entering into it.*[150]

The extent to which this warning applies to Chauvet or his interpreters is irrelevant here, but we should note that this is the same warning, *mutatis mutandis*, that Lanfranc of Canterbury and Guitmund of Aversa made to Berengar,[151] that Thomas made to Bernard of Clairvaux,[152] that the Council of Trent made against some of the Reformers,[153] and that Paul VI made against the advocates of transsignification.[154] No amount of weight given to the sign quality, for example elevating it to the status of symbol, or tying together the concept of sign and being, is sufficient to capture the entirety of what a sacrament is. In the words of Thomas, the problem with these approaches is that they do not transcend the logic of the sign—*non transcendit rationem signi*—and thus place a rational limit, no matter how sophisticated, on Christ's eucharistic presence. For Lacoste, and certainly for Balthasar, the sacraments operate always under the mode of excess. This requires that ascetic self-limitation we have discussed above: for Balthasar, recognizing the limits of aesthetic analyses, and for Lacoste, those of phenomenology. There is then a marginalization and a limit that must be the start of sacramental theology, but that is not where it needs to end.

A SACRAMENTAL PHENOMENOLOGY

Balthasar has placed the sacraments in a marginal location in his aesthetics. Then, in a sudden reversal of fortune, they are changed from playing a minor supporting role to being a lead character: "The sacraments are an essential part of ecclesial aesthetics."[155] How can Balthasar, in the same work (*GL* I), claim that sacraments are both marginal and essential to the project of theological aesthetics? For Balthasar, these are not two contradictory adjectives, nor is one in play in one way and the other in another way, but rather, for Balthasar, marginality and centrality must be considered together. Their marginalization is precisely what makes them central. Perhaps even more than central, we can say that sacraments are *the* center of a theological aesthetics, precisely because they illustrate the same law of manifestation and hiddenness that is evident in the Incarnation. As we move from the previous section and its various prohibitions, there will be a shift in language, from the primarily negative concept of hiddenness to the positive notion of excess.

It would indeed be an ironic accusation, but one could say that Balthasar's initial lack of attention to the liturgical rites and the sign-quality of the sacraments indicates that he is still indebted to the scholastic bifurcation between sign and cause that was supposedly foreign to the patristic period and to the Eastern Church. De Lubac traced the growing distance between liturgical symbolism and the "reality" of the Eucharist in his *Corpus Mysticum*, a book so influential that its basic thesis has become a truism. There is no doubt that Balthasar agrees with at least the basic thrust of de Lubac's argument, but de Lubac is successful in pointing out the problem, not in proposing a solution. For sacramental theology after de Lubac, if one is to take his considerations to heart, it seems that there are a variety of options available. One option, which has gained considerable traction among the Eastern Orthodox, is to return to the patristic vision of "symbol," which operates with a much richer, fuller sense than the scholastic notion of sign.[156] Concomitant with this decision is the need to return to the *Weltanschauung* of the Fathers, and their understanding of the created order such that "symbol" would be a participation in the archetype of that which it symbolizes.[157] From our previous glance at Balthasar's interpretation of the Fathers, it is clear that he would immediately resist any theology of "return," despite his commitment to *ressourcement*.[158] To repeat, the danger in the Fathers is that "symbol" can end up either as equally disjunctive as a *signum*, or it can tend to collapse the symbol into that which is symbolized. The baroque, with its turn to "representation," is for Balthasar a crystallization of this attempt at a return to a Greek, sometimes Platonic and sometimes patristic, conception of the symbol. For Balthasar, the fact of Luther and modernity means that the patristic or Platonic vision is simply no longer a possibility.[159] Another option, more popular among Catholic and Protestant theologians, is to propose new, contemporary understandings of "symbol" that can more faithfully render the patristic vision, while also taking responsibility for developments in thought and using insights from contemporary philosophies. Chauvet's concept of symbol borrowed largely from Heidegger has already been surveyed, but David Power's use of Ricoeur (at least in *Unsearchable Riches*) and Rahner's proposal of a *Realsymbolik* should also be mentioned as examples.[160] Balthasar belongs to this second group because of his borrowing of the concept of *Gestalt* from Goethe, but more so than these others, Balthasar attempts to distance his use of the concept from its original source.[161] Thus, although *Gestalt* is from Goethe, Balthasar's use of it is intended not to point to the superiority of one philosophical position over another (it is certainly this also), but rather to the primacy of the revealed phenomenon itself.

In sum, what Balthasar hopes to accomplish with his concept of *Gestalt*, as it is applied to the sacraments, is to more closely unify the *sacramentum et res*, such that it would be considered as *one* reality, not two. It is thus directly an answer to de Lubac's challenge. Nevertheless, Balthasar does not propose that the *sacramentum/res* distinction should be abolished altogether, for it points to an absolutely necessary aspect of the sacraments, even if it has led to a deficient appreciation of the ecclesial context of the sacrament. What the distinction points to is that all of God's revelation, indeed all of creaturely being, is fundamentally constituted by excess. Even in a form of worldly beauty "we must see something invisible," because the reality that gives itself outstrips one's ability for conceptual mastery. There is always something "more" to beauty: "You are never finished with any being, be it the tiniest gnat or the most inconspicuous stone. It has a secret [*geheime*] opening, through which never-failing replenishments of sense and significance ceaselessly flow to it from eternity."[162] Turning from worldly beauty to divine glory, the same law is magnified. The law applies to such an extent that for Balthasar revelation and concealment grow together in exact proportion, so that "in Jesus Christ, God's revelation in concealment reaches perfection."[163] In Christ, God is not partially manifest and partially concealed (not part *sacramentum* and part *res*) but "revealed in concealment," such that the hiddenness of the cross is the chosen speech of God to fully reveal his inner life.[164] The *Gestalt* of Christ, and by extension the *Gestalt* of the Church and its liturgy (and it has no form but Christ's), is to be perceived not by moving from the sign to the referent, but by remaining with the superabundant form, even in its apparent poverty and hidden mode of expression. The *sacramentum*, then, as the mode of Christ's concealment, is not a mere sign of a distant reality, but it does remain in the order of signs. Catherine Pickstock expresses a position consonant with that of Balthasar: the Eucharist "is not wholly other from the sign, although it cannot be exhausted by the sign."[165] *Gestalt* is a placeholder for excess, for the inexhaustibility of God's self-manifestation, such that no philosophical system can adequately place revelation into a predetermined category, and such that no one person, nor even the totality of persons, could claim to be finished with any aspect of revelation.[166] There is an infinity of approaches to the same polysemic reality.[167] But this is not an excess that moves away from the *Gestalt*, such that one could arrive at the same destination by another, certainly quicker, route, but is instead an appeal to the excessiveness of the *Gestalt* itself. The temptation to move quickly from sign to reality is a difficult one to avoid, and can be found in various two-tiered ecclesiologies (pneumatics vs. regular Christians who cling to visibility), and also in more transcendental approaches that cannot adequately find a manner of uniting prethematic faith with the need for external expression.[168]

Because Christ's self-manifestation is one of hiddenness, to see this form correctly one needs to have a developed capacity for vision. This can be formulated in a variety of ways, several of which have already been mentioned. The most generic mode of describing this capacity would be the supernatural virtue of faith, but this can also be made more specific by referring to the spiritual senses: "The spiritual man judges all things."[169] These senses are pneumatic in the sense in which Christ's resurrected body is pneumatic, and in fact must follow the same pattern of dying and rising: "For our senses . . . must die with Christ and descend to the underworld in order then to rise unto the Father in an unspeakable manner which is both sensory and suprasensory."[170] We could also speak with Lacoste of a sacramental intuition, or a sacramental intention, such that one would believe, in advance, that one was looking at a sacrament. Or one could turn to Cardinal Newman and his "sacramental principle," whereby visible nature is seen as a parable of a greater, invisible reality, which is then the epistemic *sine qua non* for there being particular, ecclesial sacraments.[171] There are differences in intention and in method for each of these approaches, but they each in their own way point to the same principle of presuming excess rather than exhaustion. For Balthasar, as for Newman, this presumption would apply to all levels of creaturely being ("the tiniest gnat"), especially the human person, and is likewise indispensable when assessing the sacraments. Whatever this capacity for vision is called, and it takes on a variety of expressions in Balthasar's writing, at its most basic it is Paul's prayer that the Ephesians have "the eyes of your heart enlightened" (Eph. 1:18). Balthasar connects this verse with Rousselot's "eyes of faith," and interprets it as "a synthesizing power to penetrate the phenomena, a power that derives from God and is capable of interpreting phenomena so that they disclose what God wishes to reveal of his own depths in them . . . it is not possible to look on the form of revelation and to decipher it in a position of intellectual neutrality."[172]

Doxological Theology: Theology and Prayer

Presuming excess is thus methodologically necessary, but it is void of specific content. One must know *how* each object is excessive, and in the case of the sacraments, how Christ is present under the appearance of bread and wine. This brings us to a direct consideration of whether, and the extent to which, Balthasar could be considered a liturgical theologian. Initially, it would seem to be a claim that is widely off the mark. In addition to his initial marginalization of the sacraments and the liturgy, his claim that one needs a theological a priori to understand the liturgy suggests that he is no liturgical theologian if this is defined as one who receives the primary data of theology directly from the rites themselves.[173] This is indeed how Alexander Schmemann, at least on one occasion, defines it: "Liturgical theology is therefore an independent theological discipline, with its own special subject—the liturgical tradition of the Church, and requiring its own corresponding and special method, distinct from the methods of other theological disciplines."[174] Balthasar does indeed cite liturgical texts at key places in his theology, but this cannot be taken to be anything more than his desire to draw upon a wide range of sources for his theology. Liturgical texts do not feature more prominently or carry more authoritative weight for Balthasar than scripture, the saints, the Fathers, the mystics, or even poets. If, then, a case is going to be made, it cannot be made along the lines of his supposed indebtedness to the rites of the Church as a primary source for his theological speculation. Nevertheless, there is every reason to consider Balthasar's theology as a form of liturgical theology when that term is understood as a reflection of its *Grundaxiom*: *legem credendi lex statuat supplicandi*, "the law of prayer establishes the law of faith."[175] This axiom expresses well Balthasar's own intentions regarding the nature and task of theology, which is why Balthasar is so well known for his proposal of a "kneeling theology," a theology that is not detached speculation, but rather an act of adoration.[176] And this form of theology, he says, "is most intimately bound up with the liturgy."[177] For Balthasar, the *lex supplicandi/orandi* is not just the liturgy as understood in the narrow sense of the Church's cultic rites, though this is a privileged source, but rather prayer understood in its fullest sense. Balthasar's entire theology can be understood as a liturgical or doxological theology, in that its purpose is to reflect the attitude of the Church at prayer and to assist the Church in its adoration of God.

The *lex orandi* axiom must be interpreted correctly, because it has been the cause of not a little theological confusion. First of all, to call the "law of prayer" the "law of belief" "does not mean that theology in its individual details could be lifted out of the formulations of the liturgy."[178] This would be to turn the *statuat* into an *est*, and would result in a strange form of liturgical positivism whereby the Church's faith is nothing more than its ritual expression. A far more difficult issue that must be sorted out is disassociating the axiom from modernism. It should not be forgotten, even though it is hardly ever remembered, that one of the first explicit proponents of a *lex orandi/lex credendi* theology was the modernist George Tyrrell.[179] Balthasar shares the modernists's desire to give greater emphasis to spirituality and the interior life of individual Christians, but he thinks that they err in doing this to the detriment of the objective, external aspect of the Church, with its doctrines and laws. According to Balthasar, "For modernism, dogmas are but crystallized forms of the existential faith-relationship to God . . . valid as long as they foster the existential reality, but harmful once the life has gone out of them and they have stiffened into dead formulae."[180] For Tyrrell, the relationship between the *lex credendi* and the *lex orandi* is the total subordination of the former to the latter, with the latter defined as the subjective impulses of prayer and devotion: "It is timely to insist on the general subordination of Theology to Devotion, and to show that the Creed is ultimately a creation and an instrument of the Church's spiritual life."[181] This also maps onto the *sacramentum/res* distinction, by denigrating the type (*sacramentum*, doctrines, objectivity) in favor of the archetype (*res*, subjective union with God): "In virtue of our twofold nature we live in two worlds—one bodily, the other spiritual; one the shadow and the sacrament; the other, the substance and the signified reality."[182] Balthasar wants to complicate this too tidy division, by showing the necessary interpenetration of the two "laws" and the objective dimension of prayer and liturgy. For Balthasar, we do not live in two worlds, but one. Prayer is not, for Balthasar, a simple spontaneous impulse of the believing spirit toward that indeterminate Infinity we happen to call "God," an inner principle that cannot be captured by doctrinal specificity that is its outer expression. Rather, prayer, if it is to be Christian, is "doctrinal" from the outset. Or, as Guardini expresses it, "The prayers of the liturgy are entirely governed by and interwoven with dogma."[183] Although this is true of the objective form of liturgical prayer, the liturgy does in fact especially clarify and direct the ambiguities of subjective prayer.[184] Prayer is doctrinal in that it does not address God as *mysterium tremendum et fascinans*, but as the God who is known as Father, Son, and Holy Spirit, as the God who is known to be self-gift by the Incarnation in the historically particular life of Christ.[185] Balthasar insists on the unity of theology and sanctity for the sake of theology, but this is equally for the sake of spirituality. The life of the Christian must be a "mirror" of the divine life, and thus "Christian *praxis* or spirituality would have to mirror the whole Christian theory or dogmatics."[186] Prayer is then "not only a relation between man and God," but also a relationship *between* the divine persons, to which the Church is called to participate. The Church comes to share the space of the Holy Spirit, and can thus "pray within the Trinity."[187] The dramatic element of prayer will be considered shortly, but the key here is that prayer, private or liturgical, is oriented toward a God who is doctrinally specified rather than left as an impersonal deity on whom one feels dependent.

Balthasar's claim that we "pray within the Trinity" can only be understood when we see that personal prayer and corporate, liturgical prayer have a theologically more expansive definition than what Tyrrell meant by the *lex orandi* or what sociologists mean when they speak of cultic activity. The liturgy for Balthasar is not first of all a set of rites, secondarily infused with theological significance, but from the outset can only be understood as part of the divine-human drama. The *lex orandi* truly does support the *lex credendi*, then, but no specific formula can be given as to their interrelation. As he says of Maximus, "a genuine polarity remains in force, by which the cult of the sacraments and that of theological knowledge only come to their fullness through each other."[188] This "polarity" between the liturgy and theological expression is one of dynamic movement, with the liturgy representing and performing the truths of the Creed, and doctrine giving precision and clarity to the enacted truths of the liturgy. No doctrine, according to Balthasar, is irrelevant to the life of the believer, and no spiritual insight is devoid of doctrinal import: "From the standpoint of revelation, there is simply no real truth which does not have to be incarnated in an act or in some action."[189] The liturgy in particular, which is the Church's glorification of God, is thus a response to the prior action of God, but these two elements, God's action and the Church's response, cannot be entirely separated. Liturgy is the response to theology, understood as God's word of revelation: "*Liturgy* grows directly out of the innermost substance of scriptural revelation, in so far as God's demonstration of his glory is always necessarily answered by the glorification (doxology) of God."[190]

Balthasar's doxological theology has several implications. First, liturgy is always-already theological. Second, theology is to be an act of adoration, and is thus also a "liturgical" exercise. Third, liturgy and theology interpenetrate in this way because they share the same object, and are functions of the same ecclesial reality. The Church at prayer, for Balthasar, is the Church in its ideal state, in which all that it believes theologically is ratified and performed: "For when she prays, the Church is entirely what she ought to be and, through the infusion of the Holy Spirit from her Head, also is at every moment: the body, the glory of the man, the bride without spot, purified in the bath of water. How could it be possible for her, therefore, to strike the wrong note when she prays?"[191] The fact is, certainly, that the Church often *does* strike the wrong note at prayer, but this is only when it has already betrayed something essential of its own nature, a nature typified in the person of Mary. The Church *as* prayer can only be fully understood in the light of its ideal member, Mary, and its future, eschatological state (to be explored in chapter 4). At issue here is the fact that theology and prayer, and we could add all of the charisms in the Church, from works of mercy to the mystics to the hierarchical structure, are all part of the same body, and are thus centered around the same object, Christ. It is not just that what the mystic says "poetically" is roughly equivalent to what the systematic theologian says with precision. These various sources are not united by being interchangeable with one another, but rather by having the same object of reflection, which admits of an infinitely plurivocal attestation: "Whatever truth is, it is judged, aligned and instituted from this center [Christ]."[192] Liturgy and theology, because they have the same object, must (maximally) be mutually reinforcing, and (minimally) be noncontradictory.[193] For example, this alignment between liturgy and theology is essential to Balthasar's argument in *Dare We Hope*, in which he notes that whereas the liturgy frequently directs the Church to pray for the "salvation of all," the standard theological position would prohibit the hope for universal salvation. This disjunction creates an opening whereby this *theologoumenon* can be considered again, in light of all the evidence, including the Church's liturgy and the prayers of the saints.[194] Because Christ is the definitive center of the Church's life, there is then a total relativizing of every particular aspect of its life in light of the whole. One need not weigh the relative value of each part of the Church's self-expression, for all have their value in respect to the common center. Liturgy is then not made redundant by the superior clarity of theological language, nor is theology rendered otiose by the liturgy's more direct, existentially more relevant and explicit mode of glorifying God. Again, one does not need to specify the exact, scientific relationship between liturgy and theology (as if we could specify an appropriate "exchange rate"), for it is an oscillating movement that has its center not inherent to the relationship of the two terms, but in its unmoved center around which each revolves, Christ.[195]

The Saint as Liturgist

There is thus a reciprocal relationship between theology and prayer/liturgy for Balthasar, such that one would be incomprehensible without the other, and without their common center. Yet, the theology/prayer dyad is by itself unbalanced and risks becoming unhinged, and thus must be turned into a triad. The tension between the *lex orandi* and *lex credendi* must be supplemented and balanced by a third category, as several other theologians have noted. For example, Chauvet proposes the three elements of scripture, sacrament, and ethics as the structure of Christian identity, and David Fagerberg has theology, liturgy, and asceticism as the three legs of his stool.[196] Ratzinger also notes a triad that is as old as the Mosaic covenant: worship, law (the Mosaic law, or revelation in general), and ethics.[197] For Balthasar, the triptych is theology, prayer, and holiness. Although the selection of words in each case is not a trivial matter, but in fact points to important theological decisions, all agree that the intellectual formulations of the faith (scripture/theology/law) must be corporately enacted by the Church (sacrament/liturgy/prayer), but also appropriated and lived by concrete individuals (ethics/asceticism/holiness). In the words of Fagerberg, *"Liturgy* without asceticism and theology is a species of ritual studies; *asceticism* without liturgy and theology is athletic or philosophical training; *theology* without liturgy and asceticism is an academic discipline in higher education."[198] One can also map, when transferred to a more abstract level of speculation, the transcendentals (truth, beauty, goodness) onto these three elements. For Balthasar, theological truth that is believed (theo-*logic*), God's salvific acts that make us holy (theo-*drama*), and the splendor of God that must be met with praise and adoration (the *Glory* of the Lord) all exist concomitantly. Thus liturgy, as a response to God's glory, is structurally implicated with the prior actions of God, and so liturgy is *not* exclusively (or even primarily) an aesthetic category, but a dramatic one.[199] And if it is dramatic, then we must know who the actors are.

For Balthasar, one corner of this methodological triangle, holiness, plays the privileged role of being methodologically regulative for the other two. This is because holiness participates in a privileged way in the center, in Christ, in such a way that the saint has an eye for how the various peripheries fit proportionally around the center. This returns us to the question of a sacramental phenomenology, but also adds a new element previously missing. Beyond the minimum epistemic requirement of a sacramental intuition, or a theological a priori in order to correctly judge sacramental phenomena, in Balthasar's schemata, it is holiness that functions as the instrument that is properly attuned to measure the appearance of Christ in the Eucharist.[200] For just as a healthy person is a more fit judge of flavor than the infirm, so the saint is a more fit judge of revelation than the sinner.[201] This is both because the saints have a heightened sense of perception, like a seismograph, but also because they are the main actors in the drama. The "eyes of faith," then, admit of a minimalist and a maximalist reading, of which Balthasar chooses the latter.

Minimally, the eyes of faith can be understood as an assent to "all that the holy Catholic Church teaches, believes and proclaims to be revealed by God," or at a medium level of intensity it would mean what Paul says to the Philippians, "Have this mind among yourselves, which was in Christ Jesus," and maximally it is allowing Paul to finish his sentence, "who, though he was in the form of God, did not count equality. . . ."[202] Balthasar refuses to allow the "spiritual senses," or the eyes of faith, to be abstracted from Christian attunement to the pattern of the crucified, eucharistically self-giving Christ. In his mind, these grow in proportion to one another. Those who are "expropriated," who have cleared a space within themselves in order to be determined not by themselves, but by the will of God, are truly capable of "seeing the form."[203] This is why, for Balthasar, the liturgist must be the saint, the one who understands the liturgy, not necessarily (and most likely not at all) in its textual history or ritual structure, but in its true purpose and dramatic intent. In other words, not just the material and efficient causes, but the formal and the final. The saint will then be the one to tell us what is truly occurring during the liturgy, not the uninitiated. Like must measure like, and the saint and the liturgy are alike in that they share the same "style," that of holiness.[204]

It is necessary to ask, as canon law does, about the bare minimum required for liceity and validity in the sacraments, or about the objective efficacy of the sacraments despite a defective intention, but this is not yet theologically productive, no matter how pastorally and canonically necessary these clarifications may be. According to Balthasar, in order to arrive at the theologically rich aspect of the liturgy and the sacraments, one should ask not about these limit cases, but about the proper and intended use, which is exemplified by the saints: "Much would appear in a very different light were we to apply our reflections to the archetypal function of the saints rather than to the figure presented by the average sinner, for example in the understanding of what a sacrament is and of what its reception means. What does it mean for a saint, when he communicates? He should know, and be able to teach us."[205]

How does the saint live the liturgical year? How does the saint approach confession? What does the marriage of two true lovers tell us about the sacrament of matrimony? These are the questions that Balthasar is interested in, not in the questions that are typically asked about the limit cases of sacramental efficacy; for example, is there an infusion of grace when there is an *obex* (obstacle)?, what about a communicant who is *fictus* (insincere)? As an example of how this shift in perspective affects Balthasar's theology, one could look at Adrienne von Speyr's reflections on the Mass and confession,[206] which find their way into Balthasar's own theology quite conspicuously. Further, if one wants to understand the liturgical year, with its various feasts and seasons, one need look no further than St. Francis: "The *hodie* of the liturgy on the great feast was the *hodie* of his life."[207] Gleaning an interpretation of the liturgy from the saints *is* not to arrive at one, clearly defined interpretation of the liturgical rites, which is one way of reading patristic mystagogy and medieval allegory, but rather points to an infinite plurality of possible contemplative insights into the meaning of Christian cult. Not that just any interpretation is allowed, for some will be positively excluded, but one cannot decide in advance what may emerge from liturgical contemplation.[208]

Even this is stopping too soon. The saint, for Balthasar, does not merely understand the essence of the liturgy, thus transmitting this perspective to the rest of the Church, but at an even more basic level, the saint is the interpretation of the liturgy, the liturgy-made-parable. To recall the "existential sacramental theology" we discussed in chapter 2, if one wants to understand the nature of the Eucharist, not necessarily in order to answer the *how* of transubstantiation, but to understand it in light of the *ordo salutis*, one should look at Ignatius of Antioch, or Charles de Foucault, or even at one of the characters in a novel by Bernanos. That is to say, what the liturgy performs through types and symbols, by way of figuration and prolepsis, the saints perform through their concrete acts of witness. Typically, for Balthasar, this means a life lived in imitation of the hiddenness of the liturgy, the concealment of Christ in the Eucharist. This does not mean that the saint captures or exhausts all that is theologically true, which would render theology redundant.[209] Nor does this mean that the saint, as a lived interpretation of the liturgy, does not also need to be interpreted. What Balthasar is suggesting is that the intended effects of the liturgy and the sacraments, the "transubstantiation" of the communicant, shed light retrospectively on the liturgy itself. We can catch a glimpse of what baptism truly is when we hear of a martyr who quite literally is "united with Christ in a death like his," which shows us the profundity of what was meant at the end of the blessing of the baptismal waters: "May all who are buried with Christ in the death of baptism rise also with him to newness of life."[210] Ratzinger makes the same point: "The baptized man himself becomes a spring. When we think of the great saints of history, from whom streams of faith, hope, and love really came forth, we can understand these words and thus understand something of the dynamism of Baptism, of the promise and vocation it contains."[211] To speak in dramatic categories, one should consider a well-acted performance of *Hamlet* to be a more authentic rendition than a poorly produced version with unconvincing actors. Likewise, the saint is the best "actor" of the liturgical drama, and it is against his or her performance that the rites should be measured, not the unrehearsed participant who, even if remembering most of the lines, does not know how to speak them with conviction.

The Dramatic Setting

To fill out Balthasar's sacramental phenomenology, and as already implied by the dramatic enactment of the liturgy in the lives of the saints, it is necessary to move from aesthetics to dramatics.[212] This is the case for several reasons: first, the sacraments are immediately misunderstood when they are considered as static objects subject to perception rather than as events; second, for Balthasar, the "excess" of the sacraments is a dramatic excess, such that the drama of the sacrament is in excess of its aesthetic appearance; third, in accordance with the principle of the saint as the primary liturgist, the liturgical experience of the saint is a dramatic encounter, more akin to Jacob wrestling with the angel than the observation of a work of art; fourth, the categories of aesthetics and dramatics are permeable, such that Balthasar admits in his volumes of *Glory* that "the 'theological drama' has already begun," because "God's revelation is not an object to be looked at: it is his action in and upon the world."[213] Even if the liturgy must be portrayed in dramatic categories, some precautionary measures must first be taken. Balthasar is hesitant about patristic mystagogy in which the rites of the liturgy themselves become allegories for higher, spiritual realities. This was, again, because it tends to make the drama of the liturgy more representational than operative. In other words, the drama being played out is illustrative of either Christ's historical life or of the mystical ascent to God, rather than the concrete drama that is occurring *in* the liturgy, not just *through* it, between God and the Church.

For Balthasar, the Mass, in its essence, is not a play. The opening volume of *Theodrama* provides a useful summary of how he views the distinction, yet relation, between liturgy and drama, which applies directly to his interpretation of the Fathers:

> The mystery of God's stepping into the world had to be clearly distinguished from everything mythological. Only at a later stage of reflection, if at all, could this mystery by understood—primarily in its cultic side—as the true drama. . . . This celebration, for the Christian, is much more "serious" than any Greek initiation into truth, since here the death of Christ for me and for all men is realized and 'proclaimed' through sacramental participation (1 Cor. 11). . . . *What liturgy brings forth is both more and less than itself.*[214]

The liturgy is "both more and less than itself" in that it is representational, demonstrating its truth through sensible media, but not exclusively representational: merely viewing the liturgy with one's eyes is not the same thing as entering into the depths of its symbolism; personal appropriation is necessary. At issue is the mode in which one can say that the liturgy and the sacraments are representative. For Balthasar, they are representative of the truths they signify (*sacramenta causant quod figurant*) in the sense that they do truly make present and available the saving actions of Christ, but only partially because the visible aspect of the liturgy is not an eidetic representation of what it signifies.

As a matter of historical fact, however, the liturgy and drama have been closely connected, and with good theological reason: "In her actions (*drāma*, that is, 'doings,' from the Greek *drāō*), the Church is always related, at least indirectly, to the Paschal drama. As a result, the celebration of the Eucharist has often been described as a dramatic action."[215] He provides the example of medieval allegories, but the mystagogical catecheses of Germanus and Maximus should also be mentioned, in addition to the "theatrical" aspects of Corpus Christi processions and the liturgical dramas, the *autos sacramentales* of the baroque era, particularly those of Calderón de la Barca.[216] We could also add the operatic masses of Mozart or Bach, which magnified the naturally dramatic aspect of the liturgy.[217] None of this is what Balthasar has in mind with regard to the liturgical drama, but they are important analogues. The primary drama, as we saw in chapters 1 and 2, is the Trinitarian life that communicates itself in the creaturely sphere. As he makes explicit in *TD* I, Balthasar's various uses of dramatic categories "remain at the level of image and metaphor," and thus there is a "greater dissimilarity" between the world drama and God's action, but there is also an important similarity that justifies the use of these categories.[218] There is thus an undeniable and necessary dramatic element to the Church's liturgy when considered at the purely immanent level: priest and laity play their roles, the altar or the church building as a whole functions as a sort of stage, and the author and director of the play is the universal Church that establishes the rites. All of this has some truth, in an analogous sense, and an analysis of the liturgy as drama along these lines would bear a certain amount of fruit.[219] For Balthasar, though, this purely immanent, horizontal drama must be understood as intersected by the primary, vertical drama. To do so requires shifting our understanding of the drama, which necessarily means a shift from the sociologically verifiable aspect of ritual to the claims of theology, based as they are on revelation. Certainly, the Eucharist could be verified, legitimized, through some other means, psychological or sociological, but for Balthasar, the Eucharist is, *per definitionem*, an "unverifiable mystery."[220]

When the horizontal drama is illuminated by being crossed by the vertical, new actors appear on the stage. These actors, however, do not appear in addition to the actors discernible in the horizontal drama: "The triune God does not appear onstage alongside other characters but in them."[221] Especially at the dramatic climax, the eucharistic prayer, Christ shifts from being addressed in the third person to speaking in the first person. But even more than just at this instance where Christ most evidently plays a role, from the very outset the liturgy is marked as an intra-Trinitarian event (*in nomine Patris* . . .). As we discussed in chapter 1, the Eucharist, and this can be expanded to include the liturgy and all of the sacraments, is the meeting of the closed, intra-Trinitarian circuit and the narrower circuit of creaturely being, such that the latter is caught up and included in the former, without losing its own integrity and freedom. For Balthasar, the Trinitarian shape of the liturgy distinguishes the Church's cult from all other religious cults, and it is only within this Trinitarian circuit that it is understood. "It is solely in view of the entire triune God that the worshipping community is gathered together to celebrate God's generosity and liberality."[222] The Church's Eucharist is the entry point into Christ's everlasting *eucharistia* to the Father, into the particularity of his mission, which becomes universally applicable.[223] The liturgy is therefore "re-presentative," in the sense of "making present again," and not as "presenting" again in a quasi-visual or illustrative sense.[224] The two dramas thus meet: the horizontal drama of a religious cult making an offering and the self-offering of Christ to the Father on behalf of the world, with the latter made present in the former.

We can now see, finally, the place of the seemingly mythological aspect of the liturgy for Balthasar. The liturgy is given in a form that is both entirely objective and also clearly the result of a definite and particular decision, which thus demands a sacrifice of previous subjective expectations: "In the sacraments, the Christ-form itself in turn appears before us and impresses its shape upon us in a valid form which is free of all subjective ambiguities."[225] The liturgical form is then the meeting of finite and infinite freedoms, which does not result in the obliteration of finite freedom, but in its expansion.[226] This is not to say that the form of the liturgy and the chosen matter of the sacraments are entirely arbitrary, even if they clearly come from a decision and not from an intracreaturely need for self-expression. For instance, in chapter 1 we saw how the bread, with its inertness and edibility, and the wine with its ability to be poured out and drained, are particularly suited to illustrate Christ's eucharistic humility and his desire to give himself over, without reserve, into the hands of sinners. These, or any other, contemplative insights into the fittingness of the chosen elements or the shape of the liturgy are not to be given exclusive rights of interpretation but rather seen as one of many possible entry points into the same inexhaustible mystery, which is given in an entirely objective, positively willed, form.

This is to say, even though Balthasar insists that the horizontal drama of the liturgy must be seen as crossed by the vertical, this is actually in the service of preserving the importance of the horizontal, not in order to render it illusory. The Church's liturgy redeems and preserves the positivity of pagan cult, and in the post-Enlightenment West, it is the only institution that preserves pagan dignity. The temptation, within religions themselves, toward spiritualization is a strong one, and results in viewing the external cult "as embarrassing and unreligious": "The Christian cult, however, is based not on this (demythologising) spiritualisation, but on a wholly different kind of spiritualisation . . . which nonetheless salvages the bodily and corporeal element in the cult of highly developed cultures and ensures its continued existence in a world that is ever more desacralised, disembodied and technicised. What is at stake is always the Incarnation."[227]

The combination of many religions' own native tendencies toward spiritualization and the lingering Enlightenment critique of all cult and prayer as "superstition"[228] results in religious cult being, at best, rendered metaphorical (and thus for "the weak") or, at worst, totally prohibited. Instead, for Balthasar, the vertical drama of the forgiveness of sins occurs *in* the horizontal drama of the sacrament of confession, and the soul's union with Christ is enacted *in* the visible cult of the Mass.[229] Balthasar's understanding of the liturgy stabilizes the place of religious cult by neither absolutizing it, and thus sliding into pure *mythos*, nor spiritualizing it, thus sacrificing *mythos* in favor of *logos*. The mythic, the cultic, is thus saved because it is essential to a sane, nontechnocratic, human culture, and becomes the site of the vertical meeting of the finite with the infinite.[230] To say that the Eucharist is "the primal drama in the world"[231] is to admit of two senses of the dramatic, which stand in an analogous relation to one another. First, it is the primal drama in that it fulfills the intramundane, cultural need for communal worship (again, not originating by any necessity), and, second, it is the primal drama that comes, as it were, from *outside* the world, from the very life of God made present *hic et nunc*. The basic structure of the liturgy illustrates this cooperation between these two senses, in that some elements come clearly from a dominical decision (e.g., the words of consecration, the elements of bread and wine) and some are added and freely chosen by the ecclesial community itself. The Church "remains aware that she is giving structure to her own work."[232] The liturgy is thus the site of synergy between the head and the members of the *totus Christus*, a synergy that is a continuation of the interpenetration without confusion of the two natures and wills of Christ.

CONCLUSION: LITURGICAL BEAUTY

Even after the journey through Balthasar's proscriptions against aestheticizing the liturgy and his emphasis on the hiddenness of Christ, it must be noted that he does insist that the liturgy should be beautiful.[233] Christ is assuredly only manifest in his concealment, but there is no excuse for concealing him even more with kitsch or with the banal. There must simply be an acknowledged distinction, which is one of the major intentions of *The Glory of the Lord*, between divine glory and earthly beauty, the former of which attests to its own validity, and the latter of which is ideally a reflection of the former.[234] The reflection, however, neither establishes nor legitimizes that which it is a reflection of: "Glory is eternal love descending into the uttermost darkness. The liturgy is a mirror for this."[235] The mirroring of divine glory in the liturgy is the Church's response (*Antwort*) to God's original word (*Wort*), and thus its beauty is in the service of returning glory to its source in God. This liturgical answer is not something over and against God's glory: "It would be ridiculous and blasphemous to want to respond to the glory of God's grace with a counter-glory produced from our own creaturely reserves."[236] Instead, like the heavenly liturgy of the book of Revelation, the liturgy should be "completely dominated and shaped by God's glory."[237] Just as the liturgical drama is analogous to the primal (*Ur-*) drama of the Trinity, so earthly beauty, even as it is heightened and chastened by the liturgy, stands in a similar, yet even more dissimilar relationship to divine glory. No matter how glorious, sublime, and even rapturous a baroque liturgy in a magnificent cathedral might be, its indubitable superiority in terms of earthly beauty when compared to a simple low mass in any average parish does not "increase" the presence of divine glory. What makes a difference, the only thing that makes a difference, is something that admits of no measure and also of no guarantee: the Church's own receptivity to the influx of divine grace.

Balthasar's understanding of the liturgy stands suspended between two of the most important books on the liturgy that frame the twentieth century, both named *The Spirit of the Liturgy*, by Guardini (1918) and Ratzinger (2000). And it is in proximity to these books that Balthasar's most important liturgical concerns can be analyzed.[238] Guardini's influence on Balthasar is significant, particularly on the question of the liturgy,[239] and Balthasar's shaping of Ratzinger's thought is beyond doubt, and he exerts a strong, even if unacknowledged, presence in Ratzinger's *Spirit of the Liturgy*.[240] With regard to the question of the role of aesthetics and the possibility of a liturgical manifestation, there is remarkable continuity between these three. Guardini noted the problem with aestheticism in the liturgy long before Balthasar: "Aesthetes are everywhere looked upon as unwelcome guests, as drones and as parasites sponging on life, but nowhere are they more deserving of anger and contempt than in the sphere of sacred things."[241] Even more than Balthasar's marginalization, Guardini prohibits the aesthete from entering into the liturgy. There is simply no place for liturgical voyeurism, which can be read as a reaffirmation of the ancient practice of the *disciplina arcani*. Certainly, Guardini highlights the "playfulness" and the "symbolism" of the liturgy, and this is often what his text is most remembered for. But for Guardini, and he repeats this point throughout, the symbol and the play of the liturgy are not primarily of a cognitive or aesthetic nature, but are *dramatic*: "The many people who, barren of feeling and perceiving nothing of the beauty and splendor of word and sound which surrounds them, but merely seek strength for their daily toil—all these penetrate far more deeply into the essence of the liturgy than does the connoisseur who is busy savoring the contrast between the austere beauty of a Preface and the melodiousness of a Gradual."[242] Those who come to the liturgy to encounter Christ, or even more basically, to "seek strength for their daily toil" are the true participants, the true liturgical actors, even if they fail to grasp the marvelously arranged liturgical performance.

Ratzinger, who is far more interested in questions of liturgical performance and reform than Balthasar, retains the same position as Guardini and Balthasar about the appearance of the liturgy. Certainly drawing on the same source as Balthasar, Rousselot's "eyes of faith" appear throughout Ratzinger's text as a stable and underlying theme. Ratzinger insists on certain concrete reforms of the liturgy, such as prayer *ad orientem*, but this is not because this allows the glory of God to *appear* to a greater extent, but precisely the opposite, because it demonstrates an eschatological posture, which means that the liturgy is itself self-effacing when properly performed. The great liturgical temptation, not only with regard to physical posture but also with the Church's self-understanding, is to become a "self-enclosed circle," whereby the community is content with its own immanence and "no longer opens out on what lies ahead and above."[243] This applies equally to the question of liturgical beauty, where a modern understanding of aesthetics leads to "the vision of a beauty that no longer points beyond itself but is content in the end with itself, the beauty of the appearing thing."[244] To "see" the liturgy properly, one needs "a new kind of seeing, which perceives the Invisible in the visible," which also must be "a fruit of contemplation."[245] For Guardini, Balthasar, and Ratzinger, this subordination of the visible and aesthetic aspect of the liturgy is a theological necessity when one gives precedence to dramatic action of the liturgy. This drama is not the intraliturgical drama akin to a play, or what Guardini calls "spiritual theater" or Ratzinger "parody," but the drama of salvation whereby Christ descends to dwell with his Church and sinners are forgiven and healed.[246] To assume that the external rites themselves constitute the liturgical drama is, in the Balthasarian words of Ratzinger, to have "radically misunderstood the '*theo-drama*' of the liturgy."[247] Ratzinger summarizes well the position shared by all three: "But this properly liturgical level does not stand on its own. It has meaning only in relation to something that really happens, to a reality that is substantially present. Otherwise it would lack real content, like bank notes without funds to cover them. . . . Without the Cross and Resurrection, Christian worship is null and void, and a theology of liturgy that omitted any reference to them would really just be talking about an empty game."[248]

We have seen throughout this chapter how Balthasar subordinates questions of liturgical structure to the primary impetus of personal and ecclesial holiness, even to the extent that he offers essentially no practical suggestions for liturgical reform. Balthasar can be forgiven for this because he was more concerned with systematic and historical theology than with the liturgy, but Guardini and Ratzinger, whose liturgical pedigrees are unquestionable, demonstrate the same priorities as Balthasar, even if their suggestions for liturgical reform are more nuanced and developed than anything Balthasar ever proposed. Even in these two towering liturgical theologians, we have the admission of the need for a healthy credulity with regard to the ability of holiness and obedience to produce worthy liturgical forms. Guardini takes Christ's command to "seek first the kingdom of God and his righteousness, and all these things shall be added unto you," and adds "all else, even the glorious experience of beauty."[249] In other words, the beauty of the liturgy is a fruit, a by-product, of a salvific encounter with God, and not the other way around.[250] And Ratzinger, who was thoroughly convinced that liturgy shapes subjective experiences and contributes to a properly Christian attitude toward God, says that "the uniqueness of the eucharistic liturgy lies precisely in the fact that God himself is acting and that we are drawn into that action of God. Everything else is, therefore, secondary."[251] True liturgical reform, then, is not a distinct movement from a renewal of holiness in the Church, just as Balthasar said that the liturgical movement must be firmly attached to the contemplative movement.

Guardini and Ratzinger knew and loved, more than most, the beauty of the liturgy. Neither, however, understood the nature of beauty or of aesthetics to the same extent as Balthasar did. Guardini, did, however, hope that a Balthasar would be coming, and if one might be so cavalier to suggest it, prophesied his arrival: "What profound penetration and insight was shown by Plato, the master of aesthetics, in his warnings against the dangers of excessive worship of beauty! *We need a new artist-seer* to convince the young people of our day, who bend the knee in idolatrous homage before art and beauty, what must be the fruit of such perversion of the highest spiritual laws."[252]

With regard to questions theological and specifically liturgical, Balthasar's restraint in his deployment of aesthetic categories shows him to be precisely this theological "artist-seer" that Guardini awaited. Because Balthasar knew earthly beauty, whether in musical or literary form, he knew what it could and could not provide in the service of theology and in an analysis of the liturgy. It may be that those who love to praise the liturgy as a work of art, as a coherent ritual structure, and think that this will provide sufficient theological data on its own, simply love neither beauty nor the visible liturgy well enough. A true lover would never require of the beloved a task that he knows she simply could never accomplish. And, for Balthasar, love, *eros* in particular, is what is essential to the liturgy. Liturgy is *both* the Church's erotic ascent toward God, bringing with it all of earthly beauty, the horizontal drama, and the desire for manifestation and vision, *and* God's erotic descent toward the creature, which comes in the form of humiliation and hiddenness, and totally overtakes the creaturely *eros*.[253] Even if the second, divine *eros* overtakes the human, it does not thereby negate it and render its strivings either representative or illusory, for the descent on God's part and the elevation of humanity occur as one single movement. Liturgy is thus the purification of *eros*, it is the fire at the top of Mount Purgatory where earthly *eros* is transfigured into the heavenly. The beauty of the liturgy, like Virgil's goading of Dante, can be, in the end, that which is transformed into divine splendor: *Lo dolce padre mio, per confortarmi, pur di Beatrice ragionando andava, dicendo: "Li occhi suoi già veder parmi,"* "My sweet father [Virgil], in order to encourage me, while he proceeded continued to speak of Beatrice, saying: 'It seems that her eyes can already be seen.'"[254]

CHAPTER 4

Sub velamento

The Eucharist between This World and the Next

Behold, there he stands behind our wall, gazing in at the windows, look-ing through the lattice. My beloved speaks and says to me: "Arise, my love, my dove, my fair one, and come away; for behold, the winter is past, the rain is over and gone. The flowers appear on the earth, the time of prun-ing has come."

—Song of Solomon 2:9b–12a

The transfiguration of creaturely *eros* at the top of Dante's Mount Purga-tory, with which we concluded chapter 3, is for Balthasar an index of the ecclesial liturgy's proximity to and distance from its celestial goal. But this distance is not merely a matter of the proper distinction between the infinite God as *actus purus* and the creaturely mode of becoming that is a mix of act and potency, for it is a question of temporal and ontological distance. The reason the lover in our epigraph from the Song of Solomon is "looking through the lattice," that is, marked both by vision but also obscurity and obstruction, is that the beloved must "arise" and "come away" in order to realize that, indeed, "the winter is past" and that "the time of pruning has come." Everything we discussed regarding eucharis-tic vision and nonvision in chapter 3, primarily in epistemological terms, is ultimately only comprehensible in light of eschatology. According to

Balthasar, the ultimate reason that the sacraments evince as much obscurity as clarity, that Christ is behind the lattice of the Eucharist rather than in full sight, is that the sacraments testify to a ratio between the "already" of eschatological fulfillment and the "not yet" of the delay of final consummation that is proportionate to the vision/obscurity ratio of liturgical manifestation in hiddenness.[1] Virgil says atop the mountain, "it seems that her eyes can already be seen," but Beatrice will only be seen on the far side of the fire that demarcates this world from the next, this form of temporality from the next.

As we stated explicitly in chapter 1 as something of a methodological "rule," and have demonstrated in the subsequent chapters, the Eucharist only functions for Balthasar insofar as it is brought into tandem with other doctrinal subjects, such as the Trinity and the Incarnation. Better put, these other subjects only function insofar as they are able to retain their balance when brought into the orbit of a eucharistic logic that acts as the axis around which all other doctrines move centripetally. Eschatology is thus no exception to this rule. The only possible exception would be the argument that it is eschatology that is, in fact, the central axis for all of Balthasar's speculative dogmatics, an argument for which evidence could be quite easily garnered.[2] Leaving aside the likely fruitless question of whether the Eucharist or eschatology is "more central," we can proceed with the obvious: both Eucharist and eschatology are nearly ubiquitous topics in Balthasar's work, and often the sites in which he deals with his most consequential positions. In this chapter, I make an implicit argument that the Eucharist and eschatology are so intertwined in Balthasar's mature theological position that his eschatology is nothing more (and nothing less) than a bringing of what is implied by eucharistic theology and practice to its logical conclusion. More explicitly, in the three main sections, I shall explore (1) how Balthasar relates various conceptions of time, including sacramental time; (2) the simultaneity of celestial worship and historical strife, and thus the question of theodicy; and (3) questions relating to the continuance of the Eucharist in the eschaton, and thus the eucharistic state of the blessed dead. My conclusion will then ask what Balthasar means when he says that not only does God give himself totally to creation in the Eucharist, but that he likewise enables the creature to return a gift to himself, thus making God a "recipient" of the eucharistic exchange.

TIME, SUPERTIME, AND SACRAMENTAL TIME

Eschatology and apocalyptic discourse may seem, *per definitionem*, to be concerned principally with questions of time, but this is not so clearly the case. Any eschatology will have to deal, even if tangentially, with the question of time and its fulfillment, but eschatological and apocalyptic thought is taken by Balthasar to be broader than temporal considerations, and may even be resolved before arriving at the question of time.[3] Thus, the opening lines of the first volume of *Apokalypse der deutschen Seele* give a definition of the apocalyptic that is itself quite revealing as to what Balthasar has in mind: "Apo-kalypsis means disclosure just as much as it means revelation: revelatio. The exterior lies open, however, while the interior is veiled. . . . Whatever is always vital in philosophy, poetry, and theology moves towards the interior, to what Novalis called the mysterious [*geheimnisvollen*]."[4] His three-volume study is then an attempt to discover, to unveil, the central concerns of German thought, even the implicit attempts to think of the meaning and purpose of reality as a whole. Eschatology is thus ontology, and in this Balthasar agrees with Heidegger regarding the inseparability of Being and time.[5] Some, especially the German idealists Fichte, Schelling, and Hegel, will think explicitly of the meaning of temporality and how the contingency and seeming relativity of historical development can be understood alongside the Absolute, while others, such as Goethe, will not consider time to be a "problem" at all, representing as it does the totality of nature's flux. For Balthasar, however, those eschatologies that fail to account for the vagaries of time, what Balthasar so trenchantly refers to as the "slaughter" of history, or what Paul Griffiths more recently refers to as "the devastation," are failures of the exercise of faith and of reason.[6]

Attempts at a rational justification of the suffering concomitant to historicity include rendering such suffering as a logical necessity, either as an unfortunate side effect for some higher good (Leibniz) or the means by which that higher good is reached in the first place (Hegel). Whatever the demerits of these philosophical positions, and Balthasar is keenly aware of them, the culpability of inadequate theological responses to the question of time and suffering is all the greater. For Balthasar, the march of time, which indeed does appear as a slaughter bench, cannot be rendered illusory without simultaneously surrendering what is, in fact, the true *novum* of Christian faith: the God-man's earthly sojourn culminating on a specifiable date on a rocky outcrop of an Israelite city. Because of Christianity's clear dependence on the validity of a historically identified event, Balthasar thinks that even more pressing than the relation between beings and Being is the relationship between time and eternity. Especially in the wake of rational and rationalist attempts to justify the flux of time, but also because of Christianity's own native concerns, Balthasar thinks that metaphysics is only a subset of the larger question of metahistory.

Balthasar's first article on Gregory of Nyssa, in 1939, which was later expanded into his 1942 book *Présence et Pensée*, was published the same year as the last volume of the *Apokalypse*, and in many ways insights from the Greek Fathers function as answers to his own immediate context of Franco-Germanic philosophy and literature. There is every reason, then, to interpret the following quote from *Présence et Pensée* as a riposte to any modern critique that suggests that Christianity renders history the mere reverse image of stable eternity: "Now Christianity brings to religious philosophy a complete reversal of its point of departure. It is no longer a question of knowing how the soul can approach God but of learning how, indeed, God has approached us. Through a historical fact that is exterior, Christianity teaches us a historical fact that is interior. For metaphysics, it substitutes metahistory. In a more profound way, these two facts are, to be sure, but one sole event."[7]

For Balthasar, modernity's fascination with history is a lingering effect of Christianity, such that even though the cause has been largely forgotten or even actively banished, the gift of historical sensitivity remains, even without proper citation. This is what makes Balthasar far less generous and accommodating to post-Christian philosophers than he is to the pre-Christian variety, who are generally forgiven on the basis of invincible ignorance. First, however, before analyzing Balthasar's understanding of sacramental time, we need to briefly look at the larger scene of contemporary eschatological speculation to see how Balthasar's understanding of the essentially eschatological nature of the Eucharist serves to hold off various temptations of eschatological excess, by stressing the axiological pole to the detriment of the teleological, or vice versa. The liturgical fact of the Eucharist, and the Church's doctrinal affirmations about it, inherently suggest an eschatology of moderation incompatible with the eschatologies of excess, as Balthasar is wont to demonstrate. Although his critics would suggest that Balthasar is anything but moderate, the best reading is that his eschatology is, indeed, one of sober inebriation.

Eschatological Directions

In *Apokalypse*, Balthasar treats such a wide variety of forms of "apocalypse" that establishing something like a basic, at least marginally orthodox, Christian consensus, as this differs from the options represented by Schelling, Nietzsche, and Scheler, is neither very difficult nor very informative. For the sake of precision, we will here narrow the range of possible eschatological postures to those that are operating within the ambit of Christian theology and thus also feel at least some duty to address questions of sacramentality. The various philosophical, literary, or radically heterodox positions will function here as merely additive or illustrative. The question of time, in Balthasar's judgment, is *the* question that attempts to see how the part fits into the whole. Or, stated even better, and stated so as to already indicate the eventual solution, the question is how the whole can fit into the parts, as the title to his largest treatment of the question of time makes clear: *Das Ganze im Fragment*.[8] However, understood aright, the justification of time is not a mere intellectual puzzle that aims at a solution regarding the proper conjugation of temporality and eternity, but is instead really a *justification* of time; it is about salvation.[9]

In the opening volume of *Apokalypse*, Balthasar (thinking with an intellectual reflex inherited from Przywara) characterizes the two main modes of eschatological thought as a polarity: on the one end is the axiological, or what could just as easily be characterized as the existential, and on the other is the teleological.[10] Neither is satisfactory on its own, nor will the right formulation be a mean between the two, but the solution will rather do justice to the fact that the "concrete mind" is directed to the "irresolvable dialectic" of both the axiological and the teleological.[11] This tension can be characterized, *mutatis mutandis*, as that between the *already* and the *not yet* or, in terms of theological figures from the twentieth century, between the existentialism and realized eschatology of Rudolf Bultmann and the future-oriented eschatological orientation of figures such as Jürgen Moltmann and Latin American liberation theologians. Here we will see how Balthasar asks the following question to both sides of the dialectic: Can either pole, on its own, account in any meaningful way for sacramentality in general, or the startling fact of the Eucharist in particular?

Inasmuch as Balthasar considers a purely axiological eschatology to be a failure of thought, a refusal to consider the question of time and its culmination, he does nonetheless think that, as he writes in 1957, "in constructing a sound and comprehensive eschatology of man, history and the cosmos, it is the task of Catholic thought to take up the themes of present-day existentialist philosophy and theology."[12] Balthasar answers his own call for a Catholic existentialist eschatology, most explicitly in *A Theology of History* (1959), *A Theological Anthropology* (1963), and *Theo-Drama* IV and V (1980, 1983). Thus, even if he grants Karl Barth the status of blessed (sainthood would perhaps be going too far) for saving Protestantism from the morass to which Bultmann's existentialism led it, Balthasar is not ungenerous toward Bultmann and freely acknowledges a sympathy for his desire to root dogma in the subjectivity of Christian experience.[13] Bultmann's greatest error, however, is simply an excess of a virtue. Bultmann's eschatology is so thoroughly "Christian" that it has lost touch with Judaism, thus resulting in a form of eschatological Marcionism. Yet another pair of descriptors for the same eschatological polarity of the axiological and teleological that recurs throughout Balthasar's work is the tension between "Christian" and "Jewish" eschatologies. The "Jewish," which Balthasar consistently connects to Marx, Bloch, Moltmann, and liberation theology, looks toward a "horizontal" fulfillment of eschatological hope, and in its most excessive forms results in chiliasm or utopianism. "Christian" eschatology is first and foremost "vertical," for the Messiah is no longer awaited, thus resulting in Christian hope based entirely in the Lord and in the Pauline belief that "Christ lives in me."[14] A purely vertical eschatology, however, one entirely unmoored from Judaism, also ceases to account for the genuine Christian position that does indeed have a horizontal element and a hope for temporal resolution.

The temptation of an existential eschatology is to render history as illusory, or at least as irrelevant to the inbreaking of the Kingdom of God. Thus Bultmann writes: "The meaning of history lies always in the present . . . do not look around yourself into universal history, you must look into your own personal history. Always in your present lies the meaning in history, and you cannot see it as a spectator, but only in your responsible decisions. In every moment slumbers the possibility of being the eschatological moment. You must awaken it."[15] For Balthasar, this position chafes against the Church's sacramentality. Sacramentality is necessarily tied to time, and in fact, according to Aquinas, is so tied to time that the Eucharist is temporally significant three times over (*signum rememorativum, signum demonstrativum, signum prognosticum*).[16] Saying this, however, is no affront to Bultmann, who saw as clearly as anyone else that his position was essentially antithetical to the sacraments. In fact, Bultmann knew that the sacraments function somewhere in the middle between the chiliastic expectations of the early Church and his own purified and atemporal eschatology.[17] The confrontation between Bultmann and Balthasar can then be reduced to the former's refusal of sacramentality and the latter's acceptance thereof. Sacramentality functions as something of an a priori (though not in the Kantian sense) decision on the part of Bultmann and Balthasar, respectively, and both seem to largely acknowledge the fact. Balthasar never seemed tempted by Bultmann, and thus his generosity is an admiration from afar, from a position in which one recognizes that no agreement could ever be reached. For Bultmann, the fact that the Church attributes to the sacraments a real efficacy means first of all that grace is not immediate, that it comes through the mediation of the institutional Church, and thus the Kingdom is at best partially present, but ultimately delayed in coming. The Church awaits a time when mediation and sacramentality give way to the immediacy of eschatological fulfillment. Balthasar would want to rephrase Bultmann's presentation, especially in its historical reconstruction about the emergence of sacramentality, but he does grant that no matter how much the sacraments are already moments of eschatological disclosure, they are equally an indication of distance and nonconsummation. A eucharistic eschatology, such as Balthasar's, does indeed affirm real presence and the intimacy of the Holy Spirit, but Christ's status as veiled and a clear gap between Christ's gift and the Church's capacity for reception indicate that Christian hope is still operative. And this hope includes a resolution to the horizontal movement of history and the groanings of creation, and not merely a vertical hope for individual integration.

More consequential than Bultmann's existentialism, both for Balthasar's own work and for contemporary eschatology, is the horizontal dimension of intrahistorical resolution. This could lead to analyzing Balthasar's engagement with liberation theology,[18] or a whole host of other political theologians, such as Johann Baptist Metz, but here the treatment will be restricted to Ernst Bloch and Jürgen Moltmann, who function as a pair for Balthasar. Balthasar typifies Moltmann as insistent upon the teleological dimension of eschatology, a feature, again, that he thinks characteristic of the Old Testament, and survives in the forms of the secularized Judaism of Marx and Bloch. Moltmann never hid the fact that his eschatology is, albeit not exclusively, an attempt to provide a Christian answer to Bloch.[19] Balthasar perhaps overplays Moltmann's reliance on Bloch, but is right to insist that Moltmann's eschatology is unthinkable without Bloch, and in a real sense is propelled by the conception of prophecy in the Old Testament with its future-oriented posture.[20] Whereas Bultmann balks at an eschatology that awaits some further good in the future, for Bloch, and to a slightly lesser extent Moltmann, the idea of a realized eschatology is vulgar, blind to the most obvious facts of imperfection and suffering, and thus ethically reprehensible. A purely existential mode of eschatological fulfillment is ethically problematic precisely because of its focus on individual experience, thus neglecting to account for the masses of people who will not be interiorly transformed by the eschaton. Even more damning, however, is that a singularly axiological posture does not even attempt to account for the carnage of human suffering.

All in all, then, even if Balthasar thinks that for a Christian, and specifically Johannine, eschatology the individual is indeed vertically related to an eschatological yet ever-present Lord, the historical and communal dimension cannot be neglected without major losses. The question of communal salvation and the attempt to render intelligible history's winding path are indeed the driving impetuses of Balthasar's eschatology, and thus he is much more eager to analyze figures such as Bloch and Moltmann rather than someone like Bultmann, not only to highlight points of similarity and possible mutual enrichment but also to more accurately demonstrate the key differences. To begin with a major point of convergence, Balthasar is in agreement with this horizontal, futurist mode of eschatology precisely because he acknowledges that the fragility of the past and the present can only be brought into the light of a totality on the basis of a "borrowing" from the future.[21] It is the future that justifies the present and the past, a future that is indeed yet to come. One can then understand Balthasar's (perhaps insensitive) use of the adjective "Jewish" to modify this type of eschatology, because it is one, even when secularized in Bloch and Walter Benjamin,[22] of messianism, a hope for a future in which God, or whatever functions as an ersatz Messiah, will indeed "rebuild the walls of Jerusalem," as the psalmist prays (Ps. 51:18).[23] The crucial issue with these futurist proposals, at least from Balthasar's perspective, is that they disallow any axiological, vertical dimension in which the eschaton could be considered at least partially present, and they concomitantly have in-built resistances to sacramentality. These two issues are, of course, one and the same.

Bloch, the atheist Jew, does not need to take any account of the sacraments, as will the Reformed Moltmann. Bloch is indeed free to dismiss them as simply encrustations of the established order of things, as cultic reenactments of the past that solidify the status quo. They are, in this reading, fundamentally opposed to the new, to a hope in a future that disturbs and supersedes that which is. Bloch has the support of the Calabrian Abbot Joachim and renders Joachim as a great exception to the normal rule of Catholicism: "the sympathy of the Vatican for fascism."[24] Only a heretical Christianity, one that is willing to dispense with priests, sacraments, and the era of Christ, is able to herald the third age of the Spirit, and Joachim is for Bloch its representative:

> And the monstrance which priests of this Christianity show to those that labor and are heavy laden testifies to no new aeon but gilds the old one. Together with the cowardice and obsequiousness which the old aeon needs in its victims, but without the day of judgment and the triumph over Babel, without intending towards a new heaven and a new earth. Resignation to fear, servitude and empty promises of the other world are the social principles of a Christianity which are despised by Marx and cast into Orcus by Joachim; but they are not the principles of a long-abandoned early Christianity and a social-revolutionary history of heresies that sprang from it.[25]

Balthasar will strongly contest the characterization of the monstrance as an encapsulation of the past and as a block on the future, but he is quite willing to allow even the fiercest attacks against Christianity to stand as witnesses against the Church's seemingly endless failures. Bloch is wrong, in Balthasar's estimation, to equate sacramentality with stagnation, but he is certainly right in noting that sacramentality *does* necessitate a strong tie to the past, and also an enduring state in the present that is not entirely relative to a future reevaluation. With the sacraments, the future cannot have exclusive reign.

Moltmann, although not obliged by his Reformed tradition to have an overly high conception of the sacraments, cannot dispense with them as easily as Bloch, and certainly cannot render the Son as merely the forerunner of the Spirit. First, it must be said that Moltmann's reading of Joachim is far more nuanced and historically accurate than Bloch's, and he admits that, regardless of how Joachim is appropriated by later history, Joachim's trifold periodization is gradual and overlapping rather than given to evaluating the new as in opposition to and as the obsolescence of the old.[26] Yet, Moltmann does follow Joachim, and thus Bloch, in allowing for an absolute priority of the future over that of the past, and most definitely over that of the present. The way this functions, when applied to sacramental theology, is, as would be expected, quite telling. He will do something quite different with the supposition, but Moltmann adopts the same essential schema as already seen in Bultmann, namely, that sacramentality is a real fall from the original eschatological posture of early Christianity. When Christianity became a cultic religion, it forsook its task of hoping for a future eschatological inbreaking of the Kingdom, because now, in the sacraments, it already had a controllable and verifiable hold on that Kingdom, thus blunting any notion of a future hope. For Moltmann, whatever "efficacy" the sacraments are to have, it is only either as a residue from the past (Christ's death and resurrection) or as a promissory note on the future, but not anything stable, localizable, and ineluctably belonging in the present tense.

Timothy Gorringe nicely summarizes Moltmann's position of affirming sacramental practice while denying any notion whatsoever of real presence: "The claim that Moltmann's theology fails to acknowledge God's present reality in turn fails to see that God is present in and through the promise. To illustrate what this means we can see that there is all the difference in the world between the eucharist which is really a glorified form of benediction, focused on the 'real presence' of Christ in the elements, and the presence of God in word and sacrament which strains after the kingdom of God."[27] Balthasar agrees: there is all the difference in the world. In Moltmann's *Church in the Power of the Spirit*, which contains his largest treatment of sacramental theology, it is clear that he wants to affirm the two times of the sacraments, their efficacy as derived from the past, which in reality only comes from the future. But any notion of an *abiding* presence or a realization of the future that is not purely under the sign of a promise is vigorously denied. The sacrament is only *sacramentum*, without *res*. In affirming the double sacramentality of the *signum rememorativum* and the *signum prognosticum*, Moltmann skips over the *signum demonstrativum* of a present reality as a potential contaminant of the second theological virtue.[28] Both in terms of sacramental theology and in terms of metaphysics, Balthasar's difference from Moltmann on these issues is simply the second round of his battle with Karl Barth, even though in terms of Trinitarian theology Moltmann is both closer and further way from Balthasar. At the end of his 1951 book on Barth, when Balthasar is attempting to provide the contours of a Catholic response to Luther's *simul*, Balthasar notes that the Catholic theologian is obliged to take account not only of the scriptural evidence of final redemption as an eschatological hope but also the clear statements of the Christian already being freed from sin and given a share in God's own life. Balthasar summarizes the two poles: "The *in spe* of the first perspective does not abolish the *in re* of the second."[29]

Just as Moltmann later, so Barth earlier insisted on the forward and backward nature of the sacraments, but could not admit to any abiding efficacy, and as Barth himself implicitly acknowledged, his prior stance regarding the *analogia entis* prohibited any sense of ecclesial mediation.[30] Barth's is then a clearly antisacramental theology,[31] and as his final, slim volume of *Church Dogmatics* indicates, the sacraments do not really have a place in his dogmatic work, other than as an *explicandum* that a Christian theologian must at least acknowledge. Moltmann is far more willing to grant the importance of sacramental practice, but all the while holding onto the established thesis of a "fall" into a cultic religion. The distinction between a decrepit, cultic view of the sacraments (represented by Catholicism) and a healthy, evangelical sense is precisely, to put it negatively, whether or not eschatological hope is surrendered to an immediate presence that is ecclesiastically controlled. Moltmann, in *The Theology of Hope*, repeats the basic narrative of the notion of "early

Catholicism": "History thus loses its eschatological direction. It is not the realm in which men suffer and hope, groaning and travailing in the expectation of Christ's future for the world, but it becomes the field in which the heavenly lordship of Christ is disclosed in Church and sacrament. In place of the eschatological 'not yet' [*noch nicht*] we have a cultic 'now only' [*nur noch*], and this becomes the key-signature of history *post Christum*."[32]

For Moltmann, this denigration of presence in favor of the future has massive implications for his Trinitarian theology and for how he conceives of the God–world relation, as Balthasar noted.[33] Nevertheless, to address only the question of the eschatological implications of sacramental practice, we can conclude with the same observation already given by Bultmann, but now from the opposite perspective: for Moltmann, sacramental theology and practice in the Catholic sense acts as a prohibition of a purely horizontal, future-oriented eschatology. It functions as a mean between the horizontal and the vertical poles, a mean that Balthasar tries to hold in his own eschatological ponderings. We have seen how the Eucharist can indeed function negatively to prohibit certain eschatological positions, namely, an exclusively vertical, existential position or one that denies an abiding eschatological immediacy in favor of the future. Yet for Balthasar, the Eucharist also functions positively within this middle space between extremes, and gives certain indispensable indications regarding the relationship between creaturely time and God's time, between earth and heaven.

Futurae gloriae nobis pignus datur

To borrow the idiom of William Desmond, Balthasar's eschatology is at root metaxological. It functions "in-between" the extremes outlined above, and this status in-between serves to demonstrate clear limits in either direction and provides generous space that has not been dogmatically defined and is thus open to theological speculation. The Christian is neither potentially in heaven if only she would adopt the appropriate perspective regarding the kerygma, nor is she ever removed from it because of its permanent status in the future. Instead, the "future," or better, the *eschaton*, can be considered present, but never in such a way as to pronounce eternity exhausted by the present moment. Thus Balthasar is content to live with a good deal of ambiguity regarding the relationship between time and eternity, once certain options are ruled out: "This presents us with the ultimately insoluble question of the relationship between temporal life and eternal life. Our notions of time are deceptive: eternal life is not a continuation of transitory life; it does not begin 'after death' but is perpendicular to it; it is the manifest face of a totality that, for the present, is accessible only in veiled form. So while this veiled form is essentially transient, it nonetheless prepares us for what is not yet manifest."[34] The perpendicular intersection of eternity and temporality, rather than their horizontal succession or simultaneity, means that time and eternity are constituted wholly dissimilarly (like verticality and horizontality), but not so dissimilarly as to render their intersection impossible. God's time and human time are, according to Balthasar, constituted such that the latter is enfolded and included in the former.

To state the matter succinctly, Balthasar thinks that even though there is a qualitative difference between finite time and the existence of God, it is better to consider God's life to be a sort of "supertime," rather than a simple lack of time or a *nunc stans*. Balthasar thinks that "everything that, in the created world, appears shot through with *potentiality* is found *positively* in God."[35] The attributes proper to the created order, such as the flow of time, are truer when applied (analogically) to God. Not, of course, that Balthasar attributes change to God, strictly speaking. The perichoretic flow of Trinitarian love is changeless, if by "change" we mean a movement from one state or nature to another. But change, movement, and time can indeed be used when speaking of God, if by these terms we mean that it is of God's very nature to be an inexhaustible life issuing from a plenitude that is ever new. The *nunc stans*, then, is more a picture of hell than heaven, for Balthasar.[36] Balthasar has at least Gregory of Nyssa and Maximus the Confessor as witnesses to the possibility of inverting the typical scale from *stasis* to movement, and Dante can, of course, be marshaled for a literary portrayal of the same point: at the base of hell, the devil is frozen, barely moving at all, but the Empyrean and the vision of God is one of light and reflection, both cause of movement and moving itself. For Dante, it seems, the nearer one arrives to the *primum movens* ("the love which moves the sun and the other stars"),[37] the more movement occurs, not less. As occurs in *Paradiso* 28, Dante undergoes something of a metaphysical reversal, in that his geocentric cosmology, "from below," is supplanted by this celestial vision whereby God is, in fact, the true center point of all movement that radiates outward. And the closer to this divine center one approaches, the faster, not slower, is the movement: "From that point Heaven and the whole of nature depend. Look at the circle which is nearest to it, and know that its movement is so fast because of the blazing love by which it is pierced."[38] Balthasar simply extends this logic one step further, by thinking through the consequences of Trinitarian theology more consistently, and thus claiming that the ultimate source of external movement is a result of an infinite internal movement.[39] Thus, from the perspective of human logic and the finite experience of temporality, there is indeed something more appropriate in restricting time to creation and thus considering God beyond all time and anything like movement. But in addition to this analogical approach, which soars upward and purifies thought as it reaches beyond its sphere of competence, Balthasar insists that theology is also privileged to go with Dante and see creation from above in a catalogical descent.[40] From *this* perspective, the one that Balthasar often prefers, movement and thus time appear as pale radiations of an original dynamism of which they are only faint echoes.

This is in no sense a trivial matter, but it can be bracketed for now whether Balthasar's use of "supertime" is warranted or not, and simply note that this is his usual vocabulary. More important for our purposes here is what comes between creaturely time and God's time: namely, sacramental time, which is a modified continuation of Christ's presence in the Church during the forty days after his resurrection. Balthasar argues that Christ's forty-day sojourn on earth after the Resurrection "belong[s] both to his earthly time and to his eternal time. They are a part of the Gospel in which his relations with his disciples are continued, the gulf between the here and the beyond is lovingly, redeemingly bridged, and his intimacy with them is renewed."[41] The "supertime" of eternal life and the creaturely time of Christ's incarnate state are both on display and are united in the one person of the *Logos*.[42] What Balthasar calls "sacramental time," or variously "eucharistic" or "ecclesial time," is the extension of those forty days for the remaining history of the Church. Christ continues to exist in the Church in both modes of temporality, but with regard to sacramental time it is a concealed and veiled form of what was clearly visible and often public during the forty days: "In this communion between the Lord and his Church there comes into existence a kind of time which is sacramental, and most especially eucharistic. Its peculiar character is that the eternal Lord is constantly coming afresh into contemporaneity with his Bride, but without becoming subject to or measurable by passing time."[43] Eucharistic time, a *novum* with regard to the various modes of time, is not, per se, a new "time" between eternal and finite time. Rather, it is the presence of Christ's eternal-historical time (historical because he has raised up and elevated his own historicity) within creaturely time without thereby being reduced to the usual strictures of the chronic temporality of creatures.[44]

Eucharistic time is, therefore, an eschatological time. But it is an eschatological *time*; it is not yet the eschaton, but rather a temporal manifestation thereof. Between God's time and creaturely time, thus between heaven and earth, there is something of an *admirabile commercium* because of Christ and his sacraments. Quoting Speyr in *TD* V, Balthasar writes: "The risen Son is earth in heaven; his Eucharist is heaven on earth."[45] In addition to any "supertime" ascribed to God because of the Trinitarian relations, according to Balthasar's incorporation of Speyr, Christ has essentially "brought" his finite time with him into heaven in his resurrected and glorified body. But Christ's kenosis was not a pillaging raid, whereby God came as a reverse Prometheus to steal what is proper to the creature, but instead, it was intended as an exchange of gifts: Christ receives and elevates creaturely time, but also gives his divine temporality in the form of the sacramental economy of the Church. To understand exactly what Balthasar is hoping to accomplish with his eschatology, it is essential to note that his eschatology is something of an expansion of his Christology (and thus eucharistic theology, by extension). That is to say, the "end" of creation is also its middle point: the incarnation of Christ. Christ's return to heaven is for Balthasar the inauguration of eschatology, not only as to temporal succession but also as to the actual mapping of the eschatological terrain. The pneumatic flesh of Christ is for Balthasar the Church's entrance into the Triune life. It is, as it were, holding the place for the *ecclesia triumphans*, which will come to share fully what it now enjoys in part. Christ embeds his historical life into God and returns that life to the Church in a sacramental form: "It is the Eucharist, however, that must reveal the most profound truth about heaven's presence to earth. . . . The Son's return to the Father with his transfigured earthly body, which also pours forth and radiates eucharistically, causes his human nature to acquire trinitarian dimensions."[46] The Eucharist is an epistemically privileged locus for eschatology (again, in that it holds the tension between manifestation and delay), but its epistemic function is a product of the Eucharist's actual mediation of eschatological fulfillment, the epistemology being a reflection of ontology. The world has already been embedded into God by Christ, but only archetypically and representatively. It is actually brought therein by the continuing kenotic movement of Christ's Eucharist, which brings the world into himself.

As the eucharistic poem *O Sacrum Convivium* expresses, the Eucharist is a *pignus futurae gloriae*, "a pledge/assurance of future glory." It points to a glory that is not yet consummated, and thus comes "vertically" in the Eucharist, but only on the basis of a "horizontal" fulfillment that is still in the future. The *body* of Christ, which we have already established as a pneumatic and fleshly body, is for Balthasar a historical and transhistorical (or future) body. The body received in the Eucharist is the same body born of the virgin and crucified on the cross (*sit idem numero / idem per Omnia Christus*),[47] but these historical notations have gained such an eschatological significance after Christ's ascension that within this historical body is contained the entire history of the world, the strivings and sufferings of all humankind, including its eventual redemption and healing. As will become clear later in this chapter, Balthasar often turns to literature when attempting to elucidate what he means regarding the relationship of time to eternity and slaughter to liturgy. In his book on the German poet Reinhold Schneider, Balthasar gives what is perhaps his best summary of how he views the interaction between history, eternity, and the Eucharist:

> If Christ's historicity has gone to heaven through his Resurrection, then he is no longer historical in the temporal sense: he has been made eternal and is enthroned above time, and yet he has time within himself, as the one who has lived time and does not separate himself from what he has lived, the one who lives time in his brethren and in all the members of the cosmos, thereby communicating to them something of the eternal substance of his Being. In the Eucharist, this mystery of the suprahistorical historicity of the very basis of the world is realized.

There the truth without fate continues to rule
and crowns the sacred chaos of earthly being
visibly-invisibly in the sacrament.

Through the Eucharist, the basis of every human fate becomes something that has no human fate itself but that has experienced every human fate.[48]

Having outlined the far easier, even if foundational, issues of Balthasar's eschatology (horizontal vs. vertical, God's time and creaturely time, sacramental time), we can now see how what could be a purely logical question has dramatic contours. For Balthasar, the "problem" of time is less its temporal succession vis-à-vis stable eternity, but more its seemingly generous hosting of natural and human evil.

LITURGY AND SLAUGHTER

"Theodicy" is neither a regular occurrence in Balthasar's vocabulary nor is it particularly welcome as a concept or as a problem. It is, strictly speaking, a problem arising from modern presuppositions that Balthasar simply refuses to concede.[49] Granting this, and sparing the need to enter into endless polemics regarding the utility of a theodicy project, the problem of evil remains, ontologically and existentially. Balthasar spends little time, mostly because he finds such questions fruitlessly speculative, addressing the ontological portion of the question, namely, how sin and evil have come to be so intertwined with a supposedly good creation. He does, controversially, provide a Trinitarian framework that indicates the conditions for the possibility of evil,[50] but he is less concerned to prove that evil does not compromise God's goodness or omniscience, and more concerned with demonstrating that Christianity already has a robust and coherent answer to evil in the person of Christ. Without worrying as much about providing an etiology of evil, Balthasar is convinced that a teleology of evil is comprehensible when seen in the light of the cross.[51] Theodicy was originally a question concerning evil, time, eschatology, and particularly Christology, but I will show how for Balthasar issues surrounding the question of theodicy can only be answered by appeal to the Eucharist.

Consider one instance when Balthasar brings together liturgy and slaughter: "This raises once more the pressing question of how the liturgy of adoration can be connected with the theme of slaughter, in other words, the question of the union of the aesthetic and the dramatic. From the vantage point of heavenly worship, the entire maelstrom of world history, with all its punishments, atrocities and sufferings, is a cause of jubilation."[52] Without a nuanced understanding of Balthasar's intention, this claim seems to be nothing but a callous minimization of real human suffering in light of the comparative greatness of the heavenly banquet. Or worse, it could be read as if the atrocities are nothing more than grist and cause for the celestial jubilation that laughs at the costs incurred for such festivities. Or it could be akin to the Calvinist notion that the suffering itself is an addition to God's greater glory, simply by its being foreordained by the inscrutable, and terrible, divine will. Balthasar, of course, means nothing of the sort. He does, however, enter into such dangerous company because he knows that an ultimate justification of a celestial liturgy can only be accomplished by taking into account its seeming opposite: earthly lamentation. This quote again recalls that the category of the aesthetic, and thus liturgy, is in itself insufficient, but needs to be balanced by the dramatic, and thus slaughter. Balthasar's theology of glory must simultaneously be a theology of the cross, and it is this *simul*, not its more famous counterpart (either the Lutheran or the Barthian), that ultimately accounts for Balthasar's eucharistic bridge over the chasm separating the liturgy above from tragedy below.

Balthasar lauds Karl Barth's reformulation of Luther's "very ambiguous formula" of *simul justus et peccator* such that it no longer applies to the individual Christian, but more originally to Christ: "It is *Christ on the Cross* who is *simul justus et peccator*; he is the sinless one who was made sin for our sake (2 Cor. 5:21) and who was turned into a curse (Gal. 3:13) so that we might be redeemed from sin and its curse."[53] Ultimately then, the one who will account not only for sin but also for suffering is Christ, who takes upon himself the entire horror of humanity's history. Balthasar writes in the *Epilogue*:

What can we say about human history, this grinding, pulverizing witches' millhouse of blood and tears, unless all these baffled, uncomprehending, and stunned victims finally come before God, embedded inside a final, conscious, and all-encompassing Victim

[*Opfer*]? Not as if they come before a perverse tyrant, but before him who is in himself absolute surrender [*absolute Hingabe*], who indeed is surrender beyond all imaginable forms of recklessness and who reveals this on the summit of the world![54]

Now we see the ultimate justification for Balthasar's overly realistic and almost macabre eucharistic vocabulary. Yes, it is a means of keeping sacramental theology close to its cruciform source and its scriptural presentation, but this needs to be extended to note that the suffering on the cross is not only representative but likewise propitiatory. Up to this point, where the disharmony of sin and strife can only be reconciled in Christ, Balthasar is not only in agreement with Barth but also in some measure indebted to him. However, beyond Christ ultimately picking up the check of suffering, as it were, Balthasar thinks that the more Catholic and more human answer cannot be one in which evil and suffering are entirely removed from creaturely province. Balthasar's Catholic evaluation of Barth is one that rejects any notion of *Alleinwirksamkeit Gottes*, that God works alone as the single cause of salvation, which renders all *causae secundae*, such as the sacraments, superfluous: "Too much in Barth gives the impression that nothing much really *happens* in his theology of event and history, because everything has already happened in eternity. . . . Then there is his ascription of the effects of the sacraments to the cognitive order alone, since he rejects the Catholic and Lutheran doctrine that the sacraments effect and cause real change."[55] That is to say, when God acts alone, even in Christ, there is no drama, and history is merely the phenomenal detritus of an eternal event.

Within the historical life of Christ, the entire history of the world unfolds. This summarizes Balthasar's use of Irenaeus's notion of recapitulation: in Christ, the macrocosm of natural flux and evolution and the microcosm of fetal gestation to bodily dissolution is redone, refashioned.[56] This is why Balthasar has a twofold notion of existential sacramental theology: Christ's life is now normative for all, *and* this norm can now be applied and lived subjectively by all peoples without exhaustion or simple repetition. An eschatological solution to the world's tragedy based on a Christological synthesis of time and eternity is, for Balthasar, indispensable but insufficient. This Christological synthesis must be applied *willingly* to creatures. Inasmuch as Balthasar is ecumenically sensitive, one point that makes him not only Tridentine but even Erasmian is the freedom of the will and the necessary cooperation with saving grace: Christ can redeem me, Balthasar says, "but never without my permission: I must continually *accept* this deed, letting it be true for me. Free men are not pieces of luggage, after all, that can be 'redeemed' from the lost and found."[57] Because people are not luggage, the cross is not in itself sufficient (God forgive the expression).[58] Balthasar links the cross and the Eucharist as a theological couplet, and the ultimate reason for this "dialectical relationship between Cross and Eucharist" is that it is the latter that makes salvation a work of the creature: "He gives back to us what once was ours and now is his."[59] This is the *analogia libertatis*, so central to Balthasar's theological project,[60] the relationship between divine and human freedom, which, when the two are brought into harmony, is essentially what Balthasar means by salvation.

Balthasar extends the notion of concomitance far beyond its typical range in arguing that the Eucharist gives to the Church the eschatologically healed resolution between slaughter and liturgy, which is given along with Christ's body and blood. Nevertheless, the Eucharist for Balthasar remains patterned on Christ's kenotic descent. Thus, even though it is an eschatological gift, it is a gift given entirely in the finite sphere, and not one that functions as an escape from finitude.[61] The ecclesial liturgy remains firmly planted in the soil of this earth, and there is thus no celestial transportation granted by the sacraments (as in Calvin).[62] Speaking with the *pathos* of Charles Péguy, to whom we will turn shortly, Balthasar insists that any eschatology that maintains that the world cannot be the site of divine manifestation and redemption, that temporality, finitude, and creation itself must be negated in order to flee to a distant heaven, is simply un-Christian by its denial of what the Incarnation affirms. To borrow a phrase from Emmanuel Falque,[63] for Balthasar the Eucharist is less a transcendence of finitude and more of its metamorphosis: "This eucharistic and spousal relationship between Christ and the Church (in which we are all members) is not, however, some Idealist process hovering above the abyss of this world and its resistance to God. It takes place in world-time, and so it must be seen in the deadly realism of world-time."[64] It is that "deadly realism," the slaughter of world history, which cannot be set in opposition to liturgy, whether of the celestial or terrestrial variety. Again, without attempting anything like a theodicy, Balthasar thinks that eucharistic participation ("real" or "spiritual") can transform even the greatest of horrors into a form of self-giving suffering that aids in the salvation of the world: "And if it is true that the suffering of the Crucified One can transform even worldly pain, unintelligible to itself, into a co-redemptive suffering, then the most unbelievable, most cruel tortures, prisons, concentration camps and whatever other horrors there may be can be seen in close proximity to the Cross, to that utter night, interrupted only by the unfathomable cry of 'Why?'"[65]

The reception of an eschatologically healed world in the form of the Eucharist does not, for Balthasar, give the communicant a panoptic optimism in which all the mysteries of innocent suffering are somehow demonstrated as necessary for the great cosmic mechanism. Quite the opposite. Receiving this recapitulated world, both by means of intellectual assent and by a personal mission of cooperating with Christ's self-gift, is for Balthasar the way in which one can truly utter, with God, a statement of perplexity about how things have turned out so poorly. Christ's response on the cross was not understanding, but eucharistic self-abandon in order to transform slaughter into liturgy.

Literary Choices

Questions of time and eternity can be discussed with some level of abstractness and precision, but the more difficult issue of "liturgy and slaughter," which is as much an existential and ethical concern as a speculative one, is often better accessed through literature. Balthasar himself usually turns to literary sources when discussing eschatology, as is obvious from *Apokalypse* but is also carried through in *Theo-Drama* and other late works. He does this because form (*Gestalt*) and content (*Gehalt*) cannot be separated, and it is the description and elucidation of creaturely drama that best gives access to a philosophical or theological analysis thereof. To then deepen our analysis of Balthasar's eschatology, and to clear up some remaining questions, we will turn to see how he variously interprets three main literary sources: Calderón de la Barca, Charles Péguy, and the book of Revelation. By moving from the baroque Calderón to the modern Péguy we will see exactly what Balthasar prefers regarding imagistic representations of how the eternal liturgy connects to (or fails to connect to) earthly tragedy. It is St. John's Revelation, however, that Balthasar chooses as ultimately preferable, not only because of its canonical status but because of the essential role played by the slaughtered lamb at the heart of the heavenly Jerusalem.

The *autos sacramentales* of the Spanish Golden Age were very much beloved by Balthasar, and none more so than those by Pedro Calderón de la Barca (1600–1681).[66] It was *El Gran Teatro del Mundo* that Balthasar translated, and what he repeatedly returned to as perhaps the height of Spanish baroque literature. Balthasar does not commend Calderón uncritically, but the very plot of *El Gran Teatro del Mundo*, with the entire tension built upon God's choice of an individual mission for all the actors, who go out onto the great stage of the world to perform their parts and are ultimately judged eschatologically for how well they played their respective roles, provides Balthasar with the constituent elements and themes for his own *Theo-Drama*.[67] The drama for Calderón is the same as it is for Balthasar: the ultimate liturgical resolution of the vicissitudes, failures, and successes of ordinary human life, with all its heroism and its shame. *El Gran Teatro* puts into stark relief the main framework by which Balthasar judges almost every thinker, from Plotinus to Aquinas to Hegel, namely, the tension between the absolute and the relative, the infinite and the finite. But Calderón does so in such a way that remains, for Balthasar, entirely Christian in its presentation and attentive to creaturely difference.

Passing Balthasar's metaphysical test, Calderón refuses the absorption of the creature into the Creator, which is tempting to any story ending in an eschatological resolution: "Between God, the most high Spectator, and the world (Fortuna) there is a relationship, but their distinctness from each other is even clearer. Initially the roles stand in lonely juxtaposition, appointed from on high, but they only have meaning through their dialogue relationship."[68] The creature remains a creature while finding its place only in the whole determined by God: "Rarely was *theologia naturalis* built into Christian theology as intimately as here."[69] Nevertheless, although Calderón's stage construction is impeccable, his casting retains one major deficit. Balthasar registers on several occasions his dissatisfaction with Calderón's portrayal of God as less an actor and more a simple spectator in the great world drama: "In his *Theatre of the World*, Calderon put God enthroned above the stage, as Spectator and Judge. Given the way he appears there, it would have been impossible for him to descend and take a part—however important—in the drama."[70] God does not appear on the stage, but instead assigns each actor his part and gives out prizes and demerits only after the curtain falls. Albeit consistent with the baroque insistence on free will and the striving of the human spirit, it fails to have the Word himself take on an integral human nature and join as an actor on the stage of the world.

What saves Calderón, in Balthasar's estimation, is precisely what makes this genre such a landmark of Catholic literature: it is a *sacramental* play. Strangely skipping over Christ within the play itself, Calderón arrives at the Eucharist as that which both unites and distinguishes God and the creature. "The world is in no way reabsorbed into God: here we have a christological conclusion looking toward the messianic, eucharistic meal."[71] Not appearing on stage during the play, Christ appears "only at the end, in heaven, veiled in the eucharistic forms."[72] Calderón's explicit notion of a celestial Eucharist, against the traditional stance of its expiration, will also win him favor with Balthasar, as will be seen later in this chapter.[73] God's liturgy and the creaturely drama do not cross on the world stage explicitly, but Balthasar does think that the eucharistic conclusion must be read back into the world theatre as its presupposition and its entelechy. Unlike Greek tragedy, which suffered under the weight of an inevitable, foreordained conclusion, such that human freedom and striving is ultimately revealed to be nothing more than an illusion in light of cosmic determinacy,[74] much of baroque literature is the "apogee of the drama" because it allows for full creaturely freedom that is not abnegated by the divine conclusion.[75] Especially in the *autos sacramentales*, it is the Eucharist that allows for the retention of both poles of the drama, the freedom of the creature to accept or reject the given "roles" (for Balthasar, "missions"), and an ultimate, liturgical harmony in which concord has overtaken strife. There is then something unrepeatable about the baroque, according to Balthasar: the idea that the ancient cosmos is brought into the light of Christian revelation without being totally disfigured. Nevertheless, what Calderón left as implicit, namely, that God himself takes on a role in the world-theater, is explored with much greater urgency and poignancy by the poets and novelists of the early twentieth century, particularly Charles Péguy, Paul Claudel, Georges Bernanos, and Reinhold Schneider.

Almost any of the aforementioned writers could have been chosen, even given some of the important differences among them, but Péguy is for Balthasar the modern poet that best sees the Christological entrance into and transformation of mutable history. And although Balthasar spent far more of his life translating Claudel, the beleaguered Péguy often triumphs in Balthasar's estimation over his aristocratic compatriot.[76] *GL* II and III contain twelve portraits of lay and clerical styles, beginning with Irenaeus and ending with Péguy, which Balthasar notes is intentional: Péguy "completes the circle back to our own point of departure, to Irenaeus," because Péguy evinces the same sensitivity to horizontal history that animated Irenaeus's notion of recapitulation.[77] This is especially a question of a Christian evaluation of the Old Testament, and thus returns us to our discussion above about Balthasar's notion of a horizontal "Jewish" form of hope. Péguy, perhaps better than anyone else, gives history a permanence and tenaciousness, even when faced with eternity. In the confrontation between temporality and eternity, it is eternity that makes accommodations, which is for Péguy most evident in the Incarnation. Nowhere is this clearer than Péguy's "Clio I," where history speaks for herself. There, the figure of History says, "As God he made an eternal leap into the world, a frontal entry, as it were, into the temporal. He incorporated himself. And by that incorporation we might say he made a *maximal* entry, coming from infinity."[78] From this quote alone it is clear how Péguy differs from Calderón regarding whether God remains an actor or a spectator during the play of the world.

Péguy took the side of Judaism against the ecclesiastical support of the political charade condemning Captain Dreyfus, and beyond the particularities of that controversy, Péguy affirms everything about the idea of Jewish hope, along with his own proclivities for socialism, but without renouncing the Christian, vertical axis.[79] For Péguy, the Old Testament's ideal of changing the actual structures of the world to match the divine will is not superseded by Christian eschatological hope. Not only for ethical and political reasons (though surely these), but for theological reasons Péguy insists that Christianity must remain wed to Israel and the prophetic tradition: "Where this mediation [of Israel] is absent, Jesus is no longer seen as emerging from a race and a particular history, but drops straight out of heaven in Gnostic fashion."[80] Instead, for Péguy, Christ binds himself irrevocably to finitude and historicity, and despite the spiritualizing tendencies of the Church, Christianity remains an affair of the flesh, of the earth, which means historical solidarity with all flesh.[81] This solidarity with human misery is true not only of Christ, but of the saints, as this is put on vivid display in Péguy's portrayals of Joan of Arc.[82] It is for all of these reasons that Balthasar uses Péguy in *TD* V as a "foil" to the secularized form of Jewish hope as represented by Bloch and later adopted by Moltmann. He is a foil because he is an ally: Péguy takes on all the concerns put forward by the desire for intrahistorical fulfillment, but he does so by ultimately demonstrating the futility of a hope based solely on a particular point at the end of the historical timeline.[83] Péguy's poem on the second theological virtue, hope, is for Balthasar the antidote to Bloch's *Principle of Hope* and also to Moltmann's *Theology of Hope* because of its portrayal of hope as a reality in the present tense, as opposed to something akin to an expectation of a still-future state.[84]

Péguy did not so much convert from socialism to Catholicism as realize that the ideals of the former are only possible in the latter. It is the concept of solidarity that is the red thread connecting all his thought, which moves from a political and ethical basis to a mystical and theological notion of vicarious suffering.[85] According to Balthasar, "Péguy was bound to see that Christianity had always been his starting point: real solidarity cannot be had more cheaply than on the basis of true biblical *caritas*. Ultimately this means the Cross and the Eucharist through which it is distributed among men."[86] Thus, although his theological poetry is very often a meditation on the earth and the flesh, Péguy comes to appreciate that ultimately "nothing earthly is self-sufficient."[87] Hope transforms the horizontal, but does so in a manner far excessive of anything our earthly plodding can accomplish on its own. *Le porche du mystère de la deuxième vertu*, a poem in praise of faith's and charity's "little sister," hope, concludes with a reflection on the tireless monotony of life. We walk the same paths over and over again,

> With difficulty, with much effort, with much straining,
> Painfully
> The same point of disappointment.
> Of earthly disappointment.[88]

And our going over the same path day after day erases yesterday's tracks; thus our walking passes away into forgetfulness and futility.

But the paths of heaven eternally preserve every layer of tracks
All of our footprints.
Lining the paths of earth there is only one material, earth,
Our earthly paths are always made from the same earth. . . .
But the paths of heaven eternally receive imprints.
New ones.[89]

But hope, like a little child, runs back and forth along this path, the path that we plod along in anguish. What we do simply to complete a journey, hope does out of joy.

Children don't even think about being tired.
They run like little puppies. They make the trip twenty times.
And, consequently, twenty times more than they needed to.
What does it matter to them. They know well that at night
(But they don't even think about it)
They will fall asleep
In their bed or even at the table
And that sleep is the end of everything.[90]

Hope makes the same, earthly path, which Christ himself walked and sanctified,[91] eschatologically significant (our steps make tracks in heaven). Instead of an earthly future at the end of the journey, "now" is the time for Christian hope.

In Péguy's praise of hope, according to Balthasar, "the 'hope principle' has become Christian."[92] That is to say, the horizontal dimension of eschatological hope is at center stage, refusing to take refuge in a purely vertical, a-temporal account of fulfillment. And far more than in Bloch or Moltmann, in Péguy the horizontal dimension is actually a site of redemption: instead of a perpetual waiting for the future, for Péguy it is *these* rather disappointing paths, thus the actual horizontal plane that we experience, that take on eternal significance because it is God who makes himself responsible for them. For Péguy, Christ is so wed to history that everything that happens makes its mark on his flesh, but not as in a Hegelian process whereby God develops by means of world history.[93] Speaking as history again in "Clio I": "The least of sinners, the least of sins, wounds Jesus eternally. There you have Christianity. And I, history, throughout my long history, can do nothing which does not interest Jesus, God, naturally as though physically. I cannot commit anything temporally which is not inserted, physically as it were, into the body of God himself."[94]

Péguy's is no happy optimism, and he does not allow even for a moment that suffering is somehow justified or understandable in light of a greater synthesis: "One submits: but one does not, my child, get accustomed to it."[95] But in the end (after, it should be noted, a Corpus Christi procession), *Le porche* does conclude with what Balthasar calls a "praise of self-surrender" (*sich-überlassens*), a praise of sleep. It is ultimately a summons to a renunciation of one's own ability to set things aright, or even to comprehend how things might be set aright. It is the child "laughing secretly because of his confidence in his mother" as he falls asleep, which is an echo of the silence that preceded creation and ultimately of the silence of night and death in which the Son was "dead in the midst of men. Dead among the dead."[96] For Balthasar this brings everything to its Trinitarian foundation, as Christ's sleep is his "ultimate self-surrender [*Hingabe*] to the Father," and in the end, the vagaries of history will be resolved only insofar as they are brought into this self-gift: "This is because self-surrender is the last thing [*weil die Hingabe das Letzte ist*]; it is the last in God the Father, in the Son and in the Spirit, and it is the last in man too, when he has reached the end of his tortuous path."[97] Balthasar sees in Péguy a truly Christian answer to the liturgy/slaughter tension because Péguy neither produces a theodicy nor does he advocate for a utopia. Instead, Péguy commends hope, hope that Christ's *Hingabe* on behalf of history is itself effective to make tragedy penultimate,[98] a hope that in the end the liturgical consummation of the Son to the Father is extended to include and heal the winding paths of history.[99]

Calderón and Péguy, however much they provide insight into our theme of liturgy and slaughter, are for Balthasar secondary when compared with the book of Revelation. There is nothing obvious about this, and even though its canonical status does lend to Revelation an authority that the others lack, many other theologians have concluded that its propensity for producing eschatological mischief, particularly its seeming delight in the torture and damnation of sinners, is enough validation for finding more suitable sources. Yet Balthasar not only occasionally cites Revelation as a source, but actually frames his main eschatological texts,

TD IV and V, in light of Revelation's dramatic denouement. Immediately, however, he cuts off the possibility that Revelation can or should be read as either a prognostication of how and when the "end times" will play out, or as merely a coded description of the author's own historical situation.[100] Instead, what Revelation provides with its "all-pervading leitmotif" of the simultaneity of heavenly liturgy and divine judgment is something of a symbolic representation of what happens when God and the world intersect, and the repercussions this has on the individual, on the community at large, and even on God. It is thus the archetypical dramatic portrayal of the Christian solution to the tension between historical variability, including all of its sorrow, and the ceaseless heavenly liturgy, lauding God's sovereignty and goodness.[101]

John's Revelation is not innovative with his simultaneous portrayal of liturgy and slaughter, but rather he extends and expands what was already something of a doxological imperative in the Old Testament: "It was possible, even in the Old Testament tradition, to worship God's majesty amid the confusions and collapses of the world as such."[102] The Psalms of Lament indicate that Israel still prays even when all cause for praise and thanksgiving seem to be taken away, and even when the cultic infrastructure has been laid low.[103] This should already indicate that a total deferral of liturgy until a horizontal rectification of wrongs is not, according to Balthasar, truly representative of even Jewish eschatological hope. The difference between this Old Testament simultaneity and what is portrayed in Revelation comes with the crucial role of the "lamb that was slain." As opposed to its thematic foil in the apocalyptic beast from the sea, a beast that has a *healed* wound (13:3, 12), the lamb, referred to twenty-eight times in the text, is introduced as a lamb standing "as though it had been slain" (5:6), or more simply "that was slain" (5:12, 13:8). The lamb clearly functions as a continuation of the prophetic tradition of unmerited or helpless suffering,[104] but for Balthasar there is a major discontinuity stemming from the fact that the lamb becomes the very image of God and the agent of the liturgical unfolding, from the slaying of the lamb to its eventual reign.[105] This signals not only that it is the lamb who "absorbs" the wrath of God, but also that the slain lamb's victory over death paradoxically both encompasses and gives meaning to history and is radically constituted by it: "The paradoxical result— the apparent contradiction—is that he who encompasses all things, the

Alpha and Omega, seems ultimately to be encircled by the final act: this will have to form the central object of faith's pondering on this drama."[106] The lamb's prior and eternal victory, it seems, is a result of an intra-historical event (the cross), which Balthasar thinks can only be grasped when Christ's eucharistic self-gift is put within the horizon of Trinitarian self-giving.

Revelation depicts the struggle and frequent opposition between creaturely freedom and the divine freedom, and the fact that the closer these two freedoms encounter one another there arises an increase in tension and strife rather than harmony. Loving acceptance of the divine will (those who "follow the Lamb wherever he goes"; 14:4) is accompanied by violent resistance and hostility ("the woman, drunk with the blood of the saints and the blood of the martyrs of Jesus"; 17:6). The anti-Trinitarian *mysterium iniquitatis* lashes out against its divine other, but the *mysterium Trinitatis*, represented by the lamb, remains eternally vulnerable. This is then the pattern for the Christian response to evil: "In the Book of Revelation, there is only one way to combat the trinity of hell, which is the final shape of evil: believers must bear witness in their lives and in their blood, thus fully incarnating their faith as they pit it against utter, satanic dis-incarnation."[107] For Balthasar, this does not mean indifference or passivity in the face of evil, but rather a creative absorption and transformation of evil that can only be modeled on the Eucharist. Christ "manifests the glory of divine power in lowliness, defenselessness and a self-surrender that goes to the lengths of the eucharistic Cross [*Selbsthingabe bis zum eucharistischen Kreuz*]," which is itself an unveiling of "God's internal, trinitarian defenselessness."[108] Because for Balthasar the world exists "in God," creaturely freedom, including its abuse, has already been resolved within the wider circuit of Trinitarian gift and reception, which is itself the condition for the possibility of creaturely freedom in addition to being its ultimate salve. Not that God is entangled in the tragedy of the world, but rather that the tragedy of the world is, as it were, entangled within a God that is marked not only by infinite gift but also by infinite reception. And it is this latter quality that allows Balthasar to say that creaturely tragedy is in fact penultimate, that even this can be turned into a gift by a Trinitarian God who is turned toward the world as a slain lamb. What the world offers to God as contempt, the lamb returns as self-gift, as the gift of his divine flesh.[109]

Balthasar's affirmation of Revelation continues his ultimate preference for a form of "vertical" eschatology, whereby the resolution occurs
above history rather than at its temporal conclusion. He is not, however,
one of the "despisers of life" that Nietzsche excoriated: "I conjure you,
my brethren, *remain true to the earth*, and believe not those who speak
unto you of superearthly hopes! Poisoners are they, whether they know it
or not. Despisers of life are they, decaying ones and poisoned ones themselves, of whom the earth is so weary: so away with them!"[110] Balthasar is
not weary of the earth such that he longs for the heavenly liturgy above,
but instead is convinced that the only true joy to be found "here below" is
a willing acceptance of and participation in the great liturgy of history, of
history transformed and returned to earth. The Eucharist for Balthasar is
Christ's gift to earth of his recapitulating and healing of history, turning
what could be considered tragedy into a hymn of divine praise. Thus it is
the communicant who can see the value in the earth, who "remains true
to the earth" in its glory and its tragedy, because, to return to Péguy, the
only true "progress" is God's own prostration on the earth:

> *Lux fiat. Voluntas fiat.* In the beginning, a God in all his glory, in the
> glory of his power, in the (young) majesty of his creation; and more
> than fifty centuries after, after more than fifty centuries of progress,
> a God prostrate upon the ground, *procidit in faciem suam*, a God
> fallen upon his face, on the earth, humble, humbled, in the humble-
> ness of man. There, my child, is your progress. Such is its form: its
> marvellous, singular form. A failure in the eyes of men. A decline.
> And that is what you call progress.[111]

God answers God, according to Péguy. God speaks the *fiat lux* and God
responds, as man, and on behalf of men who have forgotten how to speak,
with the *fiat voluntas*. It is in the Eucharist, Balthasar insists, that the
earth learns to speak this *fiat voluntas*, that it is given the power to suffer
finitude and temporality with a transforming, and thus liturgical, joy. If
Balthasar then has no theodicy, as in an etiology and explanation for the
initial appearance of evil, he does provide what can only be called a eucharistic teleology of evil, whereby evil is absorbed and returned into a
gift of self on the other side of suffering. That is to say, with John of the
Cross, "the deeper the wound, the greater the healing."[112]

COMMUNIO SANCTORUM

In this section, we turn to Balthasar's understanding of the *res* of the Eucharist in its eschatological fulfillment, with regard to the question of the status of sacraments in the eschaton and to the implications this has for the *communio sanctorum*. What I will analyze here is a step beyond what was discussed in chapter 1, namely, Balthasar's understanding of the intra-Trinitarian love as itself archetypically "eucharistic," insofar as it is the foundation for all other acts of *Hingabe*. For Balthasar, it is not just that creatures are eschatologically inaugurated into the eucharistic love of God, but that this love is still communicated to the creature in a manner that is not wholly discontinuous with the sacramental system of ecclesial life. This is indeed one of Balthasar's more speculative claims regarding sacramental theology, but it has traditional warrants and a consistency with his overall advocacy for a theology that matches the devotional life of the Church. If the Eucharist is as important as ecclesial practice indicates, and itself generative of theological thought, then the dominant theory of the expiration of the sacraments may indeed be in need of revision.

The Celestial Eucharist

Balthasar's use of poets and mystics as theological sources does not function as a simple tool for validating his own proposals that might otherwise lack the support of the theological tradition. The testimony of a poet or a mystic is not in itself sufficient to warrant departure from long-accepted theological opinions, and thus Balthasar's use of them is anything but a *deus ex machina* or post hoc justification. Rather, Balthasar often finds that particular insights from sources beyond the classical theological luminaries serve to illuminate forgotten or even buried-over truths represented in the best of the theological tradition. Nowhere is this truer than in Balthasar's forays into eschatology, and in particular the question of the perdurance of sacramentality.[113] Take, for instance, Paul Claudel: "How can we suppose that in the next world there will be nothing corresponding to eucharistic Communion and that we will not be provided with 'the bread of angels'? In that world we will meet the naked realities of which the physical manifestations on this earth are but the poor shadow and image."[114] Balthasar, like Claudel, thinks that the decision against celestial sacraments is just as daringly speculative and without firm dogmatic support as is the decision in favor of it. In fact, the standard Thomist account has enough difficulties and a lack of scriptural warrants to make it at least subject to reconsideration. Balthasar's proposal of a celestial Eucharist is then not somehow a fanciful flight of the imagination, at least not any more than Thomas's denial. The Thomist premise, namely, that sacraments exist as remedies to a situation of sin, leads to its logical conclusion concerning the cessation of the sacraments. Balthasar does not accept the initial premise and thus dares to think again about the question of what happens to the Eucharist when the veil is drawn back.

Before arriving directly at Balthasar's understanding of the matter, it must be noted that he and Aquinas are not as opposed as it seems at first, and the difference is largely a matter of defining terms. The cessation of the *sacramenta*, when *sacramentum* is defined precisely as it functions as a sign (*sacrum signum*) and not yet the simple reality to which it refers, is certainly accepted by Balthasar. If the eschaton is precisely an immediate contact with God, then signs that are defined precisely as signals of a lack of immediacy are necessarily excluded from eschatological fulfillment. If this is what is meant by *sacramenta*, then even Balthasar could agree with their expiration. But moving from the broader category of sacrament to the Eucharist in particular, the question does remain: Does the Eucharist perdure in some meaningful way? Even Geoffrey Wainwright repeats the standard position, also advocated for by both Augustine and Aquinas, at the end of his *Eucharist and Eschatology*: "But [the Eucharist] remains a sign that can be contradicted (cf. Luke 2:34). It exemplifies the *clair-obscur* of 'the time of the church.' When the mystery of God has been completed (Rev. 10:7), sacraments will cease and the eucharist will give way to vision of God in his incontestable kingdom."[115] Why, though, speak of the Eucharist "giving way" to an eschatological vision when the entire tension of the *sacramentum et res* distinction is to affirm that the *res* (what is most profoundly true about the Eucharist) is what will be experienced eschatologically in a pure form without the veiling *sacramentum*? To identify the Eucharist with its purely phenomenal aspect (*sacramentum*) and thus to assume that the loss of this veil would also entail the loss of its true essence (*res*) is simply to allow Berengar in by the back door. If the Catholic answer to the *quid est* of the Eucharist is going to be heavily weighted towards the *res*, then it is indeed most appropriate to say that with the unveiling of the *res* there will be the fullness of the Eucharist, rather than its evaporation. The *res* of the Eucharist is also most accurately what is meant by eschatological fulfillment, in terms not only of a vertical union with God but also a horizontal orientation of humanity: *res sacramenti est unitas corporis mystici*, "the reality of the sacrament [of the Eucharist] is the unity of the mystical body."[116]

And although Aquinas does say explicitly that the sacraments were not necessary before the fall and will no longer be in heaven, he seems to be referring almost entirely to the *sacramenta* and not the *res*, which is again not *really* what we are talking about when we refer to the sacraments *in se*.[117] Further, when Aquinas speaks about the "bread of angels," he points to a much more lively sense in which the Eucharist is enjoyed both by angels now and by humanity in the eschaton: "The receiving of Christ under this sacrament is ordained to the enjoyment of heaven, as to its end, in the same way as the angels enjoy it; and since the means are gauged by the end, hence it is that such eating of Christ [*ista manducatio Christi*] whereby we receive Him under this sacrament, is, as it were, derived from that eating whereby the angels enjoy Christ in heaven [*derivatur ab illa manducatione qua Angeli fruuntur Christo in patria*]."[118]

Thus even for Thomas there is a celestial "eating" of Christ, which is signaled here below by sacramental signs and a sacramental eating. By no means against the best understanding of the scholastic tradition, many of the mystics have brought into greater light the idea that the "marriage supper of the Lamb" is the fulfillment and maximization of the ecclesial Eucharist.[119] For example, Balthasar cites Mechthild von Hackeborn, the thirteenth-century Benedictine nun, and notes that she "glimpses a kind of transfigured celebration of Mass in heaven."[120] When an episcopal interdict prevented Mechthild from receiving the Eucharist, Christ took her hand and showed her a Mass in which he himself was both priest and sacrifice: "After the *pax Domini* [peace of the Lord] was said, a table was set there; the Lord sat down at it, with his Mother beside him. The whole congregation approached the table, and as each one genuflected beneath the blessed Virgin's arm, she received the Lord's body from his own hand. The Virgin held a golden bowl to his side with a golden pipe, through which they all sucked that sweet liquid that flowed from his chest."[121] For Mechthild, the transition from *sacramentum et res* to *res tantum* is not a movement from the ecclesial Eucharist to an immediate vision of the divine essence, but from a mediated sacramentality to an immediate one in which the communion is not less bodily and Christologically focused, but more so.

Balthasar suggests that our understanding of the eschatological state needs to look far more continuous with ecclesial life, especially concerning the liturgy, than is often implied by notions such as the *visio beatifica*. In *A Theology of History*, Balthasar wrote that Christ's "eucharistic time" as manifest in the individual's life and in the history of the Church will not be "withdrawn or cancelled, it is only that this *form* of encounter will have become superfluous, because the Lord will no longer need to give himself under the veils which have been instituted for this part of time, which is the time of the Church."[122] In other words, Joachimism needs to be avoided not only intrahistorically but also eschatologically. One does not overcome Joachim by simply moving his third age of the spirit to a posthistorical eschaton, which is what Balthasar worries has often been done with the downplaying of the role of the (still) incarnate *Logos* in heaven.[123] The movement from history to eschaton, according to Balthasar, is one of perfecting and heightening rather than abolishing or replacing, at least as a rule. The two main metaphors that Balthasar claims as central to both Jewish and Christian notions of union with God, and particularly as this is understood eschatologically, are those of "meal" and "marriage," and this is most abundantly clear from the book of Revelation. These two images in particular "arise from fundamental human gestures and needs, they are elevated 'apophatically' in order to portray heaven fulfilling (and overfulfilling) the dimension of human intimacy through an entirely different intimacy with God."[124] And even though Balthasar does state unequivocally that the body's sexual functions and its need for food as nourishment will cease, he notes that even these natural urges have a theological significance beyond their clearly carnal utility.[125] Thus the "mystery of the marriage between heaven and earth that is celebrated in the Eucharist is both *now* and *in eternity* a mystery of body and spirit."[126] That is to say, the wedding feast of the Church and Christ, the Bride and the lamb, is a union not only of wills but of bodies. The artificiality of the symbols will give way to an "organic sacramentality" in which the grace of divine life penetrates the entirety of the "spiritual-physical creation."[127]

Balthasar does not attempt to overexplain the state of a celestial Eucharist, but instead attempts to outline what seems to be implied by scripture and tradition. And the key notion on which Balthasar bases much of his eschatological speculation is one we have addressed on numerous occasions: Christ's postresurrection pneumatic flesh. In addition to the qualifications regarding the analogical relationship between earthly and heavenly bodies, Balthasar also retains a catalogical notion whereby Christ's resurrected body would shed light back upon the original purpose of bodies as we know them. With this back-and-forth movement, he can claim that the eschatological state will be just as much a matter of flesh and blood, even if we have serious epistemological limitations regarding precisely what this would mean:

> We should not fancy that words like flesh and blood hold true only up to the Resurrection, even if we cannot imagine how a transfigured body is still to contain something that we normally understand by *blood*. Yet we should consider: from the very beginning blood has been *the* life element in man belonging to God (Gen. 9:4–6). The central vision of Catherine of Siena, now officially proclaimed a Doctor of the Church, was that of the Blood of Christ continually circulating to give life and purification in the Church and mankind.[128]

Whatever the particulars of our eschatological state, for Balthasar this new mode of life will not abolish the fact that we are essentially finite and bodily, these being neither the result of the fall nor limited to the span of creaturely history.[129] It thus remains that contact with God, which is now a matter of both spirit and of flesh, will continue to occur through and in the fleshly pneumatic Christ. Why exactly, in eschatologies that put such enormous weight upon the *visio beatifica*, such as Thomas's, would we even have bodies? The answer has obviously to do with the clear scriptural indications in this direction, but other than adding a sense of *conveniens*, eternal beatitude is one solely of a mental-spiritual contemplation, with even the body's connection to cognition in our earthly state ceasing to function.[130] Instead, calling for a far greater continuity with the *oikonomia*, eschatology for Balthasar really is a heavenly *liturgy*, with Christ given to the Church in his pneumatic-corporeal totality. When, for instance, *Sacrosanctum concilium* speaks about this heavenly liturgy, it simply echoes the entirety of the tradition: "In the earthly liturgy we take part in a foretaste of that heavenly liturgy which is celebrated in the holy city of Jerusalem toward which we journey as pilgrims, where Christ is sitting at the right hand of God, a minister of the holies and of the true tabernacle."[131] Either this language of celestial "liturgy," "hymns," "tabernacle," and "city" is somehow just a metaphor for the vision of the divine essence, or it points to that same reality that Claudel, Mechthild, Catherine of Siena, Speyr, Antonio Rosmini-Serbati, and the book of Revelation understood as an actual celestial liturgy centered on the slain lamb.

Balthasar's position is closely related and partially indebted to the idea of an eternal sacrifice of the lamb in some French theological literature, particularly related to the thought of Pierre de Bérulle, Charles de Condren, Jean-Jacques Olier, and most recently Maurice de La Taille. One important place in which Balthasar notes the significance of the "French School" is in *Mysterium Paschale*, where he says that the school's use of the notion of the "Lamb slain before the foundation of the world" functions as a middle way between positions that would either view the Incarnation and suffering as entirely unrelated to the divine immutability or view God as becoming mutable in Christ. For this French mystical tradition, there is an eternal and abiding state of Christ as sacrificed: "The 'slaying' is in no sense conceived in a Gnostic manner, as a heavenly sacrifice independent of that of Golgotha. It designates, rather, the eternal aspect of the historic and bloody sacrifice of the Cross (Apocalypse 5, 15)—as indeed Paul everywhere presupposes."[132] For them, picking up Thomas's notion of Christ present in the Eucharist as *Christus passus*, Christ remains in a "sacrificial state" even as he is risen.[133] There are important differences among these thinkers. For instance, La Taille (whom Balthasar is likely most dependent upon for this issue, but his interest in Bérulle is also significant) objects to the previous notions that suggest Christ is being "annihilated" eternally or that there is some renewed offering of Christ in heaven. Instead, for La Taille, it is simply that there is a "virtual duration" of the one sacrifice on Golgotha.[134] Balthasar follows La Taille in this, ever attempting to avoid any notion of tragedy within God, but he thinks that all of these insights can only be upheld when Christ's sacrifice is taken as a reflection of the *dreipersönlichen Hingabe*, the Trinitarian self-gift.[135] Christ's eternally sacrificial state is the incarnate Son's expression of his eternal generation from the Father, but in such a way that creaturely freedom and tragedy are absorbed and made into an eternal liturgy, a *eucharistia* back to the Father in the Holy Spirit. As a bodily event, it is, as it were, the mode by which resurrected bodies are both nourished and given over as gifts: "There will be a Eucharist; it will no longer nourish our mortal bodies [*Körper*] but those vital bodies [*Leiber*] which will simply be the 'expression' of our freedom and essentiality, what Hengstenberg calls 'bodying-forth' [*Darleibung*]; and for this very reason they will not be able to do without God's eternal nourishment. Eucharist, as an event of love, will remain something reciprocal."[136] The marriage between God and creation, or more specifically between the lamb and the Church, depicted in the final canonical book, will then truly fulfill the intracreaturely manifestation in the first: "They shall become one flesh" (Gen. 2:24).

Communio as Permeability

It is impossible to understand why the notion of an eternal Eucharist is so important for Balthasar without understanding its relation to the communal nature of the eschatological state. This is also where many of the lines we have drawn in previous chapters come together and intersect. In chapter 1, we saw Balthasar's proposal of Christ's "eucharistic ubiquity," such that Christ's body (*Leib*) exists no longer simply for himself, but for the Church, and chapter 2 saw this same principle applied as an ethical imperative such that Christian life is essentially one of becoming eucharistically extended and permeable. Balthasar's notions of Christ's unique form of ubiquity and the eucharistic form of life of Christians is brought into much greater clarity when the partial forms of manifestation and enactment give way to consummation. To begin then with the status of Christ's eschatological flesh, although Balthasar himself only hints at this conclusion, it follows logically from his position regarding Christ's eucharistic ubiquity that, when there is no longer any resistance to Christ's body, Luther's best intentions with regard to ubiquity will be vindicated. That is to say, Balthasar thinks Luther erred greatly by devaluing the particularity of Christ's resurrected flesh (considering it thus only as pneumatic) and by underestimating creation's ability to positively resist the encroachment of Christ's presence, but eschatologically speaking, Luther's notion of ubiquity will be somewhat accurate. It remains inaccurate inasmuch as it considers Christ's flesh to be coextensive with the divinity rather than coextensive with (redeemed) creation. Nevertheless, Balthasar thinks that Christ's flesh will indeed be the material, as it were, out of which the New Jerusalem is built.

As this topic indeed stretches theological vocabulary, Balthasar is not overly eager to describe in detail how Christ's pneumatic flesh and the materiality of the new heavens and the new earth are both united and distinguished. Rather, he employs several different notions to help point to what seems to be the basic constitution of eschatological flesh. One image is taken from Teilhard de Chardin: "The 'liquefaction' of the earthly substance of Jesus into a eucharistic substance is irreversible. It does not continue to the 'end' of world time—like some 'means'—but is the radiant core crystallized around that of the cosmos (according to the vision of the young Teilhard de Chardin). Or better: it is the core from which he transfigures the cosmos with his glowing radiance."[137]

Christ's willingness to be "liquefied," to be given out entirely on the cross and in the Eucharist, is for Balthasar an irreversible gesture, meaning that he remains forever given-over to the nourishment and benefit of the entire cosmos. In this image of Christ as the "core," it is not that Christ's flesh is simply identified with the materiality of the cosmos. Christ's body does not become some sort of "cosmic soup," but is rather the animating principle. Another image Balthasar uses is very telling, but unfortunately not developed at any great length: that of Maurice Blondel's interpretation of Leibniz's notion of the *vinculum substantiale*.[138] After quoting Revelation's image of the "Lamb as though it had been slain," Balthasar writes that Christ "becomes the creaturely prototype and sacrament of the omnipresence and total self-giving of the triune God. At the same time, he becomes the *vinculum substantiale* of all creation, which he recapitulates in himself."[139] Stated roughly, the omnipresence of the divine nature is made concrete and creaturely by Christ and his flesh. And just as God's omnipotence does not logically result in pantheism, so Christ's extended flesh does not result in a kind of panchristism that leaves no room for redeemed creation's own unique materiality. Christ as the "substantial bond" of creation means, to use Leibniz's vocabulary, that the individual "monads" can indeed be united into a composite substance, that the persons who constitute the *communio sanctorum* remain both individuals and bonded together as the body of Christ.[140]

Whatever the metaphor, Balthasar's understanding can perhaps best be seen in his interpretation of John 14:3: "I go to prepare a place for you." For Balthasar, the place that Christ goes to prepare is simply himself. He quotes John Scotus Eriugena, to whom he is indebted on this issue: "It is *he* who is the only, the most spacious house: in him everything is contained and ordered as in a state [*res publica*]; in him the universe is established by God and in God, in innumerable and manifold dwellings . . . Christ is this house."[141]

Beyond this bare sketch, Balthasar is hesitant to elaborate. More central to his thought, in any case, were the implications of Christ's eucharistic ubiquity for an understanding of the communion of saints, both during the current *ecclesia triumphans/militans* divide and after. As we saw in chapter 2, a mission "deprivatizes" the ego, it makes one already ecstatic and implicated with the rest of the mystical body. The saints are bound up with one another, sharing, as it were, but one life: "There is a mutual interpenetration of the diverse missions and the persons who identify themselves with them: this is what is meant by the *communio sanctorum*."[142] Although already begun here on earth, the *ecclesia triumphans* lives this as an ontological reality. Basing much of his theology on the consistent liturgical practice of the Church, Balthasar notes that if we truly believe that the saints can be invoked at any time and at any place, as is indeed ecclesial custom, then the saints must have the "same eucharistic openness toward us" as does Christ.[143] Thus, the saints share in Christ's eucharistic ubiquity. One might be tempted to compare this to Rahner's early notion of the "pancosmic" situation of the blessed dead, but Balthasar's conception has more positive Christological content and is intended to describe not only souls in the "intermediate state" but also the status of resurrected bodies.[144] The saints can be called upon in multiple places and at multiple times not only because of how eternity intersects with time, but also because the eschatological state is one that is defined by a eucharistic "permeability" of each person to another. Not that, per se, the saints give themselves out in the ecclesial Eucharist (though this position is not without some traditional support),[145] but that they share in the same logic that reigns in the Trinity and in the risen Christ: a complete abandon and self-gift (*Hingabe*) to the will of God and the good of the *communio*, without thereby losing their own spontaneity and unique identities.

We have no need to examine his *Dare We Hope?* in any depth, but it is clear that one of Balthasar's central points in that text, along with the *Short Discourse on Hell*, is that it is the saint above all who feels herself utterly bound to the fate of the rest of humanity. For example, after calling up an enormous list of supporters of his position, from Przywara to de Lubac to Blondel to Péguy to Ratzinger to Rahner, he turns to his most valuable support: "The last word, here as well, will go to the saints. Regardless of whether they think that there are or are not men in hell, the thought of that possibility remains unbearable to them."[146] The witness of the greatest saints suggests that sanctity is coterminous with a heightened sensitivity to the sufferings and failures of all. Balthasar, of course, does not use this as evidence for *apokatastasis*, a position he explicitly rejects,[147] but rather as confirmation that the theological virtue of hope leads to an increase in solidarity and a willingness to "suffer together with Jesus for the redemption of mankind."[148] This intimate relationality in which one's own identity is implicated in that of others is essential to Balthasar's understanding of a person as opposed to a mere individual.[149] There is thus already a firm ontological basis in the solidarity of the human race that the *communio sanctorum* can be said to elevate and perfect. Although a lived reality for the saints on earth, this becomes perfectly realized and expressed in heaven. How else could one make sense of Thérèse's desire to "pass her heaven doing good on earth," not as a pious but unrealizable wish, but as a real foresight into the permeability of the *ecclesia triumphans* and *militans*: "Unlike any previous saint, she regards heaven as the scene for her most intense missionary activity."[150] For Balthasar, the only way to understand such a solidarity with the saints in glory is by noting that they have come to share in Christ's eucharistic mode of life, which, again, is the mode by which creation can share in the Triune life: "By accepting the Son's total surrender [*Vollhingabe*], [the Father] opens up for him the path of the Eucharist, through which he can integrate the Church and the world into his sacrificial spirit and so assimilate them to the mode of existence of the Trinity."[151] By being brought into this sacrificial spirit, the saints not only perfectly share the divine will, but also share the bodily life proper to the state of blessedness. This means a eucharistic mode of bodily life in which solidarity means more than empathy, but even a bodily co-presence and a co-suffering. However difficult it may be, then, Balthasar thinks that the traditional affirmation of the immediate beatitude of holy souls (Benedict XII) needs to be held simultaneously with the belief that the saints retain a "perseverance, an expectation and hope within world history," which is based on Christ's continual "agony until the end of the world" (Pascal). That is, the beatitude of Christ and the saints does not exclude their continued "cosuffering" with the rest of creation until the final consummation.[152]

It has already been stated several times, but it needs to be repeated that Balthasar knows well that eschatological speculation needs a measure of restraint. Nevertheless, he does think that the simple stipulation that the fullness of eschatological life can be reduced to the *visio beatifica* is far too restrained and fails to consider how the positive features of finite life perdure. One such issue that Balthasar is not willing to compromise is the fact of personal freedom. No matter, then, how much he speculates about the sharing of Christ's body and the spiritual and even physical unity of the *communio sanctorum*, Balthasar does not consider this unity to be a leveling out of the differences between people, the differences that make it possible to live in community here below. These differences are the origin for our ability to surprise one another and to give ourselves as a gift to others: "However we try to portray the unimaginable eternal life in the communion of saints, one element of it is constant: we shall be filled with astonished joy, constantly being given new and unexpected gifts through the creative freedom of others; and we for our part shall delight to invent other, new gifts and bestow them in return."[153] The logic of self-gift that governs eternal life will then not only be between the individual soul and God, but even horizontally, among the saints.[154] Just from this, we can see that the eschaton, according to Balthasar, in addition to being bodily and communal, is also constituted by some sort of temporal framework, is open to (creaturely) development and movement, and brings about an absolute harmony of wills by maximizing rather than equalizing individual freedoms. It is, in short, a vision of the eschatological life as a celestial liturgy. All of the positive elements of creaturely liturgy are retained, having left behind the realm of artificial signification and the all-too-frequent disjuncture between personal sentiment and liturgical rites. Balthasar then takes the notion of the Eucharist as a "foretaste" of heaven to its logical conclusion. The foretaste is not like an appetizer, a smaller and entirely different food from the main course (even if selected precisely for its compatibility), but rather a literal tasting in advance of that eschatological banquet in which all limited and fumbling uses of the body, community, and time are brought into perfection at the wedding feast of the lamb.

CONCLUSION: TO GIVE AND TO RECEIVE

Throughout this book we have strayed into topics that seem initially far from the province of traditional sacramental theology, only to see how Balthasar attempts to find eucharistic implications therein. This final chapter's foray into questions of time, tragedy, and eschatological fulfillment is the most extreme case of his prodigality with sacramental attribution. As we have seen, Balthasar believes that the Eucharist is the best means of providing a Catholic answer to some of the most intractable of philosophical and existential questions: time's relationship to eternity, the suffering of innocents, and communal and individual identity post mortem. It would be too much to say that the Eucharist "solves" these issues, and Balthasar is not so dense as to think that his eucharistic solutions would convince anyone who does not accept the givens of supernatural revelation. Rather, the main difficulties remain, and his solutions are nothing more than a hope that the promises of Christ would indeed be fulfilled. Thus, given that Christ has poured out his very substance for the salvation of the world on the cross and in the Eucharist, the full realization of individual and cosmic healing will look very much like the means used to accomplish it.

The ecclesial practice of the Eucharist signals to Balthasar that the experience of earthly life does indeed have a secret key beyond the existentials that can be discerned by any patient phenomenologist dealing with the givens of finite existence. A resigned fatalism or Nietzschean aplomb may indeed be two perfectly coherent means of facing one's own suffering and imminent death and also the horrors that bedevil the larger social and cosmic spheres. And, perhaps, one cannot be blamed too harshly for these responses. Yet Balthasar sees in the *sacramentum sacramentorum* not only a way to understand the whither of evil and suffering (cruciform absorption transformed into eucharistic gift) but also a moral imperative whereby one can suffer representatively as a repetition of the same Christic pattern. And nowhere does Balthasar claim that the decision in favor

of the eucharistic option would be the obvious choice, nor certainly that
it would be the easiest choice. For him, instead, it is the most difficult of
choices, but the only one in which there is hope. Not even the more proximate theological options, not even a "theology of hope" (Moltmann) nor
an existential faith (Bultmann), are able to provide a hope based on an
honest assessment of our utter inability to rectify the situation within time
and the fact that this rectification does indeed need to occur. Not only
does the Eucharist act as a witness regarding the partial (*sacramentum*)
fulfillment (*res*), this being our situation in the *chiaroscuro*, but it acts as
the agent that moves what remains partial toward fulfillment.

Balthasar's use of literary and mystical sources, in general but particularly concerning eschatology, can be regarded as perhaps further evidence for his recalcitrant obscurity, either out of delight for so-called
paradox or because he has nothing substantial to say. As his critics say,
it is simply fodder for him to say "too much," to know more than one is
allowed to know.[155] This criticism is fairly strange given that theologies
have never been condemned for range or extent of knowledge but rather
according to categories such as veracity versus falsity or orthodoxy versus heterodoxy. Be that as it may, Balthasar recognizes that we are all at
a loss with regard to an accurate description of the eschatological state,
and decisions regarding the expiration of the sacraments and the focusing of all eternal beatitude on the *visio beatifica* are equally subject to the
accusation of knowing "too much." Reducing the images found in scripture, above all from Revelation, and the intuitions and visions of mystics
to some purer form that fits better in the procrustean bed of our own as-
pirations to transcend finitude is for Balthasar a dangerous yet constant
temptation for the theologian. Instead, Balthasar prefers to stay with the
symbols and images that are given in scripture, and to presume that what
is enacted liturgically on earth is intrinsically related to that for which it
is a preparation. Christ's spiritual-corporal gift of self to the Church in
the Eucharist is for Balthasar an indication that when the veil of the *sacramentum* is removed, the *res* will confirm rather than negate the centrality of the sacramental practice. According to Balthasar, the heavenly
Jerusalem centered on the "Lamb as though it had been slain" means
that the *res* of the individual soul's union with God, the *actus essendi*
and infinite font of all Being, will be inseparable from the Church's corporate union with Christ in which his blood, God's blood, will circulate

freely in the *totus Christus*. The mutual self-surrender that constitutes the Trinitarian persons, their infinite nature as self-gift and reception of the other, is God's "'blood circulation,' the mutual exchange of blood between Persons."[156] This divine "blood" becomes real incarnate blood in Christ, which translates, as it were, the Trinitarian life into a finite form such that creation is able not only to receive from God but to also give in that infinite circulation. *Die Hingabe ist das Letzte.*

Balthasar's Cosmic Liturgy

Despite his absence from the halls of those traditionally recognized as major sacramental theologians, an important but rather trivial goal of this book was to demonstrate that Balthasar wrote extensively and systematically about the Eucharist, and thus, whether he receives recognition for it or not, he at least considered himself to be something of a sacramental theologian. This is in evidence most conspicuously by how extensively he wrote on the sacraments, in the form of articles, book chapters, and translations, or otherwise simply interwove them throughout his major theological writing, particularly but not exclusively in the *Trilogy*. The more consequential argument has been that beyond an impressive quantity of texts on the sacraments, Balthasar's work on the Eucharist is internally coherent with his broader theological project and generated some of his better-known theological positions. That is, he more often than not thinks from the Eucharist toward other topics, as we saw with Christology and Trinitarian theology in chapter 1, pneumatology, ecclesiology, and theological ethics in chapter 2, aesthetics in chapter 3, and eschatology in chapter 4.

It is his insistence on the unity between the structure and practices of Christian sacramental life and dogmatic theology that makes Balthasar a "liturgical theologian," even given the significant reservations he has with overvaluing the liturgical rites as sites of manifestation. And even though similar arguments could be made by turning to Balthasar's interpretation of the other sacraments, a project that would indeed bear much fruit,[1] he is above all a eucharistic theologian. It would be a strange argument indeed to accuse Balthasar of being a theological rationalist, but he is committed to the belief that no aspect of the Christian faith can be left to the side as intellectually irrelevant. On the Eucharist, especially as this sacrament has been the occasion of interminable debates since the Reformation and consistent critiques since the Enlightenment, Balthasar thinks that if it is to retain the central place it has always held in Christian spirituality, then it must be shown to be, not logically necessary, but constitutive for a particularly Catholic theological vision and for a sane humanistic one. Balthasar thus raises the stakes: either the Eucharist is theologically indispensable or Catholicism as a whole is no longer viable.

Balthasar, even if often falsely hailed as something of a traditionalist, could be quite iconoclastic regarding certain aspects of the received theological inheritance. That is to say, he was no theological positivist, assuming that the given forms of Catholicism's self-expression are necessarily constitutive to its identity. Reform and revaluation are possibilities for Balthasar, and are often required. Nevertheless, he considers Catholicism to be ineluctably tied to sacramentality, and thus no *aggiornamento* or internal reform can minimize the sacraments without incurring a major distortion. Procedurally, then, Balthasar's theology can be seen as a consistent attempt at eucharistic maximization.[2] Balthasar has staked his entire theological project on the bet that the Eucharist can indeed be maximized and stretched theologically without arriving at a breaking point. There are, of course, minor breaks, breaks such that sacramentality needs to be complemented by interiority and personal appropriation so as to avoid automatism, or by an eschatological caveat whereby certain aspects of the sacraments (such as their sign quality) must be seen as provisional. But for Balthasar, rightly understood, these are not so much complements from outside the sacraments but rather the best mode of understanding sacramentality in the first instance. He is rightly considered a dogmatic theologian, but Balthasar's *Trilogy* is not a *Summa theologiae* or a *Kirchliche Dogmatik* or even a *Handbuch der katholischen Dogmatik*. In other words, whatever his analysis of beauty, goodness, and truth may be, it is not an attempt at an exhaustive presentation of all major points of Catholic doctrine. But were he to have written a *Summa* instead of his *Trilogy*, it is clear that his *Prima Pars* would be as sacramental as his *Tertia Pars* would be Trinitarian, and the *Prima Secundae* and the *Secunda Secundae* would be equally infused by both the eucharistic foreground and the Trinitarian background.

This book has thus focused on the particular contributions that Balthasar makes to a theology of the Eucharist and on his theology as a whole as eucharistically structured. With regard to the former, Balthasar has specific and unique proposals concerning the Church's central sacrament. For instance, in chapter 1 we saw his argument that only the Eucharist completes the Incarnation, his use of kenotic language to describe Christ's humble state under the species of bread and wine, his notion that *the* Eucharist, properly speaking, is to be found within the eternal Triune processions, and his (partial) recovery of the notion of Christ's postresurrection ubiquity. In chapter 2, we saw how Balthasar proposes the notion of synergy as a more accurate description of what is typically described with causal language, his existential notion of the sacrifice of the Mass, and how he unites ethics and eucharistic theology, all placed within a discussion of the Holy Spirit. Chapter 3 placed Balthasar in conversation with other contemporary liturgical theologies and phenomenological eucharistic theologies to demonstrate how his particular understanding of theological aesthetics acts as a restraint upon unfettered valorization of liturgical appearance. A major issue there was Balthasar's insistence on the continuing relevance of the *sacramentum/res* distinction. Finally, chapter 4 raised questions of the "time" of the sacraments, the relationship between adoration and the horrors of history, and the eschatological permanence of the Eucharist. These many issues alone make it clear that Balthasar's *de sacramentis* is unique, expansive, traditional, and innovative.

These particular issues regarding eucharistic theology, however, were subservient to demonstrating that Balthasar's theology as a whole is concerned, one could say consumed, with making the Eucharist the linchpin for all speculative dogmatics. His entire theological project is one that begins, remains, and terminates in the liturgical cult. Revelation as a whole, for Balthasar, is a sacramental happening: "The revelation of the Son has from the very outset a eucharistic structure, which implies also that the Faith that answers this revelation as its echo has the same structure."[3] For Balthasar this means primarily that revelation must be understood not simply as the contents of knowledge that exceed the capacity of the human mind, but as the mode in which God gives himself out to the creature in order to be received by a reciprocal gift of self. For Balthasar, this sacramental logic extends even beyond the sphere of revelation, and into that of reason and reason's grasp of creaturely being. Not only is Christ's movement toward humanity oriented to its eucharistic conclusion, but creation is already positively disposed to the same place: "'Substanz ist da zur 'Transsubstantiation,' zur 'Kommunion'" ("substance" is there for the purpose of "transubstantiation," for "communion").[4]

This is to say that Balthasar puts no limits on the extent to which the "compelling and transparent logic" of the Eucharist must change everything about our previous conceptions.[5] In Balthasar's fertile theological mind, the sacramental *cultus* not only manages to be justified within a comprehensive theological system but, even further, the Eucharist is allowed to become the adjudicator of every other object of speculation. The doctrine of God is put to the test, and only a eucharistic God, a God whose Trinitarian life is one of infinite self-gift, is determined to be adequate. At the opposite extreme, finite being is only comprehensible to Balthasar insofar as it becomes the site of finite self-gift, actualized particularly in humanity's epistemological and ontological *ecstasis*. And even this finite self-gift makes a eucharistic synthesis, to use Blondel's idiom, both necessary and impossible. That is, finitude absolutely must be completed by a eucharistic incorporation into the *totus Christus*, by demands native to its own constitution, even if it has on its own neither the resources nor a clear conceptualization of what it implicitly demands.

Nowhere has it been claimed that Balthasar's work is the nearest thing we have to an exhaustive eucharistic theology. In fact, as we have noted on numerous occasions, he actually writes very little on the traditional topics in sacramental theology, preferring instead to elaborate the broader theological implications of the Eucharist that are more often than not forgotten. His theology as a whole, then, is based on the sacramental span in which everything from a mother's smile to God's own life can be seen to confirm and require the liturgical practice of the Church, to make ecclesial *mythos* essential to theological *logos*. Balthasar portrays everything from Christian experience and spirituality[6] to the enigma of human tragedy in a eucharistic light, and not simply to add a veneer of piety to weighty dogmatic issues, but as thematically illuminative. It is in this sense that Balthasar could arguably be considered the most expansive eucharistic theologian of recent times. This is so not only because what he writes about the Eucharist *in se* should be taken as a major boon to sacramental theology, but that he makes the Eucharist the heart of all theological topics, refusing to allow it to remain solely the province of professional liturgists or merely of interest to canon lawyers or as a dogmatic afterthought that one should really say something about, if one has the time. In the theologian's *ordo cognoscendi* it is the Eucharist that is the epistemic basis for looking downward to the goodness of creation, upward to God's infinite *Hingabe*, and to each side to see other dogmatic *topoi*. To then quote again Balthasar's depiction of Maximus's theology: "The liturgy is the midpoint, around which everything revolves, from which—as the single bright point into which one cannot look—everything is explained, whether left or right, up or down (as in Raphael's *Disputa*). . . . the liturgy is everywhere presupposed as the act that makes real the universal presence of the hypostatic Christ—at the midpoint between God and creation, heaven and earth, new age and old, Church and world."[7]

Chapter 1 concluded with a meditation on Raphael's *La Disputa*, and it is in that same room in the papal apartments (Stanza della Segnatura) that we can appreciate the full implications of Balthasar's eucharistic theology. Standing opposite the eucharistic "disputation" is the better-known *School of Athens*. With all the notable figures of classical philosophy represented, and centered on Plato and Aristotle, the *School of Athens* is not only set in apposition to *La Disputa*, but the two philosophers are literally walking toward the eucharistic scene across the room.[8] The two paintings are the same size, fit within the same parameters, and are equally structured. In the *School of Athens*, however, the vaults of heaven are blank; it is a space that is waiting to be filled in. The philosophers stand in a newly built cathedral that still awaits the iconography on the dome. *La Disputa* shows the definitive traversing of the heaven/earth division, but this traversing is only possible when the barrier is even more firmly established. The *School of Athens* exists on one plane: there are the heavens, but there is nothing dividing it from the earth. If there is a real distinction between the heavens and the earth, it is a porous one. *La Disputa*, on the other hand, has a thick layer of clouds between heaven and earth, thus confirming and even magnifying the philosophical structure, not negating it.

La Disputa fills out the content not only as to the dyad of heaven and earth, but in its introduction of a third, a triad.[9] The third that is new here is the Eucharist, placed *on* the earth, but elevated upon the altar. It is halfway between heaven and earth, as it simultaneously comes down from heaven, poured out from the Father through the Spirit, and is offered up from the earth toward heaven. The Eucharist moves in two directions at the same time. It is offering and reception, gift and counter-gift, created and uncreated, terrestrial and celestial. The most important difference between the two scenes is that the one is academic, the other cultic. The *disputa* over the Eucharist is set within the context of adoration, and is less of a "disputation" than a "revelation."[10] As the theologians are speculating about how the Eucharist is the real presence of Christ's body and blood within the species of bread and wine, they circle around the monstrance on the altar, awaiting the Benediction.[11] The movement from the *School of Athens* to *La Disputa* is a movement from cogitation to adoration: "Because love is ultimate, the seraphim cover their faces with their wings, for the mystery of eternal love is one whose superluminous night may be glorified only through adoration."[12]

It is on this hinge between thought and adoration that all of Balthasar's theology is balanced, and nowhere more so than in his eucharistic theology. For, as Balthasar explains by giving epistemic priority to love, "the lover wants to know only as much of the beloved as the beloved wants to communicate to him."[13] If this is so for finite knowledge, it is especially the case concerning revelation, which is why Balthasar's theology attempts to be nothing more, and nothing less, than a meditation on how the divine lover has chosen to communicate himself: in an utter abandonment of self into the hands of fallible humanity. It is from this eucharistic center, in which Christ is manifested only in his concealment, that all other mysteries are illuminated.

NOTES

INTRODUCTION

1. Aquinas notes a variety of possible explanations for the fittingness of bread and wine in *ST* III, 74. 1. co., including those of Ambrose and Augustine.

2. Jean Leclercq provides a helpful description of how, at least schematically, more "monastic" and "scholastic" theologians responded to the eucharistic debates stimulated by Berengar of Tours. Some focused on the precise questions of the mode of presence, but what interested others, such as Baldwin of Ford (d. 1190), "is not the way in which the Eucharistic mystery takes place; it is the mystery itself and its connection with the other mysteries in the totality of the Christian Mystery. . . . [the more scholastic questions] were considered as secondary matters in relation to the content of Revelation itself and the illumination which was obtained through contemplation" (Leclercq, *The Love of Learning and the Desire for God*, 211).

3. Balthasar, *Geschichte des eschatologischen Problems in der modernen deutschen Literatur*, originally published in 1930. He later revised and greatly expanded this between 1937 and 1939 as the three-volume *Apokalypse der deutschen Seele*.

4. Published in Rome in 1935. In the Balthasar Archiv in Basel, which contains Balthasar's personal library, there is a copy of this text, which, depending on when Balthasar studied the sacraments (he finished his studies in 1937), seems almost certainly a text he would have read in seminary (rather than purchasing a copy later!). The copy in the Balthasar Archiv has his marginalia throughout the first half of this text, which then stop abruptly.

5. Originally published in 1907. English translation of the third edition: *Theology of the Sacraments*. In addition to this being a widely used text, especially given that his theological studies were in France, it is also clear that he had read this before writing his articles on Origen in 1936 and 1937 that would later become *Parole et mystère chez Origène*, in which he cites Pourrat positively. In the later book, the citation is at 141n34, which appears exactly as the original article from 1937, "Le Mystère d'Origène," 54n2.

6. See Schwartz, *Sacramental Poetics at the Dawn of Secularism*. Schwartz's remarkable book is confined to English letters, but her thesis applies equally to the

Germanic. She argues not only that the Eucharist is relocated in modernity, but, more strikingly, that this relocation was a necessity for modernity to be born at all.

7. *TD* I, 321–22.

8. See Guerriero, *Hans Urs von Balthasar*, 21–30, for a brief description of his pre-Jesuit studies.

9. *Apok.* I, 328, 575–77, and 716.

10. *Apok.* III, 62; from Trakl's poem "Herbstseele." Interpretation of Trakl, much like Hölderlin, is a point of divergence with Heidegger, who in both cases attempts to erase the eucharistic tenor of their poetry.

11. For his commentary on Guardini's reading of Rilke, see Balthasar, *Romano Guardini*, 83–85.

12. *Apok.* II:117. Here Balthasar calls attention to Rilke's Third Elegy.

13. Hölderlin, "Brod und Wein" (1801), trans. Susan Ranson.

14. *Apok.* I, 433–40. With regard to Rilke, Guardini says, "Basic to Rilke's poetry is the will to shed the transcendence of Revelation and to ground existence absolutely on earth" (Guardini, *The End of the Modern World*, 103). See also Guardini, *Rilke's "Duino Elegies*," 239.

15. *TD* I, 92–93, 115–19, and 312.

16. Balthasar, *Tragedy under Grace*, 69.

17. Balthasar, "Review of *Die Messe* by Paul Claudel," 270 (emphasis added). Balthasar later translated *La Messe là-bas* as *Die Messe fernab*, in Claudel, *Gesammelte Werke*, Bd. I, *Lyrik*, which was later reissued as Claudel, *Die Messe des Verbannten*.

18. *GL* V, 26.

19. David N. Power, however, deserves credit for at least noting that although what he calls Balthasar's "aesthetic theology" (a term Balthasar explicitly rejects) has not been applied to sacramental theology as often or as comprehensively as the method of Karl Rahner, it still "clearly has application there" (Power, "Sacramental Theology," 663). See *GL* I, 38. Note also that Edward Kilmartin dedicates two pages to Balthasar in Kilmartin, *The Eucharist in the West*, 301–2.

20. *Parole et mystère chez Origène* has its origins in two earlier essays that were later incorporated into the book: both titled "Le Mystère d'Origène"; Balthasar, *Origenes: Geist und Feuer*; English translation of the second edition as Origen of Alexandria, *Origen: Spirit and Fire*, trans. by Robert J. Daly.

21. Balthasar, *Kosmische Liturgie*; English translation of the second edition: *CL*. Balthasar, *Présence et pensée*, which is an expansion of Balthasar's 1939 essay "Présence et Pensée, La philosophie religieuse de Grégoire de Nysse." English translation of *Présence et pensée* by Sebanc, *Presence and Thought*.

22. Balthasar, "Sehen, Hören und Lesen im Raum der Kirche"; later republished in *ET* II, 473–90.

23. Balthasar, "Liturgie und Ehrfurcht"; later republished in *ET* II, 461–71.

24. First published in *ET* II, 503–13, in 1961, but first presented on television in 1960.

25. First published in *ET* II, 491–502.

26. First published in *ET* III, 185–243.

27. First published as "Christus, Gestalt unseres Lebens: Zur theologischen Deutung der Eucharistie"; later published as "Mysterium Eucharistie/The Mystery of the Eucharist," in *NE*, 111–26.

28. First published in *E*, 181–90.

29. First published in *ET* IV, 209–43.

30. "Die Würde der Liturgie." Later republished in *NE*, 127–40.

31. First published as *Eucharistie—Gabe der Liebe*; English translation by Ciraulo, "Eucharist: Gift of Love" (2016).

32. *GL* I, 556–604.

33. See, especially, *GL* VII, 100–102, 148–52, 182–84, and 405–6.

34. *TD* III, 428–35, being the most explicit.

35. See *TL* III, 335–52.

36. Balthasar, *Epilogue*, esp. 99–123. Nicola Reali is in many respects correct to begin his book on Balthasar's sacramentality with the *Epilogue*. Cf. Reali, *La ragione e la forma*. The *Epilogue* is, according to Reali, the "chiave d'accesso" to Balthasar's thought in general and his theology of the sacraments in particular.

37. Calderón de la Barca, *Das große Welttheater*. As the publication itself mentions, Balthasar translated this precisely so that it would be performed on stage: "Übertragen und für die Bühne eingerichtet von Hans Urs von Balthasar."

38. Claudel, *Die Messe Des Verbannten*, with an afterword by Balthasar.

39. Corbon, *Liturgie aus dem Urquell*, with an introduction by Balthasar.

40. Paschasius Radbertus, *Vom Leib und Blut des Herrn*, with an introduction by Balthasar.

41. Bätzing, *Die Eucharistie Als Opfer Der Kirche Nach Hans Urs von Balthasar*; Reali, *La ragione e la forma*; Hesse, *Die Eucharistie als Opfer der Kirche*.

42. Roccasalvo, "The Eucharist as Beauty"; Mahoney, "The Analogy between the Eucharist and Marriage according to Hans Urs von Balthasar"; Zahatlan, "Das Eucharistieverständnis in Der Perspektive Der Theologischen Aesthetik Bei Hans Urs von Balthasar."

43. Miller, "The Sacramental Theology of Hans Urs von Balthasar"; Casarella, "The Expression and Form of the Word"; Casarella, "Analogia Donationis"; Worgul, "Balthasar's Kneeling Theology, Liturgics and Post Modernism"; Healy and Schindler, "For the Life of the World"; Ade, "Église Famille"; Wallner, *Eucharistie Bei Hans Urs v. Balthasar*; McPartlan, "Who Is the Church?"; Koerpel, "Hans Urs von Balthasar on Mary, Peter, and the Eucharist"; Kereszty, "The Eucharist and Mission in the Theology of Hans Urs von Balthasar"; Ide, "L'Eucharistie selon Balthasar"; Ciraulo, "Sacramentally Regulated Eschatology in Hans Urs von Balthasar and Pope

Benedict XVI"; Healy, "Christ's Eucharist and the Nature of Love"; Feichtinger, "Leo the Great and Hans Urs von Balthasar on the Eucharist."

44. *ET* V, "Peace in Theology," 390.

45. Balthasar's early essay "The Fathers, the Scholastics, and Ourselves" makes this very clear.

46. I am referring to the story that Jacques Servais tells of his time with Balthasar, de Lubac, and others at a chalet in the Swiss Alps, in which the group was doing a difficult puzzle together: "Finally, Balthasar walked up and joined us, picking up a piece, and putting it into place, then the next, and the next, until the whole puzzle was finished, and in less than ten minutes. We, quite frankly, would have been there for ten hours" (Servais, "Balthasar as Interpreter of the Catholic Tradition," 191).

CHAPTER 1

1. "Seeing, Believing, Eating," *ET* II, 499.

2. Chauvet, *Symbol and Sacrament*, 159 (emphasis original).

3. "After considering those things that concern the mystery of the incarnate Word, we must consider the sacraments of the Church which derive their efficacy from the Word incarnate Himself" (*ST* III, 60, prologue). See also *SCG* IV, 57. 1.

4. Scheeben, *The Mysteries of Christianity*, 469. And in addition to the Eucharist–Incarnation connection, Scheeben adds the Trinity to create a triptych of three primal mysteries that "mutually support, promote, and explain one another" (479). In this, as we shall see, he is an important precursor to Balthasar's position.

5. Pourrat, *Theology of the Sacraments*, 32–37. It should be added that Pourrat does not discuss the Incarnation or the Trinity in his treatise to any extent. Another example of this "confusion," as Pourrat calls it, is ready at hand with Hugh of St. Victor, whose most comprehensive work, treating all the major theological topics, is titled *De sacramentis christianae fidei*.

6. This is most evident in that when Balthasar sets about to discuss the sacraments explicitly, he almost always discusses all seven. For example, *GL* I, 576–83, *TD* III, 428–35, and *TL* III, 335–52.

7. *ST* III, 62. 5. co. Note that Balthasar employs Thomas's use of *instrumentum coniunctum* in *A Theology of History*, 17, and later notes its limits, 74.

8. For how Thomas derives these terms from Aristotle, see Yocum, "Aristotle in Aquinas's Sacramental Theology," 205–32, esp. 230–31.

9. Thomas only uses *instrumentum separatum* with regard to the sacraments twice in his entire oeuvre, both of which are in the article cited in note 7, above. Both references are concerned also with questions of causality. Lonergan explains, "An instrument is a lower cause moved by a higher so as to produce an

effect within the category proportionate to the higher" (Lonergan, *Grace and Freedom*, 83).

10. *GL* I, 582. Interestingly, in the context of this quote, Balthasar is warning against an overly aesthetic approach to the sacraments that would view their sign-value and ritual structure apart from the theological claims about them. This will be explored in more depth in chapter 3, but here it is important to note that he links scholasticism (with its concept of *instrumenta separata*) with the secularization of the study of the sacraments.

11. Of course, however, Balthasar's presumption is that this is a very bad reading of Thomas indeed. Thomas's linking of *missio* and *processio* is the cornerstone of Balthasar's own Trinitarian theology, even if his expansion of Aquinas could be justly considered a move beyond the intentions of the Angelic Doctor.

12. *GL* II, 43–44 (emphasis added).

13. *TD* IV, 349.

14. The frequency of this word in Balthasar's work will become evident in what follows, but we can also note here that he wrote a small leaflet titled "Hin-Gabe" in 1975. Two secondary works that focus on this word are Stinglhammer, *Freiheit in der Hingabe*, and a very helpful Balthasarian lexicon in Ide, *Une Théo-logique du Don*, 27–34. Ide does note the importance of *Hingabe* throughout the work, but in this *vocabulaire de la kénose* he focuses on the closely related words *Freigeben*, *Preisgabe*, and *Weggeben*. Aidan Nichols notes the importance of *Hingabe* in Balthasar's early work (particularly *Apokalypse*) in Nichols, *Scattering the Seed*; and *Hingabe* is given sustained attention by Schumacher, *A Trinitarian Anthropology*.

15. *TL* I, 42, 78, 126, and 127. For example, Balthasar treats *Hingabe* and *Opfer* (sacrifice) as virtual synonyms in *TD* V: "in die Hingabehaltung des Sohnes—in sein 'Opfer'" (*Theodramatik* IV, 443).

16. Balthasar seemed to work primarily from the French, but he owned and made some marginalia in this German translation, as can be found in the Balthasar Archiv.

17. In *Theologik* III, 217, he equates a word related to *Hingabe*, *Selbstübergabe*, with *exinanitio* (emptying).

18. *GL* V, 51.

19. Cf. ibid., 133.

20. Ibid., 139. Balthasar, *Herrlichkeit* III/I, 491 (emphasis original).

21. Balthasar calls the *fiat*, for Speyr, "the fundamental attitude." This "unconditional, definitive self-surrender" (*bedingungslose, endgültiger Hingabe*) is "the highest achievement made possible by grace" (Balthasar, *First Glance at Adrienne von Speyr*, 51; *Erster Blick auf Adrienne von Speyr*, 45).

22. *TD* IV, 322. See also Balthasar, *Mysterium Paschale*, 25.

23. It is worth comparing Balthasar's position to Bulgakov's, particularly the latter's suggestion of a "necessity of love." See Martin, *Hans Urs von Balthasar and*

the Critical Appropriation of Russian Religious Thought, and Gallaher, *Freedom and Necessity in Modern Trinitarian Theology*.

24. *TD* IV, 348. *"die Eucharistie des Sohnes, die seine Inkarnation erst wirklich vollendet"* (*Theodramatik*, III, 325). See also *TD* III, 235 and 333.

25. "The Mass, A Sacrifice of the Church?," *ET* III, 222.

26. "Eucharistic Congress 1960," *ET* II, 509.

27. Balthasar, *Life Out of Death*, 63.

28. "The Mystery of the Eucharist," *NE*, 117.

29. As noted most recently by Brendan McInerny, *The Trinitarian Theology of Hans Urs von Balthasar: An Introduction* (Notre Dame, IN: University of Notre Dame Press, 2020).

30. That is why the words of institution must be understood both in their allusion to Exodus 24:8 ("See the blood of the covenant that the Lord has made with you") and in the history of noble deaths and martyrdoms in the Old Testament and in the intertestamental period. See Evans and Johnston, "Intertestamental Background of the Christian Sacraments," esp. 44–49. For the cultic language used during the Last Supper, particularly in Luke, see Barber, "The New Temple, the New Priesthood, and the New Cult in Luke-Acts."

31. *ST* III, 73. 6. co.

32. Balthasar, "Eucharist: Gift of Love," 143. He even calls the cross the "Eucharist of the Cross," *GL* VII, 226.

33. Balthasar, *Does Jesus Know Us—Do We Know Him?*, 49.

34. Cf. *TD* III, 123, n1, and "The Mystery of the Eucharist," *NE*, 114.

35. *TD* IV, 319.

36. *TD* I, 426.

37. Cf. Balthasar, *Mysterium Paschale*, 97. On the consciousness of Christ regarding his mission, see "'Fides Christi': An Essay on the Consciousness of Christ," *ET* II, 43–79, and *TD* III, 149–202.

38. Balthasar, *The Heart of the World*, 180; Balthasar, *The Moment of Christian Witness*, 42; *TD* II, 33–36; *TD* V, 266; Balthasar, *Das Buch des Lammes*, 82. For a variety of examples of these images, from the fourteenth to the eighteenth centuries, see http://imaginemdei.blogspot.com/2017/06/corpus-christ-of-blood-all-price.html.

39. Cf. *TD* V, 266.

40. The most comprehensive survey of this phenomenon is Bynum, *Wonderful Blood*. An excellent article that analyzes this more from the perspective of artistic expression is Timmermann, "The Eucharist on the Eve of the Reformation," esp. 384–90, which also notes the dark underside to this phenomenon, namely, the accusation of Jews as desecrators of the Host.

41. *TD* V, 477.

42. Balthasar, *The Moment of Christian Witness*, 41–42.

43. Cf. *TD* IV, 495.

44. Ibid., 231–316.

45. Ibid., 260–66.

46. Kilby, *Balthasar: A (Very) Critical Introduction.* He admits, in *TD* V, 13: "We have tried to go as far as revelation permits," which nicely summarizes Balthasar's expansive speculation within the limits set by revelation itself. And he says about these five motifs, "It is clear that they belong together. It is also clear that they cannot be reduced to an allegedly higher integration, to a 'system'" (*TD* IV, 243).

47. *TD* IV, 330.

48. Ibid., 348.

49. Ibid., 406. The freedom *from* and *for* tension is seen on 367–83. *TD* II, 207–316, is the foundation for this distinction.

50. *TD* IV, 357.

51. Balthasar, *Mysterium Paschale*, 99. Compare how Aquinas treats this question, concluding, perhaps surprisingly, that it is indeed appropriate to say that "bread is the body of Christ" (*panis sit corpus Christi*) or "the body of Christ is made of bread" (*de pane fit corpus Christi*), given the requisite distinctions between bread as substance and its remaining presence uniquely as accidents; see *ST* III, 75. 8.

52. Gardiner, "The Dubious Adrienne von Speyr."

53. For instance, Speyr speaks in the most traditional terms of transubstantiation throughout *The Holy Mass* (e.g., 54, 63, 70), and in *Confession*, she speaks about the "unprecedented miracle, the miracle of transubstantiation" (221).

54. Miller, "The Sacramental Theology of Hans Urs von Balthasar," 65. Hauser also says, very incautiously, that "the danger of dehistoricizing the faith lingers in von Balthasar's theology, stemming from his suspicion of the traditional eucharistic language such as transubstantiation and *ex onere* [*sic*] *operato*" (Hauser, *Church, Worship and History*, 193).

55. Miller's work is confined almost entirely to *GL* I (where Balthasar does nonetheless affirm transubstantiation explicitly, cf. "The Sacramental Theology of Hans Urs von Balthasar," 573, and Hauser's *Church, Worship and History*, though it has a wider reach, even misses the fact that in *A Theology of History*, one of Hauser's main texts, Balthasar chooses to affirm "the miracle that achieves the sacrifice, transubstantiation" (100).

56. Instead of giving an exhaustive list of citations, I will give examples throughout this book. He even says that banishing *ex opere operato* to the realm of myth is a "flashing red 'danger' symbol" of bad theology ("Peace in Theology," *ET* V, 394–95). Also, throughout *Parole et Mystère chez Origène*, Balthasar, especially in the footnotes, attempts to transfer Origen's language into that of scholastic sacramental vocabulary.

57. Balthasar shares this understanding of the role of the concept of transubstantiation with Martelet, whose *Résurrection, Eucharistie et Genèse de l'Homme* is both influenced by Balthasar and later quoted by Balthasar himself (e.g., see *TD* II, 409). Martelet says that transubstantiation should not be understood "as though it were by itself the *nec plus ultra* we may say about the Lord's Supper. Correctly

understood, transubstantiation is, much more certainly, what we might call the *nec minus infra*: the lowest point below which we must not go if we are not to suffer a diminution of faith" (Martelet, *The Risen Christ and the Eucharistic World*, 107).

58. Cf. "Peace in Theology," *ET* V, 391.

59. "The theologian's task is not limited to repeating venerable formulae, much less in the tone of an old governess scolding foolish children who (constantly) forget their manners" ("Peace in Theology," *ET* V, 397).

60. Speyr, *The Passion from Within*, 31; *Passion von innen*, 27 (emphasis added).

61. Speyr, *The Passion from Within*, 39; *Passion von innen*, 34.

62. *GL* I, 572. *Herrlichkeit* I, 550.

63. *ST* III, 76. aa. 1–6.

64. Guitmund of Aversa, *On the Truth of the Body and Blood of Christ in the Eucharist*, 97; *Patrologia Latina (PL)* 149:1430C–D.

65. For an excellent historical discussion of this formula and its eventual acceptance at Constantinople II in 553, see Riches, *Ecce Homo*, 107–27.

66. *ST* III, 46. 12. co.

67. *GL* VII, 152.

68. *In Evangelium Ioannem*, tractatus 62.3. It is not exhaustive, but a good summary of varying patristic interpretations can be found in Joel C. Elowsky, ed. *Ancient Christian Commentary on Scripture: John 11–21*, 104–6.

69. *Sent.* IV, distinction 11, chap. 6 (65), and *ST* III, 81. 2.

70. See Speyr, *The Farewell Discourses: Meditations on John 13–17*, 51–54, and Speyr, *The Passion from Within*, 77–78.

71. *ST* III, 80. 3. s.c. One exegetical connection that Balthasar notes is that John uses the same verb "to gnaw," τρώγω, when Judas consumes the morsel (13:18), as is used in John 6. See "The Mass: A Sacrifice of the Church?," *ET* III, 232.

72. Balthasar, *Bernanos*, 522 (emphasis original). See also *TD* V, 281, and note also that the pre-Communion prayer in the Liturgy of St. John Chrysostom says, "I will not reveal your mystery to your enemies, nor will I give you a kiss like Judas."

73. "Eucharistic Congress 1960," *ET* II, 507.

74. Balthasar notes a particular connection between Christ's infancy and his eucharistic state: in both cases he is entrusted to the hands of another, first Mary, and then the Church (which is, of course, thoroughly Marian); cf. *TD* IV, 397.

75. "The Mystery of the Eucharist," *NE*, 114; German: "Christus, Gestalt Unseres Lebens," 175 (emphasis original).

76. David Bentley Hart has also used the word "scatter" to describe the prodigality of the Eucharist: "The consecrated elements 'scatter' him among his worshippers" (Hart, "'Thine Own of Thine Own,'" 157). Aquinas interestingly rejects the use of the word "scatter" to describe the Eucharist (*SCG* IV, 62.8), but it is based in his opposition to the idea that Christ is in the Eucharist "moveably."

77. Claudel, *L'Evangile d'Isaïe*, as cited in *I Believe in God*, 52.

78. A position that is partly endorsed by Pius XII: "Now the eucharistic species under which he is present symbolize the actual separation of his body and blood. . . . Jesus Christ is symbolically shown by separate symbols to be in a state of victimhood" (*Mediator Dei*, as cited in *Denz.* 3848). Note, however, that Pius only claims that the separation symbolizes (*figurant*) the sacrifice, not that it constitutes it. Balthasar even alludes to the separation of the species in *The Heart of the World*, 16.

79. De Lugo, *Treatise on the Venerable Sacrament of the Eucharist*, XIX, v. 67; as quoted by Stone, *A History of the Doctrine of the Holy Eucharist*, 2:376.

80. This is traced in detail by Pomplun, "The Theology of Gerard Manley Hopkins."

81. Hopkins, *The Sermons and Devotional Writings of Gerard Manley Hopkins*, 197; cited by Balthasar in *GL* III, 382.

82. Scheeben, *The Mysteries of Christianity*, 473, n4.

83. Ibid., 472.

84. Thérèse of Lisieux, *Histoire d'une âme*, 311–12, as cited by Balthasar, *Two Sisters in the Spirit*, 167.

85. Cf. *TD* V, 511.

86. Balthasar, "The Holy Church and the Eucharistic Sacrifice," 144. We can also note that Thomas says that bread and wine were chosen because they are among the things most frequently used by men: *sub speciebus illorum quae frequentius in usum hominis veniunt, scilicet panis et vini* (*ST* III, 75. 5. co.). See also Hugh of St. Victor, *De sacramentis*, bk. II, pt. 8, VIII.

87. Speyr, *The Discourses of Controversy: Meditations of John 6–12*, 38–39. See also Speyr, *The Cross, Word and Sacrament*, 44.

88. "The Mystery of the Eucharist," *NE*, 116–17.

89. Speyr, *The Holy Mass*, 70–71.

90. Guitmund of Aversa, *On the Truth of the Body and Blood of Christ in the Eucharist*, 100–101; *Patrologia Latina* (*PL*) 1432B–1432C (emphasis added).

91. Balthasar, *Mysterium Paschale*, 27, citing Hilary of Poitiers.

92. *TD* IV, 399.

93. Ibid., 359.

94. Pitstick, *Light in Darkness*, 250.

95. *ST* III, 73. 6. co. See also *ST* III, 62. 5, particularly obj. 3 and ad. 3, which raise a question quite similar to Pitstick's. That is to say, if so inclined, Balthasar could answer along with Aquinas that sacramental efficacy is ascribed to the Resurrection as to the *whither* (ad quem) and to the Passion (and Balthasar would add Christ's death and descent) as to the *whence* (a quo). Balthasar and Aquinas do indeed evaluate the descent into hell, along with the actual death of Christ (as distinct from the passion of the living Christ) quite differently, but that does not directly touch the issue raised by Pitstick in *Light in Darkness*.

96. *ST* III, 76. 1.

97. *Sacrosanctum concilium* 47 (*Denz.* 4047).

98. John Paul II, *Ecclesia de Eucharistia*, 11.

99. "'For as often as you eat this bread,' Paul tells us, 'you proclaim the death of the Lord' (1 Cor. 11:26). This is why we refer to the eucharistic celebration as the *'memoriale passionis Domini*,' as the 're-presentational memorial of the passion of Christ'" ("Eucharist: Gift of Love," 143). John Chrysostom, as one example, far outstrips Balthasar in his dramatic language about the relationship between cross and Eucharist.

100. Balthasar, *Does Jesus Know Us?*, 51.

101. "Spirit and Institution," *ET* IV, 228.

102. *TD* V, 325.

103. *GL* I, 298.

104. "The Mass, A Sacrifice of the Church?," *ET* III, 218 (emphasis original).

105. *GL* I, 573.

106. *ST* III, 76. 1. co.

107. *TD* IV, 391–92.

108. I will note Casel's influence on Balthasar throughout the book, but here we can say that, according to what is found at the Balthasar Archiv, he owned many books and articles by Casel, having read and made marginalia primarily in his copies of *Das christliche Kultmysterium*, *Das christliche Opfermysterium*, and "Die Heilige Eucharistie der Quellgrund der Seelsorge." It is clear that he read *Das christliche Kultmysterium* particularly closely. There is also a personal connection between Balthasar and Maria Laach Abbey: after leaving the Jesuits, Balthasar renewed his religious vows at the monastery (see Schindler, *His Life and Work*, 23).

109. Leo the Great, *Sermo* 74, 2; cited in Casel, *The Mystery of Christian Worship*, 7.

110. *TD* III, 426.

111. Balthasar, "The Mass, A Sacrifice of the Church?" is structured as an analysis first of Casel, then of Bouyer, but ultimately with an analysis of John as the more adequate answer to the title's question.

112. "The Mass, A Sacrifice of the Church?," *ET* III, 218 (emphasis added).

113. Second edition (Balthasar, *The Office of Peter and the Structure of the Church*) in 1989, from which the English translation is made.

114. *OP*, 337.

115. *OP*, 142–43 (emphasis original).

116. Note especially Blondel, *Action* (1893), 234–62. "Individual life is forced to open itself up and to spread itself out. It makes other forces concur in its ends. It seeks a complement from the outside. . . . He aspires to live in another" (234).

117. In addition to *TL* I, see the short article by Balthasar, "On the Concept of Person." This is also the position of Ratzinger, "Concerning the Notion of Person in Theology," 452: "relativity toward the other constitutes the human person. The human person is the event or being of relativity." John Paul II also equates

personhood and the gift of self to another in *Mulieris dignitatem*, 18. Also see Zizioulas, *Being as Communion*.

118. See *TD* V, 339–46, esp. 344–45.

119. "No Holy Communion is like another, although it is the same Christ who gives himself" (Balthasar, *Razing the Bastions*, 34). See also Balthasar, *A Theology of History*, 73. Balthasar is thus in total agreement with Schillebeeckx's understanding of the *personal* nature of sacramental grace. See Schillebeeckx, *Christ the Sacrament of the Encounter with God*, esp. 80. A similar approach is O'Neill, *Meeting Christ in the Sacraments*.

120. See Balthasar, *Christian Meditation*, 77–78. For Balthasar's interpretation of the *Exercises*, and their influence on his theology, see Servais, *Théologie des Exercices spirituels*.

121. Balthasar, *Herrlichkeit* I, 557; *GL* I, 579.

122. Cf. *TD* V, 345.

123. *ST* III, 48. 2. ad. 1.

124. This is not to call into question the fact that both "the Eucharist makes the Church" *and* "the Church makes the Eucharist," for the Church, for Balthasar, has been given authority to validly confect the sacraments, and thus they depend in a very real way upon the mediation of the Church. See Balthasar, *Christian Meditation*, 75.

125. Zwingli, "On the Lord's Supper," 216.

126. Council of Trent, *Decree on the Eucharist* (*Denz.* 1636).

127. Luther, "The Sacrament of the Body and Blood of Christ," 342.

128. "Heaven and earth are his sack; as wheat fills the sack, so he fills all things" (ibid., 342–43).

129. An issue Luther attempts to solve by appealing to the Word that instructs the Christian where to find him: "He is present everywhere, but he does not wish that you grope for him everywhere" (Luther, "The Sacrament of the Body and Blood of Christ," 342). Hermann Sasse summarizes Luther's position nicely: "Luther answers that there is a difference whether Christ's body is there or whether it is there *for you*; whether it is there or whether you can find it" (Sasse, *This Is My Body*, 156; emphasis original).

130. Luther, "The Sacrament of the Body and Blood of Christ," 342. Here Luther is imagining what his opponents suppose about his position.

131. *Mysterium fidei*, 39 (*Denz.* 4412). Almost at random, we cite Hugh of St. Victor to show that the rejection of ubiquity was not merely a post-Luther decision: "[Christ] is not to be thought diffused everywhere, according to this form [ascended body]. For we must beware lest we so build up the divinity of man that we take away the truth of the body" (Hugh of St. Victor, *De sacramentis*, bk. II, pt. I, XIII).

132. *ST* III, 76. 1. ad. 3.

133. Cf. *Denz.* 1636.

134. "Spirit and Institution," *ET* IV, 229. This is again a position shared with Martelet. Cf. Martelet, *The Risen Christ and the Eucharistic World*, 157.

135. "It would be wrong to regard the eucharistic state of Christ's body as 'figurative'—that is, confined to his sacramental mode of presence on earth and only valid in this mode—as compared with his 'real' or intrinsic body in heaven" (*TD* V, 382).

136. Thomas says the same: *ST* III, 54. 1. 2.

137. *TD* IV, 503.

138. See *GL* VII, 362.

139. "In death, in hell, his pregnant Heart will have to dissolve and—now as a wholly ruined Heart which has melted into a shapeless sea—he will give himself to them as their drink: the love-potion which will at last bewitch their all-too-sober hearts" (Balthasar, *The Heart of the World*, 64).

140. *GL* VII, 403.

141. See *TL* III, 94.

142. *TD* V, 476–77; *Theodramatik* IV, 438. Balthasar himself defines the difference between *Körper* and *Leib*: "The former [*Körper*], though informed by the soul, is subject to the powers of the external world; the latter [*Leib*] . . . *can* incarnate itself in the *corporal* world but does not *have* to. (Thus the risen Christ *can* eat but does not *need* to.)" (*TD* V, 475; emphasis original.) This distinction between *Körper* and *Leib* is frequently used in philosophical circles, particularly in phenomenology, first by Husserl and especially later by Merleau-Ponty. For Balthasar, the distinction seems to be simply ready to hand rather than as an implicit endorsement of or affiliation with any particular stream of phenomenology.

143. *Hingabe* and Christ's resurrected body are intrinsically connected for Balthasar, as seen by his section in *TD* V titled *Leib und Hingabe* (The Body and Self-Surrender). *Theodramatik* IV, 437–42. *TD* V, 475–82.

144. Seneca, *Letters from a Stoic*, 2.33.

145. *GL* VII, 403.

146. Balthasar notes how earthly *eros*, even sexual *eros*, prefigures Christ's eucharistic self-gift in "Eucharist: Gift of Love," and *TD* V, 475.

147. *TD* V, 382.

148. *GL* VII, 160.

149. See Taylor, *A Secular Age*, 37–43. Taylor here uses the distinction in a historical sense: the premodern self-understanding was of a porous self that is open to outside influence, whereas our modern understanding is such that the self is conceived of as buffered, as an unassailable ego.

150. *TD* V, 382; see also *TD* III, 431. For a very good treatment of the relation between Christ (and Eucharist) and the Holy Spirit, see Healy and Schindler, "For the Life of the World," 55–59.

151. "The Veneration of the Holy of Holies," *E*, 183–84.

152. And even this can find support in Thomas, who admits that Christ "ascending above the heavens" does not mean that he or his body is then contained by the heavens: "But glorified bodies, Christ's especially, do not stand in need of being so contained, because they draw nothing from the heavenly bodies, but from God

through the soul. So there is nothing to prevent Christ's body from being beyond the containing radius of the heavenly bodies, and not in a containing place" (*ST* III, 57. 4. ad. 2). This, however, is in tension with Thomas's distinction of Christ's presence "as in a place" (presumably in heaven) and his substantial presence in the Eucharist (*ST* III, 76. 5–6). He does say that "Christ's body is at rest in heaven." For Balthasar, Christ's presence in heaven, which is not a presence that can be contained and so is not locally circumscribed, does not need to be in contrast to his substantial presence elsewhere, as there is nothing to prevent his body from being elsewhere, as Thomas himself said.

153. Peter Vermigli, the Italian Reformer, protested against Luther's notion of ubiquity precisely because he thought ubiquity to be antithetical to human nature; see Vermigli, *Dialogue on the Two Natures in Christ*, 89–107. Balthasar would agree with this with regard to *Luther's* notion of ubiquity, which seems to dissolve Christ's body of any corporeality, but would protest that his eucharistic ubiquity is in fact the paragon of human nature.

154. We could say, then, that although Balthasar accepts the causal implications regarding Thomas's use of instrumental causality, he would be less inclined to accept that the Eucharist is a "separated instrumental cause," whereas his own body is a "conjoined instrumental cause." Although it is a distinction doubtless important for the other sacraments, it seems to presume that Christ's eucharistic body is something external to his "real" body. Recently, however, Lawrence Feingold has suggested that we should not read Thomas as saying that the Eucharist is an external instrumental cause, but rather as a conjoined instrument. See Feingold, *The Eucharist*, esp. 190.

155. And there is no reason, according to Thomas, why Christ's body cannot also be in the same place as another body (*ST* III, 57. 4. ad 3). But Christ and the Church can be considered as one flesh *only* when this does not imply a collapse of the distinction between head and members. Later Balthasar cautions against an error to which he himself is tempted, thus wanting to retain some notional difference between Christ's natural and mystical body: "What is excluded, of course, is any suggestion that believers, who are, after all, created spiritual subjects, are brought into the hypostatic union of the God-man. Excluded too, therefore, is any form of eucharistic union that would be understood as an incorporation into what the encyclical *Mystici Corporis* calls Christ's 'physical body'" (*TL* III, 292). He goes on, however, to speak precisely of Christ giving back to us our own bodies "in the form of his transfigured body" (293).

156. Origen of Alexandria, *Origen: Spirit and Fire*, 285. The quote originally comes from Origen's *Commentary on the Gospel of Matthew*, 14, 16–17. Also, see de Lubac, *History and Spirit*, 411–15. We can also add the influence of Gregory of Nyssa. Balthasar notes in his early *Presence and Thought* (1942), esp. 138–39 and 176–78, that Nyssa shares Origen's predilection for the language of ubiquity. But if indeed Origen could be credibly accused of making the incarnate Christ a penultimate

reality, and if his concept of ubiquity was used toward that end, the same could in no way be said of Balthasar, who uses "eucharistic ubiquity" as an index of the permanence of the Incarnation.

157. See Hegel, *Lectures on the Philosophy of Religion*, 479–81.

158. See O'Regan, *The Anatomy of Misremembering*, esp. 199–204.

159. This is Jean-Luc Marion's main argument against Hegel's rendition of the Eucharist: "Only distance, in maintaining a distinct separation of terms (of persons), renders communion possible, and immediately mediates the relation. Here again, between the idol and distance, one must choose" (Marion, *God without Being*, 169). Chauvet, *Symbol and Sacrament* (e.g., 94–95), makes the same point throughout, but whereas this distance for Chauvet is from the presence-of-the-absence of Christ in the sacramental mediation (405), for Balthasar it is a positive imitation of the *diastasis* between the divine persons.

160. Cf. *GL* I, 559 and 563.

161. See *ET* II, 462.

162. William Desmond nicely expresses the difference between Hegelian dialectic and his idea of metaxological intermediation, which is consonant with Balthasar's position (and a host of others, particularly Erich Przywara and Ferdinand Ulrich): "The agapeic absolute is already full in itself and hence does not constitute *itself* via the detour of the other as a moment of its own dialectical self-mediation; rather from this overwholeness . . . it gives itself to the other, which in this is given to be other, in a sense irreducible to the agapeic other: the other is loosed as a free other" (Desmond, *Beyond Hegel and Dialectic*, 135–36; emphasis original).

163. "The gift which is offered is indeed truly crystallized [*kristallisierte*] (and at the same time liquefied [*verflüssigte*]) love of the giver" ("A Verse of Matthias Claudius," *E*, 14–15). Balthasar, *Klarstellungen*, 13.

164. Two of the more influential critics of appropriation are Rahner, *The Trinity*, see esp. 3–15, 76–77, 86–87, and LaCugna, *God for Us*, esp. 100.

165. See *TL* III, 181–84, where he critiques the "modern sense" of appropriations, by which he means neoscholastic. Also see *ET* III, 118.

166. "Peace in Theology," *ET* V, 392. Balthasar, *Homo Creatus Est*, 315. See also *TD* III, 432.

167. Rahner, *The Trinity*, 22.

168. *TD* V, 63. He quotes Thomas's commentary on the *Sentences* (I, d. 14, q. 1, a. 1) to support his position: "Sicut processio temporalis non est alia quam processio aeterna essentialiter, sed addit aliquem respectum ad effectum temporalem, ita etiam missio visibilis non est alia essentialiter ab invisibili missione."

169. David Bentley Hart, "'Thine Own of Thine Own,'" 165, says much the same.

170. As quoted by Balthasar, *Two Sisters in the Spirit*, 433.

171. Catherine of Siena, *The Dialogue*, 210 (emphasis added).

172. See *TD* V, 478.

173. *E*, 190. "Denn was Gott ist, das ist uns kundgetan und geschenkt in seiner Eucharistie" (Balthasar, *Klarstellungen*, 116). See also *TD* V, 478, and *Light of the Word*, 313.

174. "Liturgy and Awe," *ET* II, 469.

175. Speyr, *The World of Prayer*, 35.

176. The virtue of religion, for Aquinas, is a natural or a moral and not a theological virtue (*ST* II-II, 81. 5).

177. See especially Speyr, *The World of Prayer*, 28–74. This book is essentially a collection chosen and arranged by Balthasar of key texts on prayer by Speyr.

178. *TD* V, 399.

179. Ibid., 96.

180. Balthasar quotes Speyr in ibid., 401: "This also applies to *prayer*, which, as we have seen, has its original shape in the life of the Trinity: in heaven 'we do not pray our own prayers: we are taken up into prayer.'"

181. Ibid., 389 (emphasis original).

182. One much discussed example would be Balthasar's discussion of supermasculinity and superfemininity in God. See ibid., 91.

183. Ibid., 516.

184. Ibid.

185. Ibid., 483; *Theodramatik* IV, 443.

186. See *TD* V, 245.

187. "While the will of the Father and the completion of his work were the continuing 'eucharistic' food for the earthly Jesus (John 4:34), in intertrinitary life all the divine hypostases are 'eucharistic' food for each other" (Balthasar, *Life out of Death*, 70).

188. This is the same impetus that led Vladimir Soloviev to posit the notion of *Sophia*: "But it is in order that God be unconditionally distinguished from our world, from our Nature, from this visible reality, that it is necessary to acknowledge in Him His particular eternal nature. His special eternal world. Otherwise our idea of Divinity will be poorer, more abstract, than our conception of the visible world" (Soloviev, *Lectures on Godmanhood*, 155). For Balthasar, though, nothing "additional" needs to be posited of God that is not already included in the divine persons and their shared nature (if indeed Sophia is understood as something besides the persons or nature, which is not always clear, either in Soloviev or Bulgakov).

189. Balthasar, *Presence and Thought*, 153.

190. Cf. *TD* V, 79. He often repeats the same point without acknowledging the analogous use of the term, but it should be kept in mind that "surprise" is only used analogously to point to God's quality as "ever-more." He even admits that speaking of "surprise in God" is "to use anthropomorphic terms" (*ET* IV, 233).

191. *TD* V, 514.

192. "In this sense he is, as Son, the Eucharist: that is, thanksgiving absolutely" ("Spirit and Institution," *ET* IV, 230).

193. *TD* V, 373.

194. See Leeming, *Principles of Sacramental Theology*, xxxi, for a clear articulation of this principle. Leeming's manual, first published in 1956, remains a remarkably useful and even subtle text. It represents the best of the manual genre and proves that Balthasar's critique of the manual tradition does not apply to every text.

195. "Theology and Sanctity," *ET* I, 202. Also *GL* I, 104–17. For Scheeben, the great linking idea of all his theology is *eros* and the nuptial unity of Christ and the Church, which is a close analogue to *Hingabe*, which functions in much the same way for Balthasar.

196. This theme is found throughout Balthasar, *Cosmic Liturgy*, but even more so in his work on Origen, both *Parole et Mystère* and his anthology, *Spirit and Fire*. In his introduction to the last, he notes the "fundamentally sacramental character of the whole plan of salvation (which in turn rests on a quasi-sacramental structure of being itself)" (15).

197. Cf. *E*, 20, and Balthasar, *Convergences*, 15. In 1984, upon his reception of the Paul VI prize, he claimed that in his theological work, in Aidan Nichols's words, "he wanted to overcome fragmentation by showing the unity of all the theological treatises" (Nichols, *Divine Fruitfulness*, 18).

198. Anne Barbeau Gardiner accuses Speyr of having a "metaphorical sacrament" by her extension of the concept (Gardiner, "The Dubious Adrienne von Speyr," 32). There is of course no question that Balthasar uses metaphorical language, such as the concept of "gift." But as Richard of St. Victor said, "Allegory is engaged especially with the sacraments of our faith and with such things as are believed more than understood" (Richard of St. Victor, *The Mystical Ark*, 365). Aquinas affirms that "sacra doctrina utitur metaphoris propter necessitatem et utilitatem" (*ST* I, 1. 9. ad. 1). The question here then is not whether Balthasar uses metaphorical language (he does), but whether he renders the Eucharist itself as a metaphor. The same questions regarding Balthasar's theology of the Eucharist have been asked of one of his main influences, Origen. See de Lubac's answer to the accusations that Origen "spiritualizes" or "allegorizes" the Eucharist in de Lubac, *History and Spirit*, 406–15.

199. *GL* I, 561.

200. Ibid., 313–14.

201. *GL* II, 206–7. Balthasar even goes as far as to affirm that in Denys the "mystery of the God-man, his humiliation, his suffering, death and descent is perfectly present" (208), a claim that would not be uncontroversial. This evaluation of Denys is significantly different from the portrayal in *Cosmic Liturgy*.

202. *GL* II, 153. See Golitzen, *Mystagogy* for a more sustained argument regarding the ecclesial and liturgical nature of Denys's theology.

203. *TD* V, 505.

204. *CL*, 316.

205. Balthasar thinks that the terms "heaven" and "earth" are indeed appropriate and necessary when discussing the drama between God and the world (*TD* IV, 23–26). Giorgio I. Spadaro notes, however, that in *La Disputa* whereas the earthly is "angular and linear (dividing)," the heavens are "curved (encompassing)" (Spadaro, *The Esoteric Meaning in Raphael's Paintings*, 28). Further, it seems that Giovanni Reale is correct to say that there are not two levels (heaven and earth) but three, including the "sopraceleste," which cuts through the heavenly and "conguinge la realtà sopraceleste con quella terrestre" (Reale, *Raffaello*, 23).

206. This *taxis* also demonstrates the "Trinitarian Inversion," as Balthasar calls it, as Christ is both "above" the Spirit in the immanent sphere (as the Spirit proceeds from the Father and the Son) and "below" and obedient to the Spirit in the economy. See *TD* III, 183–91.

207. Spadaro, *The Esoteric Meaning in Raphael's Paintings*, 32, thinks da Vinci here represents the ability to transcend the ritual and go straight to the spiritual, but this seems neither necessary nor probable, especially considering da Vinci's own *Last Supper*.

208. "Although theories explaining sacramental causation can be traced at least to Augustine, they tend to be formalistic rather than existential. In other words, they emphasize defining the causal mechanics that obtain between the sacrament's signs and its grace. Insufficient attention is given to the origins of these mechanics in the divine freedom that offers the grace and in the human freedom that integrates the effects of the grace into the dynamics of personal consciousness" (Fields, *Analogies of Transcendence*, 82–83).

CHAPTER 2

1. Endean, "Von Balthasar, Rahner, and The Commissar," 33. Endean presents a defense of Rahner, but here we are not concerned with whether Balthasar presents Rahner's position equitably or not, but merely with Balthasar's understanding of the dangers of theological modernity.

2. Balthasar, *The Moment of Christian Witness*, 130. Balthasar uses "liquidation" in the negative sense on multiple occasions. For example, he says that Bultmann's disciples liquidate Christianity (Balthasar, *Convergences*, 40), and even in his very early essay on "The Fathers, the Scholastics, and Ourselves," Balthasar notes how "the spiritual and cultural traditions" of the West are "being liquidated" (347).

3. Dupré, *Symbols of the Sacred*, 122.

4. See *TL* III, 243–44.

5. Balthasar, *The Theology of Henri De Lubac*, 124. Perhaps Balthasar's best reflection on Joachim can be found in "Improvisation on Spirit and Future," *ET* III, 135–71. See also Balthasar, *A Theological Anthropology*, 131–36.

6. Schleiermacher, very much like Hegel, seems to conflate the human and the divine Spirit: "The Holy Spirit is the Union of the Divine Essence with human nature in the form of the common Spirit animating the life of common believers . . . the Spirit as a common consciousness" (Schleiermacher, *The Christian Faith*, §123. Cf. *TL* III; see 422 on Tillich). A good overview of Spirit Christology is found in Del Colle, *Christ and the Spirit*, esp. 195–216.

7. Pannenberg, "Ekstatische Selbstüberschritte als Teilnahme am göttlichen Geist," as quoted in *TL* III, 423.

8. *TL* III, 427. We can add that he interprets Irenaeus's tripartite anthropology (body, soul, and spirit) not to mean that the Holy Spirit is a natural element of human nature, but rather that the Spirit comes by grace to dwell in the soul as in a temple. Cf. *GL* II, 64.

9. "Spirit, Love, Contemplation," *ET* III, 175.

10. Balthasar's engagement with Nygren is long and multifaceted. He wrote a review of Nygren in 1939 ("Eros und Agape"), and the Eros/Agape dialectic recurs as a theme throughout Balthasar's career. In general, Balthasar aligns his own understanding of purified *eros* with Denys, Dante, and Ficino. The end of the introduction to *GL* I, 119–27, is a nice summary of his position.

11. And this partly explains Balthasar's lifelong engagement with Plotinus, for whom religious mysticism and the heights of speculation were seamlessly united. It was in Hans Eibl's lectures in Vienna in the 1920s that Balthasar first encountered Plotinus.

12. This would include Husserl and Heidegger, but far more importantly Maurice Blondel. From the latter he would have learned that "every thought is autochthonous; and there are no true truths for us except indigenous truths. . . . The clear idea is inert" (see Blondel, *Action (1893)*, 111 and 114).

13. *GL* I, 146.

14. This is essentially how Rahner presents it, but Rahner's subtlety assures us that it is not so simple. Even if the Spirit is universal and Christ particular and historical, each is oriented toward the other in a manner similar to Balthasar, but certainly from a different starting point. See Rahner, *Foundations of Christian Faith*, 318.

15. *TD* IV, 433 (emphasis original). Also see *TL* I, 13.

16. For example, see Przywara, "Image, Likeness, Symbol, Mythos, Mysterium, Logos," in *Analogia Entis*, 438.

17. Cf. Balthasar, "Afterword" to *Meditations on the Tarot*, 559–665. There Balthasar provides an *apologia* for this type of Hermeticism, showing how the author brought the Hermetic tradition of Tarot into Christian meditation along the lines of a *spoliatio Aegyptiorum*. Note also Kevin Mongrain's lucid examination of this text in Mongrain, "Rule-Governed Christian Gnosis."

18. E.g., cf. *Didache* 9; Ignatius of Antioch, *To the Philadelphians* 4; and Augustine, *Sermo* 272.

19. *TL* II, 234, 301, 304, and 306.

20. For example, Vladimir Lossky divides the economies of the Son and the Spirit into a divinizing of nature and of persons, respectively. See Lossky, *Mystical Theology of the Eastern Church*, 167.

21. E.g., cf. Romans 8:16, Galatians 4:6, Acts 5:32, John 3:8, and 2 Corinthians 3:17.

22. "Spirit and Institution," *ET* IV, 233. Balthasar, *Pneuma und Institution*, 225. See also *TL* III, 74, 141, and 307–10, and *TD* III, 187.

23. *TL* III, 199.

24. Balthasar discusses the "Trinitarian inversion" in several places, esp., *TD* III, 183–91. This is Balthasar's shorthand for discussing how the Son participates in the spiration of the Spirit (*filioque*) from all eternity, yet in the economy is obedient to the Spirit as the Spirit of the Father. See Sutton, "A Compelling Trinitarian Taxonomy."

25. "Incarnation and 'anointing' simply coincide" (*TL* III, 184). "The Spirit assumes the directing role in the Incarnation" (*ET* IV, 232).

26. Cf. Balthasar, *A Theology of History*, 81–82. Also: "The Spirit will impart an infinite fluidity to the flesh, yet it will not dissolve it into Spirit" (*TL* III, 245).

27. Chauvet has also argued for this strong link between Spirit and body: "A constant feature of ancient liturgies is their linking the Spirit and the body. . . . The Spirit is the agent of this *enfleshment of the word*" (Chauvet, *Symbol and Sacrament*, 525–26; emphasis original). A more recent phenomenological analysis of the flesh and the Eucharist, which is in large part indebted to Balthasar, is Falque, *The Wedding Feast of the Lamb*.

28. The obvious reason is that although Balthasar did in fact reject Rahner's notion of anonymous Christians, this was not because of a more pessimistic understanding of the saved/damned ratio (as Balthasar, *Dare We Hope That All Men Be Saved?* makes clear), but rather because of theological commitments concerning the inseparability of subjective dispositions and their proper object.

29. Balthasar, *A Theology of History*, 83.

30. *TL* I, 13. The qualification "working in a mysterious way" should not be read as an evasion of giving a more theoretically convincing account, but more likely as an implicit reference to Odo Casel and his mystery theology.

31. One exception is Tóth, "Diaphany of the Divine Milieu or the Epiphany of Divine Glory?"

32. See "Movement toward God," *ET* III, 15–55.

33. *TL* III, 201–2.

34. And although there are certainly some differences, Balthasar's position is not far from Rahner's highly instructive essay on the question of spiritual communion: Rahner, "Personal and Sacramental Piety."

35. *TL* III, 429.

36. See Bulgakov, *The Comforter*, 161 and 181.

37. *TL* III, 448. Also see Balthasar, *A Theological Anthropology*, 69.

38. *TL* III, 310 (emphasis original).

39. Rahner, *Foundations*, 414.

40. Rahner, *The Church and the Sacraments*, 27.

41. The best contemporary presentation of issues of sacramental causality, which is both historically nuanced and creative in its own presentation, is without a doubt Revel, *Traité des sacrements*.

42. *TD* III, 300.

43. On some of the issues involved in Zizioulas's virtual equation of personhood with the sacrament of baptism, see Ciraulo, "Sacraments and Personhood."

44. *TD* III, 263.

45. "The Mass, A Sacrifice of the Church?," *ET* III, 227.

46. See *TD* III, 324.

47. *TD* III, 267.

48. "Mary and the Holy Spirit," *ET* V, 181. Balthasar, *Homo creatus est*, 146.

49. *OP*, 168; Journet, *L'Église du Verbe incarné*, 2:438–46, as cited in *OP*, 220.

50. Balthasar, *Truth Is Symphonic*, 139.

51. As Balthasar suggests was the understanding in the patristic era. See *GL* I, 248.

52. Cf. *TD* III, 129 and *TD* V, 333.

53. Balthasar, *Mary for Today*, 35–45.

54. Ibid., 41.

55. "Mary and the Holy Spirit," *ET* V, 182.

56. *GL* I, 224; see also 409–10.

57. Guardini, *The Spirit of the Liturgy*, 38–39.

58. "Spirit and Institution," *ET* IV, 237 (emphasis original).

59. "However fervent we may be at Communion, we know that we cannot receive the sacrament in an adequate manner or respond to it adequately; and, in all probability, the closer we get to a reception and a response that *is* adequate, the more we shall be aware of this" (*TL* III, 309; emphasis original).

60. Corbon, *Liturgie aus dem Urquell*.

61. Balthasar, "Vorwort des Übersetzers," 9.

62. However, even before his encounter with Corbon, he did briefly note the importance of the *en Christo* becoming a *syn Christo*, a cooperation with the work of Christ (*TD* III, 247).

63. *TD* V, 416. He is here commenting on and agreeing with Corbon.

64. Balthasar cites the following from Maximus the Confessor's *Quaestiones ad Thalassium*, which exactly reproduces the analogy: *Logos* is to Jesus's human nature, as Spirit is to saints: "For as the Logos accomplished divine works in the flesh, but not without the cooperation of a body animated by a rational soul, so the Holy Spirit accomplishes in the saints the ability to understand mysteries, but not without

the exercise of their natural abilities or without their seeking and careful searching for knowledge" (*CL*, 73).

65. Balthasar, *The Theology of Karl Barth*, 389.

66. Cf. ibid., 286.

67. The most obvious is John Paul II's use of Balthasar in his teaching on the theology of the body. See also Scola's indebtedness to Balthasar in Scola, *The Nuptial Mystery*.

68. See especially Beattie, *New Catholic Feminism*; Kilby, *Balthasar: A (Very) Critical Introduction*, 123–46; and Crammer, "One Sex or Two? Balthasar's Theology of the Sexes."

69. In his emphasis on catalogy in addition to analogy, Balthasar says that it is not human sexuality as a metaphor for the Christ/Church union, but rather that the latter is the prototype of the former. See *TD* III, 433.

70. *TL* I, 114–15.

71. Ibid., 115 (emphasis added).

72. *GL* VI, 228. Balthasar also uses the occasion of Hosea to bring up the theme of God's *supra*sexual (not *a*-sexual) relationship with humanity. It is in this biblical register, most explicitly in Ephesians 5, but also throughout the Old and New Testaments, that Balthasar's understanding of gender should be primarily located. See also *TD* III, 433.

73. Cf. "Who Is the Church?," *ET* II, 162.

74. Balthasar, *The Theology of Karl Barth*, 366. In the sentence before this Balthasar calls infant baptism "exceptional," because he wants the sacramental encounter to be modeled more explicitly on the activity of God and the receptivity of the person, rather than as a simple act of God that may or may not be personally ratified. Balthasar repeats his claim that infant baptism is more of an exception rather than a rule (theologically, not numerically speaking) many times, for instance, at the beginning and end of the *Trilogy*: *GL* I, 579 (infant baptism "was perhaps the most portentous decision in the entire history of the Church"), and *TL* III, 335 (infant baptism is a "borderline situation"). Balthasar's seeming inability or lack of desire to understand infant baptism in a theologically rich manner is a lacuna in his thought, but there is good reason to think that infant baptism is indeed highly compatible with Balthasar's theology.

75. Long provides an invaluable insight into Balthasar's attendance at and contributions to Barth's seminar on Trent's teaching on the sacraments in Long, *Saving Karl Barth*, 239–65.

76. *GL* I, 563. Cooperation is "both possible and necessary," but "nowhere do God and man work together on the same plane."

77. For instance, see "Who Is the Church?," *ET* II, 171–72. Balthasar's emphasis on receptivity while also avoiding quietism is another instance where a fruitful comparison to Caussade is in order. According to Caussade, "It is foolish to picture

any kind of self-surrender in which all personal activity is excluded. When God requires action, holiness is to be found in activity" (Caussade, *The Joy of Full Surrender*, 27).

78. This theme of "theosis as kenosis" derives in large measure from Erich Przywara, in particular with how the *maior dissimilitudo* between God and the creature becomes not merely a negative distance, but a positive attribute of creatureliness. See Ciraulo, "Divinization as Christification in Erich Przywara and John Zizioulas."

79. *GL* I, 564.

80. "Who Is the Church?," *ET* II, 163. Balthasar, *Sponsa Verbi*, 171.

81. "Who Is the Church?," *ET* II, 187. Balthasar, *Sponsa Verbi*, 198.

82. "Who Is the Church?," *ET* II, 188: "The dissimilarity is ever greater than the similarity—the opposition, that is, of God and creature. In the hypostatic union (and its imperfect participation in the Church), even this irreducible abyss, without being eliminated, is bridged and tunneled by the power of God's love."

83. "Who Is the Church?," *ET* II, 165–66. Balthasar, *Sponsa Verbi*, 174. See also *GL* I, 564.

84. "The Mass, A Sacrifice of the Church?," *ET* III, 218 (italics original).

85. *GL* I, 573. See also "Who Is the Church?," *ET* II, 157.

86. *GL* I, 583. This is also how Balthasar interprets Maximus's sacramental theology. See *CL*, 324–25.

87. Leeming notes that the first to apply "form and matter" to all of the sacraments was Stephen Langton (d. 1228), and is of Aristotelian origin. See Leeming, *Principles of Sacramental Theology*, 404. Note that Augustine speaks of *verbum* and *elementum*, which are precursors, but not necessarily exact parallels, to form and matter.

88. Cf. *GL* I, 573, and Balthasar, "Eucharist: Gift of Love," 142.

89. The choice of this analogy is not to suggest that Balthasar considers that "bread is only for eating, not for looking at," as a critique of the practice of eucharistic adoration. Balthasar's defense of adoration can be seen in "The Veneration of the Holy of Holies," *E*, 181–90.

90. "Who Is the Church?," *ET* II, 187.

91. Thomas used these terms in a different way, but this was essentially his position: *ST* III, 80. 1. co.

92. Bätzing, *Die Eucharistie als Opfer der Kirche nach Hans Urs von Balthasar*, and Michael Hesse, *Die Eucharistie als Opfer der Kirche*. See also Lösel, "A Plain Account of Christian Salvation?"; Levering, *Sacrifice and Community*, esp. 25n75; Di Girolamo, "Peccato, Croce ed Eucaristia in Hans Urs von Balthasar," esp. 443–47; Feichtinger, "Leo the Great and Hans Urs von Balthasar on the Eucharist."

93. A good summary of the history of the sacrificial nature of the Mass can be found in Journet, *The Mass*.

94. In "The Mass: A Sacrifice of the Church?," Balthasar notes that both Protestants and Catholics will have to make renunciations on this question. On the Catholic

side, "It would be necessary to revise the whole traditional separation between the Mass as sacrificial act and the Eucharist as a sacrificial meal; it would not be possible any longer, as with de La Taille, to limit the sacrificial act to *oblatio* and *immolatio* (on the Cross or, liturgically, in the Consecration) and to handle the meal as an almost irrelevant postlude" (*ET* III, 237–38n98).

95. This critique is found first in Lösel, "A Plain Account of Christian Salvation?," which is repeated by Levering, *Sacrifice and Community*, 25n75.

96. This is one particularly noteworthy instance of Balthasar's "liturgical theology," as the entire force of the essay is trying to come to terms with the liturgical fact of the language of *sacrificium, hostia, offerre, oblatio*, etc: "Whence comes the urgent *offerimus* in the Roman Canon? Can it be justified?" ("The Mass, A Sacrifice of the Church?," *ET* III).

97. "The Mass, A Sacrifice of the Church?," *ET* III, 215.

98. "Here there is somehow missing the radical distinction between Christ's deed and our own, there is missing the absolute, solitary priority of his commission that comes from on high, from the Father, and of his carrying out of this commission" ("The Mass, A Sacrifice of the Church?," *ET* III, 215).

99. "And [Christ] wanted the sacrifice offered by the Church to be the daily sacrament of his sacrifice, *in which the Church*, since it is the body of which he is the head, *learns to offer its very self through him*" (Augustine, *De civitate Dei* 10.20; emphasis added).

100. In the context of Hebrews, the "behold, I have come to do your will" is invoked precisely as the abolition of all previous forms of cultic sacrifice.

101. Thus, he calls the dogma of the Immaculate Conception a "strict postulate of ecclesiology" ("The Mass: A Sacrifice of the Church?," *ET* III, 239).

102. *CL*, 271.

103. Balthasar, *Engagement with God*, 38; *In Gottes Einsatz Leben*, 45.

104. "The Mass, A Sacrifice of the Church?," *ET* III, 227.

105. Ibid., 221 (emphasis original).

106. Ibid., 232–33. Balthasar, *Spiritus Creator*, 208 (emphasis original).

107. "The Mass, A Sacrifice of the Church?," *ET* III, 234.

108. Ibid., 235. He points to Maurice de La Taille, who compiled these texts in de La Taille, *Mysterium Fidei*.

109. He cites Jeremias, *Die Abendmahlsworte Jesu*, 200 and 202, and points to such verses as Luke 22:15 for support of this position.

110. "The Mass, A Sacrifice of the Church?," *ET* III, 236. *Spiritus Creator*, 211.

111. Ratzinger ratifies Balthasar's position, but sidelines the destruction theories to an even greater degree. See Ratzinger, *The Spirit of the Liturgy*, in *Collected Works*, 11:15.

112. "The Mass, A Sacrifice of the Church?," *ET* III, 222.

113. For Balthasar's interpretation of the *Exercises*, and their influence on his theology, see Servais, *Théologie des Exercices spirituels*; Löser, "The Ignatian

Exercises in the Work of Hans Urs von Balthasar." Also see McInroy, *Balthasar on the Spiritual Senses*, 84–91.

114. Balthasar insists on the bodily nature of the "application of the senses" in *GL* I, 373–80.

115. *TD* IV, 234. See also Balthasar, *A Theology of History*, 71, and *TD* V, 81.

116. "The Mass, A Sacrifice of the Church?," *ET* III, 240.

117. On this, see his short but important essay, "Drei Formen der Gelassenheit," translated as "The Serenity of the Surrendered Self: Three Variations on a Theme," *ET* V, 38–46. The three forms of *Gelassenheit* are those of the sinner, of Mary, and of Christ.

118. Caussade, *Joy of Full Surrender*, 147.

119. Cf. "The Mass, A Sacrifice of the Church?," *ET* III, 240.

120. Caussade, *Joy of Full Surrender*, 157.

121. "The Mass, A Sacrifice of the Church?," *ET* III, 241. *Spiritus Creator*, 216.

122. See also the Liturgy of St. John Chrysostom: "Thine own of Thine own we Offer unto Thee, in behalf of all and for all!" Even consider the prayer from the Chaplet of Divine Mercy: "Eternal Father, I offer you the Body and Blood, Soul and Divinity of Your Dearly Beloved Son, Our Lord, Jesus Christ, in atonement for our sins and those of the whole world."

123. Balthasar, *A Short Primer for Unsettled Laymen*, 96.

124. Calculated based on pages 234–473 out of the total of 540 in Balthasar, *Gelebte Kirche: Bernanos*.

125. Every sacrament, that is, besides matrimony, because Balthasar does not find sufficient analysis of marriage in Bernanos's work. See Balthasar, *Bernanos*, 389.

126. "Theology and Sanctity," *ET* I, 204.

127. Balthasar, *Bernanos*, 284.

128. Balthasar, *Bernanos*, 287. In *A Theological Anthropology*, one can hear Balthasar bemoaning the fact that the Joachimite impulse in the Franciscan Order prevented the kind of analysis that Balthasar seems to be carrying out in *Bernanos*: "The significance of everything institutional and sacramental could have been read by means of the 'model' of St. Francis and given a better and more comprehensible theological setting" (133).

129. Chauvet, *Symbol and Sacrament*, 277 (italics original).

130. For example, see Leo XIII, *Mirae caritatis* 11; John Paul II, *Veritatis splendor*, 107; Benedict XVI, *Deus caritas est*, 14; Pope Francis, *Laudato si'*, 236–37.

131. On Balthasar's "ethics," see Ouellet, "The Foundations of Christian Ethics according to Hans Urs von Balthasar," and Christopher Steck, *The Ethical Thought of Hans Urs von Balthasar*.

132. Aubert, "Débats autour de la morale fondamentale," 207–8, as cited and translated in Ouellet, "The Foundations of Christian Ethics according to Hans Urs von Balthasar," in *Hans Urs von Balthasar: His Life and Work*, 231–32.

133. Caussade, *Joy of Full Surrender*, 125–26.

134. Cf. "The Mystery of the Eucharist," *NE*, 116–17.

135. Balthasar, "Nine Propositions on Christian Ethics," 79.

136. Ibid. Note the liturgical reference in this quote, which is a confirmation of what he says on the following page: "Leiturgia is inseparable from ethical conduct."

137. *TD* III, 29.

138. "The Mystery of the Eucharist," *NE*, 122.

139. For example, although indeed there are *some* hints at a eucharistic reading of *The Diary of a Country Priest*, such as the fact that the sick Curé is only able to consume bread and wine, it is by no means the obvious reading.

140. Balthasar, *Bernanos*, 504.

141. Ibid., 517. A similar point is made by Claudel: "We are the Body of the Church through our acceptance of her form, that is, the sacraments that are her arteries" (Claudel, *L'Épée et le Miroir*, as collected in Claudel, *I Believe in God*, 33).

142. Bernanos, *The Diary of a Country Priest*, 30. Also quoted in Balthasar, *Bernanos*, 518. The Country Priest is also important as a character because here Bernanos has no illusions of his character as heroic. As the Curé himself notes of his diary, it is full of "very simple trivial secrets of a very ordinary kind of life" (Bernanos, *Diary of a Country Priest*, 7).

143. *Bernanos*, 526. Balthasar notes earlier in the book that there is historical precedence for this connection too, as Bernanos gave a paper on death and transcendence the same year that Heidegger's *Being and Time* was published (*Bernanos*, 82).

144. Ibid., 483.

145. Ibid. It seems that the "denuding of being" likely relates to Ferdinand Ulrich's concept of the *Durchnichtung* of Being, one of the key concepts in Ulrich, *Homo Abyssus*.

146. Ibid., 487, 490 (emphasis original); Balthasar, *Gelebte Kirche: Bernanos*, 436.

147. Ibid., 520–21 (emphasis added).

148. *TD* IV, 234; *TD* V, 81.

149. Cf. *TD* III, 527–28, *TD* IV, 407, and "Spirit and Institution," *ET* IV, 242.

150. Cf. Balthasar, *Engagement with God*, 51.

151. On this, see Marion, *Believing in Order to See*, 113.

152. We find here again the meeting of the Eucharist and the Holy Spirit, both of which claim the title of *vinculum caritatis/amoris*.

153. "A Verse of Matthias Claudius," *E*, 15; *Klarstellungen*, 13.

154. "A Verse of Matthias Claudius," *E*, 15; *Klarstellungen*, 13.

155. Cf. Balthasar, *Unless You Become Like This Child*, 52.

156. Balthasar, *Engagement with God*, 15.

157. Cf. "Martyrdom and Mission," *NE*, 279–305.

158. Balthasar, *Two Sisters*, 71.

159. See *TD* IV, 422.

160. Cf. *Engagement with God*, 93.

161. From Thérèse's *Collected Letters*, as cited in Balthasar, *Two Sisters*, 249 (emphasis original).

162. "This is your mission: being sent away from the Son, you yourself repeat the way of the Son, away from the Father and out to the world" (Balthasar, *The Heart of the World*, 214).

163. Henrici notes this as the content of his first homily; cf. Schindler, *Hans Urs von Balthasar: His Life and Work*, 14. Nichols notes that this was on his ordination card, under a picture of St. John leaning on Jesus (Nichols, *Divine Fruitfulness*, 17).

164. Balthasar, *The Grain of Wheat*, 110.

165. Balthasar, *Principles of Christian Morality*, 79. See also *GL* V, 633, where Balthasar contests Kant's categorical imperative by expanding its import. See also Steck, *The Ethical Thought of Hans Urs von Balthasar*, 25.

166. As argued by Barrett, *Love's Beauty at the Heart of the Christian Moral Life*.

167. Cf. Balthasar, *The God Question and Modern Man*, 143. See also Hart's critique of Levinas in Hart, *The Beauty of the Infinite*, 75–93.

168. *The God Question and Modern Man*, 146–47.

169. Ibid., 151. Balthasar then cites Origen to substantiate this claim.

170. See, for example, *GL* V, 649.

171. Benedict XVI, *Sacramentum caritatis*, 82 (emphasis original). See also John Paul II, *Veritatis splendor*, 107.

172. Benedict XVI, *Deus caritas est*, 13 (emphasis added). There is good reason to think that this German edition represents Benedict's original text, as the official Latin renders "*Hingabeakt*" as *actu oblationis*. It is more improbable that *Hingabe* would be used to translate *oblatio* than the other way around, as *Opfer* or *Opfergabe* would be the more natural rendition.

173. Peter Casarella gives expression to the connection between Balthasar's eucharistic theology and ethics in Casarella, "*Analogia Donationis*," by using Dorothy Day as a dramatic enactment of Balthasar's sacramental theology.

174. Balthasar, *My Work in Retrospect*, 51.

175. Balthasar, *Test Everything*, 13. In 1965, he wrote that subsequently "the blast did not die away unheard, but now it forced the trumpeter [i.e., himself] to reflect more deeply." In particular, he notes that openness to the world must be matched by purification and the Church's "centering of its idea" (Balthasar, *My Work in Retrospect*, 51).

176. In this regard, it should be remembered that Balthasar wrote *The Office of Peter* (more aptly titled in the German: *Der antirömische Affekt*) in defense of the papacy.

177. See also "Kenosis of the Church?," *ET* IV, 137.

178. Holiness lived hidden in the world is, incidentally, Balthasar's program for the *Johannesgemeinschaft*, the secular institute that he founded with Speyr. See Balthasar, *Our Task*. For Balthasar, with regard to the world, the Church is, as in the biblical parable, like yeast: "The yeast must be plunged into the dough; it must sink into it and disappear, in order that its energy may be released and the dough transformed into bread" (Balthasar, *Engagement with God*, 11).

179. Balthasar drew attention to Bernanos's devotion to Thérèse; see esp. Balthasar, *Bernanos*, 185 and 328–30. Note even how her little way makes its way into Bernanos, *The Diary of a Country Priest*: "Little things—they don't look much, yet they bring peace" (209).

180. As cited in Balthasar, *Two Sisters*, 328–29 (emphasis original).

181. *TD* V, 521. From this quote, and from the argument of this entire chapter, it should be clear just how much the following comment by George Worgul is a mischaracterization of Balthasar: "It seems that Balthasar presents us as mere observers or spectators with our roles fulfilled by little more than watching or gazing at the divine drama" (Worgul, "Balthasar's Kneeling Theology, Liturgics and Post Modernism," 267).

182. "The Church as the Presence of Christ," *NE*, 103.

CHAPTER 3

1. Plato, *Republic*, bk. 2, 377a.

2. *GL* I, 17.

3. Balthasar, "The Fathers, the Scholastics, and Ourselves," 391.

4. Balthasar, *My Work In Retrospect*, 49.

5. Both Balthasar, *Parole et Mystère*, and his introduction to *Geist und Feuer* make this clear with regard to Origen, and though Denys is sometimes held at a distance, the text of *GL* II, 144–210, puts him to productive use.

6. *CL*, 318.

7. Ibid., 316.

8. "Seeing, Hearing, and Reading," *ET* II, 485.

9. *GL* I, 313–17.

10. Cf. "Seeing, Hearing, and Reading," *ET* II, 483.

11. Schmemann, *Introduction to Liturgical Theology*, 31.

12. I am referring, of course, to Plato's appeal to the demiurge in the *Timaeus*. In Casel's case, there is never a clear explanation of how the *mystery* of Christ is made present in the Church's *liturgy*, and especially because he closely aligns Christian cult with the mystery religions, there remains something necessarily inexplicable about the connection.

13. *TD* IV, 393.

14. Balthasar cites Gottlieb Söhngen's two works that correct Casel on this point: Söhngen, *Symbol und Wirklichkeit im Kultmysterium*, and Söhngen, *Der Wesenaufbau des Mysteriums*. See *TL* III, 335. Balthasar wrote a review of these two books, "Söhngens Begriff des Mysteriums." Balthasar says that these books "search for the connection between Casel's platonic teaching on mystery and the scholastic theology of the sacraments" (ibid., 60).

15. Casel, *The Mystery of Christian Worship*, 72.

16. See Balthasar, *Prayer*, 121, and "Unmodern Prayer," *E*, 178. Balthasar's critique of romanticism in the liturgical movement has been documented historically; see O'Meara, "The Origins of the Liturgical Movement and German Romanticism." Also see Geldhof, "German Romanticism and Liturgical Theology."

17. A good summary of the "archeologism" of some in the liturgical movement is Van Slyke, "The Study of Early Christian Worship." See also Taft, *Through Their Own Eyes*, 2–4.

18. E.g., Lathrop, *Holy Things*, esp. 15–85.

19. Cf. "Liturgy and Awe," *ET* II, 462.

20. Ratzinger holds these two in tension: "[The worship of God] contains its measure within itself, that is, it can only be ordered by the measure of revelation, in dependency upon God" (Ratzinger, *The Spirit of the Liturgy*, 7).

21. See Balthasar, *Love Alone Is Credible*, 45n15.

22. "Seeing, Hearing, and Reading," *ET* II, 489. Balthasar originally published this essay in 1939.

23. *ST* I-II, 111. 2.

24. "Eucharistic Congress 1960," *ET* II, 508.

25. Cf. ibid.

26. Cf. Balthasar, *Test Everything*, 9. See also Lacoste's reflection on the pilgrim's, the xeniteia's, relationship with *topoi* and what this means for the liturgy in Lacoste, *Experience and the Absolute* (here, 32).

27. "The Worthiness of the Liturgy," *NE*, 137.

28. He even speaks for Speyr, saying that she "would not have resisted the new form of the liturgy in any respect" (Balthasar, "Editor's Introduction" in Speyr, *The Holy Mass*, 9). See also Balthasar, *Paul Struggles with His Congregation*, 63.

29. *Sacrosanctum concilium*, 1.12

30. "The Worthiness of the Liturgy," *NE*, 134.

31. In one particularly harsh analysis of the state of the Church in Switzerland in the 1970s, Balthasar noted the "clergy gone wild [wildegewordener Klerus]" who celebrate "fantasy liturgies" with additions, omissions, new canons of the Mass, and even asking the laity to speak the words of consecration ("Voraussetzung Einer Geisterneuerung," 2925). This is Balthasar at a bit of rhetorical excess, but the context of the Church in Switzerland and the pastoral nature of this journal (*Theologisches*) should be taken into account. See also "Liturgiereform Und Zukunft Der Kirche," 20, and *E*, 178.

32. Cf. Balthasar, "Eucharist: Gift of Love," 146–47.

33. "The Worthiness of the Liturgy," *NE*, 135–36.

34. O'Meara, "The Origins of the Liturgical Movement and German Romanticism," 342.

35. Hegel, *Lectures on the Philosophy of Religion*, 479–81, and Hegel, *Philosophy of Mind*, para. 552. See also Stepelevich, "Hegel and the Lutheran Eucharist." See also the analysis of Marion, *God without Being*, 167.

36. See especially Barth, *Church Dogmatics*, I.1, 34–44, and Balthasar, *The Theology of Karl Barth*, 30–38

37. Balthasar, *Who Is a Christian?*, 39.

38. *GL* I, 575.

39. As members of the *Johannesgemeinschaft* told me in Basel, Balthasar celebrated the liturgy "ganz einfach" (very simply), with no additions of his own to the liturgy, with a short, five-minute homily (even on Sundays), and always (after the council) facing *versus populum*. The chasuble and stoles he used at the end of his life (which are still used in the community) are monochromatic but elegant.

40. See Balthasar, "Liturgiereform und Zukunft der Kirche."

41. He mentions the painter Georges Rouault, the composer Olivier Messiaen, and the churches Notre Dame du Haut in Ronchamps and the Wotruba Church in Vienna ("On the Christian's Capacity to See," *ET* V, 76). Balthasar was also good friends with Albert Schilling, the Swiss sculptor, who made Adrienne von Speyr's tombstone and later Balthasar's bust. In many ways, Balthasar's aesthetic predilections match those of Basel: integration of the modern into the antique.

42. "On the Christian's Capacity to See," *ET* V, 75.

43. Also see Nichols, *Scattering the Seed*, 13–15. Anne Carpenter also provides a nice distinction between the type of *Hingabe* advocated for by Heidegger and Rilke, and the one Balthasar recommends in Carpenter, *Theo-Poetics*. She also helpfully points to the importance of sacramentality for Balthasar's evaluation of art in the final chapter.

44. "Liturgy and Awe," *ET* II, 463. See also *E*, 177–78.

45. "The Worthiness of the Liturgy," *NE*, 135.

46. Cf. *GL* I, 583.

47. "The Worthiness of the Liturgy," *NE*, 130.

48. For example, on Husserl and Scheler, see *Apok.* III, 84–192, and on Heidegger, see Balthasar, "Heideggers Philosophie vom Standpunkt des Katholizismus," 193–315, and *GL* V, 429–50; Husserl, Scheler, and Heidegger are not mentioned by name in *TL* I, but it is clear that Balthasar has them in mind. According to what is found in the Balthasar Archiv, it is clear that he read Heidegger far more than Husserl.

49. D. C. Schindler highlights Balthasar's explicit disagreements with Husserl in Schindler, "Metaphysics within the Limits of Phenomenology."

50. *GL* I, 26.

51. Speyr says of the words of consecration: "Bread and wine become flesh and blood, the body of the Lord made visible to the *eyes of faith*" (Speyr, *The Holy Mass*, 61; emphasis added).

52. *GL* I, 447.

53. Ulrich, *Homo Abyssus*, 55; originally published in 1961.

54. The classic text for this discussion is Janicaud, *Phenomenology and the "Theological Turn."*

55. See especially Przywara, "*A Priori* and *A Posteriori* Metaphysics," in *Analogia Entis*, 132–54.

56. *GL* I, 146.

57. Ibid., 148.

58. Ibid., 151.

59. *GL* VII, 318.

60. "The Eyes of Pascal," *ET* V, 90.

61. *GL* III, 180–81.

62. Pascal, Letter to Charlotte de Roannez (October 1656), as cited by Tilliette, *Philosophies Eucharistiques de Descartes à Blondel*, 28. See Marin, *La parole mangée et autres essais théologico-politiques*, 11–35.

63. *GL* III, 238.

64. *GL* VII, 384–85. "The Johannine insight [is] that God's *doxa* already radiates Christ's mortality from within; indeed, it shines at its brightest in the consummation of his suffering and death" ("Fides Christi," *ET* II, 66).

65. *GL* I, 172 (emphasis original).

66. *GL* I, 247. See Schindler, *Hans Urs von Balthasar and the Dramatic Structure of Truth*, 207–19, and 386–94, on Balthasar's proximity to and distance from Rousselot.

67. Rousselot, *The Eyes of Faith*. Rousselot is not adopted by Balthasar without remainder but is criticized: "He does not sufficiently attribute this synthesis to the efficacy of the objective evidence of the form of revelation" (*GL* I, 177). In this, Rousselot remains too "Kantian."

68. The quote is from Newman, *Fifteen Sermons Preached before the University of Oxford, Sermon 10*, but the concept is developed with greater precision in Newman, *An Essay in Aid of a Grammar of Assent.*

69. On the relationship between love and knowledge of God, in a phenomenological key, see Lacoste, *La phénoménalité de dieu: Neuf etudes*, 87–110.

70. Marion, *Givenness and Revelation*, 41 (emphasis original).

71. *GL* I, 531. Balthasar, *Herrlichkeit* I, 510 (emphasis added). On another occasion, he speaks about a "relativization of the liturgy" ("Liturgy and Awe," *ET* II, 464).

72. For a helpful analysis of the history of this division, see King, "The Origin and Evolution of a Sacramental Formula." More specifically on Thomas's

sacramental vocabulary, see Dondaine, "La définition des sacrements dans la Somme théologique."

73. Leeming, for example, prefers to translate *res et sacramentum* by "symbolic reality" (Leeming, *Principles of Sacramental Theology*, 251–56).

74. "For any one who eats and drinks without *discerning* the body eats and drinks judgement upon himself" (1 Cor. 11:29) (emphasis added).

75. For a perceptive, phenomenological analysis of the use of citation in the eucharistic liturgy, see Sokolowski, *Eucharistic Presence*, 82–100.

76. In Balthasar's thought, the interplay between the Word and the sacrament is most evident in his work on Origen, in both his early *Parole et Mystère* and his anthology, *Spirit and Fire*. For an excellent overview of the history of the distinction between *Schein* and *Erscheinung*, and the related terms *Phänomen* and *Offenbarung*, see Cassin, ed., *Dictionary of Untranslatables*, 281–86.

77. Augustine, *Essential Sermons*, 317–18.

78. *GL* I, 583. The citation of Dz 849 (*Denz.* 1606 in the 43rd ed.) is to the Council of Trent's canon 6 on the sacraments in general. See also *GL* III, 427.

79. It is interesting to note, however, that Chauvet does not categorize his work as phenomenological in *Symbol and Sacrament*. This is another reason to think that the social sciences in general, and psychology and anthropology in particular, are more regulative for Chauvet than philosophical discourse. Nevertheless, both push him toward his antimetaphysical stance. Hal St John critiques Chauvet's "anthropological Heidegger" and shows how this is against Heidegger's own evaluation of anthropology (St John, *The Call of the Holy*, 4–5).

80. In fact, early scholasticism can indeed be thanked for bridging the gap between *signum/sacramentum* and *res*, by creating the middle term *sacramentum et res*, out of the crucible of the Berengarian controversy, which, using patristic and particularly Augustianian categories, struggled to articulate a third term between sign and reality.

81. Tertullian, *De baptismo*, 2. Emphasis added. Tertullian continues, however, following the same method we observed in Augustine, with a valorization of the symbol itself, but only *after* noting the incongruity: "Since in fact that substance has had conferred upon it a function of such high dignity, I suppose we need to ask what is the significance of the liquid element" (ibid., 3).

82. *GL* I, 320. One can also discern here the influence of Gregory of Nyssa in this passage.

83. Guitmund, *On the Truth of the Body and Blood of Christ in the Eucharist*, 1.24, 112. Or one could add Richard of St. Victor: "In the divine sacraments the exterior form that is outwardly accessible is one thing; that intrinsic power which lies deeply hidden is another" (*The Mystical Ark*, appendix, 351).

84. Hopkins, "Godhead here in hiding," in *The Poetical Works of Gerard Manley Hopkins*, 112.

85. *TD* II, 275–76 (italics added). Balthasar also quotes this hymn in "Eucharist: Gift of Love," and comments: "How could God hide himself more humbly than beneath a little bit of bread and a few drops of wine, and how better to teach us the divine humility and majesty than in this inconspicuousness" (150).

86. As cited in *GL* I, 483.

87. *GL* I, 484.

88. *ST* III, 60. 1. ad. 1: *sacramenta novae legis simul sunt causa et signa. Et inde est quod, sicut communiter dicitur, efficiunt quod figurant.* Earlier, in *De veritate* (27. 4, ad. 13), Thomas says *quia sacramenta significando causant*, but because this text is so much earlier than his position in the *ST*, to claim that "cause by signifying" is Thomas's position (as does Powers, *Eucharistic Theology*, 89–90) is to fail to see this potential development.

89. Cf. Chauvet, *Symbol and Sacrament*, 18.

90. Rahner, "Introductory Observations on Thomas Aquinas' Theology of the Sacraments in General," 155–56. Also: "The sign is therefore a cause of what it signifies by being the way in which what is signified effects itself" (Rahner, *The Church and the Sacraments*, 38). However, to understand how symbols are still metaphysical for Rahner, which is one aspect of how he differs from Chauvet, see Rahner, "The Theology of the Symbol," 4.

91. See Long, *Saving Karl Barth*, 251–65. Long shows how in 1941 Balthasar and Barth agree to the formula *significando causant* as a way to mediate between Trent and the Reformers, but they still remained in disagreement about *causae secundae*. Balthasar also draws a diagram, illustrated in Long's book, on the relationship between *sacramentum, sacramentum et res*, and *res*.

92. *TD* IV, 394 (emphasis original). See also *GL* I, 418 and 581.

93. Each of them consciously tries to avoid such a conclusion: Rahner by appealing to the metaphysical nature of the symbol, Schillebeeckx by admitting that "I cannot personally be satisfied with a *purely* phenomenological interpretation without metaphysical density" (Schillebeeckx, *The Eucharist*, 150; emphasis original), and Chauvet's position will be seen shortly.

94. Power, *The Eucharistic Mystery*, 270.

95. *Denz.* 4411. Paul VI of course acknowledges the importance of the symbolism of the Eucharist in *Mysterium fidei*, but calls an error the opinion that symbolism "fully expressed and exhausted the manner of Christ's presence—*totam exprimat et exhauriat rationem praesentiae Christi.*" See O'Neill, *New Approaches to the Eucharist*, for an analysis of the transsignification debate, some of the major issues involved, and the significance of *Mysterium fidei.*

96. Balthasar uses the phrase "transsignification" in his early book on Origen, but he heavily qualifies it with the adjective "ontological" and connects it not to the *res* but only to the *sacramentum*: "la manducation typique est une vraie manducation (*res* et sacramentum), qui, comme telle, signifie (res et *sacramentum*) une

manducation plus spirituelle et par consequent plus réelle. La matérialité du pain symbolise par une trans-signification ontologique le Christ hors du temps et du lieu" (Balthasar, *Parole et Mystère*, 109).

97. *ST* III, 60. 5. ad. 3.

98. *ST* III, 60. 6. co. Balthasar makes this distinction explicitly in his book on Origen, citing in fact P. Pourrat's sacramental manual: "La définition du signe . . . n'a aucun rapport avec 'les' sacrements et il faut se garder d'en tirer quelque chose pour ou contre l'efficacité du signe matériel" (*Parole et Mystère*, 141n34).

99. *GL* I, 422 (emphasis added). See also *GL* III, 427.

100. Morrill, in his Catholic Theological Society of America address in 2012 ("Sacramental-Liturgical Theology since Vatican II") proposes that social sciences are precisely the way forward: "Sacramental-liturgical theology can make its proper, original contribution at this moment, I propose, precisely by 'eradicating illusions of immediacy' with the help of such social-scientific disciplines as ritual and performance studies."

101. *GL* I, 203.

102. "Spiritual senses, in the sense of Christian mysticism, presuppose devout bodily senses which are capable of undergoing Christian transformation by coming to resemble the sensibility of Christ and of Mary" (*GL* I, 378).

103. *GL* I, 370. For Balthasar on the spiritual senses, see McInroy, *Balthasar on the Spiritual Senses*.

104. *CL*, 285–86 (emphasis original).

105. And we can add Catherine of Siena's reflection: "So the spiritual must be the principal vision, because it cannot be deceived. It is with this eye, then, that you must contemplate this sacrament. . . . So you see, the body's senses can be deceived, but not the soul's" (*The Dialogue*, 211).

106. De Lubac, *Corpus Mysticum*. See Balthasar, *Henri de Lubac*, esp. 35–43 and 105–21.

107. See Balthasar, *Christen sind einfältig*, 63–72. See Mongrain, *The Systematic Thought of Hans Urs von Balthasar*, for reflections on the use to which Balthasar puts the *corpus triforme* in his theology.

108. *GL* I, 528.

109. "Since the network of tensions in the Church is visible—as was the man Jesus—she has naturally a sociological and psychological exterior that should not be underestimated, because we cannot (adequately) separate the visible from the invisible Church" (*OP*, 18).

110. For a large collection of citations regarding the Church's sinful-yet-pure nature, see "Casta Meretrix," *ET* II, 193–288.

111. *OP*, 88 and 18.

112. John Paul II, *Ecclesia de Eucharistia*, 21. Also see Benedict XVI, *Sacramentum caritatis*, 14.

113. There are also precedents in the Tübingen school, as Balthasar notes in *TD* III, 429n7. For Vatican II, see *Lumen gentium* 1, and *Sacrosanctum concilium* 5.

114. See Rempel, "Anabaptist Theologies of the Eucharist," 115–37. "In most of Anabaptism, bread is more commonly a sign of the Church as Christ's sacramental presence rather than a sign of his person" (126).

115. Balthasar, *Bernanos*, 502.

116. *TD* III, 430.

117. See *TD* III, 428.

118. "The Experience of the Church," *ET* II, 34.

119. Balthasar, *A Short Primer*, 128–29.

120. "Eucharistic Congress 1960," *ET* II, 507.

121. "Seeing, Hearing, and Reading," *ET* II, 488–99.

122. Balthasar, "The Fathers, the Scholastics, and Ourselves," 363–64.

123. Cf. *GL* I, 530–31.

124. "On the Christian's Capacity to See," *ET* V, 71.

125. For a nice overview, focusing particularly on Chauvet and L. Boeve, see Sweeney, *Sacramental Presence after Heidegger.*

126. The title of "philosopher/theologian" is intentional, in that Lacoste has been a major proponent of troubling a too tidy distinction between these two disciplines. Cf. Lacoste, *From Theology to Theological Thinking.*

127. Murphy, *A Theology of Criticism.* Also see O'Regan, "Balthasar: Between Tübingen and Postmodernity."

128. It must be noted that several recent dissertations have tried to find ways to get beyond some of the problems in Chauvet's thought. For instance, Joseph Mudd uses Lonergan's critical metaphysics (Mudd, *Eucharist as Meaning*), Hal St John looks at Ratzinger and questions Chauvet's use of Heidegger (St John, *The Call of the Holy*), and Conor Sweeney uses Balthasar's concept of the mother's smile (Sweeney, *Sacramental Presence after Heidegger*).

129. Chauvet, *Symbol and Sacrament*, 397–98.

130. Ibid., 398 (emphasis original). This is precisely how Paul VI formulates it, which perhaps Chauvet has in mind: "While Eucharistic symbolism is well suited to helping us understand the effect that is proper to this Sacrament—the unity of the Mystical Body—still it does not indicate or explain what it is that makes this Sacrament different from all the others" (Paul VI, *Mysterium fidei*, 44).

131. We can also note that Chauvet seems to be growing even *more* suspicious of this approach to the Eucharist as a *Ding* as time goes by. For example, whereas in *Symbol and Sacrament* Chauvet looked for a homology between his approach and Heidegger's, in an article from 2001, he again uses *Das Ding*, but now he says it is only *an* approach, and instead of a homology, the similarity is "nonetheless interesting." There is indeed an "abyss" between the two approaches. See Chauvet, "The Broken Bread as Theological Figure of Eucharistic Presence."

132. Chauvet, *Symbol and Sacrament*, 76.

133. A Wittgenstein that Chauvet receives as interpreted by Jean Ladrière.

134. Lacoste, *Experience and the Absolute*, 12.

135. Heidegger, "Language," in *Poetry, Language, Thought*. Here is what Heidegger makes of the reference to bread and wine: "Bread and wine are the fruits of heaven and earth, gifts from the divinities to mortals. Bread and wine gather these four to themselves from the simple unity of their fourfoldness" (*Poetry, Language, Thought*, 203). Lacoste notes Heidegger's noneucharistic interpretation in Lacoste, "Présence et Affection," 223, and Lacoste, *Être en Danger*, 116. In this latter text, Lacoste says that Heidegger's noneucharistic interpretation was *deliberate*.

136. Lacoste, *Experience and the Absolute*, 104.

137. Schrijvers notes that "Lacoste conceives of the liturgical experience in a somewhat Barthian fashion" (Schrijvers, "Jean-Yves Lacoste: A Phenomenology of Liturgy," 315). Yet we should note that from a purely phenomenological perspective, the distinction between whether the nonexperience of God is due to original sin or to a particular theology of creation would be irrelevant.

138. He notes this explicitly in Lacoste, "Le désir et l'inexigible," 25–54. This position is ratified by Falque, *The Metamorphosis of Finitude*, esp. 159n2.

139. Lacoste, "Liturgy and Coaffection," 99.

140. Lacoste, "L'Intuition Sacramentelle," in *L'intuition sacramentelle et autres essais*, 74. See also Balthasar's qualification of the use of the term "natural sacraments" in *TD* III, 412–13n22: "The term is misleading because what is distinctive of sacraments, namely, the *ex opere operato*, is lacking; it is only used to justify the objectification of personal religiosity in the form of religion."

141. For an example of the *total* collapse of sacrament and symbol, albeit his purposes are more poetic and suggestive than systematic, see Boff, *Sacraments of Life, Life of the Sacraments*. Of course, with a very different understanding of "symbol," one more patristic than Heideggerian, which does admit of a genuine transcendence and metaphysical implications, the two concepts can in fact be made harmonious. For example, see Schmemann, *For the Life of the World*, 135–51.

142. *GL* I, 249.

143. Lacoste mentions *les yeux de la foi* in connection to the Eucharist in Lacoste, "L'apparaître du révélé: Sur le clair-obscur," in *Présence et parousie*, 336. For Husserl, one can only see a few sides of a cube, but one perceives the entire cube. One sees what is visible, and one perceives what is invisible.

144. Lacoste, "Liturgy and Coaffection," 97.

145. Lacoste, "L'Intuition Sacramentelle," 85. Also, and this example is perhaps only rhetorically useful, Lacoste notes that whereas Heidegger is interested only in the jug, and only marginally in what it contains, the situation is the reverse for a theology of the Eucharist: the chalice and the monstrance are really of little interest compared to their contents.

146. "L'Intuition Sacramentelle," 94.

147. Lacoste, *Être en Danger*, 108.

148. Ibid., 85, notes the similarity and difference between Augustine and Berengar.

149. For the same point, see also Newman, *Apologia Pro Vita Sua*, 215; Ratzinger, "The Problem of Transubstantiation and the Question about the Meaning of the Eucharist" [originally 1967], in *Collected Works*, Vol. 11. According to Ratzinger, the *being* of the bread and wine cease to be *beings* in their own right and become purely *signs*. See also Benedict XVI, *Sacramentum caritatis*, 7.

150. "L'Intuition Sacramentelle," 77 (emphasis added). Could this perhaps be a veiled allusion to Heidegger's "Letter to a Young Student" (June 1950), about *Das Ding*? There he says that "any path always risks going astray, leading astray" (Heidegger, *Poetry, Language, Thought*, 184).

151. Berengar says explicitly: "I use the word sacrament synonymously with the words: sign, figure, likeness and pledge" (Berengar, *Epistola contra Almannum*, 532, as cited by Vaillancourt, "Sacramental Theology from Gottschalk to Lanfranc," 195). Lanfranc of Canterbury, *On the Body and Blood of the Lord*, and Guitmund of Aversa, *On the Truth of the Body and Blood of Christ in the Eucharist*.

152. *ST* III, 62. 1. co.

153. *Denz.* 1651: condemned are those who say that Christ is in the Eucharist "only as in a sign or figure or by his power—*ut in signo vel, figura, aut virtute*."

154. Paul VI, *Mysterium fidei*, 11.

155. *GL* I, 582.

156. E.g., Schmemann, *For the Life of the World*, last chapter. Even Schmemann admits, however, that "symbol" does not occur very frequently among the fathers (146). In addition to "returning" to the symbolism of the Fathers, this approach also necessarily has to label all Western, scholastic influences on Eastern theology, such as the *sacramentum/res* distinction, as a "Babylonian captivity."

157. In the highly interesting Borella, *The Crisis of Religious Symbolism*, he traces the loss of a symbolic cosmology and advocates for the necessary return to the symbol.

158. "There is no question of turning back the wheel of history, and proposing a renascence of patristic theology at the expense of Scholasticism. The progress wrought by Scholasticism is obvious" ("Theology and Sanctity," *ET* I, 208).

159. Cf. *GL* V, 111. But referring more specifically to the liturgy, and this time medieval and not baroque, see "Liturgy and Awe," *ET* II, 465: the medieval liturgy, with its strong "relationship of archetype and copy, portraying its meaning and its expression. . . . The decisive fact here is that we can no longer accomplish this unity as it was."

160. Power, *Unsearchable Riches*; Rahner, "Theology of Symbol." Balthasar uses "Realsymbolik" on several occasions, e.g., in *OP*, 157–67, *TD* III, 306 and 333.

161. Cf. *GL* I, 432.

162. *TL* I, 107. See also *GL* I, 441–47. The reference to the inexhaustibility of a "gnat" or a "fly" is of course an allusion to the same point made by Aquinas in

Expositio in Symbolum Apostolorum I. Note also that Ulrich, *Homo Abyssus*, begins with the same quotation.

163. *GL* I, 456.

164. Ibid., 458.

165. Pickstock, *After Writing*, 267.

166. Much as Balthasar discusses the *sacramentum/res* distinction in terms of excess, so also does he conceive of the relationship between doctrinal expression and the *res*, the matter to be believed. Cf. Balthasar, *Truth Is Symphonic*, 65.

167. "God's truth is, indeed, great enough to allow an infinity of approaches and entryways" (*GL* I, 17). Also, "Naturally, the image of Christ cannot be fully 'taken in' as can a painting; its dimensions are objectively infinite, and no finite spirit can traverse them" (*GL* I, 512).

168. Rahner of course attempted to unite a person's prethematic orientation toward the absolute horizon with the necessity of a historical and thus thematic mediation by the Church, but he admitted of the inherent difficulty of this task: "It may be that it is not easy or even possible to explain down to the last detail the harmony between these two truths . . . but any theology in any case is faced with the task of showing that such a harmony exists" (Rahner, "Consideration on the Active Role of the Person in the Sacramental Event," 176).

169. 1 Corinthians 2:15. Balthasar cites this in *GL* I, 510.

170. *GL* I, 425.

171. Newman, *Apologia*, chap. 3.

172. "Movement toward God," *ET* III, 42.

173. He does not draw attention to the important places where Balthasar does in fact use liturgical texts, but Worgul calls attention to this relative paucity: "Balthasar seems to avoid a sustained critical reflection on our 'earthly liturgy'. . . . Balthasar does not appear to emphasize liturgical sacramental theology as a central element in his theological enterprise." This betrays an unfamiliarity with Balthasar's oeuvre, but Worgul is to be credited for at least noting the following: "On the other hand, one can legitimately read the Balthasar trilogy as one great and grand theology of worship" (Worgul, "Balthasar's Kneeling Theology, Liturgics and Post Modernism," 257).

174. Schmemann, *Introduction to Liturgical Theology*, 19.

175. The origin is from Prosper of Aquitaine, *Indiculus de gratia Dei, PL* 50:555.

176. "Theology and Sanctity," *ET* I, 181–209, esp. 201–9. As he says of Denys, but this applies equally to his own form of doing theology, "the ultimate goal of this form of theology is liturgy and hymnody: pure adoration" (*TL* II, 102).

177. *TL* III, 366. For a rendering of liturgical theology that could apply quite easily to Balthasar, see Kavanaugh, *On Liturgical Theology*, esp. 143–46. If one had to decide where Balthasar belongs according to Kavanaugh's distinction between systematic and liturgical theology, a strong argument could be made for the latter.

178. "Liturgy and Awe," *ET* II, 461.

179. Tyrrell, *Lex Orandi or Prayer and Creed* and *Lex Credendi: A Sequel to Lex Orandi*. Caldwell, *Liturgy as Revelation*, esp. 70–76, is an exception in that he draws specific attention to Tyrrell and modernism. See Balthasar's reflection on Tyrrell in *OP*, 110–17.

180. *GL* I, 177. Balthasar does not mention or cite Tyrrell here, but this was almost a paraphrase from a line of Tyrrell, *Lex Credendi*: "All we contend is that a Creed has representative truth so far as it constantly and universally fosters the spirit-life; that it is false so far as it is spiritually sterilizing and decadent" (*Lex Credendi*, 253).

181. Tyrrell, *Lex Credendi*, 254.

182. Tyrrell, *Lex Orandi*, 10.

183. Guardini, *The Spirit of the Liturgy*, 21.

184. Cf. "Liturgy and Awe," *ET* II, 463.

185. Hence some of Balthasar's worries about John of the Cross and Balthasar's frequent, indeed anxious, attempts to illustrate the differences between Buddhist and Hindu meditation and Christian meditation.

186. Balthasar, *Convergences*, 44.

187. "Distinctively Christian Prayer," *ET* V, 301 and 302.

188. *CL*, 318.

189. "Theology and Sanctity," *ET* I, 181.

190. *GL* VI, 23 (emphasis original).

191. "Liturgy and Awe," *ET* II, 462.

192. Balthasar, *Truth Is Symphonic*, 34.

193. Balthasar notes that the Enlightenment has caused a rupture between the *lex orandi* and the *lex credendi*: "For the 'enlightened' Christian, the *lex orandi* can no longer be the *lex credendi*: he can in no way take literally the words that are prayed in the Canon of the Mass in the parish Eucharist. The rationalism that has penetrated theology is a new form of Gnosticism" (*TD* IV, 460).

194. Balthasar, *Dare We Hope*, 23–25n3. Balthasar cites six liturgical texts from the Liturgy of the Hours and the Mass (offertory prayers, a collect, and a preface). Also see 32–33, 57n6, 135, and 148.

195. "Everything is related only by reference to the center" (*E*, 18).

196. See Chauvet, *Symbol and Sacrament*, 172, and Fagerberg, *On Liturgical Asceticism*, 10. One could also add Irwin's proposal for *lex vivendi* to fill out the triptych, particularly in Irwin, *Context and Text*.

197. Ratzinger, *The Spirit of the Liturgy*, 8–9.

198. Fagerberg, *On Liturgical Asceticism*, 10 (emphasis original).

199. This is a fact that even Dom Gregory Dix, *The Shape of the Liturgy*, esp. 1–35, notes.

200. There is even reason to associate, for Balthasar, holiness and artistic vision: "The true artist would have to be a saint" (Balthasar, *Tragedy under Grace*, 70).

201. Cf. Aristotle, *Metaphysics* 10.6.

202. Philippians 2:5–6. See *GL* I, 253, for a reflection on this verse and what it means for Christian attunement (*sich-Einstimmen*) to the pattern of Christ.

203. *GL* VII, 399–415. See also Balthasar, *You Crown the Year with Your Goodness*, 205–6, for the Feast of All Saints.

204. "Liturgy and Awe," *ET* II, 470.

205. "Theology and Sanctity," *ET* I, 200.

206. Speyr, *The Holy Mass, The Cross: Word and Sacrament*, and *Confession*.

207. Balthasar, *Razing the Bastions*, 32. Balthasar makes the same point in *GL* VI: "Great renewals in the period of the Church always proceed from the contemporaneity with Christ, which is always presupposed and created anew by the *hodie* of the liturgy" (171n70). See also "Eucharistic Congress 1960," *ET* II, 511.

208. "Contemplation is liturgical, if we understand liturgy in its fullest sense" (Balthasar, *Prayer*, 116).

209. Balthasar says of St. Thérèse, for instance, that because she reduces everything to the present moment, she tends to "neglect certain objective, timeless aspects of the revealed truth" (Balthasar, *Two Sisters*, 71). One should also look at his analysis of holy fools in *GL* V, 141–204.

210. Romans 6:5; Blessing and Invocation of God over Baptismal Water in the Rite for the Baptism of a Child.

211. Ratzinger, *The Spirit of the Liturgy*, 142; see also 69.

212. Quash explores why it is Ignatius of Loyola who "impels the move from aesthetics to dramatics," or from contemplation to action, in Balthasar's thought (Quash, "Hans Urs von Balthasar's 'Theatre of the World'").

213. *TD* I, 15.

214. Ibid., 92–93 (emphasis added). Balthasar cites Casel in the first sentence of the quotation, demonstrating that Balthasar thinks that the liturgy for Casel tends toward the dramatic. See also *TD* II, 74.

215. *TD* IV, 389.

216. See *TD* I, 105–9, on how Balthasar interprets how the Church, in both East and West, "developed aspects of the theatre which helped to bring home the Christian reality," including processions and other local customs so central to late medieval piety.

217. The danger of these masses, no matter how beautiful, is that they led to "the obscuring of the sacred by the operatic," in the words of Ratzinger, *The Spirit of the Liturgy*, 91.

218. *TD* I, 18–19.

219. For example, see McCall, *Do This: Liturgy as Performance*. Also Schnusenberg, *The Mythological Traditions of Liturgical Drama*.

220. *GL* I, 199. With regard to the sciences such as anthropology, psychology, or sociology, Balthasar does not issue an absolute prohibition, but simply wants to draw attention to the principles (whether Christian or anti-Christian) that inform them (*TD* IV, 480).

221. *TD* III, 525.

222. "The Worthiness of the Liturgy," *NE*, 130.

223. *GL* VII, 418.

224. Cf. *TD* II, 49.

225. *GL* I, 582.

226. "This comes about through our being incorporated into the Eucharist that, in the Spirit, Christ makes to the Father" (*TD* IV, 406). On the connection between infinite and finite freedoms, the *analogia libertatis*, see Reali, *La ragione e la forma*. This theme of the sacraments as resolving the paradox of human liberty (ibid., 287) by accepting the freedom of Christ's decision is the main motif in Reali's book.

227. *GL* I, 575 (translation slightly altered). On the temptation toward spiritualizing, see also *TL* II, 221, and *Epilogue*, 99–108.

228. According to Charles Taylor, at least in the eighteenth century, "superstitious" was defined as "the enchanted dimension of religion, the rites and cults and practices which partook of magic in their understanding" (Taylor, *A Secular Age*, 239).

229. Cf. "Seeing, Hearing, and Reading," *ET* II, 486–87.

230. "Christian revelation must fulfill the inchoate yearnings of *mythos* and, at the same time, banish its uncertainties" (*TD* II, 62).

231. Balthasar, *Tragedy under Grace*, 69. He is speaking of Reinhold Schneider and Calderón.

232. "Liturgy and Awe," *ET* II, 462.

233. "Therefore, genuine life of the senses and hearing has its abiding place in this liturgy. The sacramental event *ought* to unfold visibly in as beautiful and worthy a form as possible" ("Seeing, Hearing, and Reading," *ET* II, 488; emphasis original).

234. "One of the main tasks of our *Aesthetics* (*The Glory of the Lord*) was to demonstrate the difference between inner-historical phenomena (even religious phenomena) and the epiphany of God in Jesus" (*TD* III, 206n6).

235. Balthasar, *My Work in Retrospect*, 85–86.

236. "The Worthiness of the Liturgy," *NE*, 130.

237. Ibid. Further: "There is therefore no excuse for remaining on the level of aesthetics (or of mourning over old forms of the Mass), for in the liturgy everything is relative to and oriented toward God's glory" (ibid., 137n2).

238. The titles are identical in English, but the original German admits of a slight and inconsequential difference: Guardini's is *Vom Geist der Liturgie*, and Ratzinger's is rendered as either *Einführung in den Geist der Liturgie* or *Der Geist der Liturgie: Eine Einführung*.

239. It is a curious fact, however, that the liturgy and Guardini's *Vom Geist der Liturgie* are only given minor treatment in Balthasar, *Romano Guardini*. Nevertheless, it could be said that it is Guardini's "religious phenomenology" (*GL* I, 389) that Balthasar latches onto, in his book on Guardini, but also in his own work on aesthetics, which subsequently shapes his interpretation of the liturgy, which results in an analysis much like Guardini's.

240. The more salient of these influences will become apparent in what follows, but here the following hints can be seen as an accumulation of convergent probabilities (to use Newman's term): in *The Spirit of the Liturgy*, Ratzinger uses the phrase "theo-drama" twice (108 and 118), the phrase "Cosmic liturgy" appears numerous times throughout, his understanding of "sacrifice" (15–19) seems to echo Balthasar's influential treatment in "The Mass, a Sacrifice of the Church?," the strong connection between Eucharist and the Word, which Balthasar finds in Origen (27), his understanding of God's eternity as not time-lessness, but a sort of *Ur*-time (56), he speaks of the "humility of the sacraments" (80), and he claims that the human soul is always feminine in relationship to God (123).

241. Guardini, *The Spirit of the Liturgy*, 74. Further: "Aestheticism is profoundly shameless. All true beauty is modest" (79), and that to understand beautiful works of art, "one must take the inner essence for their starting-point" (81).

242. Guardini, *The Spirit of the Liturgy*, 74.

243. Ratzinger, *The Spirit of the Liturgy*, 49.

244. Ibid., 79.

245. Ibid., 82; see also 74–75 on the need for a "new kind of seeing," which means that "the senses are not to be discarded, but they should be expanded to their widest capacity."

246. Guardini, *The Spirit of the Liturgy*, 83. Ratzinger, *The Spirit of the Liturgy*, 108.

247. Ratzinger, *The Spirit of the Liturgy*, 108.

248. Ibid., 32; see also 34: "The celebration is not just a rite, not just a liturgical 'game.'"

249. Guardini, *The Spirit of the Liturgy*, 84.

250. Ibid., 82.

251. Ratzinger, *The Spirit of the Liturgy*, 108.

252. Guardini, *The Spirit of the Liturgy*, 82 (emphasis added).

253. See the end of Balthasar's introduction to *GL* I, esp. 117–24. In particular, Balthasar quotes a preface from the Christmas liturgy that speaks of God's visible manifestation as the hook by which creatures are snatched up to things invisible, and he provides a long quotation of Denys on divine *eros* from *Divine Names* IV, connecting it explicitly to the sacraments: "Only the mysteries and sacraments of Christ's revelation effect what they signify" (123).

254. *Purgatorio* 27.52–54. See *GL* III, 34–54.

CHAPTER 4

1. For an earlier, and much briefer, account of how Balthasar, and Joseph Ratzinger, allow sacramental theology to "regulate" their eschatologies, see Ciraulo, "Sacramentally Regulated Eschatology in Hans Urs von Balthasar and Pope Benedict XVI."

2. See Wainwright, "Eschatology."

3. Karl Rahner, for instance, wants to make a clear distinction between apocalyptic and eschatological, but for Balthasar the terms seem to function more or less synonymously, as they will for us in this chapter. The best example of the exchangeability of the two terms is the fact that Balthasar's dissertation, "Geschichte des eschatologischen Problems in der modernen deutschen Literatur" (1930), is renamed *Apokalypse der deutschen Seele* (1937–39) in the greatly expanded and developed version, without any justification given for the change from *Eschatologie* to *Apokalypse*. He also says that "'Apokalypse der Seele' ist darum nur ein konkreteres Wort für Eschatologie" (*Apok.* I, 3). See Rahner, "The Hermeneutics of Eschatological Assertions."

4. *Apok.* I, 3.

5. Nicholas Healy understood this quite well, and thus Healy, *The Eschatology of Hans Urs von Balthasar*, has just as much, if not even more, to say about metaphysics as it does about temporality and eternity.

6. Griffiths, *Decreation*, 4: "But for the most part, the world appears to human creatures as it is: a charnel house, saturated in blood violently shed; an ensemble of inanimate creatures decaying toward extinction; a theater of vice and cruelty." Despite this rather lugubrious picture, it is certain that this description is at least *sometimes* true, and thus must be accounted for in eschatology.

7. Balthasar, *Presence and Thought*, 133.

8. Which is given the unfortunate English title: *A Theological Anthropology*.

9. "In this way, eschatology is, almost more even than any other *locus theologicus*, entirely a doctrine of *salvation*. This is, as we shall see, absolutely central" ("Some Points of Eschatology," *ET* I, 261; emphasis original).

10. "Axiologie heißt also Schicksalsgegenwart der letzten Dinge, Teleologie Weg der Verwandlung von Schicksalsgegenwart in Erfüllungsgegenwart" (*Apok.* I, 13).

11. *Apok.* I, 13.

12. "Some Points of Eschatology," *ET* I, 276.

13. For example, see *GL* I, 52.

14. Galatians 2:20. See *TD* V, 141–52.

15. Balthasar, *History and Eschatology*, 155.

16. *ST* III, 60. 3. co.

17. See Bultmann, *History and Eschatology*, 51–55. Here Bultmann claims that Christianity became a "community of cultic worship" as a result of its contact with the Hellenistic world. The sacraments functioned to evacuate the Church of its temporal anxieties, but also, unfortunately, to render any eschatological sense as rather enervated. This position naturally carries over into his exegesis. Note how Bultmann argues that the eucharistic overtones of John 6 are necessarily the additions of a later, ecclesial, redactor, turning an initial invitation to personal communion with the Lord into a cultic ceremony. See Bultmann, *The Gospel of John*, 218–20, 485–86.

18. See Walatka, *Von Balthasar and the Option for the Poor*, esp. 44–78.

19. Note Moltmann's description in his autobiography, *A Broad Place*, 79: "What I was looking for was a theological parallel act to [Bloch's] atheistic principle of hope on the basis of the promissory history of the old covenant and the resurrection history of the new."

20. See *TD* V, 168. It should be uncontroversial to consider Moltmann's theology as quite "Jewish," because Moltmann himself credits many of his ideas to Jewish influences. For instance, in addition to the obvious influence of Bloch, his understanding of creation is admittedly close to the kabbalistic notion of *zimsum*, and at the beginning of *The Crucified God*, Moltmann acknowledges that his controversial thesis was indebted to Heschel, rabbinic and kabbalistic ideas, Rosenzweig, Scholem, and Wiesel. Cf. Moltmann, *God in Creation*, xv, 86–87, 156, and Moltmann, *The Crucified God*, xi.

21. This is the basis of Balthasar, *Das Ganze im Fragment*, but Balthasar also provides a nice summary in "Improvisation on Spirit and Future," *ET* III, 136: "If something like a totality is to be attained within the structure of this fragment, this can be done only on the basis of a borrowing from the future, of an anticipation of the future that the promise allows."

22. And today one would need to include the thought of Alain Badiou and Quentin Meillassoux in this grouping. For them, God is indeed a "not yet" of the world, one who is currently only a virtual possibility but a possibility of the future nonetheless. Aaron Riches, "Christology and Anti-Humanism," has a nice engagement with this thought.

23. To show how indeed this characterization of Judaism functions only as a type, it is easy enough to look at *GL* VI, where Balthasar himself shows what he thinks the shape of the Old Testament and Judaism is in reality. There, although he does highlight the prophetic, futurist mode of anticipation, he equally highlights the fact that God's glory is also ever-present. There are, he says, three forms of divine *kabod*: "the 'historical' *kabod* (with its centre in Sinai), the 'prophetic' *kabod* (with its clearest expression in Isaiah and Ezekiel), and the 'cosmic' *kabod* (in the nature-psalms, in Job, and in Sirach). *The three forms are integrated beyond separation*" (*GL* VI, 79; emphasis added). These three forms of *kabod* correspond to the three directions of sacramental time, being thus natively characteristic of Judaism and not merely a novelty of Christianity.

24. Bloch, *The Principle of Hope*, II, 513.

25. Ibid., 513–14.

26. See especially Moltmann, *The Coming of God*, 143–46 and 186–87, and Moltmann, *The Trinity and the Kingdom*, 203–9. Likewise, de Lubac, Balthasar, and Ratzinger all acknowledge that some important distinctions need to be made between the historical Joachim and the later effects of Joachimism, especially as it appears in Lessing and others as a validation of the Enlightenment goals of progress.

27. Gorringe, "Eschatology and Political Radicalism," 107.

28. More accurately, in his book on ecclesiology, Moltmann does recognize the *signum demonstrativum*, but his affirmation is an immediate denial, for that presence is only a cipher for the coincidence of past and future: "In the coincidence of remembrance and hope, history and eschatology, it is the sign of present grace, which confers liberty and fellowship (*signum demonstrativum*). In the Lord's supper, Christ's redeeming future is anticipated and this hope celebrated in remembrance of his passion. In this meal his past and his future are simultaneously made present" (Moltmann, *The Church in the Power of the Spirit*, 243).

29. Balthasar, *The Theology of Karl Barth*, 372.

30. In Barth's response to Balthasar's *Barth* book, he said that the supposed "Christological renaissance" in Roman Catholicism, represented in part by Balthasar, will come to nothing and that in reality nothing has changed because "the doctrine of the sacrifice of the mass, the archetype of the whole idea of representation, is still unshaken" (Barth, *Church Dogmatics* IV.1, 768).

31. I mean this simply in the sense that the late Barth himself meant it: there are no such things as ecclesial sacraments, not even baptism or the Lord's Supper are properly called "sacraments" for Barth (see *Church Dogmatics* IV.4, 102). For a Catholic, specifically Rahnerian, analysis of Barth's eucharistic theology, see Molnar, *Karl Barth and the Theology of the Lord's Supper*. See also Barth's clear articulation of the bidirectionality of baptism in Barth, *Church Dogmatics* IV.4, 195.

32. Moltmann, *Theology of Hope*, 159. See the same essential argument in Moltmann, *The Crucified God*, in his discussion of "the cult of the cross" as a form of resistance to the cross (41–45). And Moltmann's strong aversion to "ecclesiastical control" is evident in and explains his proposal for an entirely "open table," in which baptism and confirmation are no longer prerequisites for admission to the Eucharist (and thus obviously including intercommunion among all denominations). He also entirely dismisses the notion that only the ordained are equipped to celebrate the Lord's Supper; see Moltmann, *The Church in the Presence of the Holy Spirit*, 258–60.

33. See Balthasar, "Zu einer christlichen Theologie der Hoffnung," and *TD* V, 172–75, 227–31. To state it briefly, it is not accidental that Barth and Moltmann reject both a metaphysics whereby some positive relationship between nature and grace can be established and sacramental efficacy in the present tense. There can be no stable form of grace, either in terms of the participation of being in Being or in terms of ecclesial institution. If grace is to appear here and now, it can only do so as an *Ereignis*, as an "event." In the more extreme case of Moltmann, it leads toward the view that every happening is indeed a happening *of God*.

34. *TD* V, 499.

35. *TD* V, 389 (emphasis original).

36. "A *nunc stans* would be the very picture of damnation. When theologians describe eternity in such terms, it is no wonder people fear the boredom of eternity" ("Finite Time within Eternal Time," *ET* V, 55).

37. *Paradiso* 33.145.

38. *Paradiso* 28.42–43.

39. Balthasar explicitly critiques Dante for a deficit in Trinitarian thought: "For this reason the *Comedy*'s image of God is not really trinitarian but an extraordinarily intensified, Christian version of the Eros of Antiquity" (*GL* III, 101).

40. Guy Mansini has provided perhaps the most trenchant critique of Balthasar's proposal of some sort of "change" or development in God, after what is really a fairly sympathetic and level-headed evaluation in Mansini, "Balthasar and the Theodramatic Enrichment of the Trinity." His main critique can be summarized, not unjustly, as follows: (1) "There is no other analysis of change besides that of Aristotle" (518); (2) Aristotle's notion of change cannot logically be applied to God; (3) ergo, Balthasar's attribution of change to God is illogical.

Balthasar would not, I trust, disagree that this is a healthy and necessary application of analogical thought, moving upward from the best of human reason. Balthasar, however, would reply that it is then indeed possible to allow our (apparently Aristotelian) understanding of time, movement, and change to be inverted by data coming from revelation itself. Nevertheless, Mansini does call attention to this important critique, which will not be answered here: if time and change when applied to God mean something contrary to their usual definition (and in fact mean something closer to the usual categories of immutability), why use those words at all? See also the exchange between Kevin Duffy and Gerard F. O'Hanlon: Duffy, "Change, Suffering, and Surprise in God," and O'Hanlon, "A Response to Kevin Duffy on von Balthasar and the Immutability of God."

41. Balthasar, *A Theology of History*, 83. Balthasar explores the time of the forty days most explicitly in *A Theology of History*, but he develops similar ideas in the later *Theo-Drama,* albeit with slightly altered vocabulary. Although not noted by Balthasar, it seems probable that the notion of Christ as a bridge is indebted to his reading of Catherine of Siena, who uses the image in her *Dialogue*. Balthasar admits explicitly that he borrows the emphasis on the forty days in *A Theology of History* from Speyr. See Balthasar, *Our Task*, 100.

42. Cf. *TD* V, 30.

43. *A Theology of History*, 98. The notion of contemporaneity here is indebted to Casel, as evidenced by the fact that Balthasar refers to the idea of "mystery-presence" in "mystery theology," meaning Casel primarily, just a few pages earlier (95).

44. I am borrowing this last phrase from Paul Griffith, *Decreation*. This chronic time, also called "metronomic," is opposed to the *systolic*, or the kairotic; see particularly 95–108.

45. *TD* V, 119. Quoting Speyr's commentary on Isaiah. Also quoting Speyr on 135: "The whole of nontemporal and nonspatial eternal life is projected into the small-sized host." See also 331.

46. *TD* V, 416.

47. Cf. *Denz.* 1083 and 1256.

48. Balthasar, *Tragedy under Grace*, 202–3. The italics here (not italicized in the original) are a quotation from Schneider, *Stern der Zeit: Sonette*.

49. That is to say, at least Leibniz's theodicy, in which God "chooses" the best possible world, has already presupposed that there is a criterion of goodness that is in fact separate from God's own nature. In other words, modern theodicy often tries to justify a god (more a demiurge) that Christians do not in fact believe in.

50. It is axiomatic for Balthasar, in *TD* V especially, that all things in the economy must have their foundation in the Trinitarian life, including freedom and its misuse. There is, of course, no evil within the Triune life for Balthasar, but actual evils are only possible because of a corruption of positive features when found in God.

51. Balthasar's overall approach to "theodicy" is consonant with Hart, *The Doors of the Sea*, which argues that a healthy amount of agnosticism regarding evil's etiology is in order, not only for good mental hygiene but more importantly as the only remotely ethical and Christian response.

52. *TD* IV, 53–54.

53. Balthasar, *The Theology of Karl Barth*, 369; 376 (emphasis original).

54. Balthasar, *Epilogue*, 103; Balthasar, *Epilog*, 80. Bulgakov says much the same: God's love "is disclosed here as the continuing Golgotha, as Christ's *compassion* for humankind in its human Golgotha. All human life is integrated in Christ's personal life, and all human sufferings are contained in His suffering" (Bulgakov, *The Holy Grail & The Eucharist*, 53).

55. Balthasar, *The Theology of Karl Barth*, 371 (emphasis original). It is no accident that Balthasar calls attention to sacramental theology at this point. But it does call into question Balthasar's own bracketing, at the beginning of his book on Barth, of "the obvious dogmatic differences, such as the doctrine of the Church, of the Magisterium, sources of revelation, sacraments, and so forth" (xix). It seems more likely that these dogmatic differences have their corollary implications in the metaphysical and Christological spheres.

56. Cf. *TD* IV, 76. I interpret Balthasar on that page to mean something very much like Benedict XVI's statement in *Spe salvi* (esp. para. 24), that moral progress is always individual and cannot be mapped onto the same developmental schema of natural or technological progress.

57. *Epilogue*, 119. And noting that Balthasar prefers the language of "accepting" and "receiving" rather than the traditional vocabulary of "works" or "merit" does not change this fact. For Balthasar, the highest work a creature can accomplish is indeed one of reception.

58. For Balthasar, without the Eucharist, the Incarnation would be like an unconsummated marriage: "*Only if* the most real historical body of Christ . . . is communicated to the faithful in its reality—only on the condition, then, that there is the mystery of the Eucharist—do we truly participate in the God-man's fate" ("Only If," in *Convergences*, 146; emphasis original).

59. *Epilogue*, 121.

60. Explored most in depth in *TD* II and III. One should also note that Maximus's defense of dyotheletism is likewise central for Balthasar, and provides Christological warrant and validation for a possible harmony between the divine and human wills more generally.

61. Cf. *TD* V, 478.

62. As is the usual Reformed understanding of real presence, where Christ does not so much come to earth, but rather the Church is brought up to the presence of Christ in heaven. Instead, for Balthasar, we need to feel the "healthy 'materialism,' the weighty substance, of the Eucharist and of all the sacraments, binding them to the earth" (Balthasar, *In the Fullness of Faith*, 117).

63. Falque, *The Metamorphosis of Finitude*.

64. *TD* V, 478.

65. *TD* V, 501.

66. Calderón de la Barca of course wrote much more than *autos sacramentales*, but it is only with these that we are concerned here. It is the *autos* that deal with the heaven/earth tension, while, for instance, the *comedias* "remain within the worldly sphere, and so they can refer only peripherally to this opening to heaven that heaven itself creates" (*TD* I, 363; see 361–69 for an excursus on Calderón's work beyond the *autos*).

67. Note especially Calderón, *El Gran Teatro del Mundo*, lines 409–18.

68. *TD* I, 168.

69. Ibid.

70. *TD* III, 505. He says virtually the same thing in the next volume, *TD* IV, 132. Nevertheless, in *TD* I, Balthasar had a more favorable interpretation, saying that Christ was the "hidden presupposition" in *El Gran Teatro*, and points to the other *autos* that make this more explicit (*TD* I, 165). It is clearly a problem that haunted Balthasar, as he had already discussed it in his afterword to his translation of *Das große Welttheater*: "Von Christus ist nicht die Rede, höchstens ganz indirect in der für alle 'Autos Sacramentales' obligatorischen eucharistischen Schluß-Symbolik wird seine Existenz vorausgesetzt. Von Freiheit und Gewissen wird gesprochen, aber nicht vom Heiligen Geist" ("Nachwort," 74).

71. *TD* I, 165.

72. *TD* III, 505.

73. "Suban a cenar conmigo el pobre y la religiosa que, aunque por haber salido del mundo este pan no coman, sustento será adorarle por ser objeto de gloria. . . . Pues el ángel en el cielo, en el mundo las personas y en el infierno el demonio, todos a este pan se postran; en el infierno, en el cielo y mundo a un tiempo se oigan dulces voces que le alaben acordadas y sonoras" (Calderón, *El Gran Teatro*, 1449–54 and 1561–68). Then, the play concludes with singing of the *Tantum ergo*.

74. See *GL* IV, 104–5. This position is argued even more stridently by John Zizioulas, especially in Zizioulas, *Being as Communion*, 27–65.

75. Balthasar, *Tragedy under Grace*, 69. Balthasar defines this height as the period between Shakespeare and Calderón, a very narrow window indeed. He repeats this timeframe in *TD* II, 189. Essential also to the baroque, and to Balthasar's interest in it, is the notion of "representation," which is found equally in the *autos sacramentales* and in Ignatius's *Exercises*. See Balthasar, "Nachwort" to *Das große Welttheater*; Casarella, "'Repräsentation': Zum Barockverständnis bei Hans Urs von Balthasar (1905–1988)"; and Schumacher, "The Concept of Representation in the Theology of Hans Urs von Balthasar."

76. The only complete text of Péguy's that Balthasar translated was *Le porche du mystère de la deuxième vertu*, translated into German as *Das Tor zum Geheimnis der Hoffnung* (1943). He also selected and translated a very nice anthology of Péguy in 1953: *Wir stehen alle an der Front*. There is a recent edition of these chosen texts in the original French, which includes Balthasar's introduction: *Nous sommes tous à la frontière*. Compare that, however, with the fact that Balthasar translated almost the entirety of Claudel's work into German, and admitted that he had spent "months, indeed virtually years" translating Claudel, in addition to knowing him personally. See Balthasar, "Petit mémoire sur Paul Claudel," as cited in Nichols, *Divine Fruitfulness*, 335. In *TD* IV, Balthasar uses Péguy as "the best corrective to Claudel's ambiguity," at least with regard to the question of the *communio sanctorum* (417), and in GL *III*, Péguy is "less pedestrian" than Claudel (404).

77. *GL* III, 406. He repeats later in the same work: "Here for the first time theology returns to its home port with Irenaeus of Lyons" (484).

78. Péguy, "Clio I," in *Temporal and Eternal*, 105.

79. "Péguy again saw his fate as an exile side by side with the Jewish destiny, especially that of the poor Jews. . . . Péguy the poor man felt and knew himself to be 'in a common state of *misère, dans cet enfer commun*,' with them" (*GL* III, 452). A good summary of Péguy's understanding of politics and the Church–state relation is Perreau-Saussine, *Catholicism and Democracy*, 103–8.

80. *GL* III, 435.

81. "Péguy laid the blame for the de-Christianising of the modern world almost exclusively at the door of the clergy and the religious. They have spiritualised everything in Christianity. They have betrayed the earth" (*GL* III, 472).

82. Joan is essential to Péguy not only because she is a saint of the Church, but because she is so thoroughly a *French* saint. That is to say, her sufferings were both spiritual and political in a manner that demonstrates her profound solidarity with humanity. Péguy had two plays on Joan of Arc: *Jeanne d'Arc* (1897), and *Le Mystère de la charité de Jeanne d'Arc* (1910), which was translated into English as *The Mystery of the Charity of Joan of Arc* by Julian Green.

83. Cyril O'Regan notes that "Péguy can serve as a foil for Moltmann because he shares Moltmann's genuine concerns about God's relation to the world, without sharing the latter's tendency to over-explain and thereby become trapped in the web of Hegel's master-discourse" (O'Regan, *The Anatomy of Misremembering*, 362).

84. Aquinas's definition of hope as a "future good, arduous but possible to attain" could be misunderstood to be in line with a purely horizontal expectation. But this is certainly not the case, as is clear when it is understood that the object of hope is both eternal happiness and the divine assistance necessary to obtain that end. The former, eternal happiness, is still in the "future" with regard to complete fulfillment, but hope can still be considered a virtue because of the possession of divine assistance here and now. See, esp., *ST* II.II, 17. 1. ad. 3.

85. "Der Christ Péguy wird eine tiefere misère im Menschen entdecken: die Sünde und Konkupiszenz, und dem seine Mysterien des stellvertretenden Leidens ('Jeanne d'Arc' und die Unschuldigen Kinder) entgegensetzen" (Balthasar, "Heilsgeschichtliche Überlegungen zur Befreiungstheologie," 171n5).

86. *TD* IV, 418.

87. *TD* V, 183.

88. Péguy, *The Portal of the Mystery of Hope*, 117.

89. Ibid., 121.

90. Ibid., 123.

91. This is again what makes Péguy "Irenaean": it is Christ's recapitulation of ordinary time that makes his life salvific: "How many days were any different from the others. How much of his preaching was any different and how much of it was not, temporally, a repetition" (Péguy, *The Portal of the Mystery of Hope*, 122).

92. *TD* V, 187.

93. Cf. *GL* III, 498. In other words, God's involvement with the world, God's "hope," as Péguy says, is not a result of a metaphysical necessity, but is rather the creative solution to the interaction of creaturely and divine freedoms.

94. Péguy, "Clio I," 119.

95. Ibid., 145. The saints are those who are above all sensitized: "The saints themselves, my child, the greatest saints (in a sense even more than others), all felt the blow" (ibid.).

96. Péguy, *The Portal of the Mystery of Hope*, 135, 136.

97. *TD* V, 188. I have significantly altered the English to better reflect the original German (*Theodramatik* IV, 167).

98. The entire project of the *Theo-Drama* is itself an attempt to provide a Christian understanding of the tragic, but Aidan Nichols notes that as early as 1927, in his essay "Katholische Religion und Kunst," "Balthasar points out that the Church gives full weight to tragedy while avoiding 'pantragism'—the secular dogma that would make of tragedy the final word" (Nichols, *Scattering the Seed*, 15).

99. For an analysis of the Trinitarian dimensions of Péguy's triptych (*The Mystery of the Charity of Joan of Arc*, *The Portal of the Mystery of Hope*, and *The Mystery of the Holy Innocents*), see Borras, "Péguy, Expositor of Christian Hope."

100. Cf. *TD* IV, 15. See also "Eschatology in Outline," *ET* IV, 466.

101. A few representative studies on the liturgical structure of Revelation include Ruiz, "The Apocalypse of John and Contemporary Roman Catholic Liturgy"; Vanni,

"Liturgical Dialogue as a Literary Form in the Book of Revelation"; and Shepherd, *The Paschal Liturgy and the Apocalypse*. See also Baker, *The Great High Priest*, and the enormously evocative essay by Erik Peterson, "The Book on the Angels."

102. *TD* IV, 54.

103. See the section on the "Liturgies of Lament," in *GL* VI, 256–59, but also note that throughout this volume on the Old Testament the theme of liturgy and adoration recur with great frequency.

104. On this, see an analysis of Revelation in Schillebeeckx, *Christ*, 432–62, esp. 440. Schillebeeckx, however, interprets Revelation almost entirely as if it was a mere extension of themes from the Old Testament: see esp. 432, 444, 448.

105. "The worshipper always has the unity of God's 'action' in view: the Lamb is worshipped together with God and as God, and *at the same time* is 'as though it had been slain,' . . . . Just as the drama originated in the liturgy (at the handing-over, *traditio*, of the sealed scroll to the Lamb), so now it returns to it" (*TD* IV, 54–55; emphasis original).

106. Ibid., 58.

107. Ibid., 452.

108. Ibid., 450. *Theodramatik* III, 420.

109. See "Tragedy and Christian Faith," in *ET* III, 391–411.

110. Nietzsche, *Thus Spake Zarathustra*, prologue, 3.

111. Péguy, "Clio I," 155.

112. *TD* V, 481.

113. Which is partly why in Balthasar's most important late work on eschatology, *TD* V, perhaps more than any other text, his own voice almost entirely disappears. Instead, much of the text reads as a sort of *lectio divina* and commentary on Adrienne von Speyr.

114. Claudel, *Un poète regarde la croix*, as cited in Claudel, *I Believe in God*, 314. In addition to Claudel, and other poets and mystics who speak of a celestial Eucharist, Balthasar's most important theological predecessor is Antonio Rosmini-Serbati.

115. Wainwright, *Eucharist and Eschatology*, 191. It is a very helpful resource, but Wainwright's book would more appropriately be titled *Eucharist or Eschatology*, for if there is no carryover from the realm of sacramentality to that of the eschaton, then the Eucharist is only valuable insofar as it effaces itself either now (as prognostication and foretaste) or later in favor of the eschaton. Bernard Leeming has a nice summary of the scholastics' discussions regarding when sacramentality would have been suitable for human nature in Leeming, *Principles of Sacramental Theology*, 598–614. He agrees wholeheartedly with the dominant opinion: "After the resurrection it [the sacramental dispensation] will not be so, and sounder theological thought has always maintained that it would not have been so, except for the catastrophe of sin" (604).

116. *ST* III, 73. 3. co.

117. The reasons he and other scholastics give for the existence of the sacraments are *ad instructionem, humiliationem, et exercitationem.* See *ST* III, 61. 1.

118. *ST* III, 80. 2. ad.1.

119. Revelation 19:9. Eating and drinking is a major theme throughout Revelation, with ends that are good, such as 2:17 and 3:20; bad, such as 2:14, 14:8, 14:10, 14:19–20; and mixed, such as 10:9. Note that the verb "to eat," δειπνήσω, in 3:20 is the same as in other eucharistic passages of the New Testament, such as Luke 22:20 and 1 Corinthians 11:20–25. See Perrin, "Sacraments and Sacramentality in the New Testament," 58.

120. *TD* V, 468.

121. Mechthild of Hackeborn, *The Book of Special Grace*, I.27, 102. Balthasar also uses this image to illustrate the inseparable unity between the Church and Mary.

122. Balthasar, *A Theology of History*, 99 (emphasis original).

123. See *GL* I, 301–2.

124. *TD* V, 470.

125. Cf. Ibid., 472–73.

126. Ibid., 472 (emphasis original).

127. *TD* III, 440–41.

128. Balthasar, *Epilogue*, 106. Also see *E*, 97–100.

129. For an exploration of Balthasar's understanding of the positivity of creaturely difference from the Creator, and the retention of this difference even upon "divinization," see Ciraulo, "Hans Urs von Balthasar's Indifference to Divinization."

130. Which is why, for Aquinas, there is no need for sacraments in heaven. Not only have the sacraments' function as remedies to sin ceased to be necessary, but so have their role as affirming and perfecting our ordinary mode of thinking by means of sense perception. This is true regarding the vision of the divine essence (without the eyes of the body), but it is also true that Aquinas (if the supplement to the *Tertia Pars* is to be trusted) does think we will see God indirectly by seeing his glory reflected in the bodies of the saints (*ST*, Suppl. 92. 2. co.). Also, Aquinas's hylomorphism makes it such that the soul detached from the body would be lacking in some happiness, and thus it is necessary that they be reunited with their bodies (*SCG* IV, 79.11). Therefore, although Aquinas is insistent on the resurrection of the body, the reasons he gives, beyond the clear indications in scripture, have more to do with anthropology than with the body's role in uniting the Church together and to Christ in the eschatological state. Balthasar, instead, "aims to understand eschatology, not anthropocentrically, but theocentrically and in trinitarian terms" (*TD* V, 244).

131. *Sacrosanctum concilium* 8. This passage cites Revelation 21:2, Colossians 3:1, and Hebrews 8:2.

132. Balthasar, *Mysterium Paschale*, 34. See also 206, and also *TL* II, 121–22, and the section on "The Metaphysics of the Oratory," in *GL* V, 119–40. Note that the idea of a *sacrificium coeleste* is highly debated. Abbot Vonier, for instance, takes a

very hard line on this issue, arguing from Thomas's notion of the cessation of sacramental life that Christ is in no sense still immolated in heaven. See Vonier, *A Key to the Doctrine of the Eucharist*, 172–74.

133. Bulgakov says much the same: "Until [the Kingdom is established in all of creation], although he is glorified, Christ continues to be crucified in the world in His humanity and the Lamb continues to be slaughtered in the Eucharistic sacrifice of this continuing Golgotha" (Bulgakov, *The Comforter*, 284; see also 373).

134. Matthiesen, *Sacrifice as Gift*, is an important and enormously helpful book. On La Taille's difference from the French School on this issue, see ibid., 90–91 in particular. Balthasar does not agree entirely with La Taille, particularly on the question of the sacrifice of the Mass. He thinks that La Taille's prioritization of the eternal sacrifice makes the meal element in the ecclesial Eucharist superfluous, thus separating meal and sacrifice, which must be thought in tandem. See "The Mass, A Sacrifice of the Church?," *ET* III, 238n98.

135. Balthasar, *Mysterium Paschale*, 28. Balthasar, *Theologie der Drei Tage*, 33.

136. *TD* V, 481. Balthasar is referring to Ernst Wilhelm Hengstenberg, a nineteenth-century Lutheran theologian.

137. "Spirit and Institution," *ET* IV, 228–29. In this passage (from 1974) Balthasar is recycling a thought he had already written in 1970, as seen in "The Mystery of the Eucharist," *NE*, 118.

138. It was originally an obscure notion in Leibniz's philosophy, but Maurice Blondel was the first to see the vital importance of the notion not only for Leibniz's justification of transubstantiation (which was why he invented the term) but for his entire metaphysics. Blondel's Latin dissertation, "De Vinculo substantiali et de substantia composita apud Leibnitium," was defended the same year (1893) as his more influential first thesis, "L'Action." Blondel then later published a French edition of his Latin dissertation in 1930. See Blanchette, *Maurice Blondel*, 95–97, 346–53, and Tilliette, *Philosophies Eucharistique de Descartes à Blondel*, 101–16.

139. *TD* IV, 499. Bulgakov makes a similar point: "The blood and water that came out of Christ's side hold the world together, make it indestructible" (Bulgakov, *The Holy Grail & The Eucharist*, 58). Bulgakov is specifically referring to Christ's blood spilled into the earth at Golgotha, *not* the Eucharist, a distinction that Balthasar is less concerned to make.

140. Cf. *Epilogue*, 112, and *TD* III, 440–41.

141. John Scotus Eriugena, *De divis. naturae* V, 38, as quoted in *TD* V, 378 (emphasis original).

142. *TD* III, 349.

143. *TD* V, 383.

144. Rahner, *On The Theology of Death*, 24–34. Note that Balthasar does not give much attention to the question of the intermediate state. For a summary of Balthasar's position on the matter, and a critique of his concision in this regard, see

Hofer, "Balthasar's Eschatology on the Intermediate State." With regard to the problem of separated souls, it seems like a consistent extension of Balthasar's theology (but he does not say so explicitly) to suggest that during the "intermediate state" the souls of the blessed cannot be said to be bodiless. That is, although they do not yet possess their own resurrected body, they participate and share in Christ's eucharistic flesh. Something like this is suggested in *TD* V, 358–59.

145. According to Thomas, by natural concomitance "there is also in this sacrament that which is really united with that thing wherein the aforesaid conversion is terminated [that is, Christ's body and blood]. For if any two things be really united, then wherever the one is really, there must the other also be" (*ST* III, 76. 1. co.). Thomas says this to explain why not just the body and blood are in the Eucharist, but the *totus Christus*. It seems quite consistent to extend this to include the saints in glory, who make up the *totus Christus*. Also note that John Paul II speaks of Mary's presence in the Eucharist in *Ecclesia de Eucharistia*, 57.

146. Balthasar, *Dare We Hope?*, 134.

147. At least as this term is used to convey the Neoplatonic notion that the end and the beginning are the same, in other words, that there is some logical or at least aesthetic necessity that all creation return to the One without any loss. See Balthasar, *Dare We Hope?*, 181–204.

148. Balthasar, *Dare We Hope?*, 86. See the entire chapter titled "Testimonies," where he cites Mechthild of Hackeborn, Thérèse of Lisieux, Angela of Folino, Julian Norwich, Christina von Stammeln, Mary Magdalene de' Pazzi, Teresa of Avila, Marie de l'Incarnation, and others. As an aside, it must be mentioned that even beyond his relationship with Adrienne von Speyr, Balthasar's interest in the voices of women mystics and his willingness to consider them as among the most important theological voices is perhaps without parallel in recent theology.

149. This is explored mostly in *TD* II and III, but also note how he describes Paul's "I" after his conversion: "It knows itself as utterly divested of ownership of itself; belonging wholly to Christ and the communion of saints" ("Who Is the Church?," *ET* II, 168).

150. Balthasar, *Two Sisters in the Spirit*, 201.

151. *TD* V, 484; *Theodramatik* IV, 444.

152. "Eschatology in Outline," *ET* IV, 458–60. Note that *Lumen gentium* (49) even speaks about the "exchange of spiritual goods" with the blessed dead, and says that they "serve God in all things and completing in their flesh what is lacking in Christ's suffering for the sake of his body." Also note *GL* I, 236: "Seen with the eyes of faith, bliss and sacrificial self-abandonment are identical."

153. *TD* V, 404.

154. Cf. ibid., 485–86.

155. Hofer, "Balthasar's Eschatology on the Intermediate State," implies precisely this. He critiques Balthasar's contradiction in both claiming that we cannot

say much about the intermediate state and in utilizing Adrienne von Speyr to say very much indeed regarding Christ's "activity" on Holy Saturday. Kilby, too, is suspicious about Speyr's role in giving Balthasar a more "direct" source of information, but she does conclude by advocating for a more charitable reading regarding his appeals to mystical experience. See Kilby, *Balthasar: A (Very) Critical Introduction,* esp. 156–61.

156. *TD* V, 245.

CONCLUSION

1. In particular, Balthasar's theology of the sacrament of reconciliation could be explored, given that Balthasar himself noted that in this sacrament "the full form of the sacramental event is made evident, plausible, visible," and thus reconciliation "could be taken as the model for a general doctrine of the sacraments, in so far as such a model could be sustained through all the individual sacraments, which are so different and yet interiorly analogous" (*GL* I, 580).

2. This sacramental maximization is not, per se, what makes Balthasar's eucharistic theology unique. Twentieth-century Catholic theology in general can be considered one of sacramental maximization, and this is true, *mutatis mutandis,* of Schillebeeckx, Rahner, and Chauvet, among others. The question is *how* this maximization occurs, for one mode of maximization can be absolute minimization in the end: *promoveatur ut amoveatur.*

3. "Seeing, Believing, Eating," *ET* II, 499. John Paul II also speaks of the "*sacramental* character of Revelation" (*Fides et ratio,* 13).

4. *TD* V, 74; *Theodramatik* IV, 65. Here Balthasar is citing the work of Klaus Hemmerle, *Thesen zu einer trinitarischen Ontologie.*

5. *GL* I, 571.

6. "Any Christian experience deserving the name is rooted, not in psychology, but in the sacraments or, in other words, in faith" (Balthasar, *Bernanos,* 294).

7. Balthasar, *Cosmic Liturgy,* 316.

8. For analyses of this painting, see Marcia Hall, ed., *Raphael's "School of Athens,"* and Reale, *"The School of Athens" by Raphael.*

9. The Trinity is the true "triad" in the painting, and is its dominating motif. The Trinity is likewise the theological presupposition that makes a sacramental mediation intelligible.

10. Reale makes this important point about the definition of *disputa*: "In latino, infatti, *disputare* significa non solo discutere, ma anche 'chiarire,' 'spiegare,' 'rendere evidente,' e quindi 'rivelare' . . . . la *Disputa,* in realtà, rappresenta una 'Rivelazione' della Verità del messaggio cristiano, articolata nelle sue varie componenti con una dinamica assai ricca e complessa" (Reale, *Raffaello,* 15).

11. "[In Raphael's *La Disputa*] the greatest geniuses of Christian intellectual history are gathered in throngs around the mystery and are utterly absorbed in it" ("Eucharistic Congress 1960," *ET* II, 503).

12. *TL* I, 272.

13. Ibid., 264.

BIBLIOGRAPHY

Ade, Edouard. "Église Famille: Du Principe Marial à l'Eucharistie." In *La Missione Teologica Di Hans Urs von Balthsar: Atti Del Simposio Internazionale Di Teologia in Occasione Del Centisimo Anniversario Della Nascita Di Hans Urs von Balthasar, Lugano 2–4 Marzo 2005*, 333–44. Lugano: Eupress, 2005.

Alighieri, Dante. *The Divine Comedy*. Translated by C. H. Sisson. Oxford: Oxford University Press, 1993.

Aquinas, Thomas. *Summa Contra Gentiles* IV. Notre Dame, IN: University of Notre Dame Press, 1975.

———. *Summa Theologiae*. Latin/English Edition of the Works of Thomas Aquinas. Translated by Fr. Laurence Shapcote. Lander, WY: Aquinas Institute, 2012.

Augustine of Hippo. *Essential Sermons*. Translated by Edmund Hill. Hyde Park, NY: New City Press, 2007.

Baker, Margaret. *The Great High Priest: The Temple Roots of Christian Liturgy*. Edinburgh: T&T Clark, 2003.

Balthasar, Hans Urs von. "Afterword." In *Meditations on the Tarot: A Journey into Christian Hermeticism*, translated by Robert Powell, 559–665. New York: Tarcher/Putnam, 2002.

———. *Apokalypse der deutschen Seele: Studien zu einer Lehre von den letzten Haltungen*. Vol. 1, *Der deutsche Idealismus*. Einsiedeln: Johannes Verlag, 1998.

———. *Apokalypse der deutschen Seele: Studien zu einer Lehre von den letzten Haltungen*. Vol. 2, *Im Zeichen Nietzsches*. Einsiedeln: Johannes Verlag, 1998.

———. *Apokalypse der deutschen Seele: Studien zu einer Lehre von den letzten Haltungen*. Vol. 3, *Vergöttlichung des Todes*. Einsiedeln: Johannes Verlag, 1998.

———. *Bernanos: An Ecclesial Existence*. San Francisco: Ignatius, 1996.

———. *Christen sind einfältig*. Einsiedeln: Johannes Verlag, 1983.

———. *Christian Meditation*. San Francisco: Ignatius, 1989.

———. "Christus, Gestalt Unseres Lebens: Zur Theologischen Deutung Der Eucharistie." *Geist Und Leben* 43 (1970): 173–80.

———. *Convergences: To the Source of Christian Mystery*. San Francisco: Ignatius, 1983.

————. *Cosmic Liturgy: The Universe according to Maximus the Confessor.* San Francisco: Ignatius, 2003.

————. *Dare We Hope That All Men Be Saved? With a Short Discourse on Hell.* San Francisco: Ignatius, 2014.

————. *Das Buch des Lammes.* Einsiedeln: Johannes Verlag, 2004.

————. "Die Würde der Liturgie." *Internationale Katholishe Zeitschrift Communio* 7 (1978): 481–87.

————. *Does Jesus Know Us—Do We Know Him?* San Francisco: Ignatius, 1986.

————. *Elucidations.* Translated by John Riches. San Francisco: Ignatius, 2011.

————. *Engagement with God: The Drama of Christian Discipleship.* San Francisco: Ignatius, 2008.

————. *Epilog.* Trier: Johannes Verlag, 1987.

————. *Epilogue.* Translated by Edward T. Oakes. San Francisco: Ignatius, 1991.

————. "Eros und Agape." *Stimmen der Zeit* 69 (1939): 398–403.

————. *Erster Blick auf Adrienne von Speyr.* Einsiedeln: Johannes Verlag, 1968.

————. "Eucharist: Gift of Love." Translated by Jonathan Martin Ciraulo. *Communio: International Catholic Review* 43 (Spring 2016): 139–53.

————. *Eucharistie: Gabe Der Liebe.* Antwort Des Glaubens 44. Freiburg: Informationszentrum Berufe der Kirche, 1986.

————. *Explorations in Theology.* Vol. 1, *The Word Made Flesh.* Translated by A. V. Littledale and Alexander Dru. San Francisco: Ignatius, 1989.

————. *Explorations in Theology.* Vol. 2, *Spouse of the Word.* Translated by John Saward. San Francisco: Ignatius, 1991.

————. *Explorations in Theology.* Vol. 3, *Creator Spirit.* Translated by Brian McNeil. San Francisco: Ignatius, 2012.

————. *Explorations in Theology.* Vol. 4, *Spirit and Institution.* Translated by Edward T. Oakes. San Francisco: Ignatius, 1995.

————. *Explorations in Theology.* Vol. 5, *Man Is Created.* Translated by Adrian Walker. San Francisco: Ignatius, 2014.

————. "The Fathers, the Scholastics, and Ourselves." Translated by Edward Oakes. *Communio* 24 (1997): 347–96.

————. *First Glance at Adrienne von Speyr.* Translated by Antje Lawry and Sr. Sergia Englund. San Francisco: Ignatius, 1981.

————. *Gelebte Kirche: Bernanos.* 3rd ed. Trier: Johannes Verlag, 1988.

————. *Geschichte des eschatologischen Problems in der modernen deutschen Literatur.* Einsiedeln: Johannes Verlag, 1998.

————. *The Glory of the Lord: A Theological Aesthetics.* Vol. 1, *Seeing the Form.* Edinburgh: Bloomsbury T&T Clark, 2001.

————. *The Glory of the Lord: A Theological Aesthetics.* Vol. 2, *Studies in Theological Style: Clerical Styles.* San Francisco: Ignatius, 1984.

————. *The Glory of the Lord: A Theological Aesthetics.* Vol. 3, *Studies in Theological Style: Lay Styles.* San Francisco: Ignatius, 2004.

————. *The Glory of the Lord: A Theological Aesthetics.* Vol. 4, *The Realm of Metaphysics in Antiquity.* San Francisco: Ignatius, 1989.

————. *The Glory of the Lord: A Theological Aesthetics.* Vol. 5, *The Realm of Metaphysics in the Modern Age.* San Francisco: Ignatius, 2011.

————. *The Glory of the Lord: A Theological Aesthetics.* Vol. 6, *The Old Covenant.* San Francisco: Ignatius, 1991.

————. *The Glory of the Lord: A Theological Aesthetics.* Vol. 7, *The New Covenant.* San Francisco: Ignatius, 1990.

————. *The God Question and Modern Man.* New York: Seabury Press, 1967.

————. *The Grain of Wheat: Aphorisms.* San Francisco: Ignatius, 1995.

————. *The Heart of the World.* San Francisco: Ignatius, 1980.

————. "Heilsgeschichtliche Überlegungen zur Befreiungstheologie." In *Theologie der Befreiung*, 155–71. Einsiedeln: Johannes Verlag, 1977.

————. *Herrlichkeit.* Band I, *Schau der Gestalt.* 3rd ed. Trier: Johannes Verlag, 1988.

————. *Herrlichkeit.* Band III/I, *Im Raum der Metaphysik.* Einsiedeln: Johannes Verlag, 1965.

————. "Hin-Gabe." Meditation 3. Hg. vom Informationszentrum Berufe der Kirche. Freiburg, 1975.

————. "The Holy Church and the Eucharistic Sacrifice." *Communio: International Catholic Review* 12 (Summer 1985): 139–45.

————. *Homo Creatus Est: Skizzen zur Theologie* V. Einsiedeln: Johannes Verlag, 1986.

————. *In Gottes Einsatz Leben.* Einsiedeln: Johannes Verlag, 1972.

————. *In the Fullness of Faith: On the Centrality of the Distinctively Catholic.* San Francisco: Ignatius, 1988.

————. "Katholische Religion und Kunst." *Schweizeriche Rundschau* 27 (1927): 44–54.

————. *Klarstellungen: Zur Prüfung der Geister.* Einsiedeln: Johannes Verlag, 1978.

————. *Kosmische Liturgie: Höhe und Krise des griechischen Weltbilds bei Maximus Confessor.* Freiburg, 1941.

————. "Le Mystère d'Origène." *Recherches de Science Religieuse* 26 (1936): 514–62.

————. "Le Mystère d'Origène." *Recherches de Science Religieuse* 27 (1937): 38–64.

————. *Life out of Death: Meditations on the Paschal Mystery.* San Francisco: Ignatius, 2012.

————. *Light of the Word: Brief Reflections on the Sunday Readings.* San Francisco: Ignatius, 1994.

————. "Liturgiereform und Zukunft der Kirche: Eine Rundfrage über die Auswirkungen der Volkssrpache im Gottesdienst." *Wort und Wahrheit* 20, no. 11 (1965): 653–54.

————. "Liturgie und Ehrfurcht." *Der christliche Sonntag* 12, no. 49 (1960): 393ff.

————. *Love Alone Is Credible*. San Francisco: Ignatius, 2005.

————. *Mary for Today*. San Francisco: Ignatius, 1988.

————. *The Moment of Christian Witness*. San Francisco: Ignatius, 1994.

————. *Mysterium Paschale: The Mystery of Easter*. San Francisco: Ignatius, 2000.

————. *New Elucidations*. San Francisco: Ignatius, 1986.

————. "Nine Propositions on Christian Ethics." In *Principles of Christian Morality*, edited by Joseph Ratzinger, Heniz Schürmann, and Hans Urs von Balthasar, 75–104. Translated by Graham Harrison. San Francisco: Ignatius, 1986.

————. *The Office of Peter and the Structure of the Church*. San Francisco: Ignatius, 2007.

————. "On the Concept of Person," *Communio* 13 (Spring 1986): 18–26.

————. *Origenes: Geist und Feuer: Ein Aufbau aus seinen Schriften*. Salzburg: Otto Müller Verlag, 1938.

————. *Our Task: A Report and a Plan*. Translated by John Saward. San Francisco: Ignatius, 1994.

————. *Parole et Mystère Chez Origène*. Paris: Les Éditions du Cerf, 1957.

————. "Patristik, Scholastik und Wir." *Theologie der Zeit* 3 (1939): 65–104.

————. *Paul Struggles with His Congregation: The Pastoral Message of the Letters to the Corinthians*. Translated by Brigitte Bojarska. San Francisco: Ignatius, 2012.

————. *Pneuma und Institution: Skizzen zur Theologie IV*. Einsiedeln: Johannes Verlag.

————. *Prayer*. Translated by Graham Harrison. San Francisco: Ignatius, 1986.

————. *Presence and Thought: Essay on the Religious Philosophy of Gregory of Nyssa*. San Francisco: Ignatius, 1995.

————. *Présence et pensée: Essai sur la philosophie religieuse de Grégoire de Nysse*. Paris: 1942.

————. "Présence et Pensée: La philosophie religieuse de Grégoire de Nysse." *Recherches de Science Religieuse* 29 (1939): 513–49.

————. *Razing the Bastions: On the Church in This Age*. San Francisco: Ignatius, 1993.

————. Review of *Die Messe*, by Paul Claudel, *Stimmen der Zeit* 136, no. 4 (1939): 270.

————. *Romano Guardini: Reform from the Source*. San Francisco: Ignatius, 2010.

————. "Sehen, Hören und Lesen im Raum der Kirche." *Schildgenossen* 18 (1939): 400–414.

————. *A Short Primer for Unsettled Laymen*. San Francisco: Ignatius, 1985.

————. "Söhngens Begriff des Mysteriums." *Stimmen der Zeit* 138 (1940): 60–61.

————. *Spiritus Creator: Skizzen zur Theologie III*. Einsiedeln: Johannes Verlag, 1967.

————. *Sponsa Verbi: Skizzen zur Theologie II*. Einsiedeln: Johannes Verlag, 1961.

————. *Theo-Drama: Theological Dramatic Theory.* Vol. 1, *Prolegomena.* Translated by Graham Harrison. San Francisco: Ignatius, 1988.

————. *Theo-Drama: Theological Dramatic Theory.* Vol. 2, *The Dramatis Personae: Man in God.* Translated by Graham Harrison. San Francisco: Ignatius, 1990.

————. *Theo-Drama: Theological Dramatic Theory.* Vol. 3, *The Dramatis Personae: Persons in Christ.* San Francisco: Ignatius, 1993.

————. *Theo-Drama: Theological Dramatic Theory.* Vol. 4, *The Action.* San Francisco: Ignatius, 1994.

————. *Theo-Drama: Theological Dramatic Theory.* Vol. 5, *The Last Act.* San Francisco: Ignatius, 2003.

————. *Theodramatik.* Band 3, *Die Handlung.* Einsiedeln: Johannes Verlag, 1980.

————. *Theodramatik.* Band 4, *Das Endspiel.* Einsiedeln: Johannes Verlag, 1983.

————. *Theo-Logic: Theological Logical Theory.* Vol. 1, *The Truth of the World.* San Francisco: Ignatius, 2001.

————. *Theo-Logic: Theological Logical Theory.* Vol. 2, *Truth of God.* San Francisco: Ignatius, 2004.

————. *Theo-Logic: Theological Logical Theory.* Vol. 3, *The Spirit of Truth.* Translated by Adrian J. Walker. San Francisco: Ignatius, 2005.

————. *Theologie der Drei Tage.* Einsiedeln: Johannes Verlag, 1990.

————. *The Theology of Henri de Lubac: An Overview.* San Francisco: Ignatius, 1991.

————. *A Theology of History.* San Francisco: Ignatius, 1994.

————. *The Theology of Karl Barth.* San Francisco: Ignatius, 1992.

————. *Tragedy under Grace: Reinhold Schneider on the Experience of the West.* Translated by Brian McNeil. San Francisco: Ignatius, 1997.

————. *Truth Is Symphonic: Aspects of Christian Pluralism.* San Francisco: Ignatius, 1987.

————. *Two Sisters in the Spirit: Thérèse of Lisieux and Elizabeth of the Trinity.* Translated by Dennis D. Martin. San Francisco: Ignatius, 1998.

————. *Unless You Become Like This Child.* Translated by Erasmo Leiva Merikakis. San Francisco: Ignatius, 1991.

————. "Voraussetzung Einer Geisterneuerung: Zur Lage Der Kirche in Der Schweiz." *Theologisches* 102 (October 1978): 2919–25.

————. "Vorwort des Übersetzers." In Jean Corbon, *Liturgie aus dem Urquell,* 9–10. Einsiedeln: Johannes Verlag, 1981.

————. *Who Is a Christian?* Translated by Frank Davidson. San Francisco: Ignatius, 2014.

————. *You Crown the Year with Your Goodness: Sermons throughout the Liturgical Year.* San Francisco: Ignatius, 1989.

————. "Zu einer christlichen Theologie der Hoffnung." *Münchener Theologische Zeitschrift* 32, no. 2 (1981): 81–102.

Balthasar, Hans Urs Von, and Angelo Scola. *Test Everything: Hold Fast to What Is Good: An Interview with Hans Urs Von Balthasar.* San Francisco: Ignatius, 1989.

Barber, Michael Patrick. "The New Temple, the New Priesthood, and the New Cult in Luke-Acts." *Letter & Spirit* 8 (2013): 101–24.

Barrett, Melanie. *Love's Beauty at the Heart of the Christian Moral Life: The Ethics of Catholic Theologian Hans Urs Von Balthasar.* Lewiston, NY: Edwin Mellen Press, 2009.

Barth, Karl. *Church Dogmatics.* 2nd ed. Peabody, MA: Hendrickson, 2010.

Bätzing, Georg. *Die Eucharistie Als Opfer Der Kirche Nach Hans Urs von Balthasar.* Einsiedeln: Johannes Verlag, 1986.

Beattie, Tina. *New Catholic Feminism: Theology and Theory.* London: Routledge, 2006.

Bernanos, Georges. *The Diary of a Country Priest.* Translated by Pamela Morris. Cambridge, MA: Da Capo, 2002.

Blanchette, Oliva. *Maurice Blondel: A Philosophical Life.* Grand Rapids, MI: Eerdmans, 2010.

Bloch, Ernst. *The Principle of Hope.* Vol. 1. Cambridge, MA: MIT Press, 1986.

Blondel, Maurice. *Action (1893): Essay on a Critique of Life and a Science of Practice.* Translated by Oliva Blanchette. Notre Dame, IN: University of Notre Dame Press, 2003.

Boersma, Hans. *Nouvelle Theologie and Sacramental Ontology: A Return to Mystery.* Oxford: Oxford University Press, 2013.

Boeve, L., and L. Leijssen. *Sacramental Presence in a Postmodern Context.* Leuven: Peeters, 2001.

Boff, Leonardo. *Sacraments of Life, Life of the Sacraments.* Translated by John Drury. Washington, DC: Pastoral Press, 1987.

Borella, Jean. *The Crisis of Religious Symbolism.* Translated by G. John Champoux. Kettering, OH: Angelico Press, 2016.

Borras, Michelle. "Péguy, Expositor of Christian Hope." *Communio* 35 (Summer 2008): 221–54.

Bulgakov, Sergius. *The Comforter.* Translated by Boris Jakim. Grand Rapids, MI: Eerdmans, 2004.

———. *The Holy Grail & The Eucharist.* Translated by Boris Jakim. Hudson, NY: Lindisfarne, 1997.

Bultmann, Rudolf. *The Gospel of John: A Commentary.* Eugene, OR: Wipf and Stock, 2014.

———. *History and Eschatology.* Edinburgh: Edinburgh University Press, 1957.

Bynum, Caroline Walker. *Wonderful Blood: Theology and Practice in Late Medieval Northern Germany and Beyond.* Philadelphia: University of Pennsylvania Press, 2007.

Calderón de la Barca, Pedro. *Das große Welttheater.* Translated by Hans Urs von Balthasar. Christliche Meister 56. Einsiedeln: Johannes Verlag, 2011.

———. *El Gran Teatro del Mundo.* In *Obras Maestras,* edited by José Alcalá-Zamora, José María Díez Borque, and José N. Alcalá-Zamora. Castalia Publishing Company, 2003.

Caldwell, Philip. *Liturgy as Revelation: Re-Sourcing a Theme in Twentieth-Century Catholic Theology.* Minneapolis: Fortress Press, 2014.

Carpenter, Anne M. *Theo-Poetics: Hans Urs von Balthasar and the Risk of Art and Being.* Notre Dame, IN: University of Notre Dame Press, 2015.

Casarella, Peter. "*Analogia Donationis*: Hans Urs von Balthasar on the Eucharist." *Philosophy & Theology* 11, no. 1 (1998): 147–77.

———. "The Expression and Form of the Word: Trinitarian Hermeneutics and the Sacramentality of Language in Hans Urs von Balthasar." *Renascence* 48, no. 2 (1996): 111–35.

———. "'Repräsentation': Zum Barockverständnis bei Hans Urs von Balthasar (1905–1988)." In *Reisen des Barock: Selbst- und Fremderfahrungen und ihre Darstellung,* edited by Regina Pleithner, 1–24. Bonn: Romanstischer, 1991.

Casel, Odo. *Das christliche Kultmysterium.* 4th ed. Regensburg: Friedrich Pustet, 1960.

———. *Das christliche Opfermysterium: Zur Morphologie und Theologie des eucharistischen Hochgebetes.* Graz: Styria, 1968.

———. "Die Heilige Eucharistie der Quellgrund der Seelsorge." *Die Seelsorge* 14 (1936): 241–54.

———. *The Mystery of Christian Worship.* New York: Crossroad, 1999.

Cassin, Barbara, ed. *Dictionary of Untranslatables: A Philosophical Lexicon.* Princeton, NJ: Princeton University Press, 2014.

Catherine of Siena, *The Dialogue.* Translated by Suzanne Noffke. New York: Paulist Press, 1980.

Caussade, Jean-Pierre de. *The Joy of Full Surrender.* Translated by Hal M. Helms. Brewster, MA: Paraclete Press, 1986.

Chauvet, Louis-Marie. "The Broken Bread as Theological Figure of Eucharistic Presence." In *Sacramental Presence in a Postmodern Context,* edited by L. Boeve and L. Leijssen, 236–62. Leuven: Leuven University Press, 2001.

———. *Symbol and Sacrament: Sacramental Reinterpretation of Christian Existence.* Translated by Madeleine M. Beaumont and Patrick Madigan, SJ. Collegeville, MN: Pueblo Books, 1994.

Ciraulo, Jonathan Martin. "Divinization as Christification in Erich Przywara and John Zizioulas." *Modern Theology* 32, no. 4 (2016): 479–503.

———. "Hans Urs von Balthasar's Indifference to Divinization." In *Mystical Doctrines of Deification: Case Studies in the Christian Tradition,* edited by John Arblaster and Rob Faesen, 165–85. New York: Routledge, 2018.

———. "Sacramentally Regulated Eschatology in Hans Urs von Balthasar and Pope Benedict XVI." *Pro Ecclesia: A Journal of Catholic and Evangelical Theology* 24, no. 2 (2015): 216–34.

———. "Sacraments and Personhood: John Zizioulas' Impasse and a Way Forward." *Heythrop Journal* 53, no. 6 (2012): 993–1004.

Claudel, Paul. *Cahiers*. Vol. 12, *Correspondance Paul Claudel–Jacques Rivière, 1907–1924*. Paris: Éditions Gallimard, 1984.

———. *Die Messe Des Verbannten*. Translated by Hans Urs von Balthasar. Einsiedeln: Johannes Verlag, 1981.

———. *Gesammelte Werke*, Bd. I, *Lyrik*. Translated by Hans Urs von Balthasar. Einsiedeln: Benzinger Verlag, 1963.

———. *I Believe in God: A Meditation on the Apostle's Creed*. Translated by Helen Weaver. San Francisco: Ignatius, 2002.

Corbon, Jean. *Liturgie aus dem Urquell*. Translated and edited by Hans Urs von Balthasar. Einsiedeln: Johannes Verlag, 1981.

———. *The Wellspring of Worship*. Translated by Matthew J. O'Connell. San Francisco: Ignatius, 2005.

Crammer, Karen Corinne. "One Sex or Two? Balthasar's Theology of the Sexes." In *The Cambridge Companion to Hans Urs von Balthasar*, edited by Edward Oakes and David Moss, 93–112. Cambridge: Cambridge University Press, 2004.

Daniélou, Jean. *Bible and the Liturgy*. Notre Dame, IN: University of Notre Dame Press, 2002.

Del Colle, Ralph. *Christ and the Spirit: Spirit-Christology in Trinitarian Perspective*. Oxford: Oxford University Press, 1994.

de Lubac, Henri. *Corpus Mysticum: The Eucharist and the Church in the Middle Ages*. Translated by Gemma Simmonds, C.J. Notre Dame, IN: University of Notre Dame Press, 2007.

———. *History and Spirit: The Understanding of Scripture according to Origen*. San Francisco: Ignatius, 2007.

Denzinger, Heinrich. *Enchiridion Symbolorum: A Compendium of Creeds, Definitions, and Declarations of the Catholic Church*. 43rd ed. Edited by Peter Hünermann. San Francisco: Ignatius, 2012.

Desmond, William. *Beyond Hegel and Dialectic: Speculation, Cult, and Comedy*. Albany: SUNY Press, 1992.

Di Girolamo, Luca M. "Peccato, Croce ed Eucaristia in Hans Urs von Balthasar." *Rivista teologica di Lugano* 10 (2005): 425–51.

Dix, Dom Gregory. *The Shape of the Liturgy*. New York: Bloomsbury T&T Clark, 2005.

Dondaine, H. F. "La définition des sacrements dans la Somme théologique." *Revue des Sciences Philosophiques et Théologiques* 31 (1947): 213–28.

Duffy, Kevin. "Change, Suffering, and Surprise in God: Von Balthasar's Use of Metaphor." *Irish Theological Quarterly* 76 (2011): 370–87.

Duncan, Roger. "Eucharist, Drama, and Cosmos: A Response to Nicholas Healy." *Saint Anselm Journal* 10, no. 2 (2015): 34–39.

Dupré, Louis. *Symbols of the Sacred*. Grand Rapids, MI: Eerdmans, 2000.

Elowsky, Joel C., ed. *Ancient Christian Commentary on Scripture: John 11–21*. Downers Grove, IL: InterVarsity Press, 2007.

Endean, Philip. "Von Balthasar, Rahner, and The Commissar." *New Blackfriars* 79, no. 923 (1998): 33–38.

Evans, Craig A., and Jeremiah J. Johnston. "Intertestamental Background of the Christian Sacraments." In *The Oxford Handbook of Sacramental Theology*, edited by Hans Boersma and Matthew Levering, 37–51. Oxford: Oxford University Press, 2015.

Fagerberg, David W. *On Liturgical Asceticism*. Washington, DC: Catholic University of America Press, 2013.

———. *Theologia Prima: What Is Liturgical Theology?* Chicago: Hillenbrand Books, 2012.

Falque, Emmanuel. *The Metamorphosis of Finitude: An Essay on Birth and Resurrection*. Translated by George Hughes. New York: Fordham University Press, 2012.

———. *The Wedding Feast of the Lamb: Eros, the Body, and the Eucharist*. Translated by George Hughes. New York: Fordham University Press, 2016.

Feichtinger, Hans. "Leo the Great and Hans Urs von Balthasar on the Eucharist." *Saint Anselm Journal* 10, no. 2 (2015): 17–33.

Feingold, Lawrence. *The Eucharist: Mystery of Presence, Sacrifice, and Communion*. Steubenville, OH: Emmaus Academic, 2018.

Fields, Stephen M. *Analogies of Transcendence: An Essay on Nature, Grace & Modernity*. Washington DC: Catholic University of America Press, 2016.

Gallaher, Brandon. *Freedom and Necessity in Modern Trinitarian Theology*. Oxford: Oxford University Press, 2016.

Gardiner, Anne Barbeau. "The Dubious Adrienne von Speyr." *New Oxford Review* 69 (September 2002): 31–36.

Geldhof, Joris. "German Romanticism and Liturgical Theology: Exploring the Potential of Organic Thinking." *Horizons* 43 (2016): 282–307.

Gierens, M., ed. *De causalitate sacramentorum seu de modo explicandi efficientiam sacramentorum novae legis, textus scholasticorum principaliorum*. Rome: Pontificia Universitas Gregoriana, 1935.

Golitzin, Alexander. *Mystagogy: A Monastic Reading of Dionysius Areopagita*. Edited by Bogdan G. Bucur. Collegeville, MN: Cistercian Publications, 2014.

Gorringe, Timothy. "Eschatology and Political Radicalism." In *God Will Be All in All: The Eschatology of Jürgen Moltmann*, edited by Richard Bauckham, 87–114. Minneapolis: Fortress, 2001.

Griffiths, Paul J. *Decreation: The Last Things of All Creatures*. Waco, TX: Baylor University Press, 2014.

Guardini, Romano. *The End of the Modern World.* Wilmington, DE: ISI Books, 1998.

———. *Rilke's "Duino Elegies": An Interpretation.* Translated by K. G. Knight. Chicago: Regnery, 1961.

———. *The Spirit of the Liturgy.* New York: Crossroad, 1998.

Guerriero, Elio. *Hans Urs von Balthasar.* Milan: Edizioni Paoline, 1991.

Hall, Marcia, ed. *Raphael's "School of Athens."* Cambridge: Cambridge University Press, 1997.

Hart, David Bentley. *The Beauty of the Infinite: The Aesthetics of Christian Truth.* Grand Rapids, MI: Eerdmans, 2004.

———. *The Doors of the Sea: Where Was God in the Tsunami?* Grand Rapids, MI: Eerdmans, 2005.

———. "'Thine Own of Thine Own': Eucharistic Sacrifice in Orthodox Tradition." In *Rediscovering the Eucharist: Ecumenical Conversations*, edited by Roch A. Kereszty, 142–69. New York: Paulist Press, 2003.

Hauser, Daniel C. *Church, Worship and History: Catholic Systematic Theology.* San Francisco: Catholic Scholars Press, 1997.

Healy, Nicholas. "Christ's Eucharist and the Nature of Love: The Contribution of Hans Urs von Balthasar." *Saint Anselm Journal* 10, no. 2 (2015): 1–17.

———. *The Eschatology of Hans Urs von Balthasar: Eschatology as Communion.* Oxford: Oxford University Press, 2005.

Healy, Nicholas J., and David L. Schindler. "For the Life of the World: Hans Urs von Balthasar on the Church as Eucharist." In *The Cambridge Companion to Hans Urs von Balthasar*, edited by Edward Oakes and David Moss, 51–63. Cambridge: Cambridge University Press, 2004.

Hegel, Georg Wilhelm Friedrich. *Lectures on the Philosophy of Religion: One-Volume Edition—The Lectures of 1827.* Edited by Peter Hodgson. Berkeley: University of California Press, 1988.

———. *Philosophy of Mind.* Part III of the *Encyclopedia of the Philosophical Sciences.* Translated by W. Wallace and A. V. Miller. Oxford: Clarendon, 2007.

Heidegger, Martin. *Poetry, Language, Thought.* New York: HarperCollins, 2001.

Hesse, Michael. *Die Eucharistie als Opfer der Kirche: Antwortsuche bei Odo Casal—Karl Rahner—Hans Urs von Balthasar.* Würzburg: Echter, 2015.

Hofer, Andrew. "Balthasar's Eschatology on the Intermediate State: The Question of Knowability." *Logos: A Journal of Catholic Thought and Culture* 12, no. 3 (2009): 148–72.

Hölderlin, Johann Christian Friedrich. "Brod und Wein" (1801). Translation by Susan Ranson. https://sites.google.com/site/germanliterature/19th-century/hoelderlin/brot-und-wein-bread-and-wine.

Hopkins, Gerard Manley. *The Poetical Works of Gerard Manley Hopkins.* Edited by Norman H. MacKenzie. Oxford: Clarendon, 1990.

Hugh of St. Victor. *On the Sacraments of the Christian Faith*. Translated by Roy J. Deferrari. Eugene, OR: Wipf & Stock, 2007.

Ide, Pascal. "L'Eucharistie selon Balthasar: Une relecture à partir de l'amour de don." *Annales Theologici* 28 (2014): 125–38.

————. *Une théologie de l'amour: L'amour, centre de la Trilogie de Hans Urs von Balthasar*. Brussels: Editions Lessius, 2012.

————. *Une Théo-logique du Don: Le Don dans la "Trilogie" de Hans Urs von Balthasar*. Leuven: Peeters, 2013.

Irwin, Kevin. *Context and Text: A Method for Liturgical Theology*. Rev. ed. Collegeville, MN: Liturgical Press, 2018.

Journet, Charles Cardinal. *The Mass: The Presence of the Sacrifice of the Cross*. Translated by Victor Szczurek. South Bend, IN: St. Augustine's Press, 2008.

Kavanaugh, Aidan. *On Liturgical Theology*. Collegeville, MN: Pueblo Books, 1984.

Kereszty, Roch. "The Eucharist and Mission in the Theology of Hans Urs von Balthasar." In *Love Alone Is Credible: Hans Urs von Balthasar as Interpreter of the Catholic Tradition*, edited by David L. Schindler, 3–15. Grand Rapids, MI: Eerdmans, 2008.

Kilby, Karen. *Balthasar: A (Very) Critical Introduction*. Grand Rapids, MI: Eerdmans, 2012.

Kilmartin, Edward J. *The Eucharist in the West: History and Theology*. Edited by Robert J. Daly. Collegeville, MN: The Liturgical Press, 2004.

King, Ronald. "The Origin and Evolution of a Sacramental Formula: *Sacramentum Tantum, Res et Sacramentum, Res Tantum.*" *Thomist* 31, no. 1 (1967): 21–82.

Koerpel, Robert C. "Hans Urs von Balthasar on Mary, Peter, and the Eucharist." *Logos: A Journal of Catholic Thought and Culture* 11, no. 1 (2008): 70–99.

Janicaud, Dominique, et al. *Phenomenology and the "Theological Turn": The French Debate*. New York: Fordham University Press, 2000.

Lacoste, Jean-Yves. *Être en danger*. Paris: Les Éditions du Cerf, 2011.

————. *Experience and the Absolute: Disputed Questions on the Humanity of Man*. New York: Fordham University Press, 2004.

————. *From Theology to Theological Thinking*. Translated by W. Chris Hackett. Charlottesville: University Press of Virginia, 2014.

————. *La phénoménalité de dieu: Neuf études*. Paris: Les Éditions du Cerf, 2008.

————. *Le Monde et l'Absence d'oeuvre*. Paris: PUF, 2000.

————. *L'intuition sacramentelle et autres essais*. Nanterre: Ad Solem, 2015.

————. "Liturgy and Coaffection." In *The Experience of God: A Postmodern Response*, edited by Kevin Hart and Barbara Wall, 93–103. New York: Fordham University Press, 2005.

————. "Présence et Affection." In *Sacramental Presence in a Postmodern Context*, edited by L. Boeve and L. Leijssen, 212–31. Leuven: Leuven University Press, 2001.

————. *Présence et parousie*. Geneva: Ad Solem, 2006.

LaCugna, Catherine. *God for Us: The Trinity and Christian Life.* New York: Harper-Collins, 1991.

Lanfranc of Canterbury and Guitmund of Aversa. *On the Body and Blood of the Lord* and *On the Truth of the Body and Blood of Christ in the Eucharist.* Translated by Mark G. Vaillancourt. Washington, DC: Catholic University of America Press, 2009.

Lathrop, Gordon W. *Holy Things: A Liturgical Theology.* Minneapolis, MN: Fortress Press, 1998.

Leclercq, Jean. *The Love of Learning and the Desire for God: A Study of Monastic Culture.* New York: Fordham University Press, 1982.

Leeming, Bernard. *Principles of Sacramental Theology.* Westminster, MD: Newman Press, 1956.

Levering, Matthew. *Sacrifice and Community: Jewish Offering and Christian Eucharist.* Malden, MA: Blackwell, 2005.

Lonergan, Bernard. *Grace and Freedom: Operative Grace in the Thought of St. Thomas Aquinas.* Toronto: University of Toronto Press, 2000.

Long, D. Stephen. *Saving Karl Barth: Hans Urs von Balthasar's Preoccupation.* Minneapolis, MN: Fortress Press, 2014.

Lösel, Steffen. "A Plain Account of Christian Salvation? Balthasar on Sacrifice, Solidarity, and Substitution." *Pro Ecclesia* 13 (2004): 141–71.

Löser, Werner. "The Ignatian *Exercises* in the Work of Hans Urs von Balthasar." In *Hans Urs von Balthasar: His Life and Work*, edited by David L. Schindler, 103–20. San Francisco: Ignatius, 1991.

Lossky, Vladimir. *Mystical Theology of the Eastern Church.* Crestwood, NY: St. Vladimir's Seminary Press, 1976.

Luther, Martin. "The Sacrament of the Body and Blood of Christ—Against the Fanatics." In *Luther's Works*, Vol. 36, *Word and Sacrament II.* Philadelphia: Fortress Press, 1959.

Mahoney, Shaun L. "The Analogy between the Eucharist and Marriage according to Hans Urs von Balthasar." Rome: Università Gregoriana, 2000.

Mansini, Guy. "Balthasar and the Theodramatic Enrichment of the Trinity." *Thomist* 64, no. 4 (2000): 499–519.

Marin, Louis. *La parole mangée et autres essais théologico-politiques.* Paris: Méridiens Klincksieck, 1986.

Marion, Jean-Luc. *Believing in Order to See: On the Rationality of Revelation and the Irrationality of Some Believers.* New York: Fordham University Press, 2017.

———. *Givenness and Revelation.* Translated by Stephen E. Lewis. Oxford: Oxford University Press, 2016.

———. *God without Being: Hors-Texte.* 2nd ed. Translated by Thomas A. Carlson. Chicago: University of Chicago Press, 2012.

Martelet, Gustave. *The Risen Christ and the Eucharistic World.* Translated by René Hague. New York: Seabury Press, 1976.

Martin, Jennifer Newsome. *Hans Urs von Balthasar and the Critical Appropriation of Russian Religious Thought.* Notre Dame, IN: University of Notre Dame Press, 2015.

Matthiesen, Michon M. *Sacrifice as Gift: Eucharist, Grace, and Contemplative Prayer in Maurice de La Taille.* Washington, DC: Catholic University of America Press, 2013.

McCall, Richard D. *Do This: Liturgy as Performance.* Notre Dame, IN: University of Notre Dame Press, 2007.

McInerny, Brendan. *The Trinitarian Theology of Hans Urs von Balthasar: An Introduction.* Notre Dame, IN: University of Notre Dame Press, 2020.

McInroy, Mark. *Balthasar on the Spiritual Senses: Perceiving Splendor.* Oxford: Oxford University Press, 2014.

McPartlan, Paul. "Who Is the Church? Zizioulas and von Balthasar on the Church's Identity." *Ecclesiology* 4 (2008): 271–88.

Mechthild of Hackeborn. *The Book of Special Grace.* New York: Paulist Press, 2017.

Miller, Mark. "The Sacramental Theology of Hans Urs von Balthasar." *Worship* 64 (1990): 48–66.

Molnar, Paul D. *Karl Barth and the Theology of the Lord's Supper: A Systematic Investigation.* New York: Peter Lang, 1996.

Moltmann, Jürgen. *A Broad Place: An Autobiography.* Translated by Margaret Kohl. Minneapolis, MN: Fortress Press, 2008.

———. *The Church in the Power of The Spirit: A Contribution to Messianic Ecclesiology.* Translated by Margaret Kohl. New York: Harper & Row, 1977.

———. *The Coming of God: Christian Eschatology.* Translated by Margaret Kohl. Minneapolis, MN: Fortress Press, 1996.

———. *The Crucified God: The Cross of Christ as the Foundation and Criticism of Christian Theology.* Minneapolis, MN: Fortress Press, 1993.

———. *God in Creation: A New Theology of Creation and the Spirit of God.* Translated by Margaret Kohl. Minneapolis, MN: Fortress Press, 1993.

———. *Theology of Hope: On the Ground and the Implications of a Christian Eschatology.* New York: Harper & Row, 1967.

———. *The Trinity and the Kingdom: The Doctrine of God.* Translated by Margaret Kohl. Minneapolis, MN: Fortress Press, 1993.

Mongrain, Kevin. "Rule-Governed Christian Gnosis: Hans Urs von Balthasar on Valentin Tomberg's *Meditations on the Tarot.*" *Modern Theology* 25, no. 2 (2009): 285–314.

———. *The Systematic Thought of Hans Urs von Balthasar: An Irenaean Retrieval.* New York: Crossroad, 2002.

Morrill, Bruce. "Sacramental-Liturgical Theology since Vatican II: The Dialectic of Meaning and Performance." *Catholic Theological Society of America Proceedings* 67 (2012): 1–13.

Mudd, Joseph. *Eucharist as Meaning: Critical Metaphysics and Contemporary Sacramental Theology.* Collegeville, MN: Liturgical Press, 2014.

Murphy, Michael Patrick. *A Theology of Criticism: Balthasar, Postmodernism, and the Catholic Imagination.* Oxford: Oxford University Press, 2008.

Newman, John Henry. *Apologia Pro Vita Sua.* New York: Penguin, 1994.

———. *An Essay in Aid of a Grammar of Assent.* Notre Dame, IN: University of Notre Dame Press, 1992.

———. *Fifteen Sermons Preached before the University of Oxford.* Notre Dame, IN: University of Notre Dame Press, 1998.

Nichols, Aidan. *Divine Fruitfulness: A Guide through Balthasar's Theology beyond the Trilogy.* Washington, DC: Catholic University of America Press, 2007.

———. *Scattering the Seed: A Guide through Balthasar's Early Writings on Philosophy and the Arts.* Washington, DC: Catholic University of America Press, 2006.

Nietzsche, Friedrich. *Thus Spake Zarathustra.* Translated by Thomas Common. New York: Dover, 1999.

O'Hanlon, Gerard F. "A Response to Kevin Duffy on von Balthasar and the Immutability of God." *Irish Theological Quarterly* 78 (2013): 179–84.

O'Meara, Thomas F. "The Origins of the Liturgical Movement and German Romanticism." *Worship* 59, no. 4 (1985): 326–42.

O'Neill, Colman E. *Meeting Christ in the Sacraments.* New York: Alba House, 1964.

———. *New Approaches to the Eucharist.* Staten Island, NY: Alba House, 1967.

O'Regan, Cyril. *Anatomy of Misremembering: Von Balthasar's Response to Philosophical Modernity.* Vol. 1, *Hegel.* Chestnut Ridge, NY: Crossroad, 2014.

———. "Balthasar: Between Tübingen and Postmodernity." *Modern Theology* 14, no. 3 (1998): 325–53.

Origen of Alexandria. *Origen: Spirit and Fire: A Thematic Anthology of His Writings.* Edited by Hans Urs von Balthasar. Translated by Robert J. Daly. Washington, DC: Catholic University of America Press, 2001.

Ouellet, Marc. "The Foundations of Christian Ethics according to Hans Urs von Balthasar." In *Hans Urs von Balthasar: His Life and Work*, edited by David L. Schindler, 231–49. San Francisco: Ignatius, 1991.

Paschasius Radbertus. *Vom Leib und Blut des Herrn.* Translated by Hans Urs von Balthasar. Einsiedeln: Johannes Verlag, 1988.

Péguy, Charles. *Das Tor zum Geheimnis der Hoffnung.* Edited and translated by Hans Urs von Balthasar. Einsiedeln: Johannes, 2011.

———. *The Mystery of the Charity of Joan of Arc.* Translated by Julian Green. New York: Pantheon, 1950.

———. *Nous sommes tous à la frontière.* Edited by Hans Urs von Balthasar. Paris: Éditions Johannes Verlag, 2014.

———. *The Portal of the Mystery of Hope.* Translated by David Louis Schindler Jr. Grand Rapids, MI: Eerdmans, 1996.

———. *Temporal and Eternal.* Translated by Alexander Dru. Indianapolis: Liberty Fund, 2001.

Perreau-Saussine, Emile. *Catholicism and Democracy: An Essay in the History of Political Thought.* Translated by Richard Rex. Princeton, NJ: Princeton University Press, 2012.

Perrin, Nicholas. "Sacraments and Sacramentality in the New Testament." In *The Oxford Handbook of Sacramental Theology,* edited by Hans Boersma and Matthew Levering, 52–67. Oxford: Oxford University Press, 2015.

Peterson, Erik. "The Book on the Angels: Their Place and Meaning in the Liturgy." In *Theological Tractates,* translated by Michael J. Hollerich, 106–42. Stanford, CA: Stanford University Press, 2011.

Peyrard, Olivier. *Fondements pour une théologie de la chair: La médiation christologique chez Hans Urs von Balthasar.* Paris: Les Éditions du Cerf, 2016.

Pickstock, Catherine. *After Writing: On the Liturgical Consummation of Philosophy.* Oxford: Wiley-Blackwell, 1997.

Pitstick, Alyssa Lyra. *Light in Darkness: Hans Urs von Balthasar and the Catholic Doctrine of Christ's Descent into Hell.* Grand Rapids, MI: Eerdmans, 2007.

Pomplun, Trent. "The Theology of Gerard Manley Hopkins: From John Duns Scotus to the Baroque." *Journal of Religion* 95, no. 1 (2015): 1–34.

Pourrat, P. *La Théologie Sacramentaire: Étude de Théologie Positive.* Paris: Lecoffre, 1907.

———. *Theology of the Sacraments: A Study in Positive Theology.* 3rd ed. St. Louis: Herder, 1910.

Power, David N. *The Eucharistic Mystery: Revitalizing the Tradition.* New York: Crossroad, 1995.

———. "Sacramental Theology: A Review of Literature." *Theological Studies* 55 (1994): 657–705.

———. *Unsearchable Riches: The Symbolic Nature of Liturgy.* Eugene, OR: Wipf & Stock, 2008.

Powers, Joseph. *Eucharistic Theology.* New York: Herder and Herder, 1967.

Przywara, Erich. *Analogia Entis: Metaphysics—Original Structure and Universal Rhythm.* Translated by John R. Betz and David Bentley Hart. Grand Rapids, MI: Wm. B. Eerdmans, 2014.

Quash, Ben. "Hans Urs von Balthasar's 'Theatre of the World': The Aesthetic of a Dramatics." In *Theological Aesthetics after von Balthasar,* edited by Oleg V. Bychkov and James Fodor, 19–34. Aldershot: Ashgate, 2008.

Rahner, Karl. *The Church and the Sacraments.* New York: Herder and Herder, 1963.

———. "Consideration on the Active Role of the Person in the Sacramental Event." In *Theological Investigations,* 4:161–84. Baltimore: Helicon Press, 1966.

———. *Foundations of Christian Faith: An Introduction to the Idea of Christianity.* Translated by William V. Dych. New York: Crossroad, 1982.

———. "The Hermeneutics of Eschatological Assertions." In *Theological Investigations*, 4:323–46. Baltimore: Helicon Press, 1966.

———. "Introductory Observations on Thomas Aquinas' Theology of the Sacraments in General." In *Theological Investigations*, 14:149–60. New York: Seabury, 1976.

———. *On the Theology of Death.* New York: Herder and Herder, 1963.

———. "Personal and Sacramental Piety." In *Theological Investigations*, 2:109–33. Baltimore: Helicon Press, 1963.

———. "The Theology of the Symbol." In *Theological Investigations*, 4:221–52. Baltimore: Helicon Press, 1966.

———. *The Trinity.* New York: Crossroad, 1997.

Ratzinger, Joseph. *Collected Works*, Vol. 11, *Theology of the Liturgy.* San Francisco: Ignatius, 2014.

———. "Concerning the Notion of Person in Theology," *Communio* 17, no. 3 (1990): 439–54.

Reale, Giovanni. *Raffaello: La "Disputa."* Milan: Rusconi, 1998.

———. *"The School of Athens" by Raphael.* Translated by Marco Anone. Sankt Augustin: Academia Verlag, 2008.

Reali, Nicola. *La ragione e la forma: Il sacramento nella teologia di H. U. von Balthasar.* Rome: Lateran University Press, 1999.

Rempel, John D. "Anabaptist Theologies of the Eucharist." In *A Companion to the Eucharist in the Reformation*, edited by Lee Palmer Wandel, 115–37. Leiden: Brill, 2014.

Revel, Jean-Philippe. *Traité des sacrements.* Vol. 1, *Baptême et sacramentalité*, Tome 1, *Origine et signification du baptême.* Paris: Les Éditions du Cerf, 2004.

———. *Traité des sacrements.* Vol. 1, *Baptême et sacramentalité*, Tome 2, *Don et réception de la grâce baptismale.* Paris: Les Éditions du Cerf, 2005.

Richard of St. Victor. *"The Book of the Patriarchs," "The Mystical Ark," and "Book Three of the Trinity."* Translated by Grover A. Zinn. New York: Paulist Press, 1979.

Riches, Aaron. "Christology and Anti-Humanism." *Modern Theology* 29, no. 3 (2013): 311–37.

———. *Ecce Homo: On the Divine Unity of Christ.* Grand Rapids, MI: Eerdmans, 2016.

Roccasalvo, Joan Lucie. "The Eucharist as Beauty: A Study in the Thought of Hans Urs von Balthasar." PhD diss., Drew University, 1998.

Rousselot, Pierre. *The Eyes of Faith.* Translated by Joseph Donceel. New York: Fordham University Press, 1990.

Ruiz, J.-P. "The Apocalypse of John and Contemporary Roman Catholic Liturgy." *Worship* 68 (1994): 482–504.

Sasse, Hermann. *This Is My Body: Luther's Contention for the Real Presence in the Sacrament of the Altar.* Minneapolis, MN: Augsburg, 1959.

Scheeben, Matthias Joseph. *The Mysteries of Christianity.* New York: Crossroad, 2008.

Schillebeeckx, Edward. *Christ: The Experience of Jesus as Lord.* New York: Crossroad, 1989.

———. *Christ the Sacrament of the Encounter with God.* London: Sheed & Ward, 1987.

———. *The Eucharist.* Translated by N. D. Smith. London: Sheed & Ward, 1977.

Schindler, D. C. *The Catholicity of Reason.* Grand Rapids, MI: Eerdmans, 2013.

———. *Hans Urs von Balthasar and the Dramatic Structure of Truth.* New York: Fordham University Press, 2004.

———. "Metaphysics within the Limits of Phenomenology: Balthasar and Husserl on the Nature of the Philosophical Act." *Teología y Vida* 50 (2009): 243–58.

Schindler, David L., ed. *Hans Urs von Balthasar: His Life and Work.* San Francisco: Ignatius, 1991.

Schmemann, Alexander. *For the Life of the World: Sacraments and Orthodoxy.* Crestwood, NY: St. Vladimir's Seminary Press, 1973.

———. *Introduction to Liturgical Theology.* Crestwood, NY: St. Vladimir's Seminary Press, 1966.

Schnusenberg, Christine. *The Mythological Traditions of Liturgical Drama: The Eucharist as Theater.* New York: Paulist Press, 2010.

Schrijvers, Joeri. "Jean-Yves Lacoste: A Phenomenology of Liturgy." *Heythrop Journal* 46 (2005): 314–33.

Schumacher, Michele. "The Concept of Representation in the Theology of Hans Urs von Balthasar." *Theological Studies* 60 (1999): 53–71.

———. *A Trinitarian Anthropology: Adrienne von Speyr and Hans Urs von Balthasar in Dialogue with Thomas Aquinas.* Washington, DC: Catholic University of America Press, 2014.

Schwartz, Regina Mara. *Sacramental Poetics at the Dawn of Secularism: When God Left the World.* Stanford, CA: Stanford University Press, 2008.

Scola, Angelo. *The Nuptial Mystery.* Grand Rapids, MI: Eerdmans, 2005.

Seneca. *Letters from a Stoic.* New York: Penguin, 1969.

Servais, Jacques. "Balthasar as Interpreter of the Catholic Tradition." In *Love Alone Is Credible: Hans Urs von Balthasar as Interpreter of the Catholic Tradition,* Vol. 1, edited by David L. Schindler, 191–208. Grand Rapids, MI: Eerdmans, 2008.

———. *Théologie des Exercices spirituels: H. U. von Balthasar interprète saint Ignace.* Paris: Culture et vérité, 1996.

Shepherd, M. A. *The Paschal Liturgy and the Apocalypse.* London: Lutterworth, 1960.

Sokolowski, Robert. *Eucharistic Presence: A Study in the Theology of Disclosure.* Washington, DC: Catholic University of America Press, 1994.

Solovyov, Vladimir, *Lectures on Godmanhood*. San Rafael, CA: Semantron Press, 2007.

Spadaro, Giorgio I. *The Esoteric Meaning in Raphael's Paintings: The Philosophy of Composition*. Great Barrington, MA: Lindisfarne, 2006.

Speyr, Adrienne von. *Confession*. Translated by Douglas W. Stott. San Francisco: Ignatius, 1985.

———. *The Cross, Word and Sacrament*. San Francisco: Ignatius, 1987.

———. *The Discourses of Controversy: Meditations of John 6–12*. Translated by Brian McNeil. San Francisco: Ignatius, 1993.

———. *The Farewell Discourses: Meditations on John 13–17*. Translated by E. A. Nelson. San Francisco: Ignatius, 1987.

———. *The Holy Mass*. San Francisco: Ignatius, 1999.

———. *The Passion from Within*. Translated by Sister Lucia Wiedenhöver, O.C.D. San Francisco: Ignatius, 1998.

———. *Passion von innen*. Einsiedeln: Johannes Verlag, 1981.

———. *The World of Prayer*. San Francisco: Ignatius, 1987.

Steck, Christopher. *The Ethical Thought of Hans Urs von Balthasar*. New York: Crossroad, 2011.

Stepelevich, Lawrence S. "Hegel and the Lutheran Eucharist." *Heythrop Journal* 27, no. 3 (1986): 262–74.

Stinglhammer, Hermann. *Freiheit in der Hingabe: Trinitarische Freiheitslehre bei Hans Urs von Balthasar. Ein Beitrag zur Rezeption der Theodramatik*. Würzburg: Echter, 1997.

St John, Hal. *The Call of the Holy: Heidegger—Chauvet—Benedict XVI*. London: Bloomsbury T&T Clark, 2012.

Stone, Darwell. *A History of the Doctrine of the Holy Eucharist*. Vol. 2. New York: Longmans, Green, and Co., 1909.

Sutton, Matthew Lewis. "A Compelling Trinitarian Taxonomy: Hans Urs von Balthasar's Theology of the Trinitarian Inversion and Reversion." *International Journal of Systematic Theology*, 14, no. 2 (2012): 161–76.

Sweeney, Conor. *Sacramental Presence after Heidegger: Onto-Theology, Sacraments, and the Mother's Smile*. Eugene, OR: Cascade, 2015.

Taft, Robert. *Through Their Own Eyes: Liturgy as the Byzantines Saw It*. Berkeley, CA: InterOrthodox Press, 2006.

Taylor, Charles. *A Secular Age*. Cambridge, MA: Belknap, 2007.

Tertullian of Carthage. *De baptismo*. http://www.tertullian.org/articles/evans_bapt /evans_bapt_text_trans.htm.

Tilliette, Xavier. *Philosophies Eucharistiques de Descartes à Blondel*. Paris: Les Éditions du Cerf, 2006.

Timmermann, Achim. "The Eucharist on the Eve of the Reformation." In *A Companion to the Eucharist in the Reformation*, edited by Lee Palmer Wandel, 365–98. Leiden: Brill, 2014.

Tóth, Beáta. "Diaphany of the Divine Milieu or the Epiphany of Divine Glory? The Revelation of the Natural World in Teilhard de Chardin and Hans Urs von Balthasar." *New Blackfriars* 95, no. 1059 (2014): 535–52.

Tyrrell, George. *Lex Credendi: A Sequel to Lex Orandi.* London: Longmans, Green, and Co., 1906.

———. *Lex Orandi or Prayer and Creed.* London: Longmans, Green, and Co., 1903.

Ulrich, Ferdinand. *Homo Abyssus: The Drama of the Question of Being.* Translated by D. C. Schindler. Washington, DC: Humanum Academic Press, 2018.

Vaillaincourt, Mark G. "Sacramental Theology from Gottschalk to Lanfranc." In *The Oxford Handbook of Sacramental Theology*, edited by Hans Boersma and Matthew Levering, 187–200. Oxford: Oxford University Press, 2015.

Vanni, Ugo. "Liturgical Dialogue as a Literary Form in the Book of Revelation." *New Testament Studies* 37 (1991): 348–72.

Van Slyke, Daniel G. "The Study of Early Christian Worship." In the *T&T Clark Companion to Liturgy*, edited by Alcuin Reid, 43–71. New York: Bloomsbury, 2016.

Vermigli, Peter. *Dialogue on the Two Natures in Christ.* Kirksville, MO: Sixteenth Century Journal Publishers, 1995.

Vonier, Abbot. *A Key to the Doctrine of the Eucharist.* Bethesda, MD: Zaccheus Press, 2003.

Wainwright, Geoffrey. "Eschatology." In *The Cambridge Companion to Hans Urs von Balthasar*, edited by Edward Oakes and David Moss, 113–27. Cambridge: Cambridge University Press, 2004.

———. *Eucharist and Eschatology.* 3rd ed. Akron, OH: OSL Publications, 2002.

Walatka, Todd. *Von Balthasar and the Option for the Poor: Theodramatics in the Light of Liberation Theology.* Washington, DC: Catholic University of America Press, 2017.

Wallner, Karl Joseph. *Eucharistie Bei Hans Urs v. Balthasar.* Schriften Der Wiener Katholischen Akademie 50. Wien: Wiener Katholische Akademie, 2006.

Worgul, George S. "Balthasar's Kneeling Theology, Liturgics and Post Modernism." *Questions Liturgiques/Studies in Liturgy* 83 (2002): 257–69.

Yocum, John P. "Aristotle in Aquinas's Sacramental Theology." In *Aristotle in Aquinas's Theology*, edited by Gilles Emery and Matthew Levering, 205–32. Oxford: Oxford University Press, 2015.

Zahatlan, Pavol. "Das Eucharistieverständnis in Der Perspektive Der Theologischen Aesthetik Bei Hans Urs von Balthasar." PhD diss., Graz Univeität, 2009.

Zizioulas, John. *Being as Communion: Studies in Personhood and the Church.* Crestwood, NY: St. Vladimir's Seminary Press, 1997.

Zwingli, Ulrich. "On the Lord's Supper." In *Zwingli and Bullinger*, edited by G. W. Bromiley, 176–238. Philadelphia: Westminster Press, 1953.

INDEX

abandonment, 22–24, 90, 94–95, 213
  Gelassenheit, 23, 95
admirabile commercium, 28–29, 178
aesthetics (liturgical). *See* liturgy: liturgical aesthetics; liturgy: liturgical beauty
analogy, 23, 33, 53–55, 61, 80, 176–77, 235n69, 259n40. *See also* catalogy
  analogia entis, 82, 174
  analogia libertatis, 183
Anselm of Canterbury, 28
ascetic aestheticism, 123–24, 126, 130
Augustine of Hippo, 33–34, 52, 79, 86, 89, 99, 109, 126, 134, 195

baptism, 26, 44, 48, 74–75, 78–79, 126, 140, 153–54
  infant baptism, 235n74
Barth, Karl, 82, 84, 117, 139, 169, 174, 181–82, 246n91, 258nn30–31
beatific vision, 197–98, 203–4, 206
beauty. *See* liturgy: liturgical aesthetics; liturgy: liturgical beauty
Benedict XVI, Pope. *See* Ratzinger, Joseph
Being, 18, 58, 69, 101, 122, 138–46, 166–67, 258n33
  Dasein, 101, 124, 138
beloved/lover. *See* lover/beloved
Berengar of Tours, 38, 64, 127, 141–42, 195

Bernanos, Georges, 5–6, 9, 34, 96–97, 100–101, 107, 153, 186, 239n139, 239n142
Bérulle, Pierre de, 199
Bloch, Ernst, 169, 171–73, 188–89
Blondel, Maurice, 43, 201, 203, 211, 232n12, 266n138
Bouyer, Louis, 88–89
Bulgakov, Sergei, 74, 260n54, 266n133, 266n139
Bultmann, Rudolf, 12, 168–71, 173, 175, 206, 256n17

Calderón de la Barca, Pedro, 9, 13, 155, 184–87, 190, 261n66, 261n70, 261n73
Casel, Odo, 41–42, 88–89, 91, 93, 113, 224n108, 241n12
catalogy, 53–54, 57, 61, 177, 198, 234. *See also* analogy
Catherine of Siena, 28, 54, 198–99, 247n105, 259n41
causality. *See* sacrament: causality; synergy
Caussade, Jean Pierre de, 22–24, 94–95, 98
Chardin, Teilhard de, 73, 201
Chauvet, Louis-Marie, 12, 18, 59, 81, 97, 126, 129, 136–42, 144, 150, 233n27, 245n79, 248nn130–31

Jonathan Martin Ciraulo is assistant professor of
systematic theology at Saint Meinrad Seminary.

CPSIA information can be obtained
at www.ICGtesting.com
Printed in the USA
LVHW111633250322
714399LV00003B/39